Oil Windfalls

Blessing or Curse?

A World Bank Research Publication

Oil Windfalls

Blessing or Curse?

Alan Gelb
and Associates

Published for The World Bank
Oxford University Press

Oxford University Press

NEW YORK OXFORD LONDON GLASGOW
TORONTO MELBOURNE WELLINGTON HONG KONG
TOKYO KUALA LUMPUR SINGAPORE JAKARTA
DELHI BOMBAY CALCUTTA MADRAS KARACHI
NAIROBI DAR ES SALAAM CAPE TOWN

Manufactured in the United States of America
First printing October 1988

Library of Congress Cataloging-in-Publication Data

Gelb, Alan H.
  Oil windfalls : blessing or curse? / Alan Gelb and associates.
    p.   cm.—(A World Bank research publication)
  "Published for the World Bank."
  Bibliography: p.
  ISBN 0-19-520774-2
  1. Petroleum industry and trade—Case studies. I. Title.
II. Series.
HD9560.5.G423 1988
338.2'7282—dc19   88-25256
                                                        CIP

Contents

Preface

The research project underlying this book was started in 1981 and continued for several years, during which the temporary—even if quite long-lived—nature of the oil booms became more and more apparent. This required some changes in the focus of research, but the result is a more interesting study of the impact on economic development of the large export windfalls which accompanied the two oil shocks. The later chapters of this episode, however, are still to be written. Many more years will be needed before a final assessment, especially of the downside of the cycle, becomes possible.

The study itself involved continuous interaction between the comparative component at the core and the six country reports drafted by collaborators. A certain tension existed between the analysis of any one country and the comparisons made with other countries: aspects which appeared most illuminating in the comparative context were not always those which a country expert would choose to emphasize. Therefore, although in most cases the country chapters follow the lines of the original reports, the author of the overall study cannot disclaim final responsibility for all chapters.

Boubker Abisourour, Perry Beider, Shahrzad Gohari, Carlos Medeiros, and Ann Meyendorff provided helpful assistance at various stages, and Lu Oropesa, Maria Ameal, and Raquel Luz processed the manuscripts beyond the call of duty. Arne Drud and Alex Meeraus of the Development Research Department's Analytic Support Unit made a particular contribution in the setup and solution of the optimization model which underlies the results reported in chapter 8 and, in a broader sense, underpins the whole approach. Without the expert editorial help of Jeanne Rosen it would have been much harder to keep up writing momentum. In addition to the six experts who collaborated on the country chapters, Mauricio Garcia Araujo, Bela Balassa, Martha de Melo, Jack Duloy, Joan Nelson, Graham

Pyatt, and two anonymous referees have contributed useful comments. So have many of the World Bank's country economists; their cooperation has been much appreciated. The collaborators on the country chapters deserve a special mention for their efforts and their patience over the period needed to put together this comparative volume.

The book is dedicated to Robert Alexander Simon, who arrived just in time for galley proofs.

PART I

Approach to Windfall Gains

Chapter 1

Introduction

The dramatic Arab embargo of October 1973, which quadrupled world oil prices, set in motion a chain of events that was to have a great impact on the economies of virtually all countries, industrialized and developing, oil-importing and oil-exporting. Although some signs of strain in the global economic environment had emerged earlier that year—notably the monetary crisis in February, which led to the system of generalized exchange rate floating—the first oil shock signaled the end of a quarter century of high growth and relative economic stability. In dollar terms, oil prices slumped slightly in 1975–78. But they almost tripled in 1979 with the fall of the Iranian government and cutbacks in output by major producers. These two oil price shocks, charted in figure 1-1, have dwarfed all other terms of trade movements in the postwar period.

Because oil represented the largest internationally traded commodity (having displaced coffee from this position in the late 1960s), the shocks caused unprecedented transfers of income between consumers and producers. Each of the abrupt increases in the price of oil brought about a shift from importing to exporting countries of $300 million a day.[1] Over a year, this represented the equivalent of one-and-a-half times all medium- and long-term debt owed by developing countries in 1973. The oil boom, moreover, has been of surprisingly long duration given the price movements usual for primary products. Not until 1985 and 1986, when the market for oil from established producers contracted and the price of oil plunged briefly to about $10 a barrel before returning to about $16, did the purchasing power of these countries fall back toward the pre-1973 level.

For all countries dependent on imported oil, the terms of trade shocks, followed by the "interest rate shock" and global recession, had severe adverse effects on inflation, employment, and productiv-

3

Figure 1-1. Relative Prices: Oil, Manufactured Imports, and Non-Oil Exports of Developing Countries, 1960–84

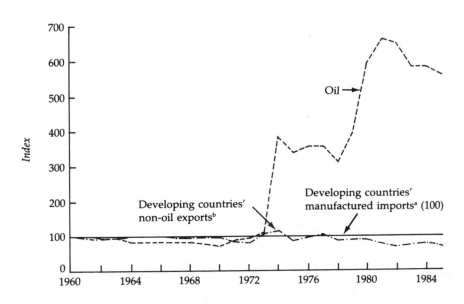

a. Unit value of manufactured exports from five industrial countries to developing countries.

b. Unit value index for thirty-three commodities excluding oil, weighted by 1979–81 developing countries' export values.

Source: World Bank data.

ity. This set of issues has been extensively researched and will not be considered here.[2] For countries with oil to export, the shocks and their effects were of course very different. It is the experience of the second group of countries—the apparent "winners" in the global oil drama—that is the subject of this study.

How important were the oil windfalls to developing exporters? Did these countries merely consume their terms of trade gains? If not, what strategies did they formulate for using their new wealth to promote growth and development? Did the windfalls actually accelerate growth and lay the framework for sustained development? Did they enhance well-being and raise consumption? Or did the difficulties of managing producer economies through volatile, poorly predicted terms of trade shifts nullify the potential gain, perhaps even turning it into a net loss? Is it in fact possible for a country receiving a large windfall gain to end up less well-off than it might have been without it? What lessons can be learned from these countries' experiences?

Many more years must pass before economists can draw up a balance sheet reflecting the full impact of the terms of trade windfalls on oil producers. Some of the projects funded by spending or borrowing against oil income cannot be expected to realize their intended benefits for a long time—as is true of development efforts in general. Moreover, many projects that are now financial disasters could eventually prove to be profitable, if poorly timed, investments should the prices of energy and primary commodities regain lost ground.

Nevertheless, enough time has elapsed to permit at least some preliminary answers to the questions raised above. If, upon careful analysis, the payoff to oil producers should appear to be small (especially when judged by their own criteria for success), then the fluctuations in oil markets since 1973 may not simply have resulted in transfers between consumers and producers. They may also have engaged the global economy in a negative-sum game of monstrous proportions.

In attempting to determine whether this is indeed what has happened, this study considers the recent experience of six developing oil exporters—Algeria, Ecuador, Indonesia, Nigeria, Trinidad and Tobago, and Venezuela. These countries differ widely in per capita income, area and population, natural and human resources, political system, and the government's entrepreneurial and regulatory role in the economy. But they also share some important characteristics. For all of them, oil represents a large share of exports but a moderate share of gross domestic product (GDP). Oil income per capita is fairly low. Proven, low-cost oil reserves are high in value at average post-1973 prices relative to the countries' estimated non-oil capital stocks, yet are insufficient to bear the burden of financing development for more than another fifteen to twenty-five years unless real oil prices exhibit a rising secular trend. In 1974 the terms of trade oil windfalls for these countries totaled $22.5 billion, about 23 percent of their GDP (see table 1-1).

Together, the six countries constitute the group of capital-deficit developing oil exporters (also referred to as the high-absorbing or capital-importing oil exporters) that have long enough experience and comprehensive enough data to make a comparative study possible. Mexico and Egypt, although sharing many features with this group, were not oil exporters in 1974. Iran is excluded because of inadequate data after 1977.

In contrast, the capital-surplus oil exporters such as Kuwait and Saudi Arabia have small populations, exceptionally underdeveloped

Table 1-1. The 1974 Oil Windfall

Country	GDP[a] (billions of U.S. dollars)	Windfall[b] (as percentage of GDP)	Windfall (billions of U.S. dollars)
Algeria	11.6	29.0	3.4
Ecuador	3.7	22.8	0.8
Indonesia	25.8	16.5	4.2
Nigeria	29.8	26.6	7.9
Trinidad and Tobago	2.1	30.4	0.6
Venezuela	26.2	21.3	5.6
All	99.2	22.7	22.5

a. 1974 GDP at market prices converted at annual average exchange rate.
b. Windfall is measured according to the method in chapter 5.
Source: World Bank, and International Monetary Fund (IMF) *International Financial Statistics*.

non-oil economies (aside from activities financed by oil revenues), and very large, low-cost reserves that guarantee the comparative advantage of oil for the foreseeable future. Their capacity to absorb revenue has been far lower than the maximum oil revenue they could extract, especially at the prices prevailing between 1974 and 1984. Their main medium-term economic problem, therefore, has been to choose an optimal asset portfolio of oil in the ground and financial and real assets abroad. The capital-deficit exporters also face a portfolio problem, as do all countries that can lend or borrow abroad. But in addition, their medium-run policy responses are crucial in determining the economic value of windfall gains and the effects of those gains on the non-oil economy. As indicated by statements of their governments, since at least the beginning of the 1970s these countries have been well aware that they could look forward to relatively few years of resource abundance.

This study focuses on the medium-term management of windfall gains and reversals caused by changes in the terms of trade. It does not consider the implications of the discovery and exploitation of oil resources; all but one of the sample countries were well-established exporters by the time of the first oil shock. It also does not emphasize a third, and important, issue—the rate at which "exhaustible" oil reserves should be depleted.

The separation of the first and third issues requires that a distinction be made between two concepts of economic rent. The first, whose magnitude, use, and impact *is* addressed in this study, is *Ricardian rent*, defined as the residual component of market price over production cost where all reproducible factors of production (labor, capital) are paid at market rates. This concept should be separated from that of *Hotelling rent*, the equilibrium rise in the unit price of a nonrenewable resource at the real interest rate as the stock is exhausted. Ricardian rent is associated with resources of a superior quality (land particularly suited to the production of certain crops, such as coffee or rubber), which may be renewable. Hotelling rent is associated with exhaustibility, and the Hotelling rule reflects arbitrage between holding the resource and holding interest-bearing assets. Given the geographical concentration of large, low-cost oil reserves and the increased dependence on a few suppliers that emerged during the 1960s and 1970s, it is not at all clear that price movements have reflected exhaustion on a global scale. It is equally plausible to explain them in terms of producer monopolies or backward-bending supply curves, as discussed in chapter 2.

The Ricardian rent element in the price of low-cost oil has been massive since 1973—far in excess of the rent element in the price of any other major product. In the largest and cheapest fields, production and transport costs absorb as little as $1 a barrel, although the average for the six countries in this study probably lies between $3 and $5 a barrel, with some extraction techniques raising costs to as much as $12 a barrel. In contrast, the average cost of extracting oil from Alaska's North Slope and delivering it to market is perhaps $8 to $12 a barrel, although the marginal cost is believed to be considerably lower. North Sea oil costs are still lower, but well above costs in the sample countries.[3]

The Oil Windfalls: Expectation and Reality

> Having long been the victims of an international division of labor which had relegated them to the classic dependency status of raw materials producers, the OPEC nations could now redefine their external relations as well as make fundamental changes in their internal models of capital accumulation. (Karl 1982, p. 3.)

The 1973–74 oil price rise fundamentally altered the relation of the oil-producing countries to the international economic system. Oil producers were elevated to a distinct status among developing countries—in political influence, in trade matters, and in access to foreign capital. Expectations for their rapid economic development were little short of euphoric. Shah Mohammed Reza Pahlavi proclaimed that Iran stood on the threshold of a "Great Civilization," while Carlos Andrés Pérez, president of Venezuela, announced his vision of "La Gran Venezuela." And indeed, the windfalls relaxed three traditional constraints on economic growth: foreign exchange, domestic savings, and fiscal revenues.

Not surprisingly, developing countries that lacked oil were envious:

> The capital-short and aspiring Third-World planners have kept telling themselves (and each other) that if only they had this black gold, the magical *elan vital* for their economic takeoff would be close at hand. (Amuzegar 1982, p. 814.)

Yet as early as 1975, this optimistic view was being questioned:

> You think we are lucky. I don't think so. We are dying of indigestion . . . I call petroleum "the devil's excrement." It brings trouble. Look around you. Look at this *locura*—waste, corruption, consumption, our public services falling apart . . . And debt, debt we shall have for years. We are putting our grandchildren in debt. (Juan Pablo Pérez Alfonso, one of the founders of the Organization of the Petroleum Exporting Countries [OPEC]; cited by Karl 1982, p. 18.)

As time went on, prominent citizens of oil-exporting countries began to voice more and more doubts. History might show, they feared, that their countries "have gained the least, or lost the most, from the discovery and development of their resources" (Attiga 1981b, p. 7). The very titles of several studies are revealing: "The Years that the Locust Hath Eaten: Oil Policy and OPEC Development Prospects" (Levy 1978); "How Oil Revenues Can Destroy a Country" (Attiga 1981a); and "Oil Wealth: A Very Mixed Blessing" (Amuzegar 1982a).[4] In his critical assessment of the Iranian experience, Katouzian (1978) concluded that the main consequence of Iran's depleting its oil reserves was to squander its agricultural resources—a case of "dual depletion." Significantly, such views emerged well before the oil glut caused a steep drop in the revenues of the oil-producing economies.

It is probably fair to say that those analysts taking the most critical view of the uses and effects of the oil windfalls have emphasized political and institutional factors more than is usual in quantitative neoclassical economic analyses. They have generally not attempted to quantify benefits and then assess them objectively in light of the potential offered by the windfalls, national priorities, and the desires of the recipients. To do so is important, however, since there is no a priori reason why certain outcomes usually deplored (such as a drop in non-oil work productivity or the neglect of agriculture) might not be appropriate responses to windfall gains in certain circumstances. Some policymakers have regarded the extent to which oil revenues have led to capital formation as virtually the only criterion of success. Others have argued that the promotion or preservation of certain favored sectors of the economy (notably industry) is an important criterion.

The present study takes the view that in the long run the level of consumption and its distribution over time and across groups are the most important criteria for assessing the use of windfalls. Sectoral structure could be a factor in achieving a desirable consumption profile (for example, if there are learning-by-doing effects or if certain changes are hard to reverse) and is considered in later analysis. The level of investment is a relevant consideration in the short term, but it should not be considered irrespective of the ultimate payoff in terms of growth and, ultimately, consumption.

In a quantitative neoclassical framework assuming perfect foresight and a consistent set of priorities, it is hard to turn windfall gains into overall losses without supposing very large divergences between private and social benefits. Some analysts, accordingly, have adopted an intermediate position. On balance, they argue, it is difficult to make the case that a revenue windfall, especially if fairly sustained, can have a negative overall value since it expands the options available to the government and therefore to the entire country. This implies that the country can follow exactly the same policies as it would have done in the absence of the windfall and give the windfall away, for example, as foreign aid. Any different outcome will be, by definition, preferred. This argument is very powerful, but it abstracts from changes in the international environment associated with the windfall, which may make it impossible for the same policy to yield the same outcome as before. It also assumes that the windfall itself does not eliminate parts of the range of previously feasible policies (for example, by changing expectations or institutions), and in this respect abstraction comes at the expense of political reality.

Further, certain sectors of the non-oil economy—especially those producing tradable goods—as well as certain groups heavily dependent on these sectors will be adversely affected by the windfall. Thus, in the absence of a costless, nondistorting system of compensation, income distribution will be changed, perhaps in a way judged to be undesirable. Also, the adjustment costs of factor relocation, accelerated obsolescence of capital, and delays in regaining equilibrium in labor markets may erase at least part of the potential benefit of the windfall. An intermediate view has probably become the dominant one, at least in those analyses restricted to a relatively narrow "economic" framework—windfall gains are "goods" not "bads," but with some adverse side effects.

Scope of the Study

In an effort to bridge the gap between institutionally based and quantitative analysis, this study takes a broad look at the impact of windfall gains on six oil-producing countries. Emphasis will be on the size of the gains, the intentions of the governments, the way the gains were actually used and how this was affected by the country's history and institutions, and the impact of increased spending on the non-oil economy—both on growth in general and on the performance of specific sectors. This approach requires some attention to macroeconomic, microeconomic, and political factors. It also requires some consideration of the strong association between the windfalls and changes in the global environment, notably the increased economic uncertainty in oil, commodity, and capital markets since 1973.

Windfall gains and rents have been approached from a number of analytical perspectives, and chapter 2 selectively reviews four strands of economic theory relevant in analyzing the exporters' experience. *"Linkage" theory* stresses the nature of the demands engendered by a leading or booming sector, both those related to production (upstream and downstream linkages) and those related to final spending of income generated in the sector (consumption and fiscal linkages). More than the other theories, it leads to a consideration of the political and administrative factors that may reduce the effectiveness of the fiscal linkage that has been especially important for oil exporters. *Neoclassical and related growth theory*, in contrast, stresses the impact of the leading sector in augmenting the quantity of factors, both domestic and imported, as a determinant of growth. *Export instability theories* consider the effect of fluctuating and uncertain terms of trade on producer countries. As the empirical chapters show, the stochastic and cyclical nature of oil windfalls has had important consequences. Prediction errors have led to serious mistakes in the composition of investments across sectors and the location of industries among countries. Moreover, macroeconomic adjustment to rising and falling demand tends to be asymmetrical, so that prediction errors in one direction are more costly than in the other. This can turn an expected windfall gain into an actual loss. "Ratchet effects", the irreversibility of policies initiated in the boom years, can have a similar result. Finally, *"booming sector" theory* stresses the impact of a booming sector on resource allocation in the rest of the economy. This approach raises the question of the appropriate degree of oil dependence and bears on strategic choices for absorbing windfall gains.

In assessing the experience of the exporters, it is useful to have in mind the long-standing and more general debate on the role of mineral resources and natural Ricardian rents in development—a debate to which this study makes a contribution. In most cases, it is not easy to distinguish the impact of mineral rents from the effects of other characteristics of mineral production. Moreover, certain nonmineral-producing activities may also generate sizable rents. The evidence on the impact of rents, which is surveyed in chapter 3, is somewhat ambivalent. This argues for approaching with an open mind the question of whether oil windfalls invariably prove advantageous.

Part I concludes with a summary, derived from the body of analytical work, of the main strategic options for handling windfall gains. These options cover decisions on the primary uses of the windfall over time and across applications—consumption, saving abroad, domestic investment (private or public), and so on. They also include macro policies—such as trade restrictions, exchange rates, and controls on commodity and capital markets—that help to determine the ultimate uses of the windfall and the outcome.

Part II is a comparative study of the evolution of the six oil-exporting economies both during and after the price shocks. In chapter 4, the introduction to part II, country characteristics are presented. A table also previews how the countries fit into the strategic options outlined in part I. The reader may wish to refer back to this table from the later empirical analysis. Chapter 5 develops and uses a simple methodology to estimate the size of the windfalls between 1974 and 1981 and how they have been used. Although the commonalities among the countries should not be overstated, in general most of the gains have been transformed into domestic capital in the public sector rather than consumed outright or saved abroad. In fact, for a representative country, the split between consumption and other uses is not very different from what would be predicted by a simple permanent income model that allows for the depletion of proven oil reserves.

This overall pattern of use reflects three important objectives of producer governments:

- To accelerate growth of the non-oil economy
- To modernize and diversify to reduce dependence on oil
- To consolidate national control over the hydrocarbon sector and other industrial sectors

The pattern also reflects a common desire, or political need, to spend rapidly. This precluded applications that would have required time-consuming institutional and social change; in fact, oil income may have reduced the ability of governments to perceive the

urgency of such change. The result was a concentration on infrastructural and certain types of social investments and on large-scale
industrial projects, since these are conducive to relatively quick disbursements.

The following chapters examine the consequences of these windfall uses, using the above four theoretical approaches. Chapter 6 considers the impact on the structure of the countries' non-oil economies and compares the outcomes with those expected from the
"booming sector" theory. By and large, the predictions of this approach are validated, although some notable exceptions point to
the wide range of possible effects and to the importance of policy
in influencing the outcome.

Chapter 7 assesses the growth record of the six producers in relation to both their own historical trends and trends in other countries. Judged in terms of neoclassical growth and other, related theories, the results are disappointing, even without considering the
post-1981 period. Given the emphasis that the producer governments have put on growth, this fact calls into question the efficiency of the crucial fiscal linkage between the oil sector and the
rest of the producing economy. In particular, fiscal linkage has
been ineffectual in developing competitive non-oil traded sectors.
This critical weakness stemmed from a number of economic factors
and management deficiencies. But the oil exporters were also in the
difficult position of being impelled by their own internal political dynamics to accelerate the implementation of long-range investment
plans at a time when global uncertainty and volatility had greatly increased. The result was that large and vital industrial components
of these investment plans performed far more poorly than expected , not only because of poor implementation and management,
but because market projections were off by wide margins. The failure of these components to generate income and consequent expenditures led, in turn, to the suboptimal use of new infrastructure. As
a result of the interplay of these effects, capital formation did not accelerate growth beyond an initial demand-side stimulus, largely to
construction.

The slump in world oil markets after 1981 revealed just how frag-
ile the development patterns of the exporters were in the face of unexpected fluctuations. Three of the countries studied experienced
debt crises. Growth rates and demand fell sharply. And even
though oil incomes were still far higher in real terms than before
1973, the oil exporters were propelled into stagflation. Chapter 8 reviews this period, for which data are still provisional, and analyzes
the downside aspects of the oil cycle. It also summarizes the results
of a simulation modeling exercise that combines elements of all

four theories noted above. The results confirm that any upside benefits are easily negated by the costs of adjusting to falling revenues when macroeconomic behavior is asymmetric. They also suggest that incautious responses to overoptimistic oil price and export projections can cost a great deal, particularly if inappropriate or reluctant adjustment policies are pursued on the downside.

Chapter 9 summarizes the main findings of the study and tries to sketch an answer to the question: What should the developing oil exporters have done differently?

Part III consists of six chapters, each a case study of one of the sample countries. It provides sequential analyses to complement the issue-focused, cross-country treatment of part II. It also considers country-specific constraints on the deployment of rents. In principle, natural rent is available for use in an "optimal" manner since it represents an income stream uncommitted to any reproducible factor of production. Such revenues, therefore, should constitute the most highly valued income stream in the economy. One of the main findings of this study, however, is that oil incomes were committed rapidly and allocated to uses determined by a country's preshock priorities and its political and economic institutions. Indeed, it is little exaggeration to say that most of the windfalls were committed *before* they were anticipated!

To understand how and why this happened, it is necessary to study the experience of oil-producing countries in more depth; hence part III. Although the case studies follow a similar format, the treatment is not uniform. Differences in emphasis among chapters reflect important differences among the six countries in their responses to windfalls and in their economic performance. To keep the study within manageable bounds, chapters 10-15 offer a focused rather than a general economic history of each country during the years of the oil booms.

Notes

1. Dollars are U.S. dollars unless otherwise specified.

2. In explaining the evolution of the main oil-importing economies after 1972, Bruno and Sachs (1985) attribute a more important role to supply price shocks than to reduced spending on investment or on research and development.

3. For an overview of extraction costs, see Adelman (1986a). Hughes and Singh (1978) discuss the incidence of rent in selected mineral extraction activities.

4. The last-named paper also assembles critical commentaries and reviews of the performance of a number of oil economies over the boom period.

Chapter 2

Theoretical Approaches to the Analysis of Windfall Effects

Analysts disagree about whether growth and development are furthered or hindered by sectors with such an unusually strong comparative advantage that those who own the scarce factors of production garner large natural rents. In this debate, at least four theoretical approaches may be distinguished. Some understanding of these approaches is very useful when trying to assess the impact of oil windfall gains on an economy.

Linkage Theory

It has been observed that growth, particularly in its early stages, is likely to rely on a sequence of staple industries rather than just one. The "staple thesis," popular before the 1960s, attempted to show how a country's development could be shaped by a succession of primary export products.[1]

To answer the crucial questions of how, and under what circumstances, "one thing would lead to another"—specifically, from a sequence of staples based on natural resources to activities in which income would be generated by reproducible factors of production—a more structured theory was required. This led to the familiar but often misinterpreted concept of linkages.[2]

Although linkage theory, and especially attempts to quantify it, are commonly associated with input-output analysis, in its original form it emphasized the dynamic stimulus to entrepreneurship rather than a static framework of existing interrelations. Unlike the growth, two-gap, and "booming sector" theories surveyed below, it stressed that "development depends not so much on finding optimal combinations for given resources and factors of production as on calling forth and enlisting for development purposes resources and abilities that are hidden, scattered or badly utilized" (Hirschman 1958, p. 5). According to this theory, in a given social, political, and economic context certain characteristics of the leading activity are conducive to its providing such a stimulus. The effects of the interaction between the leading sector and other sectors are divided into production linkage, consumption linkage, and fiscal linkage. The first category, production linkage, is relevant to the process of increasing the density of the input-output matrix. It is further split into backward and forward linkages. Backward linkage refers to the potential for stimulating the growth of (upstream) supplying industries, forward linkage to the potential for stimulating the growth of (downstream) processing activities located in the same region or country. The importance of these backward and forward linkages (given the share of intermediates and processing in the final product price) depends on their technical requirements in relation to the endowment of the producing country. The strength of these linkages is usually considered to be inversely proportional to the "alienness" of the potential upstream or downstream activity to those who might be in a position to establish it. Hirschman (1981) also distinguishes between the stimuli provided to those engaged in the leading activity itself ("inside" linkage) and the stimuli offered to others ("outside" linkage). In contrast to other theories, linkage theory de-emphasizes comparative advantage and international trade and does not single out a few "fixed factors" as the main impediments to growth.

Production linkages must, by definition, be potentially less significant for high-rent activities since intermediate inputs and returns to reproducible factors of production account for a smaller proportion of final value than in other products. The split between the potential consumption and potential fiscal linkages then rests on the extent to which surplus is taxed rather than appropriated by private owners. The *actual* stimulus to other activities reflects patterns of demand—which are influenced by the distribution of the surplus— and, in the longer run, the supply-side impact of investments made out of the surplus.

Consumption linkages may be judged as favorable or adverse from a developmental perspective. Adverse linkage is most often attributed to a propensity to import so high that it *reduces* global demand for the country's products and thus inhibits the development of other sectors. In a static analysis, this may not cause an immediate decrease in welfare. But even if some overall measure of well-being rises in the short run, it is possible for the consumption linkage to be considered unfavorable from a dynamic perspective, usually because the shift in demand inhibits the growth of an infant sector.[3]

Because oil windfalls since 1973 have overwhelmingly accrued to governments, the efficiency of fiscal linkage is the most important determinant of their ultimate benefits. If the objective is to consume windfalls directly, the focus is on the range of possible options for expanding public services and for transferring fiscal revenues to the private sector to enable private consumption to rise. Certain policy choices, such as negative indirect taxes and subsidies, tend to create allocative distortions. But direct transfers may be administratively impracticable, and it may not be possible to reach some groups at all at reasonable cost.

If, however, the country attempts a supply-side development strategy funded by oil revenues, achieving an effective fiscal linkage is also likely to be difficult:

> The ability to tax must be combined with the ability to invest productively . . . In the case of [the more direct production and consumption linkages,] existing production lines or imports to be substituted point to the tasks to be undertaken next, whereas no such guidance is forthcoming when a portion of the income stream earned in the enclave is siphoned off for the purposes of irrigating other parts of the economy. Hence the possibility of either faulty investment, or a great deal of leakage on the way. (Hirschman 1981, p. 69.)

For investments that are intended to produce commercially marketed (usually industrial) output, the problem is obvious. Governments are no more and are probably less likely to pick "winners" than those whose livelihood depends on the outcome. But infrastructural investment, too, has its useful limits. Infrastructural capital is usually created slowly and incrementally, and has normally been provided in *response* to demand emanating from other productive activities rather than in *anticipation* of demand in the hope of stimulating production.[4] The task of usefully deploying windfall gains is arguably easier for the poorest countries because a wide range of physical infrastructure and human capital endowments is seriously deficient. But even when the state restricts itself to making good such deficiencies, the fiscal linkage at best permits, rather than stimulates, long-term growth.

Fiscal linkage has another characteristic that is likely to weaken its efficiency. Surplus is concentrated in the hands of relatively few decisionmakers in the government, so that the constraint of inadequate planning capacity rapidly becomes binding. As a result, the surplus tends to be used for large-scale projects. This may seem to minimize the administrative complexity of managing disbursements, but in fact it merely shifts the problem further down the line to the stage of project implementation. The labor/capital proportions required by large projects may also be inappropriate for the producer economy, since the criterion used is (immediate) administrative ease rather than such longer-run factor endowments. Several giant projects may then move a producing country, especially a small one, away from economic diversification toward dependence on a few key investments—leaving the country more vulnerable than before.

In addition, public officials are not personally rewarded according to the economic soundness of their choices. This leaves open the possibility that a host of other considerations, political or financial, will influence investment decisions. A large rent component in national income, if not rapidly and widely dispersed across the population, is liable to divert scarce entrepreneurial talent away from commodity production into "rent-seeking" activities. This can manifest itself in many ways. Public investments may be chosen not for any potential supply contribution, but to enrich contractors and politicians. Or there may be greater pressure for import protection to take advantage of the increasingly profitable home market. Incentives to maintain checks on the use of public funds by others may vanish entirely and be replaced by incentives to secure a share of the rent for oneself. Such rent-seeking activities, therefore, can be expected to lower the quality of domestic resource allocation. Commentaries on the experience of both high-income and developing oil-producing regions suggest that such "rentier economy" effects are indeed large in some of them although they are difficult to quantify.[5]

Finally, fluctuating fiscal revenues are likely to cause marked asymmetries in public decisionmaking. Investment programs started during a boom are hard to reverse; employees once hired are hard to dismiss. Asymmetric response is discussed below in the context of export instability, but here it should be noted that it weakens the effectiveness of fiscal linkage by lowering the average quality of public spending.

Growth, Two-Gap, and Three-Gap Models

Neoclassical growth theory characterizes output growth as a process of expanding a production possibility set, the frontier of which is set by the quantity (rather than the quality) of factors of production and by the efficiency of their allocation across activities. In the simplest formulation, growth is constrained by increases in the labor force and capital formation, hence by domestic savings. If labor and other domestic inputs are abundant, imports are an important complementary factor of production and, export revenues cannot easily be increased, foreign exchange can become a second binding constraint on growth, as in the two-gap model. Further elaboration can lead to a three-gap model, in which development may also be constrained by a shortage of fiscal revenues. For this to happen, public funds must play a critical role—for example, in the process of capital formation, in ensuring access to foreign exchange, or in relaxing bottlenecks to growth—and there must be constraints on the ability to tax.[6]

Not much more needs to be said about these theories in the present context, except to observe that rent-intensive activities help to relax simultaneously all three types of constraint: domestic savings, foreign exchange, and fiscal revenues. To the extent that rents are taxed away and invested rather than consumed, these theories predict a very favorable effect of windfalls on growth, especially if the domestic labor force is not a tightly binding constraint.

Export Instability Theories

This facet of analysis bears on the question of whether adverse effects from the *variability* of oil income are likely to offset the benefits of temporarily *high* income. Typically, exports of developing countries are more concentrated than those of developed countries and consist largely of primary agricultural and mineral commodities. The former, it is commonly argued, are price-inelastic in demand and, because of harvest fluctuations, are also subject to supply shocks which then induce large price swings. Mineral commodities are price-inelastic in both demand and supply, with demand very sensitive to economic activity in consuming regions. Cyclical demand fluctuations then induce large price and revenue shifts. Terms of trade variations, it is generally agreed, tend to be larger for developing than for developed economies,[7] and some studies suggest that mineral exporters are prone to wider fluctuations in export prices and revenues than other developing countries.

There is far less agreement, however, on the significance of such conclusions, and consequently little accord on whether it would be desirable to try and stabilize commodity markets, even if it were possible to overcome the political difficulties involved in such an effort. There is also the perennial problem of how to identify the equilibrium trend about which stabilization should occur. Newbery and Stiglitz (1981) regard the microeconomic arguments for stabilization, which center on the aversion of producers to risk, as quantitatively insignificant. And indeed, no clear empirical relation has yet been found between growth rates and the degree of export stability.[8]

As conventionally measured, however, instability emphasizes short-run fluctuations, typically lasting one or two years. Possibly more important for the oil exporters have been the macroeconomic consequences of their far larger and slower fluctuations in terms of trade and fiscal revenues, and the effects of the resulting uncertainty on project selection in their public investment programs. Though very large, swings such as those in the oil market (as well as major shifts in steel, aluminum, and other commodity markets) are greatly attenuated by the filters used to compute conventional instability indices, which screen out oscillations of more than about four years' periodicity.[9] For comparison, the periodicity of large oil market fluctuations since the early 1970s has been around ten years, with the overall boom of 1973–82 corresponding to a cycle of twenty years. These periods are long in relation to the fluctuations considered suitable for buffering, either by holding commodity stocks or by first accumulating and then drawing on international reserves. But they are quite short for planning and executing major development projects and for carrying out large fiscal, sectoral, and macroeconomic adjustments to cope with huge swings in revenue and demand.[10]

There are also macroeconomic arguments in favor of stable export revenues. These point to the well-recognized asymmetry of adjustment in response to fluctuations in demand.[11] When domestic demand increases, supply is likely to hit capacity constraints. Inflation, real exchange rate appreciation, and rising imports then clear markets. But when demand decreases, unemployment is likely to rise either because of downward wage rigidity or because of sticky prices, with firms temporarily off their long-run supply curves.[12] Thus demand fluctuations (or intermediate price shocks) both raise average imports and lower average capacity use, output, and income. If savings and investment fall with income, this has an adverse impact on growth.

If changes in oil revenue are manifested primarily in changes in the rate of public investment, a further growth argument for stability follows. There are costs in terms of quality—not easily measurable but apparently considerable—associated with very large shifts in the rhythm of investment. On the one hand, rapid growth of public spending is liable to reduce the quality of capital formation and raise costs because of more hasty planning, transport bottlenecks, and the need to use progressively more costly (or lower quality) factors at higher growth rates. On the other hand, cutbacks mean costly postponement or cancellation, with partly completed ventures yielding no output. Even if they are later completed, delay will have reduced their rate of return.

Finally, some policies and government programs put into place during the boom years may prove difficult to reverse as oil income falls. For example, restrictions on dismissing civil servants may induce a ratchet effect in the public wage bill. It may be politically difficult to cut investments in the energy sector, even though declines in the world oil market reduce their profitability. Ratchet effects worsen the allocation of resources, and if sufficiently sustained they may prevent the reattainment of the pre-boom situation for a long time after the end of the windfall.

The importance of considering *changes* in oil markets, rather than just *levels* of sales and prices, is heightened by the fact that oil market fluctuations have been very poorly predicted. Although the market had been tightening in the previous three years, the first oil price increase was not widely expected, and observers disagreed about its cause. At least four theories emerged, all with different implications for the future pattern of prices.[13] The first argued that the increase reflected the gradual evolution since the 1960s of demand and supply conditions in favor of OPEC countries as reserve-output ratios fell, especially among the high-absorbing producers. The second stressed the shift of property rights from the oil multinationals to producer governments, and was sometimes invoked to explain why the gradual evolution of demand and supply had not been reflected in a similarly gradual adjustment of prices. Both of these theories suggested that price increases would be permanent, but that prices would not continue to rise sharply once a new steady-state equilibrium was attained.

Cremer and Salehi-Isfahani (1980) proposed a third theory based on the concept of "target revenue," which resulted in a backward-bending competitive oil supply curve. The higher world oil prices were, the lower the production levels a country needed to attain its revenue target. A shock to the system or a gradual outward shift in demand could then result in a jump from a low-price to a high-price equilibrium. Such an explanation points to a potentially volatile market with rapid price declines triggered by competition from new producers, which would increase the elasticity of OPEC's demand curve.[14]

A fourth theory was that the oil shock simply resulted from cartelization of the oil market; this allowed OPEC to institutionalize the sharp spot price increases that followed several significant political events threatening supplies. In this view, the path of oil prices would be set by the cohesiveness of the cartel. Some argued that

OPEC would collapse fairly quickly like other cartels;[15] but some, pointing to distinctive characteristics of oil production and of producing countries, contended that OPEC could be sustained indefinitely.

Theories of oil-price setting have continued to evolve. A recent one (see Adelman 1986b) departs from the proposition that oil exporters tend to operate with short horizons and high discount rates because their wealth portfolios are concentrated in a volatile oil sector rather than diversified. These high discount rates cause pricing decisions to be made on the basis of short-run, inelastic demand schedules for oil rather than the more elastic long-run schedule; this leads to a policy of "take the money and run" and to an inherently unstable oil market.

Whatever the theoretical views, by 1977 projections of prolonged scarcity were being taken seriously. It was asserted that by the mid-1980s OPEC production would have to rise by 50 percent, to 45 million barrels a day, or else real world prices would escalate further. The second oil price rise, which like the first was unexpected, was widely interpreted as reflecting the long-run depletion of an exhaustible resource. Many official projections after 1979 foresaw a steady rise in real prices of about 3 percent a year for a long period rather than a ballooning for a relatively brief period,[16] and some exporting countries factored even higher price increases into their national plans. In the event, OPEC's production in the mid-1980s was barely one-third of the level projected in 1977, and the price of oil fell to a third of its peak levels.

Thus neither of the price increases was widely anticipated, nor was the oil glut of the 1980s. Nor were the policy responses of major consuming countries predicted—responses that significantly changed global scenarios between the first and second oil shocks. The stochastic nature of the windfalls and reversals, and the inadequacy of predictions—not only of oil prices but of worldwide inflation, of interest and exchange rates, and of other commodity markets—must be borne in mind when accounting for the effects of the oil shocks.

Booming Sectors and the Dutch Disease

John Cairnes seems to have been the first to use this analytical approach when, in 1857, he studied the effects of the 1851 Australian gold discoveries on other sectors of the economy.[17] The extensive theoretical literature that followed has been surveyed by Corden (1984) and Neary and van Wijnbergen (1986); the treatment here is therefore concise and selective.

Unlike the three approaches already described, the "booming sector" theory focuses on the sectoral reallocation of productive factors in response to a favorable shock emanating from either a resource discovery or an increase in the price of some commodity—typically an exportable one. If income is spent rather than saved abroad, the sum of the consequences includes a resource movement effect, which draws factors of production out of other activities and into the booming sector, and a spending effect, which draws factors of production out of activities producing traded commodities (to be substituted by imports) and into nontraded sectors. The contraction or stagnation of the traded sectors is sometimes referred to as the "Dutch disease." [18]

The key equilibrating variable in this process is the real exchange rate, the importance of which in the present context requires some elaboration. In some theoretical models of an economy, production is divided into "traded" and "nontraded" sectors where the former obey the so-called law of one price. This states that their domestic prices will equal their international prices because of the flow of goods across international boundaries, although tariffs may cause the prices to diverge by some specified amounts. The market for nontraded goods, however, must clear by domestic price movements. In this framework, the real exchange rate may be defined as the relative price of nontraded goods to traded goods, P_n/P_t. When domestic spending-power increases, an appreciation, or rise, in this ratio shifts production to the nontradables and demand to the tradables. This permits increased real income, in the form of higher absorption of nontradables and higher net imports of tradables.

An alternative concept, sometimes termed the "real effective exchange rate," is commonly used in empirical analysis because categories of goods exhibit a continuum of tradability.[19] It may be measured by an index of domestic prices (for tradables and nontradables) relative to the prices of major trading partners converted at market exchange rates, p_d/ep^*. If the price of traded goods p_t is set by the level of foreign prices and a *fixed* tariff (so that $p_t = ep^*[1 + t]$), the two concepts will clearly move together; real exchange rate appreciation will imply real effective exchange rate appreciation.[20]

However, these two definitions of the real exchange rate may not *always* point in the same direction. Suppose that domestic sectors producing tradable goods are heavily protected by tariffs or quotas that are then eliminated, at a fixed *nominal* exchange rate, in response to rising oil revenues. It is then possible for the domestic price level to fall (that is, the real effective exchange rate depreciates) even though the relative price of nontradables to tradables rises. When trade policy changes dramatically, caution is therefore needed in inferring the direction of domestic resource pulls from the real effective exchange rate. As discussed below, import liberalization is, in fact, one of three policy options for limiting the inflationary impact of spending an oil windfall domestically. The others are nominal exchange rate revaluation and price controls with rationing.[21]

One other consequence of an appreciating real effective exchange rate is important if capital is internationally mobile. As domestic prices inflate at a constant nominal exchange rate, the real interest rate on foreign funds (that is, the nominal foreign interest rate deflated by domestic prices) falls. This is likely to stimulate foreign borrowing for consumption and investment and further boost domestic absorption. Conversely, as oil prices and domestic spending fall and the real effective exchange rate depreciates, it is likely that capital movements will reverse. It is more profitable to hold foreign assets than domestic ones, which experience the adverse impact of falling demand on their returns. Alternatively, real exchange rate depreciation is expected to require nominal exchange rate devaluation and loss of value of assets denominated in domestic currency relative to those in foreign currency. Unless domestic interest rates are allowed to rise sharply, capital outflows will, therefore, probably accentuate the economic contraction.

Such a pattern of capital movements, inflows on the upswing of the cycle and outflows in the downturn, accentuates the cyclical changes in demand owing to variation in oil revenues and is opposite to the pattern which would be desirable to stabilize the economy over the cycle. Even if government saving abroad were to follow a stabilizing pattern, it is possible that this could be offset by procyclical private movements.[22]

A Simple Model

Figures 2-1 and 2-2 present the essentials for analyzing the effects of a rise in the price of oil exports, followed by a fall. In figure 2-1, OWX is the domestic production set, the combinations of non-oil tradables and nontradables which the economy can produce. Equilibrium is initially at A, with the real exchange rate (the price at which the tradables and nontradables can be exchanged) given by the slope of P_0, where the collective indifference curve dd is tangent to the production set.

A windfall equivalent to ZX in terms of traded goods shifts the absorption possibility set outward to OWYZ. We assume away any factor movements into the oil sector, and also abstract from growth.[23]

Figure 2-1. The Oil Windfall Cycle

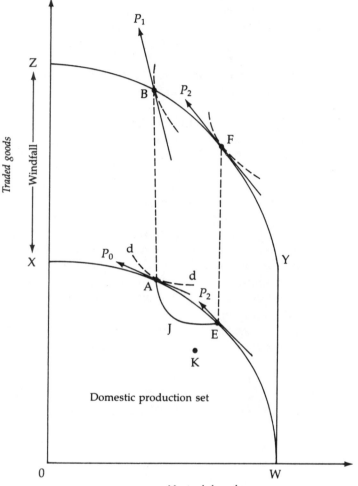

With domestic production initially fixed at A, demand shifts to B and the real exchange rate appreciates sharply to P_1, as the relative price of nontradables rises. This causes a reallocation of production toward the nontradables, and the economy shifts to production point E and demand point F. It is assumed that this shift is a smooth one along the boundary of the production set; we ignore possible factor market rigidities which could cause it to move inside the set when demand is rising.[24] The new real exchange rate is P_2,

Figure 2-2. The Oil Windfall Cycle with Government and Private Sector Distinguished

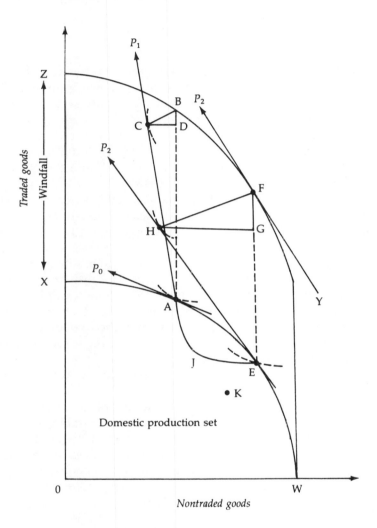

Nontraded goods

and at F the level of welfare is higher than at B, as shown by the indifference curve—the shift toward the nontraded sector is necessary to realize the full welfare gain.

Now consider the adjustment problem posed by a collapse of oil prices that eliminates the windfall gain. Production must shift back from E to A and demand from F to A. During this phase of the oil cycle the demand for nontraded goods slumps, as does real income. Unless the economy responds flexibly through smooth real wage adjustment, and unless firms remain on their supply curves (so that relative prices absorb all the reduction in the demand), adjustment will require a period of surplus capacity in the nontraded sectors such as along the path EJA. There may also be surplus capacity in the traded sector (point K) if, for example, imported inputs play a key role in production.

Oil windfalls accrue mostly to governments, however, and this introduces some changes into the analysis, as shown in figure 2-2. In this two-agent model (government and the private sector) all of the windfall is assumed to accrue to government, which initially had zero demand. Government spends the windfall on traded and nontraded goods in the fixed proportion BD/CD. Initially, with production still at A, private consumers will be at C and the public demand vector is CB. When production has shifted to E private demand is at H and government demand is HF, larger than before because the reallocation of domestic factors toward nontradables has somewhat depreciated the real exchange rate from its peak (P_1) and so reduced the cost of purchases by the public sector relative to oil prices. Note that the more the real exchange rate appreciates, the greater is the transfer of oil income to the private sector through the price mechanism, because the price index of its absorption falls relative to the cost index of non-oil production.[25] The figure shows that the more intensive the nontraded good is in public demand, the greater is the extent of real appreciation. And typically, real appreciation will be greater in the early stages, before the economy has been able to reallocate resources to the nontraded sectors.[26]

The overall value of the windfall is the integral of private welfare over the cycle ACHEJ, plus the value assigned to public absorption CB and HF, less the integral of private welfare at A over the cycle. It is likely to be *lowest* in the following circumstances: (a) public absorption has a low value; (b) traded and nontraded goods are complementary in private demand, and the private welfare function is strongly concave in income; (c) the windfall is transient and is fully absorbed, so that adjustment costs are raised; and (d) other policies also raise adjustment costs, especially in the downturn—so that the segment EJA is well inside the production set. Such policies could include a reluctance to devalue in line with falling demand, which would make relative price adjustment more difficult between traded and nontraded goods.

Some Extensions to the Model

This simple model can be extended in a number of ways, toward a full simulation system of the type which underlies the analysis of chapter 8. Without going so far, some small extensions can make it more relevant to actual experiences discussed in parts II and III.

CAPITAL FLOWS. As noted earlier, there may be a tendency for capital inflows during the boom and capital outflows in the contraction to accentuate the cycle. The latter will be especially stimulated by interest rate controls, since the real exchange rate is seen to be unsupportable. Capital flight when oil revenues are declining causes demand to fall below income, further decreases demand for domestic goods and accelerates and deepens the contraction along EJA.

TRANSPORT AND DISTRIBUTION SERVICES. All imports require transport and distribution services before they can be absorbed domestically, and these nontraded intermediate inputs may modify the conclusions of the simple model. If the rate of growth of absorption is very high or if changes in its composition are large, congestion costs in transport and distribution systems are likely to rise sharply. This will be equivalent to a fall in the efficiency of the non-oil economy, which will be manifested in a rise of consumption and investment prices relative to non-oil production costs. This tends to offset the fall in absorption prices relative to production costs that usually results from real appreciation. Part or all of the oil income transfer effected through the real exchange rate is then dissipated through lower efficiency in transforming the new mix of domestic factors and foreign exchange into final output.

INTERMEDIATE PRICE SHOCKS. So far, oil has been considered as a source of foreign exchange only, and not as an intermediate input. Once its latter role is included the sequence of intermediate price shocks will probably differ in oil-exporting and oil-importing countries over the windfall cycle. On the upswing, given their ample fiscal resources, the governments of oil-exporting countries are likely to resist raising domestic oil prices to world levels. To do so would shift resources from the private to the public sector at a time when the emphasis is on moving resources the other way. Holding domestic oil prices constant insulates these economies from the supply shock being experienced by oil-importing countries and reduces the tendency for the exporters' real effective exchange rates to appreciate against those of their trading partners. But on the downside of a cycle, falling oil export revenue will cause exporting governments to compensate by raising domestic oil prices. The non-oil economy of the oil exporter then experiences a supply shock and inflationary surge simultaneous with falling demand. Meanwhile, the opposite holds in oil-importing countries. The result may be a sudden real effective *appreciation* of the exporters' exchange rate despite falling demand on the downside of the cycle.

THE MONETARY DIMENSION. Finally, the model can be extended in the monetary dimension. Several studies, summarized in Neary and van Wijnbergen (1986), have analyzed the impact of resource booms in a monetary framework. In such studies, the supply of money normally enters, in a conventional way, as an independent policy variable. But the distinction between fiscal and monetary policy is of limited value for developing oil exporters. Money is created when their governments run a "domestic deficit," defined as the excess of domestic expenditures over domestic (typically non-oil) revenues. In the boom years, domestic deficits are extremely large, and offsetting their effect on the money supply—by open-market operations or credit controls—is not feasible. Therefore the link between monetary and fiscal policies is close and inevitable.

Nevertheless, monetary aspects can be important in several ways:

- Before imports have risen sufficiently to offset the process of money creation initiated by the domestic deficit, the expansion of credit and money via the money multiplier may accentuate the boom if not choked off by higher reserve requirements or credit ceilings.
- The government may crowd out private sector competition for scarce domestic factors of production through tightening credit policy, if it considers that its own claims on the economy are paramount.
- There is likely to be a fiscal impact from increased demand for real balances, which raises the inflation tax. This may be considerable because, in the boom years, oil economies are usually inflating and rapidly monetizing their economies; sectors such as public services and other "modern" urban activities are growing fast, pulling labor from traditional, nonmonetized activities.[27]

COMBINING THE APPROACHES. These four strands of economic analysis—linkage, growth, instability, and "booming sector"—are not, of course, mutually exclusive. Indeed, they may be combined into a unified framework such as the one that underlies the simulations reported in chapter 8. They do, however, emphasize different aspects of the set of constraints, choices and policies available to countries faced with the difficult (if enviable) task of absorbing massive windfall gains productively.

Notes

1. Canadian economists, in particular, emphasized the staple theory. It originated with Harold Innes; see Watkins (1963).

2. Linkage theory was developed by Albert Hirschman; for a concise review see Hirschman (1981), especially chap. 4, "A Generalised Linkage Approach to Development, with Special Reference to Staples."

3. A clear distinction between "absolutely adverse" consumption linkages and those which are less favorable than they could be with lower import propensities is not always made. In a static model, real incomes could fall on account of the new activity if income distribution or other changes caused a large shift in aggregate demand away from goods produced by domestic factors of production. But such an effect may not be necessary for adverse consumption linkage. Although welfare may increase in the short run, factors of production could be drawn out of activities in which learning-by-doing externalities are important, possibly through the expansion of the nontraded sectors (see van Wijnbergen 1984a). One study which examines "displacement effects" is Resnick (1970).

4. The point is discussed by Hirschman (1981) who notes that Fishlow (1965) analyzes the growth of the U.S. railway system (a vital component of that country's development) as a response to demand from existing activities. In contrast, Hunt (1973) argues that Peru's nineteenth-century guano boom failed to stimulate development because of inappropriate railway investments, rather than because rents were dissipated through imports and remittances.

5. Rentier effects are not peculiar to developing countries. As oil reveenues rose in the state of Alaska, state representatives were inclined to give up monitoring each other's proposals for development projects in favor of lobbying for their own projects. The state program eventually fragmented into numerous unassessed local programs. Rent-seeking and its costs are discussed more generally in Krueger (1974) and in Dervis, de Melo, and Robinson (1982, sec. 9.4).

6. The two-gap model was first elaborated by Chenery and Bruno (1962) and Chenery and Strout (1966). A three-gap model may be constructed along the lines of models sometimes used to analyze foreign borrowing; see Kharas (1984).

7. See, for example, Erb and Schiavo-Campo (1969).

8. Yotopolous and Nugent (1976, chap. 18) summarize the evidence then available.

9. Gelb (1979) analyzes the filters used in the construction of conventional instability indices.

10. Even the stabilization of short-term fluctuations may be academic. Davis (1983) analyzes the response of ten East African governments to export and fiscal fluctuations. His results confirm the impression that governments are ineffectual stabilizers because expenditures adjust rapidly to revenues.

11. For an evaluation of the importance of macroeconomic arguments for commodity price stabilization, see Kanbur (1984).

12. The model simulations in chapter 8 include the effects of these rigidities.

13. Gately (1984) discusses these various theories of the evolution of the world oil market and describes their implications for the role of OPEC.

14. This was the process in operation in 1985 and early 1986 as oil prices plummeted from around $30 to $12 a barrel.

15. For example, see Milton Friedman, *Newsweek*, March 4, 1974, as cited in Gately (1984).

16. With hindsight, it is apparent that projections were unduly influenced by price increases in the immediately preceding period. See, for example, World Bank (1979, p. 35; 1980a, p. 6).

17. Bordo (1975) summarizes Cairnes's analysis.

18. Holland's claim to be associated with this theory followed debate on the impact of natural gas on the Dutch economy. The term "Dutch disease" was apparently coined by the *Economist* on November 26, 1977.

19. See Dervis, de Melo, and Robinson (1982, chap. 7).

20. In some studies, the real effective exchange rate (or purchasing-power-parity-adjusted effective exchange rate) is measured as the price of foreign exchange in domestic currency corrected for changes in domestic and foreign price levels, that is, the inverse of the present variable. The present measure is preferred because it allows a natural association between the term "appreciation" and an upward move in the index.

21. Let $p_d = a \times p_n + (1 - a) \cdot p_t$ be the domestic price level, where a is the share of expenditures on nontraded goods. The price of nontraded goods is p_n and $p_t = e \cdot p^*(1 + t)$, where p^* is the level of foreign prices of nontraded goods and e is the nominal exchange rate. Then, by substitution, $p_d = a \cdot p_n + (1 - a) \cdot e \cdot p^*(1 + t)$. If t and e are constant, p_d and p_n move together. Assume that (a) there are no non-oil export sectors, (b) domestic oil prices are held constant, and (c) as world oil prices rise, t is reduced. This introduces a divergence in the movements of p_d and p_n/p_t; the former can fall while the latter rises. Reducing e can have a similar effect. For a discussion of price controls with rationing, see chapter 10.

22. Like other destabilizing speculative flows, this pattern of capital movements will probably not be profitable in the long run—unless the government absorbs losses of those who borrow abroad to finance domestic assets which later depreciate in value.

23. This analysis also disregards possible input shocks caused by rising domestic oil prices. In fact, most oil exporters stabilized domestic energy prices, at least until the early 1980s, so that input shocks were not important.

24. One such possibility, raised by van Wijnbergen (1984b), involves a downwardly rigid real wage and a consumption basket in which nontraded goods are heavily represented. In such a case, spending oil receipts could lead to more labor being released in the traded sectors than is absorbed in the nontraded sectors. This possibility is considered unlikely for cases in which real appreciation is actually caused by increased domestic spending, because it requires that investment and public consumption be so intensive in traded goods that wage earners derive none of the benefits

of real appreciation. It is significant that this analysis was stimulated by the example of Britain, perhaps the one country where rising oil revenues coincided with a government decision to *cut back* the role of the public sector in the economy. The sharp real effective appreciation of sterling, by 50 percent in 1976–80, has been attributed to tight monetary policy rather than to the spending effects from an oil bonus that represented, at best, about 5 percent of GDP; see Niehans (1981).

25. The private sector may be better or worse off at H than at C because the transfer effect and the gains from reallocating domestic production from A to E work in opposite directions.

26. This is still true in an intertemporal framework characterized by perfect product and capital markets; see Neary and van Wijnbergen (1986).

27. A simple monetary extension of the basic model is as follows: let M, CG, CP, and CF represent the money stock, credit to the government and to the private sector, and net foreign assets of the banking system. For convenience, let the money multiplier be unity. There are no private capital flows. If d represents a change in a variable, $dM = dCG + dCP + dCF = (G - T) - dO + dCP + (X - IM) + dO$, where G is government spending, assumed to be all on domestic goods, T is non-oil (domestic) tax revenue, dO is an increment of oil revenue, which was previously zero. dO is exogenous and is assumed to accrue to the government, whose domestic deficit, $G - T$, together with credit to the private sector, are controls. Let P be the real effective exchange rate, that is, the price of domestic goods relative to imports. The private non-oil trade surplus is assumed to be a negative function of dCP and P; we may then write:

$$P = 1/a_2 \left[d(G - T) + dCP(1 - a_1 - dM) \right]$$

where a_1 is the net propensity of the private sector to import at fixed relative prices, and a_2 is the response of the private non-oil trade deficit to real effective exchange appreciation. This equation indicates the dependence of the real exchange rate on fiscal policy, credit policy, import propensities (a_1 and the extent of public spending on domestic goods), the substitutability of domestic and foreign goods (a_2), and the willingness of the private sector to hold money balances. It is possible to absorb the windfall with less real appreciation if trade is not restricted so that a_2 is large, if public expenditures fall largely on imports, if private credit policy is tight, or if the private sector is willing to hold larger real balances.

Chapter 3

Absorbing Mineral Rents: The Record and the Policy Options

The composition of a country's output and exports changes continually, so that it is not possible to label an economy definitively as "mineral" or "nonmineral" on the basis of the share of minerals in GDP or trade. Despite this, categorization on the basis of general tendencies can be useful. Nankani (1979) finds that there were twenty-seven nations with a population of a million or more in which mining exceeded 10 percent of output and 40 percent of exports in the period 1967–75. These can, then, be considered "mineral economies."[1] Twelve are producers of hard minerals, twelve are capital-deficit oil producers, and three (Libya, Kuwait, and Saudi Arabia) are capital-surplus oil producers.

Do Minerals Promote Development?

Mineral production is normally associated with the Ricardian rent which accrues to owners of reserves that are particularly concentrated or that have low extraction costs. This is one of the main reasons for considering mineral economies as a distinct class of countries. Under exceptionally favorable conditions, however, the production of some agricultural commodities is also able to generate rents over and above normal returns to capital, labor, and land in alternative uses—sometimes only until the emergence of competing producers. Any assessment of the role of rent in development should therefore be broadened to include countries other than mineral exporters.

At the same time, mineral production has some peculiar features: it is large-scale, enclave, and capital-intensive, usually with close links to multinational firms, often with high wages compared with the rest of the economy and with a high degree of uncertainty (Bosson and Varon 1977). These features may prove more impor-

32

tant than the effect of spending out of mining rent in determining the evolution of the producing economy.

The available evidence concerning the impact on development of rent in general, and of mineral rent in particular, can only be described as mixed. On the one hand, as described by the staple thesis, rent—usually from a succession of activities rather than a single continuous one—has indeed played a leading role in the growth of such industrial economies as the United States, Canada, and Australia (Reynolds 1979). Profits from copper financed development in seventeenth-century Sweden (Heckscher 1963). An unusually strong comparative advantage in coffee provided funds and a source of demand to stimulate the growth of Brazil's industrial economy around São Paulo.[2] The discovery of the gold fields of the Witwatersrand spurred the development of the modern South African economy, financing imports without which expansion would have been impossible while creating demand for transport services, intermediate inputs, and capital goods (Houghton 1972, chap. 5).[3] On a more speculative note, the total of British foreign investments has been attributed to the windfall from Drake's circumnavigation in 1577–80, which paid a dividend of 4,700 percent:

> Indeed the booty brought back by Drake in the Golden Hind may fairly be considered the fountain and origin of British Foreign Investment. Elizabeth paid off out of the proceeds the whole of her foreign debt and invested a part of the balance (about £42,000) in the Levant Company; largely out of the profits of the Levant Company there was formed the East India Company . . . If this is, on the average, a fair sample of what has been going on since 1580, the £42,000 invested by Elizabeth out of Drake's booty in 1580 would have accumulated by 1930 to approximately the actual aggregate of our present foreign investments, namely £4,200,000,000. (Keynes 1930, pp. 156–57.)

Thus there is evidence that, at least in some cases, high-rent activities (including piracy) have provided an important stimulus to growth.

On the other hand, a positive causal link between high-rent activities and development is certainly not inevitable. A lengthy literature raises the possibility that the high-rent sector may inhibit the accumulation and upgrading of reproducible factors of production, and that in the long run this diversion of resources and attention can stultify growth. In the sixteenth century, discoveries of precious metals in America had an adverse effect on Spain's domestic industries by boosting wages above competitive levels (Keynes 1930) but a favorable effect on the industries of Holland—which was less

Table 3-1. Investment and Growth Rates by Developing Country Group

Measure	Hard-mineral exporters 1960–71	Hard-mineral exporters 1971–83	Oil exporters 1960–71	Oil exporters 1971–83	Other middle-income countries 1960–71	Other middle-income countries 1971–83	Other low-income countries 1960–71	Other low-income countries 1971–83
Investment/GDP								
Mean	0.21	0.23	0.21	0.28	0.20	0.24	14.30	17.20
σ	0.06	0.05	0.10	0.10	0.05	0.05	4.10	6.10
Gross IOCR[a]								
Mean	0.28	0.07	0.34	0.12	0.32	0.17	0.26	0.17
σ	0.05	0.02	0.06	0.05	0.02	0.01	0.03	0.04
Growth of GDP per capita (percent)								
Mean	2.5	−1.0	2.9	1.9	3.7	2.0	1.3	0.7
σ	1.1	1.2	1.7	3.7	1.8	2.3	1.4	2.2
Number of countries	10	10	10	10	29	29	20	20

a. Incremental output/capital ratio.
Source: World Bank data.

adventurous or perhaps less successful in its search for treasure (Williams 1970). Before the Industrial Revolution, countries of northern and western Europe were considered to be poorly endowed with natural resources compared with their neighbors in the south and east, who were soon to be outstripped economically (Southern 1952). And the most striking economic successes of the past several decades—Japan, the Republic of Korea, Singapore, and Taiwan— are all conspicuously poor in natural resources and rich in human resources.

Historical evidence also provides some support for the thesis that mineral resources encourage countries to adopt highly leveraged, overextended strategies that render them more vulnerable to shocks:

> In seeking power and glory King Philip spent the combined proceeds [of Spain's Peruvian and Mexican silver mines and revenues from the annexation of Portugal]—and more. He was the wealthiest monarch in Christendom, and went broke the most often. Accordingly, he paid increasingly high interest rates, because his creditors realized that the risk had been transferred to them. (Adelman, 1986b, p. 25.)

Table 3-1 considers the investment and growth performance, and the relationship between investment and growth, of four groups of developing countries: (a) the hard-mineral exporters, (b) oil exporters, (c) other middle-income countries, and (d) other low-income countries. It covers two periods, 1960–71 and 1971–83. Capital-surplus oil exporters and countries with incomplete data are excluded.

The table indicates, first, the extent to which there has been a general structural shift in the relationship between investment and growth. In all groups, (unweighted) average investment rates rose between the first and second periods. But this was more than offset by falls in the incremental output/capital ratios (IOCRs), so that average growth rates deteriorated by a considerable margin. Second, the averages suggest that deterioration in the productivity of investment (as suggested by the growth-investment relationship) has been more marked for the mineral exporting groups, which also experienced the greatest variation in their terms of trade (see table 3-2). The hard-mineral exporters, whose terms of trade deteriorated sharply in the second period, almost stopped growing. The oil exporters, whose terms of trade improved spectacularly and whose investment rates rose the most, saw their average IOCR fall to barely one-third of its previous value. In the first period, the hypothesis that the mineral and nonmineral economies have identical IOCRs cannot be rejected; in the second period it can, at the 90 percent level.

**Table 3-2. Terms of Trade Indices Relative to Unit Value
of Manufactures Imported by Developing Countries**

Period	Metals and hard minerals	Petroleum	Agriculture
1960–62	100	100	100
1970–72	104	92	91
1980–82	78	636	84

Source: World Bank data.

At first appearance, the mineral economies, whether facing favorable or unfavorable terms of trade movements, have therefore experienced a more serious deterioration in the efficiency of domestic capital formation than the nonmineral economies. In the hard-mineral economies this resulted in negligible growth. In the oil exporters, growth rates fell despite vastly greater investment.

Mineral economies have also been alleged to exhibit certain undesirable structural characteristics. In the cross-section study of Adelman and Morris (1973) an abundance of natural resources, together with the degree of dualism, was found to be an important explanation of the concentration of income. Labor endowments are far more evenly distributed than assets such as access to resource rents, so that an inverse long-run relation between resource abundance and income equality does not seem surprising.[4] If the government is the major recipient of rent, much depends on the pattern of public spending—and this is often asserted to be urban-biased. One reason is political: mining and urban activities provide a natural focus for efforts by organized labor to extract a share of rent.[5] To complement this effect, mineral sectors enable countries to earn the foreign exchange they need to import food. Indeed, a charge frequently levied at mineral economies is that they neglect, if not suppress, their (tradable) agricultural sectors, which suffer from overvalued real exchange rates and public indifference. The long-run consequences for the distribution of income are predictable. Migration to the urban or mining sectors is the only way to secure access to a share in the natural rent through protected employment, public services, or subsidies.[6]

More surprising, perhaps, is the observation that mineral economies have not enjoyed particularly high levels of education and health care despite the strong positive association between a large mining industry and the ratio of tax revenue to GDP.[7] Failure to allocate fiscal resources to social sectors may be related to the less crucial role played by reproducible factors of production in such economies. Mining income may lessen the pressure to ensure wide access to public goods and to develop human capital broadly across the population.

The long-run impact of these tendencies on growth could be considerable. It is generally accepted that capital markets are not sufficiently perfect for individuals to fund their own education by borrowing against their expected future earnings. At the same time, microeconomic data often suggest that human capital formation has a high private rate of return, and there may also be large externalities in such areas. Neglecting the social sectors may therefore have an adverse long-run effect on growth that offsets any positive gains derived from the mineral sector itself.

Options for Absorbing Windfall Gains

The ultimate use and impact of windfall gains depend, first, on the policy choices adopted by the producer government. These include not only extraction rates and public spending, but also possible shifts in trade and other policies in response to changes in national income, which affect the distribution of the gains across the economy. Second, they depend on how the macroeconomy responds to the surge in demand, which will create disequilibrium in some markets at prewindfall output and prices. Table 3-3 presents a framework for analyzing these policy and macroeconomic factors, which is discussed in this section.

Two underlying factors of a political and administrative nature should first be mentioned, since they affect the efficacy of any policy choices that are made. The first is the "horizon" of public decisionmaking. This is likely to be closely related to the stability of the government. If leaders change often and in a discontinuous manner, it may be futile to attribute the policy responses of the country to any consistent set of objectives through the period of windfall gains. The second factor is the "unity" or centralization of public decisionmaking. When there are powerful, competing actors (such as autonomous public enterprises or an equally strong executive and legislature), inconsistent decisions can result in an outcome different from, and inferior to, what would result if decisions were formulated by any single agent.

Together, these factors largely determine whether a country can formulate and execute any coherent strategy at all. As described in part II of this book, the six countries in this study differed considerably in these two respects. The governments of Indonesia and Algeria had long horizons and centralized power. Those of Ecuador and Nigeria, however, were subject to frequent changes and powerful re-

Table 3-3. Absorbing Windfalls: Policy Choices and Macro Variables

Oil extraction rate (1)	Net savings abroad (2)	Windfall absorption emphasis (3)	Public investment emphasis (4)	Main subsidies and rent transfers (5)	Development emphasis (6)
Increase extraction to sell more at high prices	Increase net savings abroad to reduce domestic demand and build up foreign assets	Public spending (consumption investment)	Traded: hydrocarbons, other industry, agriculture; exporting, import-substituting	Subsidies to firms	Urban
Slow extraction to keep wealth in the form of oil reserves	Increase net borrowing abroad against future oil income	Transfers to private sector (subsidies, cuts in non-oil taxes)	Nontraded: physical infrastructure, social capital (education, health)	Subsidies to households via direct transfers, subsidized credit, and subsidies on commodities (oil, food, etc.)	Rural
	Two-way flows (public capital inflows, private outflows)	Incentives to private consumption, investment	Other considerations: scale, factor intensity		Regionally decentralized (possible role of resource-based industrial projects)

Other Macro Variables and Policies

Availability of labor and skills	Trade policy	Main macroeconomic clearing method	Nominal exchange rate policy
Large: labor supply can increase in response to demand without large real wage increases	Open: clearing of markets by allowing demand to spill over onto a wide range of imports	Real exchange rate equilibrates nontradable markets (with or without nominal rate flexibility)	In boom: revaluation to reduce inflation; constant nominal rate or depreciation
Small: labor force (or skills) is a bottleneck: growth of non-tradeds requires shrinking traded sectors	Closed: try to protect some non-oil traded sectors at the expense of others	Liberal import policy allows demand to spill over onto foreign goods	In downside: flexible rate to reduce recessionary impact and cushion budget; fixed rate
Labor and skills somewhat variable through immigration policy		Price controls and rationing to limit spending on domestic goods	Large devaluations to try to restore "real" oil income

gional pressures. Trinidad and Tobago and Venezuela occupied an intermediate position, though the factors involved were quite different in the two cases.

Absorption Policy Choices

For convenience, absorption choices may be arranged as a hierarchy, even though in reality (and in an optimizing decision framework) some of these decisions would be made simultaneously. Such a choice hierarchy is set out in table 3-3.

1. The first policy choice concerns the rate of extraction. In response to a surge in world prices, should oil be kept in the ground or should reserves be depleted more rapidly? In view of the difficulty of abruptly changing the rate of depletion, this choice may be somewhat constrained. If the country can lend and borrow abroad as much as it desires at a given interest rate, oil will be left in the ground if the rate at which its value is expected to rise exceeds the interest rate. If, however, access to international funds is limited, the country might raise its extraction rate to bring forward consumption, even though the price of oil was expected to rise more rapidly than the interest rate. Optimal extraction then also depends on the opportunities for domestic investments.

2. The second choice concerns the proportion of revenues to be absorbed at home as opposed to being saved abroad. Producers are likely to have a wide range of options, with excellent access to foreign loans as oil exports soar. To hold total domestic demand to the desired level, especially when the perceived cost of foreign funds falls with real effective exchange rate appreciation (as noted in chapter 2), the government may have to constrain borrowing abroad by public enterprises and the private sector. Large two-way capital flows are possible, either with government saving abroad and the rest of the economy borrowing, or the reverse.

3. The next policy choice is the broad type of absorption. Should oil income fund public investments, public consumption, or transfers to the private sector? The last of these could be implemented in many ways—by reducing non-oil taxes, granting subsidies to selected activities or groups, or subsidizing certain products. Most of the practical possibilities (such as a subsidy on oil for domestic use) are distortionary in that they cause prices to diverge from world levels or from costs. At first

glance the policy that seems to promise the least distortion is to reduce non-oil taxes, particularly on traded goods. Indeed, such a policy promises to decrease price distortions. The tax burden is borne by rent, a totally inelastic income source, but this leaves the budget dangerously dependent on volatile oil receipts. It may also be possible to influence the composition of private demand through the method used to effect the transfer, so that the choice of how to absorb oil income extends beyond the public sector.

4. A further set of choices relates to the thrust of public investment to be funded (or encouraged) by oil revenues. Two broad strategies for "sowing the oil" to strengthen the non-oil economy can be identified. One approach is to emphasize the non-oil tradable sectors—conventionally, agriculture (both food and nonfood), manufacturing, and natural resource processing. This approach includes a wide range of suboptions: Is the focus to be on activities that are large-scale and capital-intensive or small-scale and labor-intensive, import-substituting or exporting, urban or rural? A second approach is to emphasize key infrastructural sectors that are generally nontraded. These include physical capital largely serving production (transport, communications, and power supply); physical "social" capital (housing); and human capital (education, health). Such investments do not themselves create activities that can substitute for the foreign exchange provided by the oil sector. Their contribution to economic diversification and growth must lie in the stimulation and greater efficiency they promise for the *future* production of traded goods. The first strategy is therefore a more direct attempt to diversify out of oil, the second an indirect route that can be expected to take longer to end the dependence on oil.

How the government balances these two types of domestic investment has other important repercussions as well. First, some investments—particularly in large-scale, resource-processing industry—have high import requirements, whereas others—generally in housing, infrastructure, and education—rely primarily on domestic resources.[8] Second, certain investments—notably those in the social sectors—entail high recurrent costs and so impose future claims on fiscal revenue, whereas others—notably in the industrial sector—will, in theory at least, return a profit to the treasury.[9] The spending pattern can therefore affect both the intensity of the spending effect on domestic goods and the time profile of non-oil fiscal revenues and expenditures. To assess the appropriate pattern

for a given country is a complex problem to which there are no
easy answers.

 5. The method of rent transfer to recipients has many potential
    dimensions. Table 3-3 notes two methods—direct transfer or
    commodity (or credit) subsidies—and two classes of potential
    recipients, firms and households.
 6. A final aspect of absorption policy noted in the table is
    whether the emphasis is urban or rural, and whether regional
    decentralization (perhaps through the establishment of new
    industrial centers) is an important objective.

Macroeconomic Impact and Tradeoffs

The response of non-oil output to increased domestic spending (before supply-side effects of higher investment increase capacity) depends mainly on the degree of slack in the economy. This is the
first macro variable identified in table 3-3. If labor (with necessary
skills) is in elastic supply at a given wage, non-oil growth will be vigorous and driven by demand, and the real exchange rate will appreciate less because of high supply elasticity. Any contraction exerted
on the non-oil traded sectors will be small because these do not
need to give up labor to the booming sectors. But if labor markets
are initially tight so that the non-oil economy is operating on its production frontier, the spending effect imparts less of a growth stimulus. Expansion of the nontraded sectors requires contraction (or, in
a dynamic context, slow growth) of the non-oil traded sectors and a
rise in the relative price of the nontradeds.[10]

This raises the problem of the sectoral tradeoffs posed by the absorption of oil rent, a topic which has aroused considerable concern
in producing countries. Is there a case for protecting some or all of
the non-oil traded sectors from the adverse resource pulls caused
by an oil-fueled spending effect? And, if this is desirable, how can
it be accomplished?

Whether a given sector expands or shrinks during the boom depends on three characteristics: (a) its degree of "tradability," (b) the
absorption elasticity of demand for its output, and (c) its factor requirements relative to those of the most rapidly growing sectors (typically construction and government services). Trade policy alone,
the first and most obvious option (which avoids driving a wedge
between domestic producer and consumer prices) cannot protect all
sectors simultaneously. Higher barriers against manufactured imports, for example, will simply be reflected in greater appreciation
of the real effective exchange rate since the range of traded prod-

ucts becomes narrower. Such a policy would further depress agricultural exports and therefore shift the burden of adjustment from one sector to another rather than protecting all traded sectors. The range of trade policy options is noted in table 3-3.

A second option is "exchange rate protection," a possible strategy for protecting all sectors producing non-oil traded goods (Corden 1981c). This rests on saving abroad instead of spending domestically at the rate that would be desirable were the non-oil tradables not a concern.

A third option is to launch a public spending program that is more import-intensive than would otherwise be optimal. The cost of this and of the previous strategy lies in their otherwise suboptimal profiles of rent absorption, either over time or across uses. The cost must be offset against the presumed benefits to the non-oil traded sectors.

A fourth option is to use oil income to subsidize the non-oil traded sectors. This could be done, for example, by imposing negative indirect taxes on a specific product or its inputs. In addition to administrative complexities (such as those associated with a negative indirect tax on food) this strategy has the limitation that the income injected into the economy through the subsidies itself causes a spending effect which pulls resources toward the nontraded sectors. Offsetting this entirely requires either taxation of the nontraded sectors or a cutback in public demand, to *below* the level before the windfall, to provide additional funding for the subsidy.[11]

The unavoidable conclusion is that it is inconsistent to try and implement a major development plan and at the same time protect *all* traded sectors. In the long run, however, these sectors may benefit from investments or productivity gains made possible by oil income.

Now consider the case for using windfall gains to support some of the non-oil traded sectors. In general, permanent subsidization may be justified only if the social value of an activity diverges from the private value—reflecting, for example, distributional concerns or externalities due to some market failure. Can an oil windfall make a case, or strengthen an existing case, for subsidies based on such considerations? This question has been raised by van Wijnbergen (1984a). Neary and van Wijnbergen (1986) distinguish two possibilities for a windfall whose time profile is known with certainty. In the first, the country faces perfect capital markets. The time profile of absorption and its allocation between consumption and domestic investment are optimal in the sense that they maximize some discounted sum of welfare over the entire period. If a learning-by-doing externality is introduced in the traded goods sector, so that future productivity depends on current output levels, it can then be shown that the optimal subsidy is higher if, along the optimal path, the real exchange rate depreciates in the future.

Their second possibility, which may be more relevant empirically, is that the country faces imperfect world capital markets. The government does not have the savings instruments to sterilize transient windfall gains, and the private sector is not able to save, then dissave, abroad to offset changes in the level of public spending. The subsidy to tradables then represents a form of investment in raising future levels of productivity. Its costs, notably those of distortions during the phase of high oil revenues, must be set against the benefits of increased future output. The social value of these benefits will typically be higher if real income subsequently falls, possibly due to a decrease in oil income.

A third and perhaps even more relevant scenario, however, is that no real obstacle exists to saving the appropriate portion of oil income abroad at given (not necessarily constant) interest rates, yet the government faces political constraints to running large, cumulative budget surpluses. Suppose that the private sector cannot save or borrow abroad on a sufficient scale to offset the profile of public spending. Or, suppose that it *could* do so, but that individual agents do not have a sufficiently strong incentive to save abroad during the peak years of oil income because certain costs of rapid spending are borne by society and are therefore external to the individual.[12] In either situation, any argument for subsidies that appeals to the windfall is second best; the optimal policy would be to smooth the absorption profile over time.

The column headed "Main macroeconomic clearing method" in table 3-3 shows the strong interaction between trade policies and the way in which markets reach equilibrium in the booming producer economy. If imports are limited by policy or low natural substitutability, the real exchange rate plays a major role. Liberalizing trade can permit demand to spill over onto imports by broadening their coverage. Rationing mechanisms can also be used, as further explained in the empirical chapters.

Inflation, Trade, and Exchange Rate Policy

Another set of choices is posed by the interaction of inflation, trade, and nominal exchange rate policy (the last column at the bottom of table 3-3). As noted earlier, with a fixed exchange rate and with trade policy unchanged, appreciation of the real exchange rate means appreciation of the real effective exchange rate, and is effected through domestic inflation. If price stability is an important policy objective, nominal exchange rate revaluation and trade liberalization are two ways of counteracting the inflationary effects of the boom. The more open the economy (in terms of larger import shares and fewer impediments to substitution between domestic and foreign goods) the lower will be the inflationary stimulus. Protectionist policies to shield some traded sectors (at the expense of others) will therefore also worsen inflation unless the currency is simultaneously revalued. Monetary policy can have some impact on inflation but, as noted earlier, its impact will be quite limited.

On the downside of the oil cycle, the factors influencing the inflation rate are complex. In particular, they reflect the rate at which the government curbs expenditures relative to its falling oil revenues and foreign borrowing ability, and the extent to which additional revenue-raising measures entail higher domestic prices. The least inflationary combination of policies involves sharp cuts in public spending, increases in *direct* taxation, and moderate devaluation to stimulate the traded sectors. The most inflationary choices include large, domestically financed budget deficits, tightened import controls, or massive devaluations intended to restore fully the domestic purchasing power of oil taxes.[13] As shown in later chapters, such responses can have a severely adverse effect on economic performance.

Notes

1. Some very small economies are highly dependent on minerals. A fascinating account of the island of Nauru, where phosphate sales represented $25,000 for each of its 5,000 citizens, appears in the *Wall Street Journal*, September 22, 1983. The Sultanate of Brunei is a good case of an oil ministate outside the Gulf.

2. As indicated by high rates of taxation, coffee prices have frequently embodied a large component of natural rent. Furtado (1963, chaps. 30–32) describes the substantial role of coffee in Brazilian industrialization. A classic contrast is between the effects of coffee production and those of sugar production. Coffee, partly through its propensity to exhaust the soil and induce migration to new areas, stimulated commercialization, transport systems, a processing industry, and eventually the development of the tenth largest industrial complex in the world in São Paulo. Sugar, geographically static and with less immediate links between production, processing, and commercialization, gave rise to a poor, densely populated region (Dean 1966).

3. Although gold has retained its key role since the early twentieth century, there has been a steady diversification of output and exports since the 1940s, at least until the world gold boom in 1981 raised the share of gold in exports back toward its 1946 level of 56 percent.

4. Nankani (1979) discusses the relation between mineral endowment and dualism.

5. One example is the powerful Venezuelan labor movement formed in the oil workers' camps in the 1920s and 1930s.

6. The "dual economy" case of Zambia, a mineral economy with good agricultural potential that is less exploited than that of its mineral-poor neighbor Malawi, is discussed by Baldwin (1972) and Barber (1961).

7. Nankani (1979) points to the lagging school enrollments in the mineral economies. Tait, Gratz, and Eichengreen (1979) and others who have made cross-country comparisons of fiscal effort note the overall strongly positive contribution of mineral revenues, even though this is often partly offset by lower tax rates on nonmineral sectors and incomes.

8. The direct and indirect import content of heavy industrial investment may be as high as 80 percent of total cost, whereas direct imports for a variety of infrastructural projects may be close to zero. In the countries included in this study, over 60 percent of investment in the 1970s was of domestic origin, even though these countries lacked well-developed capital goods sectors other than construction.

9. Heller (1975) estimates the ratios of annual recurrent costs to capital costs. For some investments, these ratios may be up to 20 perent.

10. The economy will respond in a Keynesian manner to higher demand, if labor supply is elastic, rather than the neoclassical mode of figures 2-1 and 2-2.

11. Using a computable general equilibrium model of Indonesia, Gelb (1985a) simulates policies to shield three traded sectors—export agriculture, food, and manufacturing—from the consequences of spending an oil windfall equivalent to 8 percent of non-oil GDP. The government maximizes public investment subject to the rate of return in those sectors not falling relative to the mean rate of return in the nontraded sectors. This yields an optimal food subsidy of 19 percent, an agricultural export subsidy of 26 percent, and indirect taxation on manufactures of minus 5 percent. However, total public absorption has to be cut back to 78 percent of its prewindfall level.

12. Congestion costs in the upswing are one example of externality. On the downside, chapter 8 of this study confirms that an important argument for smoothing the time profile of absorption is likely to be the macroeconomic cost of adjustment, in terms of negative or slow growth. Such costs should be taken into account in setting the time profile of public spending, but they are external to individual private agents and therefore will not affect the private spending decision.

13. Devaluation may temporarily restore the purchasing power of oil revenues by cutting the price of nontraded goods relative to oil. Because the aggregate resource constraint has tightened, however, continued public spending must be offset by cuts in private spending. The alternative to increasing non-oil taxes is therefore inflation.

PART II

Comparative Analysis

Chapter 4

Introduction

Having reviewed some relevant theories, described the expectations raised by the windfalls, and provided some indication of the range of policies which may be adopted to absorb them and maintain macroeconomic equilibrium, we now proceed to compare the experiences of the six countries. In chapter 5 we develop a simple method of decomposing changes in national accounts data so that the size of windfalls relative to nonmining GDP can be estimated. Then we consider the uses of the windfalls over the period 1974–81, first from the viewpoint of the fiscal response and then in terms of absorption by the economy as a whole, using the same decomposition method. Chapter 6 analyzes the "booming sector" effects of absorbing the windfalls. It deals with real exchange rate adjustments and intersectoral resource shifts between non-oil tradables and nontradables. The supply of agricultural products in the oil exporters is also considered because of the sector's importance and vulnerability.

Chapter 7 discusses the impact of the windfalls on growth through 1981. Closely related is the question of the efficiency of fiscal linkage: the composition of the massive public investment programs in each country and the reasons for their apparently low payoff are key elements of the story. As is apparent from the discussion in chapter 3, the growth performance of the oil exporters was disappointing, even before the impact of the oil glut began to be felt.

Data covering the oil glut years are still incomplete and subject to revisions. Therefore the period 1980–84 is treated separately in chapter 8 with only the broad outlines presented. In brief, the six oil exporters entered a phase of stagflation (much as the oil-consuming countries had when oil prices rose). This asymmetric response further reduced their overall gain from the oil cycle. The volatility of oil prices is central to the analysis of this chapter.

Chapter 9 draws together the main conclusions of the comparative study.

Before proceeding, it is as well to indicate some limitations of the study. The sample size of six is far from adequate to embody all the economic, political, and policy differences among the widely scattered countries that nature has endowed with oil reserves. Therefore, simple unweighted averaging is used to provide indications of central tendencies, and individual countries are judged largely by their deviation from the averages. The cross-sectional approach of part II, which is organized by topics, is complemented by the case studies in part III, which provides a country-by-country treatment.

Some indication of the diversity of the sample countries is provided by table 4-1. In 1979 gross national product (GNP) per capita ranged from $370 in Indonesia to $3,910 in Trinidad and Tobago, while population ranged from 143.9 million in Indonesia down to 1.1 million in Trinidad and Tobago—which, being tiny, is by far the most densely populated country in the sample. Oil exports per person also varied widely, from $62 to $2,135 in 1979, as did the size and diversity of non-oil exports in 1973. In one important respect, however, there was surprisingly little variation. A very rough measure of the ratio of oil wealth to the non-oil capital stock using 1975 reserve estimates and prices lies within the range of 2.3–2.7 for all six countries. The share of oil in total wealth was therefore roughly similar for the entire sample.

Table 4-1 also summarizes features of the administrations of the countries over the period 1972–84, emphasizing the two aspects stressed in chapter 3: the degree to which decisionmaking was centralized and the continuity, or "time horizon," of the government.[1] Again there has been a great deal of cross-country variation, but the sample can be grouped into three pairs. Two countries, Indonesia and Algeria, are judged to have had political continuity and a stable economic policy framework throughout the period, and also to have had a highly centralized process for determining the uses of oil income. These features are suggested by later analysis to have had some advantages for growth and to have helped to avoid a serious foreign exchange crisis when oil income fell. Nigeria and Ecuador, in contrast, both experienced frequent changes of government of a discontinuous nature. In addition, their political systems were quite decentralized along regional lines. Both these countries were plunged into crisis by the fall in oil revenues, and their growth performance was not as good as that of the first-named pair. The third pair, Trinidad and Tobago and Venezuela, are judged to occupy an intermediate position. Both had quite highly competitive, democratic political systems throughout the period. The continuous government of the former was, however, vulnerable to pressure groups which were well organized along sectoral and ethnic lines. This led to mushrooming subsidies and loss of control over public spending. The Venezuelan administration changed in the middle of the boom period, as did economic policy. Moreover, after 1978 policies of the administration and of the legislature not infrequently diverged, and this had a substantial and adverse macroeconomic impact.

In the previous chapter, table 3-3 set out a framework for the main policy decisions and macroeconomic variables affecting the absorption of the windfall and its effects. To help link the comparative study with the theory, table 4-2 places the six countries into the framework. Because of the simultaneity of macroeconomic analysis, the link between policies and effects is not simple—for example, the rate at which windfalls are absorbed (discussed in chapter 5) bears on "booming sector" effects (chapter 6), growth (chapter 7), and the severity of the downturn (chapter 8). Therefore the reader might find it useful to refer back to table 4-2 at various points in the comparative study to ascertain how the response of a particular country compares with those of the others.

Note

1. The following statements represent broad judgments in the comparative framework of the sample. They should not be taken to imply any absolute statement on the nature of the respective countries' governments and are of course subject to a variety of qualifications. More detailed discussion of each country is in part III.

Table 4-1. Economic and Political Characteristics of the Oil Exporters

Country	GNP per capita, 1979 (U.S. dollars)	Population, 1979 (millions)	Area (thousands of square kilometers)	Oil exports per capita, 1979 (U.S. dollars)	Oil reserves/capital stock, 1975[a]	Main non-oil exports, 1973[b]	Political characteristics, centralization, and continuity, 1972–84
Algeria	1,770	18.3	2,382	478	2.5	Wine, fruit	Centralized socialist state; single political party with close ties to military. Change of president, 1979, but broad administrative and policy continuity.
Ecuador	1,110	8.1	284	127	2.3	Bananas, coffee, cacao	Regionally fragmented, with decentralized public sector; executive president and legislature. Military coup, 1972; transitional military junta, 1976; elected government with populist leanings, 1979; death and replacement of president, 1982. Political discontinuity.
Indonesia	370	143.9	1,919	62	2.3	Timber, rubber, coffee, tin, animal products, palm oil, coffee tea, pepper	Centralized civilian government with dominant political party (association of groups) and close ties to military. Exceptional political and administrative continuity.

Nigeria	910	82.6	924	201	2.7	Cacao, groundnuts	Federation of states subject to strong centrifugal forces. Military government after civil war; coup, 1975; assassination of new president, 1976; civilian government installed, 1979; military coup, 1983. Political discontinuity.
Trinidad and Tobago	3,910	1.1	5	2,135	2.3	Sugar	Centralized Westminster-style government with dominant party throughout period facing strong interest groups. Death of prime minister and replacement, 1981. Political continuity.
Venezuela	3,440	14.4	912	947	2.5	Iron ore	Centralized administration but with power split between executive president and legislature. Election of AD (Social-Democrat) government, 1974; election of COPEI (Christian-Democrat) executive and AD house, 1979. Continuity subject to election cycle.

Note: The entries in this table reflect a comparative judgment within the context of the sample. They are not a statement of the country's position in any absolute sense or relative to other developing countries.

a. Estimated as (mineral value added × 0.80 × ratio of proven oil output) / (nonmining GDP × 2.5).

b. Export values greater than $20 million.

Source: World Bank.

Table 4-2. Absorption Choices and Macroeconomic Responses of the Oil Exporters

Country	Extraction rate	Net savings abroad	Windfall absorption emphasis	Public investment emphasis	Main subsidies and rent transfers
Algeria	Slower after 1979	Negative (high absorber)	Very strong public investment bias	Strongly T (heavy industry); some shift to N (housing) after 1979	Subsidies from Treasury to public firms
Ecuador	Slower than projected	Negative	Mixed	Strongly N (infrastructure, education)	Large subsidies on energy, some on basic foods
Indonesia	On trend	Slightly negative; positive after 1979	Mixed	Mixed: T (agriculture, industry), N (infrastructure, education)	Subsidies on oil, fertilizer, rice
Nigeria	On trend	Zero	Public investment bias	Strongly N (infrastructure, education, new capital); after 1979 some T (industry, steel)	Moderate subsidies on energy
Trinidad and Tobago	Increase from previous levels	Strongly positive (low absorber)	Mixed: high consumption emphasis	Mixed: T (hydrocarbon-based industry); N (roads, electrification)	Very large subsidies: sugar industry, public firms, wages, consumer goods
Venezuela	Slowdown from previous levels	Balanced: public dissaving, private saving	Mixed: high consumption emphasis	Largely T (particularly steel, aluminum)	Large subsidies: energy, public enterprises, consumer goods

T = traded; N = nontraded

Note: The entries in this table reflect a comparative judgment within the context of

Development emphasis	Labor availability	Trade and exchange policy	Main macro-clearing variables
Urban	Very large, especially relative to requirements of capital-intensive strategy	Continued tight control of trade and capital flows; pegged rates	High import leakages, household rationing, price controls
Urban	Large	Some relaxation of controls and cuts in non-oil export taxes; pegged rates	Real effective exchange rate changes
Mixed: major rural component	Very large; deep reservoir of labor in Java and Bali	Some relaxation of trade controls, free capital flows, pegged but adjustable rates	Real effective exchange rate changes rendered more flexible by willingness to devalue
Urban	Supply inelastic, supplemented by immigration	Trade policies erratic, exchange rationing, pegged rates	Very high real effective exchange rate appreciation with import controls
Urban	Large, due to initially high unemployment, but heavily unionized	Relatively open trade policy, pegged rates	High import leakages, price controls, later exchange appreciation
Urban	Supply inelastic, supplemented by immigration	Relatively open trade policy, pegged rates	Import liberalization with price controls, later exchange appreciation, massive capital flight

the sample. They are not a statement of the country's position in any absolute sense or relative to other developing countries.

Source: World Bank.

Chapter 5

The Magnitude and Uses of the Oil Windfalls, 1974–81

The size and the uses of windfalls from higher oil prices can be estimated in a variety of ways. All involve measuring deviations from some counterfactual scenario setting out what would have transpired had there been no windfall. The most complete scenarios require a full model of the economy, but this is not practical here because of the large and complex differences among the countries. This chapter develops a simple decomposition of the changes in broad demand and supply aggregates to estimate the size of the windfalls and how they were absorbed. Chapter 6 uses a further simple decomposition of the major sectoral components of the non-oil economy to assess the impact on the broad structure of production.

A Simple Decomposition of Income and Spending

In developing this approach, we begin by estimating the increase in domestic income which results from a larger current value of the oil sector relative to the aggregated non-oil sectors. To make cross-country comparisons easier, these computations are performed with the economy divided into mining and nonmining, rather than oil and non-oil, segments. Since non-oil mining is a very small part of GDP in countries without large hard-mineral sectors, this has only a minor effect on the results.[1]

By the national income identity, the trade and nonfactor service balance (which is commonly called the resource balance) is the difference between domestic output and total absorption, all at current prices. Domestic output is the sum of mining and nonmining output, and absorption is the sum of consumption and investment. Therefore we may write:

(5-1) $$R = Y + Z - C - I$$

where R, Y, Z, C, and I represent the resource (trade and nonfactor service) balance, nonmining output, mining output, consumption, and investment, all at current market prices.

Let p, pz, pc, and pi be the deflators for nonmining output, mining output, consumption, and investment respectively. In each period t, the quantity and relative price structure of the economy may then be summarized by a state vector (r, z, c, i, qz, qc, qi). The respective q's represent the mining (oil), consumption, and investment deflators relative to p, the deflator of nonmining output. The elements r, z, c, and i represent the (nominal) trade and nonfactor service balance, mining sector, consumption, and investment, respectively, relative to nonmining GDP. The state vector therefore "scales" the mining sector and the components of demand by nonmining GDP and also expresses their deflators relative to that of nonmining GDP.

From equation 5-1:

$$(5\text{-}2) \qquad r_t = 1 + z_t - (c_t + i_t)$$

A base period, denoted "0," is taken as the average for the period 1970–72. We now construct a counterfactual scenario, denoted by h, using the following assumptions:

- No changes in relative deflators from the base period 1970–72
- A constant mining sector share in total output
- No change in the ratio of total absorption to total output.

These assumptions imply that the counterfactual terms of trade .... constant (if they were not, the consumption or investment deflators would have to change relative to output deflators), and also that the counterfactual ratio of the resource balance to GDP is constant. This is consistent with a balanced growth scenario free from shocks.[2]

The composition of absorption, however, is known to change systematically with growth of income per capita, so that the balanced growth scenario must be modified. Therefore C_t^h and I_t^h (the superscript h denoting counterfactual values) are adjusted within the total absorption constraint in line with the projections of Chenery and Syrquin (1975), with real nonmining output per capita taken as the indicator of growth. In the counterfactual scenario:

$$c_t^h + i_t^h = c_0 + i_0$$

so that

$$(5\text{-}3) \qquad r_0 = 1 + z_0 - (c_t^h + i_t^h)$$

Adjustment of the exporter to the oil shock may then be written as the difference between the actual and the counterfactual scenarios, relative to nonmining output in the counterfactual scenario:

(5-4) $$(R_t - R_t^h) / Y_t^h = (Z_t - Z_t^h) / Y_t^h - (C_t - C_t^h) / Y_t^h$$
$$- (I_t - I_t^h) / Y_t^h$$

The righthand absorption terms may be further broken down into public and private components of consumption and investment.

Next each of the resulting terms may be decomposed again into price and quantity effects. Since the terms express differences in current values—of mining output, consumption, and investment—and current value equals the product of price and quantity, the change in value may be expressed as the sum of the price change weighted by quantity and the quantity change weighted by price. In such expressions, as is well known, use of the initial or final weights alone (here, counterfactual or actual weights) introduces a residual if the changes are not infinitesimal; therefore the average of the actual and counterfactual weights is used to minimize cross-effects and the residual terms.[3]

For example, scaling all base-year deflators to unity yields, for the oil windfall term:

(5-5) $$\frac{Z_t - Z_t^h}{Y_t^h} = (z_t/qz_t - z^h) \cdot (qz_t + 1)/2 + (qz_t - 1) \cdot (z_t/qz_t + z_h)/2$$

The lefthand term is the "value windfall effect." It expresses the change in the contribution of the mining sector, relative to nonmining GDP, and is the sum of two effects. The first term on the righthand side of equation 5-5 is the "real windfall effect." It indicates the contribution to the windfall of changes in real mining output relative to real nonmining output. The second term is the "price windfall effect."[4] It shows the contribution to the windfall made by relative price changes between mining and other sectors. If oil prices rise sharply but oil output falls relative to the output of other sectors, the real effect will be negative and the price effect will be positive; the windfall's value is less than it would have been had oil output grown as fast as output from other sectors.

A similar breakdown of value changes into real and relative price effects can be made for consumption and investment terms. This can be useful. If, say, investment expenditures rise relative to nonmining output, is this due to greater real investment? Or does it merely reflect a rise in the relative cost of investment goods? If consumer prices fall because of cheaper imports, real consumption can grow more rapidly for given consumption expenditures. Needless to say, the use of deflator movements to indicate price changes is not ideal, especially given the residual nature of consumption in the national accounts, but no other indicator is available.

Although the base period 1970–72 was one of reasonable stability for the world economy, it did not necessarily represent a period of stable, long-term equilibrium for each of the sample countries. Therefore economic structure in the base period is important in interpreting the results of such a decomposition. Table 5-1 provides an indication of the base absorption structures of the six sample countries plus, for comparison, Iran. These are compared with the Chenery-Syrquin norms for countries at a similar level of nonmining income per capita. The table also shows the share of oil in commodity exports in 1972 as well as the average current account, relative to nonmining GDP, in 1970–72.[5]

Iran, Algeria, and Venezuela—all with large, long-established oil sectors (and considerable remittance income in the second case)—had the highest initial ratios of absorption to nonmining GDP. Indonesia, Nigeria, and Trinidad and Tobago occupied an intermediate position. Ecuador, which became an oil exporter most recently, was least dependent on oil in terms of absorption, but it already had a higher share of oil in total exports than Indonesia, which benefited from aid inflows and maintained a diverse portfolio of non-oil exports reflecting its rich resource endowment.

In the base period, the current account deficits of the sample countries averaged 5.1 percent of nonmining GDP. This high average was due to the very large deficits of Trinidad and Tobago and of Ecuador, both of which were in a phase of rapid oil development largely financed by direct investment from abroad.

Table 5-1 also shows the breakdown of extra absorption relative to patterns "normal" for countries at similar levels of income per capita. Before the first oil shock, there were particularly strong investment biases in Algeria, normal investment rates. Private consumption was high relative to public consumption in Ecuador, Nigeria, and Indonesia, reflecting a relatively small government role.

Size of the Windfalls

Tables 5-2 and 5-3 show the decomposition estimates of windfalls and their uses for 1974–78 and 1978–81 respectively. We first consider only the windfalls. The mean windfall ("value effect") was 22 percent of nonmining income during 1974–78 (24 percent including Iran) and 23 percent during 1979–81. Particularly after 1979, slower real growth of the oil sector reduced the value impact of the "price" windfall (32 percent of nonmining GDP) by about one-fourth on average and almost eliminated the windfall in Venezuela. Table

Table 5-1. The Composition of Absorption in 1970–72 in Relation to Chenery-Syrquin Norms
(percent)

Item	Algeria	Ecuador	Indonesia	Nigeria	Trinidad and Tobago	Venezuela	Unweighted mean	Iran
Private consumption								
Actual/nonmining GDP	64.5	75.5	83.5	80.2	80.9[a]	62.8	74.6	72.2
Norm: private consumption/GDP	66	68	75	70	78[a]	62	69.8	64
Public consumption								
Actual/nonmining GDP	18	10.6	9.8	8.6	n.a.	16.4	12.7	23.4
Norm: public consumption/GDP	14	14	12	14	n.a.	15	13.8	14
Investment								
Actual/nonmining GDP	40.8	20.6	17.5	22.1	31	36.6	28.1	27
Norm: investment/GDP	20	19	15	17	22	23	19.3	22
Absorption								
Actual/nonmining GDP	123.3	106.7	110.9	111	111.9	115.8	113.3	122.7
Norm: absorption/GDP	100	101	102	101	100	100	100.7	101
Breakdown of extra absorption (percent)								
Private consumption	-6	132	96	102	24[a]	5	n.a.	36
Public consumption	17	-60	-25	-54	n.a.	9	n.a.	41
Investment	83	28	28	51	76	86	n.a.	44
Percentage of oil in exports, 1972	79	77	51	82	78	91	76	91
Current account/ nonmining GDP, 1970–72	1.4	-6.9	-3.8	-3.3	-14.5	-0.6	-5.1	-3.2

n.a. Not available.
a. Includes public consumption.
Source: World Bank, World Tables data base.

5-3 indicates that, at the time of the second oil price rise, oil sectors were relatively smaller than at the time of the first price rise (except in the case of Ecuador). This helped to mute the impact of the second boom on producing countries.

Figure 5-1 indicates the (unweighted) average time profile of the windfalls in the period 1973–81, as measured above, for the six countries. Again each year's windfall ("value effect") is expressed as a share of the nonmining economy. In 1974 the average windfall peaked at 33 percent of nonmining income, but by 1978 it had contracted to 15 percent. The second oil price increase raised the windfall to 27 percent of nonmining output in 1980 before declining sales began to reduce it. The combination of slumping prices and contracting sales in 1982–84 appears to have halved the windfall gain.

Use of the Windfalls: The Fiscal Response

With little direct linkage between the oil sector and the rest of a developing economy, and with a rapid upward adjustment of tax and royalty rates to reduce the share of surplus accruing to the oil

Figure 5-1. Oil Windfalls and Their Uses, 1973–81

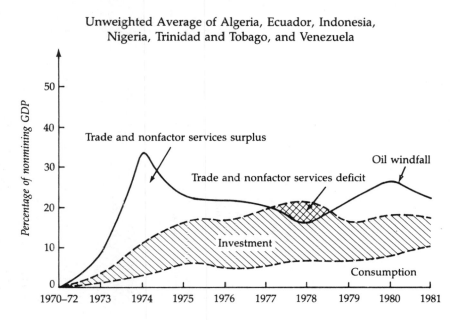

Unweighted Average of Algeria, Ecuador, Indonesia, Nigeria, Trinidad and Tobago, and Venezuela

Source: Tables 5-2 and 5-3.

Table 5-2. Oil Windfalls and Their Uses, 1974–78
(percentage of nonmining GDP)

Windfalls and uses	Algeria	Ecuador	Indonesia	Nigeria	Trinidad and Tobago	Venezuela	Unweighted mean	Iran (1974–77)
Domestic oil windfall	27.1	16.8	15.9	22.8	38.9	10.8	22.1	36.7
Real	-4.8	9.2	1.6	-2.3	2.3	-20.5	-2.4	-22.8
Price	31.9	7.6	14.3	25.1	36.6	31.3	24.5	59.5
Absorption effects								
Trade and nonfactor service	-4.3	3.5	5.3	2.8	27.2	-1.0	5.5	17.0
Current balance	-9.8	2.7	4.8	5.4	26.7	3.9	5.6	24.6
Non-oil growth effect	-7.4	15.9	-2.4	-1.5	-7.8	5.9	0.5	12.2
Allocation effects								
Value								
Private consumption	3.6	-0.9	2.1	2.9	7.1[b]	1.9	2.1	-7.0
Public consumption	1.4	5.5	2.4	4.2	n.a.	1.6	3.2	10.2
Private investment	n.a.	3.8	-1.7	-6.6	-2.6	3.3	0.6	6.7
Public investment	26.4[a]	4.8	7.9	19.5	7.3	4.9	11.8	10.0

Price								
Private consumption	−0.9	−3.0	−1.1	1.2	−18.4	−10.1	−5.4	−6.2
Public consumption	−0.2	0.3	0.7	−0.1	n.a.	3.5	0.7	2.3
Investment	4.1	4.3	−0.5	3.8	0.0	4.4	2.7	7.3
Real								
Private consumption	4.6	2.1	3.3	1.7	25.6[c]	12.1	7.5	0.8
Public consumption	1.6	5.2	1.7	4.3	n.a.	0.8	3.0	7.9
Private investment	n.a.	0.4	−1.3	−9.5	−2.6	1.8	−1.8	2.5
Public investment	22.2[a]	3.9	8.0	18.6	7.3	2.6	10.4	6.9
Real allocation plus growth effects								
Private consumption	0.0	14.0	−1.5	0.5	19.4[d]	15.8	7.5	7.6
Public consumption	0.3	6.9	1.5	4.2	n.a.	1.8	3.0	13.2
Private investment	n.a.	3.2	−3.4	−9.8	−4.6	3.3	−1.9	4.5
Public investment	19.1[a]	4.5	7.9	18.5	5.5	3.3	10.0	8.4

n.a. Not available.

a. Adequate estimates are not available because of the small share of private investment. The private investment effect is taken as zero.

b. Public consumption is included in private consumption. For computation of mean, total consumption effect is split in the average proportions for the other countries, 2.8 private and 4.3 public.

c. Price effect is attributed to private consumption. For computation of mean, private consumption effect is taken as 21.2, public consumption effect as 4.3.

d. For means, this is split into 16.0 private and 3.4 public.

Source: World Bank data.

Table 5-3. Oil Windfalls and Their Uses, 1979–81
(percentage of nonmining GDP)

Windfalls and uses	Algeria	Ecuador	Indonesia	Nigeria	Trinidad and Tobago	Venezuela	Unweighted mean	Mexico
Domestic oil windfall	29.7	22.1	22.7	21.9	34.7	8.7	23.3	3.5
Real	−17.6	10.8	−2.5	−6.1	−7.4	−28.0	−8.5	n.a.
Price	47.3	11.2	25.2	28.0	42.1	36.6	31.7	n.a.
Absorption effects								
Trade and								
nonfactor service	8.9	4.7	9.6	0.1	16.8	1.1	6.9	−1.8
Current balance	−0.6	−1.2	6.1	3.9	19.2	7.0	5.7	−0.2
Non-oil growth effect	−6.7	21.2	−3.5	−29.8	0.6	−6.6	−4.1	n.a.
Allocation effects								
Value								
Private consumption	4.6	1.1	1.2	4.1	8.6[a]	9.4	4.1	−2.9
Public consumption	3.2	6.1	3.7	5.6	n.a.	0.7	3.9	2.3
Investment	12.9	10.3	8.1	12.1	9.3	−2.5	8.4	5.9

Price								
Private consumption	-2.2	-4.0	-9.3	-4.1	-18.2[b]	-14.7	-8.8	-12.7
Public consumption	-0.1	0.1	0.3	0.6	n.a.	0.4	0.2	1.4
Investment	4.4	6.3	-0.5	4.8	-2.6	1.1	2.2	18.7
Real								
Private consumption	6.8	5.1	10.5	8.2	26.7[c]	24.1	12.9	-0.1
Public consumption	3.3	6.0	3.4	5.0	n.a.	-0.3	3.7	1.0
Investment	8.6	4.0	8.6	7.3	12.0	-3.5	6.2	4.1
Real allocation plus growth effects								
Private consumption	2.7	21.7	7.7	-15.3	27.2[d]	20.0	9.8	n.a.
Public consumption	2.5	6.8	3.0	2.3	n.a.	-0.7	3.0	n.a.
Investment	5.6	15.0	7.9	0.4	12.2	-6.0	5.8	n.a.

n.a. Not available.
a. Includes public consumption. For mean, this is split into 4.4 private and 4.2 public.
b. Price effect is attributed to private consumption.
c. For mean, this is split into 22.5 private and 4.2 public.
d. For mean, this is split into 22.9 private and 4.3 public.
Source: World Bank data.

multinationals, fluctuations in mining value added were mainly reflected in fiscal revenues. The impact is shown in tables 5-4, 5-5, and 5-6. For the six countries in the sample, the first oil price rise caused central government revenues to jump from 20 percent of nonmining GDP to 37 percent in 1974–78 (42 percent including Iran).[6] This implies that, on average, about four-fifths of the windfall accrued to producer governments. Iran, for which data after 1977 are limited, experienced a particularly large windfall, 36.7 percent of nonmining GDP during 1974–77, which was also reflected in fiscal revenues. Central government revenues relative to nonmining GDP were similar in 1979–81 to what they were in 1974–78. This would be expected, since the windfall effect in figure 5-1 is similar for the two oil shocks.

Although there were significant differences in non-oil fiscal performance among countries, almost all the increase in the ratio of fiscal revenue to nonmining income is attributable to increased taxes and royalties on oil. The only exception is Algeria, where non-oil taxes, particularly on domestic goods and services, were unusually high at 25 percent of nonmining GDP and proved to be buoyant. Non-oil taxation remained low in the rest of the sample, on average little more than half what it was for typical countries at similar levels of GNP as indicated by cross-country regressions.[7] Except for Algeria, only Trinidad and Tobago possessed a well-developed system of direct taxation. But as domestic prices rose, its brackets were adjusted to compensate for progressivity so that collection was less buoyant than in Algeria.

Tables 5-5 and 5-6 present estimates of the elasticity of non-oil taxes to growth of the non-oil economy during the first and second oil price shocks. Although most exporters relaxed import restrictions and eased import tariffs and non-oil export taxes after 1974, the rapid increase in imports made possible a substantial rise in trade taxes in 1974–78. This increase in the tax base due to oil income was compensated (except in Algeria) by a cut in the taxes levied on domestic goods and services, as shown by less-than-unit elasticities. Underlying this policy was a widespread desire to moderate inflationary pressure caused by boosting public spending. On average, non-oil tax revenues remained fairly steady as a proportion of nonmining income during the first oil price rise. They decreased slightly with the second price rise because import volumes and trade taxes did not continue to expand so rapidly.

Producer governments therefore did not generally transfer their windfalls to the private sector by sharply cutting non-oil taxes, although in some cases, notably Ecuador, non-oil tax efforts slackened. Until the early 1980s they did try to insulate domestic consum-

Table 5-4. Structure of Taxes and Government Expenditure, 1974–78

(percentage of nonmining GDP)

Item	Algeria	Ecuador	Indonesia	Nigeria	Trinidad and Tobago[a]	Venezuela	Unweighted mean	Iran[b]
Total revenue	59.9	12.9	23.1	27.7	55.9	42.1	37.0	71.1
Non-oil direct taxes	6.2	1.4	1.8	0.1	5.2	1.3	2.6	0.5
Domestic indirect taxes	14.1	2.3	3.3	0.6	3.0	1.6	4.2	1.7
Trade taxes	4.2	5.8	2.5	3.9	4.4	2.6	3.9	4.3
Total taxes	24.5	9.5	7.6	4.6	12.6	5.5	10.7	6.5
Expenditure	71.5	14.4	25.0	24.2[d]	36.7	32.0	34.0	71.6
By function								
Administration, defense	6.5[c]	4.9	9.9	9.1	5.8	5.0	6.9	23.6
Social	9.8[c]	4.8	2.7	4.3	11.0	9.6	7.0	10.1
Economic	2.0[c]	3.7	8.2	8.8	15.6	10.6	8.2	20.5
By economic classification								
Current	27.0	n.a.	14.5	13.6	21.1	20.5	19.3	49.3
(Wages and salaries)	(10.0)	n.a.	(4.1)	(4.1)	(10.9)	(11.2)	(8.1)	(16.4)
Subsidies and transfers	10.5	n.a.	5.1	3.4	3.1	5.8	5.6	13.1
Investment	44.5	n.a.	10.6	12.4	15.6	11.9	19.0	22.3
Net lending	29.0	n.a.	1.8	7.2	6.0	13.8	11.6	n.a.
Total revenue 1970–72	32.6	14.2	15.6	12.3	19.9	25.2	20.0	31.7
Total revenue 1979–81	57.4	14.2	30.9	n.a.	57.2	36.3	39.2	n.a.

n.a. Not available.
a. 1976–77.
b. 1974–77.
c. Current expenditures.
d. 1975–78.
Sources: IMF Government Finance Statistics data base; World Bank data.

Table 5-5. Elasticity of Taxes and Government Expenditure with Respect to Nonmining Output, 1974–78/1970–72

Item	Algeria	Ecuador[a]	Indonesia	Nigeria[b]	Trinidad and Tobago	Venezuela	Unweighted mean	Iran[c]
Total revenue	1.84	0.91	1.48	2.25	2.81	1.68	1.82	2.24
Non-oil direct taxes	1.15	1.00	1.25	—[f]	1.48	1.11	1.19	1.00
Domestic indirect taxes	1.25	0.85	0.92	0.20	0.71	0.90	0.81	0.72
Trade taxes	1.56	0.78	0.92	1.78	1.26	1.57	1.30	0.90
Total taxes	1.26	0.83	0.99	0.83	1.13	1.20	1.04	0.85
Expenditure	1.78	1.02	1.34	2.24[g]	1.70	1.29	1.57	1.90
By function								
Administration, defense	1.18[d]	1.32	1.25	1.44	0.89	1.16	1.21	1.92
Social	1.05[d]	1.04	1.69	4.78	1.23	1.09	1.81	1.53
Economic	—[e]	0.93	1.44	4.19	3.71	1.20	1.91	1.60
By economic classification								
Current	1.36	n.a.	1.43	1.63	1.34	1.11	1.37	1.98
(Wages and salaries)	(0.98)	n.a.	(1.11)	(1.11)	(1.10)	(1.07)	(1.07)	(1.24)
Subsidies and transfers	2.19	n.a.	1.02	3.78	n.a.	1.38	2.09	2.67
Investment	2.15	n.a.	1.53	4.96	2.89	1.83	2.68	1.74
Net lending	2.74	n.a.	1.28	3.00	n.a.	7.26	3.57	n.a.

n.a. Not available.
a. 1974–78/1973
b. 1974–78/1972
c. 1974–77/1970–72
d. Current expenditures only.

e. Negligible in 1970–72.
f. Negligible in 1972.
g. 1975–78/1972.
Sources: IMF *Government Finance Statistics* data base; World Bank data.

Table 5-6. Elasticity of Taxes and Government Expenditures with Respect to Nonmining Output, 1979–81/1974–78

Item	Algeria	Ecuador	Indonesia	Trinidad and Tobago	Venezuela	Unweighted mean
Total revenue	0.95	1.10	1.34	1.02	0.86	1.05
Non-oil direct taxes	1.11	1.29	1.00	1.63	0.92	1.19
Domestic indirect taxes	0.80	1.17	0.78	0.80	0.96	0.90
Trade taxes	0.69	0.76	0.88	0.86	0.93	0.82
Total taxes	0.86	0.94	0.87	1.16	0.93	0.95
Expenditure	1.01	1.19	1.28	1.18	0.97	1.13
By function						
Administration, defense	0.89	0.94	1.46	1.90	0.94	1.23
Social	1.07	1.46	1.26	0.92	1.05	1.15
Economic	0.90	0.91	1.22	0.99	0.72	0.95
By economic classification						
Current	0.99	n.a.	1.15	1.23	1.13	1.13
(Wages and salaries)	(1.20)	n.a.	(1.10)	(1.11)	1.03	(1.11)
Subsidies and transfers	0.80	n.a.	1.42	3.10	1.16	1.62
Investment	1.04	n.a.	1.46	1.10	0.68	1.07
Net lending	0.99	n.a.	1.06	1.50	0.50	1.01

n.a. Not available.

Note: Data were not available for Nigeria.

Sources: IMF *Government Finance Statistics* data base; World Bank data.

69

ers from the effects of higher oil prices by holding domestic oil prices at or near former levels.[8] Except for Algeria, however, governments did not attempt to restrain private competition for scarce domestic resources by increasing the non-oil tax burden.

The question of whether a government should raise or lower non-oil taxes in response to windfall gains has no simple answer. Much depends on the range of saving and spending options available to the government. But improving the non-oil tax system (broadening the tax base and improving tax administration as opposed to raising tax rates) is one way of preparing for the post-oil-boom period. Only one of the countries with weak fiscal systems, Indonesia, took advantage of the respite from revenue pressures to set in place a system to improve the efficiency of non-oil taxation. Indonesia's tax reform was implemented in 1983.

As demonstrated by the high elasticity of expenditure, especially during the first oil shock, the decade of the windfalls was marked by an unparalleled growth in the weight of the state and diversification of its role. Between 1974 and 1978, net lending by government and public investment outlays grew more than twice as fast as the non-oil economies of the respective countries (see table 5-5). Current expenditures grew less rapidly, with the notable exception of subsidies and transfers. This category, which will be discussed further below, continued to expand after 1979, whereas the relative growth of investment and net lending slowed. The growth of economic spending exceeded that of social spending during the first period, but this was reversed during the second period as other commitments began to eat into the proportion of the surplus available for economic functions.

Overall Absorption of the Windfall

Returning to figure 5-1 and tables 5-2 and 5-3, we now consider the overall absorption of the windfalls. This includes the impact of both first-round and subsequent (multiplier) rounds of expenditures. The analysis of windfall use is restricted here to the evolution of value shares. Discussion of the breakdown between real and price effects is deferred until after that of movements in the real exchange rate in chapter 6.

· As noted above, in 1970–72 current account deficits in the six countries had averaged 5.1 percent of nonmining GDP, with especially high deficits in Trinidad and Tobago (14.5 percent) and in Ecuador (6.9 percent) because of the large investments needed to develop the oil industry and because of some spending in anticipation of increased revenues. As indicated by figure 5-1 and table 5-2, during 1974–78 about one-fourth of the windfall (5.5 percent of nonmining GDP went to reduce these trade (and current) deficits. Another one-fourth (5.3 percent of nonmining GDP) was consumed. Slightly over half of this increase in consumption was public, slightly under half was private. The remainder of the windfall—almost half—was used for domestic investment. Although non-oil private investment (which is estimated as a residual) boomed in certain countries, notably in Venezuela in 1976–78, the increased investment outlays were overwhelmingly public.

Consumption and Permanent Income

Estimates of proven oil reserves are notoriously uncertain. They are also not fixed, but depend on prices and on exploration and development activity. At the extraction rates of the 1970s, the countries in the sample could have expected, on average, about fifteen years of low-cost (that is, high-rent) oil output. The equivalent flow of permanent income may be defined as that permanent flow which has the same discounted present value as the windfall. It depends on price projections and on the rate of discounting, denoted by i. If expected future prices are set to equal current prices in real terms (a random walk hypothesis for prices), projected permanent oil income, zp, is given by:

$$zp = i\int_0^{15} e^{-it}\, zdt$$

If i is taken to be 3 percent, permanent income is 36 percent of current oil income z. If instead the Hotelling rule is assumed, so that real oil rents rise with the rate of interest, permanent income will simply equal

$$i\int_0^{15} zdt$$

or 45 percent of current oil income.

Now suppose that the long-run sustainable current account deficit was zero (the average sample country was almost in current account balance in 1974–78 and 1979–81; see table 5-7). Suppose also that consumption out of windfall gains was set by a constant long-run propensity to consume (say, 80 percent) out of permanent income. Of the windfall not used to reduce the unsustainable current deficit, between 29 percent and 36 percent should then have been

Table 5-7. Current Accounts and Their Financing, 1970–83
(percentage of nonmining GDP)

Item	1970–72	1974–78	1979–81	1982–83
Current account				
Algeria	1.4	−11.4	−2.0	−0.4
Ecuador	−6.9	−4.1	−8.1	−5.0
Indonesia	−3.8	−1.6	2.3	−10.1
Nigeria	−3.3	2.3	0.6	−9.0
Trinidad and Tobago	−14.5	12.7	4.7	−15.5
Venezuela	−0.6	3.1	6.3	1.2
Unweighted average	−5.1	0.2	0.6	−6.6
Financing				
Algeria				
Portfolio + long-term capital	1.7	13.6	4.7	−2.7
(Direct investment)	(−0.4)	(1.3)	(0.5)	(−0.2)
Short-term capital + errors	−0.5	−0.8	−0.2	1.1
Reserve change and other balance items	0.2	−1.4	−2.5	2.0
Ecuador				
Portfolio + long-term capital	8.9	6.8	9.0	11.7
(Direct investment)	(3.4)	(1.0)	(1.0)	(1.0)
Short-term capital + errors	−0.8	−1.1	−1.0	−6.5
Reserve change and other balance items	1.1	−1.6	0.0	0.1
Indonesia				
Portfolio + long-term capital	4.3	4.2	3.5	8.8
(Direct investment)	(1.0)	(1.2)	(0.9)	(1.4)
Short-term capital + errors	0.6	−2.6	−3.3	0.4
Reserve change and other balance items	−1.0	0.0	−2.5	0.8

Nigeria				
Portfolio + long-term capital	2.5	1.3	1.7	3.0
(Direct investment)	(1.1)	(0.7)	(0.1)	(0.8)
Short-term capital + errors	1.4	0.0	−0.4	0.0
Reserve change and other balance items	−0.6	−3.5	−0.2	0.8
Trinidad and Tobago				
Portfolio + long-term capital	11.3	5.8	8.9	5.2
(Direct investment)	(9.6)	(8.9)	(10.4)	(10.9)
Short-term capital + errors	2.3	0.0	−0.7	1.5
Reserve change and other balance items	−0.9	−18.5	−12.8	4.9
Venezuela				
Portfolio + long-term capital	0.8	4.4	3.3	2.5
(Direct investment)	(−0.5)	(−0.9)	(0.5)	(0.7)
Short-term capital + errors	1.9	2.0	−3.3	−9.2
Reserve change and other balance items	−2.0	−9.5	−6.3	5.5
Unweighted average				
Portfolio + long-term capital	4.9	6.2	5.2	4.7
(Direct investment)	(2.4)	(−0.9)	(2.2)	(2.4)
Short-term capital + errors	0.8	−0.4	−1.5	−2.1
Reserve change and other balance items	−0.6	−5.7	−4.3	4.0

Source: IMF *International Financial Statistics.*

consumed, depending on whether future prices followed the random walk or the Hotelling rule. The actual proportion consumed in 1974–78, 33 percent, falls within this range.

The average use of the windfall in 1979–81 was similar, except that private consumption somewhat increased its value share at the expense of domestic investment, which accounted for only about one-third of the total.

The average consumption propensity of the countries was thus not out of line with that predictable from a permanent income explanation. But there were significant absorption differences among countries. In 1974–78 the use of windfalls for domestic investment was lower than average in Trinidad and Tobago and in Iran, both of which ran huge current account surpluses for very different reasons. The investment drive was far more intensive in Algeria. Taking advantage of its improved creditworthiness, Algeria absorbed the entire first windfall in investment and borrowed abroad against future oil and gas income to finance a small rise in public and private consumption relative to non-oil output and to compensate for a decline in remittance income. In 1974–78 the Algerian current account deficit was 11.4 percent of nonmining GDP. At its peak in 1977, Algerian investment reached the remarkable figure of 73 percent of nonmining GDP. Virtually all of this was public, with much going to develop heavy industry.

The other country to run substantial current account deficits in 1974–81 was Ecuador. The story is very different from that of Algeria, whose foreign borrowing was undertaken as an essential component of a long-term strategy pursued with great continuity and (possibly excessive) dedication. Ecuador's deficits, in contrast, stemmed from weak and fragmented fiscal control, exacerbated by political instability and the decentralized nature of its public sector, and from its policy of holding domestic interest rates low and expanding Central Bank credit to the private sector. Ecuador's fiscal control deteriorated seriously in 1979–81, and its current deficit rose to 8.1 percent of nonmining GDP.

For comparison, in table 5-3 estimates based on the same methodology are also presented for Mexico. An exporter of more recent vintage, Mexico experienced only a small oil windfall in 1979–81, just 3.5 percent of its non-oil GDP. But, rather like Algeria in 1974–78 or Ecuador later, it borrowed abroad against future oil earnings to boost expenditures by a further 1.8 percent of non-oil GDP. The increased Mexican expenditures, like those of the other oil exporters, mostly took the form of public investment. Development expenditure for the Mexican oil sector itself accounted for 2 percent of non-oil GDP.

The Financing of the Current Account

Table 5-7 also indicates how current deficits and surpluses were financed. It is notable that throughout the period 1974–81 all countries, whether in surplus or deficit, maintained sizable long-term capital inflows. In some cases, especially Indonesia and Trinidad and Tobago, it was considered advantageous to use excellent credit ratings to consolidate relationships with foreign lenders. Direct investment flows, however, were disappointing in 1974–78 and fell below 1970–72 levels, partly because of the stagnation of private investment and partly because of the end of the oil development phases in Ecuador and Trinidad and Tobago.

Foreign borrowing was used to accumulate reserves and to finance short-term and other capital outflows. Much of these were unofficial and unrecorded. Although in 1974–78 the sum of dollar current accounts and direct investment flows was −$12.2 billion for the six countries, the increase in their medium- and long-term debt less reserves was $16.7 billion, as shown in table 5-8.[9] Further, in 1979–81 when current accounts plus direct investment flows totaled a *surplus* of $10.3 billion, medium- and long-term debt less reserves *increased* by $4.8 billion.

Borrowing facilitated by oil income thus permitted a considerable degree of asset diversification abroad by residents of the exporting countries, and registered gross foreign debt rose over the whole period 1974–81 although current accounts were, on average, not far off balance.

Notes

1. It is not possible to obtain national accounts data which are consistent both over time and across countries and which isolate the oil sector. Inclusion of non-oil mining affects the results only if the sector is large and if its deflator changes greatly relative to that of nonmining GDP.

2. This projection should not be taken to imply that countries would actually have followed such a pattern in the absence of terms of trade changes. For example, Venezuelan constant-price mining output would certainly have declined relative to the non-oil economy during 1972–78 for technical reasons. Rather, it provides a common basis for the comparative assessment of the impact and use of windfalls. No non-oil growth effect is yet attributed to the windfalls, for reasons described below.

3. For an analysis of this (Tornquist-Theil) index as a discrete approximation to a divisia index, see Diewert (1976).

4. Residuals are small and have been subsumed into the price term. Since the actual and projected non-oil economy are identical, real apprecia-

Table 5-8. Net Borrowing and Indebtedness, 1974–83
(billions of U.S. dollars)

Item	Algeria	Ecuador	Indonesia	Nigeria	Trinidad and Tobago	Venezuela	Total
1974–78							
Current account plus direct investment	−8.2	−1.2	−2.9	−0.2	1.1	−0.7	−12.2
Change in MLT debt less reserves	9.4	1.5	6.1	−0.1	−1.5	1.3	16.7
Short-term debt, 1978	2.0	1.2	1.8	2.4	0.1	8.0	15.5
1979–81							
Current account plus direct investment	−1.3	−2.3	3.3	0.9	0.6	9.1	10.3
Change in MLT debt less reserves	0.2	2.0	0.3	1.5	−1.3	2.3	4.8
Change in short-term debt	0.3	0.8	1.5	2.0	0.1	9.0	13.7
1982–83							
Current account plus direct investment	−0.3	−1.3	−11.7	−11.4	−1.9	0.2	−26.3
Change in MLT debt less reserves	−0.6	2.0	7.1	8.8	1.5	2.1	20.9
Change in short-term debt	−0.4	−0.8	1.4	2.3	0.2	−2.4	0.3

Note: MLT debt is medium- and long-term debt.
Sources: IMF *International Financial Statistics;* World Bank, *World Debt Tables.*

tion leads to a reduction in the price effect for a sector such as oil whose prices are determined internationally.

5. Some of the following tables appeared in Gelb (1986a); the tables here correct errors in the earlier version and therefore differ in some places.

6. The unusual decrease for Ecuador is explained by (a) the fact that oil revenues also accrue to special funds outside government as defined here, and (b) the easing of certain non-oil taxes after 1974. In some cases national oil companies also received part of the windfall.

7. For cross-country tax norms and indications of the relation of non-oil taxes in oil countries to these, see Tait, Gratz, and Eichengreen (1979).

8. Domestic oil subsidies have been mostly implicit because oil production allocated to domestic use is valued at domestic rather than world prices.

9. It is possible for a country to register a negative total dollar current account over a number of years and still have a positive average ratio for the current account to GDP if the dollar value of GDP changes. For this reason the sign patterns of tables 5-7 and 5-8 may diverge, as they do for Nigeria in 1974–78.

Chapter 6

Sectoral Shifts, Real Exchange Rates, and the Dutch Disease

The standard "booming sector" three-sector model reviewed in chapter 3 predicts two main consequences of oil-led domestic expenditures. Real exchange rates will tend to appreciate as the relative price of nontraded sectors rises. This tendency will be associated with a production shift toward the nontraded sectors, which will lead to greater dependence on oil for foreign exchange. These effects are quantified in this chapter for the sample countries. Predictions of neoclassical or two-gap growth theory—that investing the windfalls domestically will cause the growth rate to increase—are investigated in chapter 7 together with the efficiency of fiscal linkage.

For various reasons, as noted in chapter 3, actual economies may deviate from the stylized patterns predicted by a simple model. Although the real exchange rate (defined as the price of nontraded goods relative to traded goods) may appreciate, trade liberalization could cause the more empirically useful measure, the real effective exchange rate (defined as the level of domestic prices relative to foreign prices), to move in the other direction. Measurement of the real exchange rate itself is complicated by the continuous rather than discrete nature of tradability. Also, services have large weight in the nontraded sector. Many of the most easily measurable service prices are those of public utilities controlled by the government. Rationing in such sectors could make the underlying pressure of demand difficult to measure. Policies which dampen multiplier effects from increased government spending can constrain resource pulls toward the nontraded sectors. If traded sectors can respond strongly to investments financed by oil revenues, product market pulls toward the nontraded sectors may be counterbalanced in the medium to long run. According to the analysis of table 3-3 this is particularly likely if labor markets are slack; then nontraded sectors do not draw labor from the traded sectors, and the economy is able to enter a phase of rapid, demand-led growth. The tendency of a particular sector to expand or contract depends on more than its tradability. It also depends on the extent to which its factor demands compete with those of the most rapidly growing sectors—notably construction—which will be heavily affected by the strong emphasis on investment that characterizes rising public demand.

Real Effective Exchange Rates

Estimates of real effective exchange rates for 1970–84 for the six exporters are shown in table 6-1. The trade-weighted real effective exchange rate is defined as the ratio of the domestic consumer price level of the oil exporter to the geometrically trade-weighted price indices of its major trading partners converted at average exchange rates. Averages for 1970–72 are taken as the base, 100; an increase indicates appreciation or loss of competitiveness. The unweighted mean (excluding Iran) indicates average real appreciation of 12.9 percent in 1974–78, 19.2 percent in 1979–81, 34.7 percent in 1982–83, and 46.3 percent in 1984.

During the 1970s, however, the unit value of manufactures imported by developing countries (MUV index) rose relative to the

Table 6-1. Real Effective Exchange Rate Movements, 1970–84
(1970–72 = 100)

Country	Average trade-weighted real effective exchange rate			
	1974–78	*1979–81*	*1982–83*	*1984*
Algeria	96.3	104.4	114.1	123.3
Ecuador	120.6	127.9	131.9	119.2
Indonesia	133.0	104.4	108.5	91.5
Nigeria	129.4	162.6	194.2	287.3
Trinidad and Tobago	105.6	115.8	139.5	169.8
Venezuela	92.9	100.1	119.8	86.9
Unweighted mean	112.9	119.2	134.7	146.3
United States	92.3	93.4	105.2	n.a.
Iran	100.4	119.2	194.2	n.a.
MUV index[a]	139	138	110	106

n.a. Not available.

a. Unit value index of manufactures imported by developing countries relative to U.S. consumer price index. The 1985 value is 111.

Sources: IMF *International Financial Statistics*; World Bank and United Nations, *Monthly Bulletin of Statistics*, various issues.

price levels of most of the trading partners of the sample countries. This rise was both because of oil and other primary intermediate price shocks, and because bursts of investment, largely in the developing oil exporters themselves, boosted costs of imported plant and equipment (an effect discussed at greater length in chapter 7). This relative price shift reduced the extent of average effective appreciation relative to the MUV index and was one factor limiting any fall in consumption and investment prices relative to the cost of domestically produced non-oil commodities. Such a fall would otherwise have been expected to result from real currency appreciation. The oil exporters were, in fact, cushioned from increased import price shocks by their own real exchange appreciation. Because of low, controlled domestic energy prices, until the early 1980s they were also spared the inflationary supply-side shock felt by their trading partners.

The Cost of Foreign Borrowing

Real exchange rates appreciated sharply relative to the dollar which, as shown in table 6-1, weakened during the first oil shock. The dollar began to recover strongly during the second shock with the adoption of a tight monetary policy after 1979. This implied that, in terms of domestic prices, real interest rates on dollar debts and returns to dollar assets were substantially negative for the sample until 1979, averaging −6.8 percent in 1974–78. Real interest rates were even lower in terms of the cost of investment goods, particularly construction prices, which tended to lead domestic inflation in the sample countries.

The highly negative returns on foreign financial assets increased the urgency of domestic spending. Countries scrambled to accelerate investment projects to avoid increases in costs and to make heavy industrial plants inflation-proof relative to competing investments which other countries were expected to make in the future. This introduced a destabilizing feedback into public decisions during the first oil cycle. The more rapidly spending accelerated, the greater was the tendency toward real appreciation and cost inflation, the more negative were real foreign interest rates, and the stronger was the incentive to absorb real resources.

This speculative bubble in real assets was abruptly punctured in 1979, when the combination of the appreciating dollar and higher real U.S. interest rates resulted in a switch to a positive real foreign interest rate, averaging 3.6 percent for the sample in 1979–81. The wide-ranging consequences of these interest rate fluctuations for the quality of large industrial programs and their returns are reviewed in chapter 7.

The Policy Impact

Table 6-1 indicates large differences, however, in the extent and timing of real effective exchange rate movements. To a great extent, these reflected differences in the policies of the various countries. By far the greatest real appreciation was experienced by Nigeria, whose effective exchange rate had doubled by the end of the second oil shock. Nigerian ports, roads, and distribution systems were particularly inadequate to handle the flood of imports and the shifts in domestic trade patterns which followed rapid urbanization. This resulted, in turn, from the urban-biased pattern of public spending. Congestion provoked initially rapid real appreciation. This was then increasingly sustained through tightened quantitative import controls as revenues and the expenditure stimulus diminished. Partly because of its restrictive and increasingly inefficient system of foreign exchange rationing, Nigeria experienced a severe deceleration in growth. The average size of its nonmining economy in 1979–81 was 29 percent lower than it would have been had the country managed to sustain its preshock growth trend.[1]

Indonesia's experience provides an interesting contrast. Its initial exchange appreciation in 1974–78 was, if anything, more violent than that of Nigeria. In November 1978, however, fearing the impact of domestic costs on labor-intensive non-oil export sectors and believing that the oil boom was at an end, Indonesia devalued by 50 percent, from 415 rupiah to the dollar to 625. As the dollar strengthened against other major currencies, the rupiah was allowed to drift downward, to 700 to the dollar by March 1983. It was then again devalued to 970 rupiah to the dollar. After 1979 the government also began to implement a more conservative fiscal policy. A substantial part of the second windfall was saved abroad. This was in spite of an official requirement that the budget be balanced rather than in surplus.[2] Thus, in tables 5-2 and 5-3, Indonesia's trade and nonfactor service effect increased from 5.3 percent of nonmining GDP in 1974–78 to 9.6 percent in 1979–81. Relative to the base period, it saved 42 percent of the second windfall abroad. The corresponding trade and nonfactor service effects for Nigeria were only 2.8 percent and 0.1 percent.

Indonesia was, in fact, the only country in the sample to implement a determined policy of expenditure reduction and exchange rate realignment before the fading of the second oil boom. In this sense, its macroeconomic management in 1973–81 could be considered as the most prudent in the sample. As is clear from table 6-1, it was fairly successful in avoiding prolonged exchange overvaluation and was quick, relative to other countries, to adopt a real effective depreciation in response to falling oil receipts. Indonesia was also quick to adjust other policies to changes in the availability of oil revenues (see chapter 12).

At least until 1981, two notable exceptions to the rule of exchange appreciation were Algeria and Venezuela. These countries actually managed to *depreciate* their effective exchange rates during the first boom period. Although price controls played a central role in both cases, the macroeconomic clearing mechanisms which substituted for real appreciation were completely different, as noted in table 4-2. Venezuela had long since completely adapted to the status of an oil monoexporter, so that virtually all non-oil sectors received some protection. After 1973 there was particularly great scope for the relaxation of tariffs and the quantitative import controls that had rendered the non-oil economy essentially noncompetitive with imports. Venezuela had historically been a low-inflation country, and the response to the inflationary burst which accompanied the start of the first oil boom was, indeed, to strengthen price controls on a wide set of wage goods and to satisfy demand, where needed, through imports. Accordingly, there was a tendency for consumer prices to rise less than the cost of non-oil output. This was reflected in the substantial real consumption effect shown in table 5-2. In addition, domestic oil prices were held constant, which shielded the economy from supply shocks and their inflationary impact, and the labor force was augmented by Colombians.

Algeria, in contrast, had a highly planned, centralized, socialist economy. Virtually all prices and wages were controlled. Throughout the windfall period, foreign trade and capital flows were tightly regulated. The public investment program was very heavily oriented toward hydrocarbon development and heavy industry. Consequently, it had a high direct import content. Labor was in elastic supply because of chronic underemployment. These factors helped to relieve pressure on the real exchange rate. In addition, private purchasing power, derived from the multiplier effects of domestic public spending, was drawn off in two distinct ways. First, non-oil taxes were heavy and buoyant in comparison with those of other exporters (see tables 5-4 and 5-5). Second, cash balances were accumulated on a massive scale. In 1973–79 the seigniorage extracted by the Central Bank averaged 7.5 percent of nonmining GDP, three times that of the other countries in the sample. This constituted a third leakage from the oil income stream (the other two being the high import propensity of public investment and high non-oil taxation). The holding of money balances appears to have been associated with rationing in markets for wage goods and housing (see chapter 10).

The Algerian strategy therefore involved deferring consumption to allow for a period of exceptionally high investment. In table 5-2 Algeria's value consumption effects total only 19 percent of the value investment effects, whereas Venezuela's consumption effects total 43 percent of investment effects. The Algerian private absorption effect is only 11 percent of total absorption, whereas the Venezuelan private sector accounted for 44 percent of the total absorption effect. As the Algerian strategy shifted after 1978 toward liberalizing markets and investing in housing (which has a higher domestic resource content), the real exchange rate began to appreciate (see table 6-1), and the share of private absorption began to rise (see table 5-3).

Real Wages during the Boom and Relative Price Effects

Information on the evolution of real wage rates is in some cases sketchy, but indicators summarized in table 6-2 suggest certain broad patterns. Algerian real wage gains were initially moderate. They became substantial, particularly in agriculture after 1976, as the heavy industrial investment strategy began to be moderated. Wage levels rose slowly at first in Ecuador, but advanced rapidly after 1979 as exchange overvaluation and fiscal and current deficits became more pronounced. Real wages in Indonesia increased after recovery in 1976 from the Pertamina crisis. There has been much controversy over the evolution of real wages in Indonesia, but the table suggests that they have, at least to some extent, reflected the country's favorable economic performance, both urban and rural. At the same time, however, the breaking down of traditional tenure and cropping patterns threatened to displace rural labor. Urban Iranian wages (not shown in the table) rose particularly strongly until 1977. This may have resulted from a policy of holding down food prices (as discussed below), which had an adverse impact on rural areas. Real wage levels appear to have been almost static in Nigeria over the boom periods, with large nominal increases (such as those granted by the Udoji civil service awards in 1975) rapidly being eroded by inflation. This was apparently caused by an acute shortage of wage goods, especially food, as domestic factors shifted toward satisfying the demands of public investment programs and imports were rationed.[3] Real wage levels rose sharply in Trinidad and Tobago, where trade union pressure, especially among the

Table 6-2. Real Wage Trends, 1974–84
(1975 = 100)

Country	1974	1975	1976	1977	1978	1979	1980	1981	1982	1983	1984
Algeria											
Agriculture[a]	108	100	114	109	133	142	157	171	n.a.	n.a.	n.a.
Nonagriculture[a]	108	100	106	101	121	127	143	144	n.a.	n.a.	n.a.
Deflated unit labor cost[b]	91	100	104	107	122	124	128	129	127	142	n.a.
Ecuador[c]											
Agriculture	105	100	111	98	87	110	180	n.a.	n.a.	n.a.	n.a.
Construction	104	100	119	105	95	116	172	n.a.	n.a.	n.a.	n.a.
Indonesia											
Urban[d]	101	100	105	118	123	135	153	n.a.	n.a.	n.a.	n.a.
Rural (1977 = 100)[e]	n.a.	n.a.	n.a.	100	n.a.	n.a.	n.a.	n.a.	n.a.	115	n.a.
Nigeria[f]											
Government	82	100	83	73	63	57	n.a.	n.a.	n.a.	n.a.	n.a.
Construction	131	100	79	70	57	82	74	62	58	63	44

Trinidad and Tobago[g]										
Textiles	95	100	111	113	122	109	113	109	157	n.a.	n.a.
Sugar	n.a.	100	193	198	205	218	246	295	313	n.a.	n.a.
Venezuela[h]										
Blue-collar workers	106	100	94	129	135	106	106	103	n.a.	n.a.	n.a.
White-collar workers	107	100	98	117	112	110	97	97	n.a.	n.a.	n.a.

n.a. Not available.

a. Until 1979, national minimum wage indices for unskilled workers in agriculture and nonagriculture; thereafter, Salaire National Global. *Source:* IMF.

b. Labor cost index from World Bank, deflated by consumer price index.

c. Legal minimum wage in agriculture and for construction artisans. *Source:* IMF.

d. Until 1975, average daily wages for skilled and unskilled workers in construction, Jakarta, *Source:* World Bank. After 1975, average real wages in manufacturing. *Source:* Warr (1986).

e. Average increase of daily wages in hoeing, planting, unskilled and skilled construction deflated by cost of living deflators for six villages in rural Java. *Source:* World Bank data.

f. Government minimum wages; construction market wages, Benin. *Source:* World Bank data.

g. Average weekly earnings in sugar, and of production workers in textiles. *Source:* World Bank data.

h. Average wages, blue-collar workers (*obreros*) and white collar workers (*empleados*). *Source:* World Bank data.

sugar workers, was strong. Real wages also increased in Venezuela during the booms, although they stabilized and then began to fall back as the economy stagnated.

These data suggest that a combination of demand-led growth, which tightened labor markets, and the price shifts discussed next, which usually favored private consumers, should have resulted in considerable increases in private consumption through the 1970s. A possible exception is Nigeria.

The price effects in tables 5-2 and 5-3 indicate the extent to which real consumption may have been increased or decreased because of relative deflator movements. Their unweighted average confirms a tendency for private consumption deflators to rise less rapidly than the deflator for nonmining GDP, and for investment deflators to rise more rapidly. This is largely because of the tendency for relative construction costs to increase with the investment boom. But except in Venezuela and Trinidad and Tobago (both of which implemented tight price controls on wage goods) and in Ecuador, the negative price effects were small. Nigerian consumers, in particular, appear not to have gained from the cheapening of imports in 1974–78, which one would expect to have accompanied the appreciating naira. Their gains in 1979–81 are more than offset by the investment price effect, a result at first sight inconsistent with the degree of real effective exchange rate appreciation observed in table 6-1.

Problems of data quality affect this measurement in particular because consumption tends to be determined residually in national accounts. Other explanations for the initial failure of real consumption and wages to increase more rapidly in Nigeria probably lie in the congestion effects already noted, which overwhelmed the distribution system. Such effects were particularly serious in the poorest countries because of their shortage of basic infrastructure.[4] The declining efficiency of resource allocation caused by the tightening of quantitative restrictions could have produced a similar effect after the first oil boom. Part of the windfall gain was then simply absorbed by the lower efficiency of Nigeria's non-oil economy, which raised prices relative to factor costs and so offset the relative cheapening of non-oil imports.

Measuring the Dutch Disease

Many observers have noted a tendency for agriculture to lag behind other sectors in oil-exporting countries, but care needs to be taken in interpreting this phenomenon. Cross-country studies such as that of Chenery and Syrquin (1975) indicate that growth of income per capita is normally associated with a considerable shift in the pattern of output, first from primary production to industry and later to services. These trends imply a "normal" shift from the non-oil sectors conventionally considered as tradable—agriculture (broadly defined to include fisheries and forestry) and manufacturing—toward services and construction. Although there are exports and imports of transport, financial, construction, and other services, these are not usually considered to be sectors where demand and supply can be easily equilibrated through net imports.

The tendency for the nontraded sectors to grow faster than the traded sectors might be weaker if measured in constant prices, however, or might not exist at all. This is because growth of income per head is also associated with an increase in the price of nontraded goods relative to those of traded goods, the so-called Balassa effect. This effect causes the currency of poorer countries to be undervalued, relative to those of richer countries, by the criterion of purchasing power parity.[5]

To assess the impact of the windfalls on economic structure, non-oil economies are decomposed into four major sectors: agriculture, manufacturing, construction, and services. Norms for shares in output (SN_i) are derived for each sector i.[6] So are changes in these norm shares owing to increased real income per capita, which is represented by nonmining output per capita. These are compared with constant-price shares (S_i) and changes in shares for the sample after 1972.[7]

The Dutch disease index, DD, is then defined as

$$DD = (SN_{ag} + SN_{ma}) - (S_{ag} + S_{ma})$$

It measures the shortfall in the share of tradables (agriculture and manufacturing) in the non-oil economy relative to their "normal levels." Changes in DD indicate the direction in which the constant-price composition of output is evolving relative to a "normal" pattern.

The results are given in table 6-3. As the initial conditions indicate, Algeria, Trinidad and Tobago, and Venezuela had severely skewed non-oil economies before the oil price rise. The exceptional initial Algerian DD value reflects the disruption of agriculture and manufacturing by the eight-year revolutionary war, which was followed by independence and the subsequent departure of French colonial proprietors. The government attempted to overcome this problem— with poor results, especially in the agricultural sector—by the strategy of *autogestion* or workers' self-management. The weakness of the Algerian traded sectors could be sustained by the foreign exchange from remittances and oil. Trinidad and Tobago and Venezuela had long since adapted to the economic structure of an oil

Table 6-3. Sectoral Structure and the Dutch Disease

Sector	Algeria Actual	Algeria Norm	Ecuador Actual	Ecuador Norm	Indonesia Actual	Indonesia Norm	Iran Actual	Iran Norm	Nigeria Actual	Nigeria Norm	Trinidad Actual	Trinidad Norm	Venezuela Actual	Venezuela Norm
	Sectoral shares in nonmining GDP and modified Chenery/Syrquin norms, 1972 (percent)													
Agriculture	11.0[b]	25	23.0	26	45.1	46	21.8	18	39.2	38	5.8[a]	16	7.6[a]	14
Manufacturing	15.8[a]	20	20.4	19	11.0	11	18.5[a]	25	5.1[b]	15	22.0	26	19.5[a]	27
Construction	13.4[b]	5	4.8	5	4.3[a]	3	6.3	6	10.7[b]	4	8.0[a]	6	6.0	7
Services	59.8	50	51.8	50	39.7	40	53.3	51	45.0	43	64.2	52	66.9[a]	52
Mining	17.9	4	2.0	4	12.1	6	28.5	3	15.1	5	8.8	2	20.5	2
	Average annual change in share at constant prices, 1972–81													
Agriculture	−0.38	−0.82	−0.91	−0.77	−1.50	−1.31	−1.44	−1.02	−1.90	−0.67	−0.31	−0.49	−0.10	−0.32
Manufacturing	0.52	0.28	0.37	0.27	0.77	0.34	0.34	0.49	0.48	0.11	−1.03	0.20	−0.04	0.06
Construction	0.82	0.09	−0.12	0.07	0.26	0.10	0.13	0.06	0.53	0.03	0.37	0.05	0.02	0.03
Services	−0.98	0.45	0.68	0.44	0.48	0.86	1.04	0.40	0.88	0.53	0.99	0.35	0.13	0.24
	Dutch disease index													
1972	18.2		1.6		0.9		2.7		8.7		14.2		13.9	
Change, 1972–81	−7.0		0.5		−2.4		5.7		8.5		10.5		−1.3	
Change in current prices, 1972–81	−3.5		12.5		−0.4		12.7		2.4		4.7		−3.2	

a. More than one standard deviation from norm.

b. More than two standard deviations from norm. Following results of Chenery and Syrquin (1975), standard deviation is approximated by 0.25 norm.

Source: World Bank, World Tables data base.

monoexporter. Indonesia and Ecuador, in contrast, had sectoral structures that were almost normal—and so, surprisingly, did Iran.

Table 6-3 also shows the average annual changes in norms and actual shares during 1972–81 and the implied change in the Dutch disease index over the decade. A negative value for the change in *DD* indicates a strengthening of the non-oil tradables relative to their expected share, whereas a positive value indicates a shrinking of the non-oil tradables relative to the norm.

Table 6-4 provides some additional indicators of sectoral evolution: indices of agricultural and food output per capita for 1974–83, with the period 1969–72 taken as the base. To facilitate comparison,

Table 6-4. The Performance of Agriculture, 1974–83
(1969–72 = 100)

Country	Index of output per capita		
	1974–78	*1979–81*	*1982–83*
Algeria			
Agriculture	89	83	70
Food	88	82	69
Ecuador			
Agriculture	109	119	113
Food	109	120	114
Indonesia			
Agriculture	109	123	127
Food	112	127	133
Nigeria			
Agriculture	91	91	84
Food	92	92	85
Trinidad and Tobago			
Agriculture	95	86	81
Food	96	87	81
Venezuela			
Agriculture	104	102	101
Food	105	104	104
Unweighted average			
Agriculture	100	101	96
Food	100	102	98
World			
Agriculture	103	104	105
Food	104	106	106
Developing world			
Agriculture	103	105	104
Food	104	106	106

Source: U.S. Department of Agriculture.

the table also shows the corresponding indices for the world and for all developing countries. These tables are complemented by table 6-5, which gives the price of food relative to other products in the sample countries and an index of world food prices relative to a price index of thirty-three nonenergy commodities.

Table 6-3 indicates that Algeria, Venezuela, and Indonesia managed to strengthen their non-oil tradable sectors over the decade. The first two, however, had very small initial non-oil traded sectors and, as noted above, were able to limit domestic market forces by price controls, import liberalization (Venezuela), and constraints on private spending (Algeria). When agricultural sectors are already small, it is less likely that they will continue to reduce their share in the "normal" manner. The exceptional case is Indonesia, which managed to sustain a rather strong performance in the non-oil traded sectors through the period of the oil price booms. This was due to a combination of good fortune and good policies. The development of high-yielding and disease-resistant rice varieties had a great impact on agricultural performance. But their dissemination would not have been possible without the unusually broad development strategy followed by the government. Input subsidies may also have played an important role; in addition, the measures taken to prevent the real exchange rate from moving too far out of line after 1978 stimulated non-oil exports (see chapter 12).

Table 6-5. The Relative Price of Food, 1974–83
(1970–72 = 1.00)

Country	Ratio of food price index to general price index		
	1974–78	1979–81	1982–83
Algeria	1.15	1.26	n.a.
Ecuador	1.15	1.13	1.20
Indonesia	1.12	1.11	1.09
Nigeria	1.09	1.09	1.11
Trinidad and Tobago	1.09	1.05	1.09
Venezuela	1.13	1.30	1.36
Unweighted average	1.12	1.16	1.17
World[a]	1.12	1.04	0.99
Iran	0.95	n.a.	n.a.

n.a. Not available.

a. Index of food prices relative to index of thirty-three commodities excluding energy; weighting by developing countries' export values, 1977–79.

Source: World Bank data.

Ecuador avoided a substantial increase in its Dutch disease index. In this, it was assisted by the rapid growth of the new seafood industry. Private manufacturing and agribusinesses were stimulated by generous tax rebates (partly responsible for poor non-oil fiscal performance), other incentives, and credit extended by the government from its borrowing abroad (see chapter 11).

The most marked shifts to the nontraded sectors occurred in Trinidad and Tobago and Nigeria. Trinidadian industry was adversely affected by the decline of petroleum refining with the falloff in world crude exports. Its agriculture (particularly sugar) contracted despite mounting subsidies as labor moved off the land into construction and other public programs. These were introduced to alleviate the chronic problem of unemployment but paid wages far above those available in rural activities (see chapter 14). Nigeria's agricultural stagnation reflected a number of factors. Its development strategy was strongly urban-biased and emphasized the nontraded sectors, especially road construction and the spread of primary education, then secondary and university education. Unlike the rural economies of Java and Bali, the Nigerian rural sector did not have a labor surplus. The manpower demands of the public construction programs had an immediate impact on the supply of farm labor. The government lacked the institutions and perhaps the will to raise smallholder agricultural productivity, and the performance of large-scale irrigation schemes was poor. As noted in chapter 13, some observers consider that much might have been done to improve Nigeria's agriculture, even though there was no revolution in dryland farming comparable to the Green Revolution in rice. With a static technology and a shrinking labor force, agricultural supply grew little.

As table 6-4 indicates, Ecuador, Indonesia, and Venezuela managed to raise domestic food and agricultural output per capita during the 1970s, although Venezuela began from an extremely small base. The table confirms the superior performance of Indonesia, both in relation to the rest of the sample and to non-oil countries. By the end of the period Indonesia's food output per capita was one-fourth larger than it would have been had supply increased at the worldwide average rate. In contrast, the performance of agriculture in Algeria, Nigeria, and Trinidad and Tobago is seen to be poor. Iran, too, experienced a rapid decline in the share of agricultural products in output over the period for which data are available.

A common criticism leveled at the policies of mineral-exporting countries is that they tend to keep food cheap because of pressures from groups in the urban areas, and that cheap food policies are sustained by spending mineral rent on imports. But table 6-5 suggests a different story for the sample in the decade of the oil windfalls. In 1974–78 world food prices were higher, relative to other non-energy commodities, than in 1970–72. This was paralleled by price movements within the sample.[8] After 1978 relative food prices fell worldwide but rose further in the oil exporters, so that the average relative increase was *greater* in the sample despite increased imports.

These relative price movements point to the importance of factor market pulls and of potential import competition as influences on sectoral evolution. In all the countries, income per capita was considerably lower in agriculture than in other sectors.[9] As public investment and construction expanded, labor was therefore drawn largely from agriculture, so that its output fell short of growing domestic demand. Although food imports by the six countries in the sample grew rapidly, this growth usually reflected the need to fill the widening food gap rather than a deliberate policy of holding down the price of food relative to, say, manufactured goods. Thus in terms of output and net import trends, Nigerian agriculture resembled a traded sector in the simple model of chapter 3 because imports increasingly satisfied demand. But in terms of relative price, it behaved more like a nontraded sector, mainly because its labor demands competed with those of construction.

One interesting exception to this pattern was Iran. As indicated in table 6-5, the relative price of Iranian food was lower in 1974–77 than in 1970–72, although domestic output had fallen short of increasing demand and imports had increased. Iran did attempt to hold down food prices through imports, and this may have been one cause of the very large increase in real urban wages indicated by official data. But at the same time, the policy limited the transmission of multiplier effects from oil spending to the rural areas, with unfortunate consequences.[10]

Table 6-3 also indicates changes in the Dutch disease index on the basis of current-price sectoral shares (rather than constant-price shares). As expected, there is a more pronounced shift toward the construction and service sectors in four of the seven countries, mainly because of higher construction and lower manufacturing deflators. The sign pattern of resource allocation shifts, as measured by *DD*, remains unchanged across countries.

The conclusion that the non-oil traded sectors remained weak or tended to weaken except in Indonesia (and possibly Ecuador) is confirmed by trade data. Total export volumes fell, on average, by 1.7 percent a year in 1972–81. Nonhydrocarbon export volumes contracted except in Indonesia (which maintained a fairly strong non-oil export performance across a wide range of primary and manufactured commodities) and Ecuador (which shifted toward processed products but experienced little overall increase). As discussed in the country chapters, Nigeria did extremely poorly in this regard, and some of its traditional exports disappeared. Trinidad and Tobago also did poorly, while Venezuela was unable to fill its coffee quota and saw a decline in cocoa exports as well. On the whole, the countries made little or no progress toward reducing the degree of dependence on oil.

Notes

1. As described in chapter 13, Nigeria entered into a vicious circle of inflation, trade restriction, and fiscal deficits.

2. Indonesia's balanced budget policy regards foreign aid and loans for development purposes as revenue; for details see chapter 12.

3. As noted in chapter 13, there is some divergence of views on Nigeria's agricultural and consumption growth. Data in this area are not strong.

4. Lagos, it was sometimes claimed, had the world's only concrete-bottomed harbor, created when ships jettisoned cement that had hardened during the delays in unloading.

5. Changes in the patterns of output with income per capita and other variables are analyzed only in current prices by Chenery and Syrquin (1975). For estimates of the Balassa effect, see Balassa (1964) and Kravis, Heston, and Summers (1978).

6. Chenery and Syrquin do not separate out construction. To do so has required additional computations using the World Bank World Tables data base to derive the share of construction in industrial output. The Chenery-Syrquin equations are used to project primary, service, and industrial shares. Industry is then split into construction and manufacturing.

7. There are no cross-country constant price norms for sectoral structures. Constant-price data are preferable for the sample because of the untypical impact of oil booms on relative prices, particularly of construction. Because of the Balassa effect the bias introduced by comparing constant-price shares and current-price norms makes it less likely that oil-exporting economies will appear skewed toward nontradeds.

8. Although energy is included in the country price indices in table 6-5, its prices were typically stabilized below world levels.

9. Some studies of villages in Java have suggested that wages are lower in certain small-scale service and manufacturing activities, but these results do not seem borne out by estimates based on economywide data. For more discussion, see Gelb (1985a).

10. The potential effects of Iran's food policy had been noted by a report of the International Labour Organisation; see Pyatt and others (1972).

Chapter 7

The Efficiency of Fiscal Linkage: Windfalls and Growth

As is clear from chapter 5, public expenditures, and in particular a vast expansion in the size and scope of public investments, constituted the main use of the windfalls. Growth, modernization, and the extension of national control over production were the main goals of these expenditures, although countries also had various subsidiary objectives. This chapter first considers the nature of public investments and the factors that affected the performance of this vital fiscal linkage. It then notes the drift toward subsidies, which assumed mounting importance in most of the sample countries. Finally, in the light of the investment drive, the growth performance of the sample is compared with that which might have resulted from the application of a simple neoclassical model.

The Composition of Public Investment Programs

It is difficult to compare the composition of public investments across countries because there is no uniform system of classification. Nevertheless, table 7-1 provides a rough indication of the broad distribution of public investments in the sample countries. It is intended simply to provide background in considering the investment strategies followed by the various governments.

Levels of development and income per capita differ greatly among the six producers. So does the role of government in the economy and the weight of the public sector. All of the countries saw extensive and growing public involvement in the hydrocarbon industry in the 1970s. The industry was nationalized in Venezuela in 1976 and almost totally nationalized in Algeria. Disputes in Ecuador with foreign oil companies over taxes and concessions resulted in CEPE, the state oil company, assuming a leading role, also in

94

1976. Moves to consolidate national control over the oil industry forged ahead in Nigeria and Trinidad and Tobago, especially during 1974–79. By the end of the 1970s national control had essentially been achieved in all of the countries. Salient features of this process of extending national control are summarized in table 7-2 to facilitate a comparison.

In all countries this process preceded the first sharp oil price increase by many years. Even in the new producer, Ecuador, state ownership of all mineral deposits had been asserted in the Constitution of 1945. The oil shocks were therefore not directly responsible for moves to nationalize the oil industry. In some cases, however, the price increases did accelerate the process. By providing more revenues to producer governments, they enabled foreign interests to be bought out at relatively little sacrifice. In Ecuador, for example, payments to multinational oil companies for CEPE's share of the industry came to $160 million between 1973 and 1979. That sum represented only 26 percent of the country's 1976 oil exports.

The extent of public involvement in sectors other than oil has differed widely. At one extreme, in Algeria the central government and public enterprises are estimated to have accounted for over 90 percent of domestic investment. At the other extreme, in Ecuador the role of the public sector outside the traditional functions of administration, defense, and provision of physical and human infrastructure has been quite limited. Differences in the public role result both from the ideological tendencies of governments and from historical accidents. For example, both the extensive involvement in agriculture of Algeria's socialist state and the considerable holdings in plantation crops and timber of Indonesia's relatively conservative government stemmed from the departure of colonial proprietors, French and Dutch respectively; they left at independence and, in the case of Indonesia, also at the time of the Irian Jaya dispute. In certain countries, notably Venezuela, public oil income had led the state to expand its role in production over a long period, even when the government was basically oriented toward the private sector. Maintaining a private economy is difficult when a government disposes of most of the investable surplus.[1]

As would be expected, all the oil exporters experienced unparalleled growth of the public sector's share in the economy after 1973. In most the public sector also extended its role as it moved toward direct participation in production, especially in the industrial sector. Although virtually all governments expanded their activities in virtually all directions, the emphases differed. Some governments, taking a direct approach, allocated public capital primarily to the trad-

Table 7-1. Sectoral Distribution of Public Investment
(percent)

Country	Period	Industry	Hydro- carbons	Agriculture and fisheries	Economic infrastructure (transport and communications)	Social infrastructure (education, housing, health)	Administration and defense	Other
Algeria	1970–73	53.2	25.0[a]	8.5	9.5	21.7	7.1	n.a.
	1974–77	53.5	25.9[a]	5.5	10.3	25.3	5.4	n.a.
	1978–79	56.5	26.9[a]	3.3	8.9	26.5	4.8	n.a.
	1980–84	38.6	15.7[a]	6.0	13.6	36.2	5.6	n.a.
Ecuador	1973–74	6.0	6.0[b]	7.6	55.9	13.5	n.a.	17.0
	1975–78	7.2	6.9[b]	8.5	53.9	28.1	n.a.	2.3
	1979–81	13.2	13.0[b]	3.9	54.0	26.9	n.a.	2.1
Indonesia	1969–72	7.6	3.3[c]	22.4	46.2	12.5	2.1	8.9
	1974–78	19.2	8.8[c]	12.8	42.8	15.4	6.7	3.1
	1979–81	17.0	8.6[c]	10.0	31.7	22.5	12.2	6.7
	1982–84	17.4	14.7[c]	8.5	32.0	24.7	6.7	10.6

Nigeria	1970–74	10.5	4.7[d]	12.9	33.3	27.9	14.5	0.9
	1975–80	13.7	5.0	7.2	37.5	24.3	17.3	n.a.
	1981–85[e]	18.8	7.7	12.6	26.0	33.7	8.8	n.a.
Trinidad and Tobago	1974–79	33.5	25.6	2.8	34.2	27.9	0.2	1.7
Venezuela	1970–74	22.5	6.3[f]	8.1	32.1	29.2	n.a.	8.0
	1976–80	41.3	20.6[b]	7.4	36.6	14.7	n.a.	n.a.
	1981–85	31.8	24.9[b]	6.4	31.2	28.5	n.a.	2.1

n.a. Not available.
a. Hydrocarbon sector.
b. Petroleum sector.
c. Mining.
d. Mining, fuel, power.
e. Projected.
f. Mining and hydroelectricity.
Sources: World Bank data; Trinidad and Tobago, Ministry of Finance (1980); Marshall-Silva (1984).

97

Table 7-2. Hydrocarbon Industries in the Oil Exporters

Country	Start of production	Major companies	Extension of national control	Gas reserves and development	Domestic energy pricing
Algeria	Oil discovered by French in commercial quantities in 1956.	Total, ERAP (French) plus Mobil, Phillips, Shell.	After 1965 a determined drive toward complete state control of hydrocarbon sector and replacement of foreign nationals by Algerians. 1963, SONATRACH, the state hydrocarbon company, established. 1971, nationalization of all non-French foreign operations and assumption of 51% public share in French interests. SONATRACH controlled 70% of crude oil production, 100% of exploration, refining, and marketing. Foreign companies could participate in exploration programs. 1980, $3 per barrel exploration fee levied on contract crude oil customers.	Major emphasis on gas exports in industrial sector plans. First LNG and later piped; SONATRACH world leader in LNG capacity (exports approximately 1 tcf a year) although pricing disputes held output well below capacity levels in some periods.	State electricity company (INECEL) heavily subsidized. Gasoline prices among lowest in world but raised from $0.18 to $0.60 per gallon in 1981. About 20% of locally sold gasoline may have been exported illegally.
Ecuador	Minor production since 1911; large deposits found by Texaco in 1967.	Anglo-Ecuadorian Oilfields (BP subsidiary) until 1963; Texaco-Gulf Consortium became major producer in 1964.	1945, Constitution asserted state ownership of all minerals. 1971, Hydrocarbon Law created state oil company CEPE. 1972, military government of General Rodriguez Lara extended state control; Anglo-Ecuadorian interests transferred to CEPE. 1974, CEPE purchased 25% of consortium; 1976, CEPE bought out Ecuadorian Gulf's 37.5% share. Exploration diminishes; 1978, Hydrocarbon Law amended to increase incentives for private investment.	Estimated gas reserves 4 tcf. Not a major focus of development.	

Indonesia	Oil discovered in 1883; commercial production by 1890.	Royal Dutch/Shell, later Caltex.	1968, state oil company Pertamina formed by merger of three locally owned companies. Foreign companies still produced 90% of oil, under contract of work, production sharing, and technical assistance programs. Although 1971 Pertamina Law made the company responsible for all petroleum activities, control was pragmatic and oriented toward raising reserves.	Estimated gas reserves 24 tcf. Output expanded rapidly to 0.5 tcf in 1980. Major LNG investments together with Japan are an important part of hydrocarbon development.	Domestic energy use, notably kerosene and diesel fuels, heavily subsidized.
Iran	Oil discovered by BP in 1908.	BP sole developer until 1951; consortium after 1954 also included Shell, Gulf, Mobil, Exxon.	1951, Prime Minister Mosadegh nationalized all petroleum resources and established the National Iranian Oil Company (NIOC). 1954, consortium deemed owner of fixed production assets and Iran owner of oil reserves; 50% tax principle established. 1960s, a number of joint ventures on 50-50 basis between NIOC and foreign companies. 1973, NIOC took over all operations but the consortium was allocated a marketing function. After 1978, trend to reduce foreign participation in energy industries.	Gas reserves 400 tcf. Ambitious program to export gas to Soviet Union and Europe via IGAT I and IGAT II pipelines in 1970s; curtailed after 1978.	
Nigeria	Oil discovered in 1956; exports began in 1958.	Shell/BP partnership and others.	Mid-1960s, political and economic significance of oil recognized. 1969, Petroleum Decree established state's option to part ownership of hydrocarbon industry at 51%. 1971, National Oil Company (NNOC) established. 1973, ultimate objective announced to be a nationalized industry; NNOC began production-sharing. 1974, public equity	Gas reserves about 75 tcf. Plans for major LNG facility at Bonny Island for gas use in steel production and for power generation.	Some subsidization of petroleum products and other energy forms.

(*Table continues on following page.*)

Table 7-2 *continued*

Country	Start of production	Major companies	Extension of national control	Gas reserves and development	Domestic energy pricing
			share in all oil operations increased to 55%; 1979 to 60%, and BP's crude oil and marketing interests nationalized. 1977, new incentive package to accelerate exploration.		
Trinidad and Tobago	Oil discovered in 1857; Shell became first producer in 1918.	Shell, Textrin, and others.	1969 Petroleum Act and 1970 Petroleum Regulations laid regulatory foundation. 1970, Trinidad-Tesoro (50.1% government-owned) established. Bought out Shell; 1974, established National Petroleum Marketing Company; 1976, bought out Texaco's marketing operations. 1979, National Energy Corporation (NEC) established. 1980 on, drive to increase public control of hydrocarbons, but 1981 Petroleum Act amended to increase private incentives to production and exploration.	Estimated gas reserves: 12 tcf probable, 21 tcf possible. Output about 0.5 tcf. Shift to gas-based industry a central part of development strategy, which implies continuing good relations with private capital and expertise.	Domestic petroleum prices subsidized; domestic sales of natural gas underpriced.

Venezuela	By 1928 leading exporter and second largest producer in the world.	Standard Oil of New Jersey (Exxon), Shell, Gulf, Texaco, Mobil, Sun, and others.	Gradual forty-year process of increasing domestic control and knowledge of industry; culminated in nationalization of oil in 1976. 1935–48, extension of regulation and establishment of the 50% tax principle. 1960, state-owned Venezuelan Petroleum Corp. (cvp) established to receive all future oil concessions, with foreign investment through service contracts. 1971, Hydrocarbon Reversion Law called for reversion of existing concessions to state ownership in early 1980s. 1974, President Carlos Andrés Pérez called for early reversion. 1976, total nationalization under Petroleos de Venezuela (pdvsa, formerly cvp).	Proven gas reserves 42.5 tcf. Nationalized in 1971. Gas for domestic use plays a role in the heavy industrial strategy developed after 1974.	Domestic petroleum and energy prices heavily subsidized throughout period.

tcf = trillion cubic feet.

Sources: U.S. Department of Energy, Office of International Affairs (1977); U.S. Embassy, Jakarta (1982); World Bank data.

able sectors to ensure a source of non-oil export revenues and to substitute for imports, if and when oil revenues faltered. Others
adopted the indirect strategy of strengthening the nontraded sectors
—transport, communications, housing—and augmenting human
capital. It might be argued that in the long run such infrastructural investments are necessary to develop efficient non-oil traded sectors.
The strategies of the sample countries, which have been outlined in
table 4-2, are summarized here. The use of the term "strategy" is
not intended to obscure the fact that the outcome did not always reflect a comprehensive, consistent plan.

Algeria possessed limited oil reserves but the fourth largest gas reservoirs in the world. It placed high priority on the development of
the gas industry, mainly for sale in primary form, both liquefied
(LNG) and piped under the Mediterranean through Sicily to Europe;
Algeria's LNG capacity rapidly became the world's largest. The cost
of Algeria's gas investments, at about $18 billion, was roughly
equal to its gross foreign debt at the end of 1981. The gigantic Algerian public investment program displayed by far the strongest bias
in the sample toward heavy industry: together with hydrocarbons,
heavy industry accounted for almost half of all investment. Little investment was allocated to agriculture. But the share going to social infrastructure, particularly housing, rose markedly during the second
windfall years, which also saw a gradual deceleration of the total investment effort. This shift represented an effective expenditure-
switching policy. The domestic resource content of investment was
increased as the total level was cut, which sustained domestic demand and growth despite a rapid reduction in the current account
deficit.

In its public programs Ecuador emphasized the building of economic infrastructure. This was mostly urban, with particular attention to transport, electrification, and water supply. Education, too, received a large share of the oil revenues. (Ecuador's uniquely
complex system of revenue earmarking effectively reserved por-
tions of the windfall for specified institutions.) Public industrial investment went mainly to the oil sector and refining. Although the
government had inherited a number of public manufacturing firms
at the time of the first oil price increase, the state's role in manufacturing was actually cut back in the windfall periods, a tendency
unique in the sample. Instead, the private manufacturing and agricultural processing industries were encouraged by generous credit, tax
and tariff rebates, and subsidies. This policy resulted in slackened
non-oil tax collection but did stem the proliferation of loss-making
public industrial plants that plagued some of the other countries.

The Ecuadorian government initially intended to use oil revenues to fund land reform. But only limited initiatives were carried out, and these involved the colonization of new lands rather than the purchase and redistribution of existing farms.

Indonesia pursued a strategy finely balanced between physical infrastructure, education, agricultural development (both smallholders and estates) and capital-intensive industry. A $20 billion pipeline of industrial projects including fertilizer, LNG, and steel plants was in place by the early 1980s. But half of this pipeline was speedily postponed or canceled with the onset of the oil glut. As described in chapter 12, Indonesia was fortunate in that the 1974 Pertamina crisis helped to delay the buildup of an irreversible investment momentum.

More than any other exporter, Indonesia directed a high proportion of its development spending to rural areas for irrigation works, roads, schools, and other small-scale infrastructural improvements. This distinctive emphasis followed from the critical role assigned to rural reconstruction and to self-sufficiency in rice when the Suharto government came to power in the mid-1960s (Timmer 1975). Indonesia's rural investments were labor-intensive. The successful INPRES programs funded productive public works at the *kabupaten* (county) level, in some cases supplying only materials and relying on self-help for labor. Although the administrative problems involved in this wide distribution of investments should not be glossed over, Indonesia seems to have had a relatively effective rural administration. An extensive dual civilian-military system had previously been established at the level of the 373 counties and towns and in many of the 60,000 villages as well.

Another notable use of oil income was for heavy subsidies on fertilizer.[2] Indonesia's gas reserves, used for fertilizer plants, were a key component of its rural strategy. An econometric assessment of these subsidies by Timmer (1985) finds that they were effective in promoting the use of fertilizers and raising yields, and concludes that their benefit-cost ratio was high (see chapter 12). Although INPRES loan programs later ran into difficulties, oil income was thus used to raise productivity and output in a key non-oil traded sector.

The public investment strategy of Nigeria, which also started the period with a large agricultural sector, was very different from that of Indonesia. A substantial part of public investment was decentralized to the states, but relatively little was spent to promote agriculture. Moreover, agricultural spending was directed to large-scale, capital-intensive projects with a low rate of return.[3] Bienen (1983) has estimated that actual capital expenditures in agriculture made by the federal government under the third plan (1975–78) were only 2.5 percent of the total, compared with a budgeted 6.5 per-

Table 7-3. Social Indicators in the Oil Exporters

Indicator	Algeria	Ecuador	Indonesia	Nigeria	Trinidad and Tobago	Venezuela	Unweighted mean	Comparator
Primary enrollment rate								
1970	76	97	77	37	94	94	79	88[a]
1982	93	114	100	98	99	105	102	102[a]
Secondary enrollment rate								
1970	11	22	15	4	42	33	21	25[a]
1982	36	56	33	16	61	40	40	42[a]
Radio receivers per thousand								
1970	63	290	22	19	226	155	129	
1982	211	357	131	73	281	359	235	251[b]
TV receivers per thousand								
1970	8	26	1	1	58	72	28	
1982	66	69	23	5	266	111	90	86[b]
Population per nursing person								
1970	2,730	1,580	7,680	5,070	330	560	2,992	
1982	740	570	2,300	3,010	380	380	1,230	1,636[b]
Infant mortality rate								
1970	144	108	121	141	43	59	103	
1982	107	76	101	113	28	38	77	62[b]

a. Middle-income countries.
b. Unweighted mean: middle-income countries in Asia and the Pacific and in Latin America and the Caribbean.
Sources: World Bank, *World Development Reports* and Social Indicator Data Sheets.

cent. Disbursement was a serious problem because of the lack of an effective rural administration.[4]

The bulk of Nigerian investment went to the nontraded sectors for roads, ports, and the extension of universal primary education and later secondary and higher levels. In June 1977 a master plan for a new capital city at Abuja was commissioned; Abuja was partly built when the revenue constraints of the oil glut halted construction.[5] At the end of the 1970s the country committed itself to an integrated iron and steel industry against the advice of feasibility studies which projected—correctly—low returns, especially since the industry was to be geographically dispersed for political reasons. These commitments began to have an impact on budgets by the end of the 1970s.

The investment programs of Trinidad and Tobago, like those of Algeria, laid heavy emphasis on the exploitation of natural gas reserves. However, Trinidad chose to establish gas-based industries—ammonia, methanol, urea, and steel—rather than to sell gas in primary form. (Although the option of exporting LNG was assessed at various stages, it never adopted.) Trinidad and Tobago's investment programs also placed considerable emphasis on physical infrastructure, notably road building and transportation. Agriculture was not a major focus for investments (as opposed to subsidies) despite a concern, frequently expressed, about the poor performance of both the export and food subsectors.

Public investment in Venezuela emphasized the metals industries. Studies of effective protection in the early 1970s had confirmed the view that the country's non-oil comparative advantage was greatest in such industries. Public manufacturing investments centered on steel and aluminum plants and their associated infrastructural needs, particularly the massive hydroelectric capacity of the Guri dam. Investment in the Venezuelan oil industry also picked up sharply after nationalization. This was needed to make up for a period of rundown which had occurred as the years of foreign ownership had drawn to a close. Physical and social infrastructure, too, were well funded,[6] and there was also an attempt to reverse the decline in the output share of the smallholder agricultural sector.

Overall, some 60 to 70 percent of the public investment spending of the exporters appears to have been on physical and social infrastructure. The effect of this on the efficiency of transport, distribution, and communications systems is not easily quantifiable, but in some countries it was substantial. As table 7-3 shows, although in 1970 the sample countries had been considerably behind middle-income comparators in education, by 1982 they had caught up in

Table 7-4. Macroprojects in Oil-Exporting Countries

Country	Number of projects included	Total cost (billions of U.S. dollars)	Average cost (millions of U.S. dollars)	Total cost/ 1980 GNP	Total cost/ 1980 oil windfall	Rank among developing countries[a]	Project sector (percent)			
							Hydro-carbons	Metals	Other industry	Infra-structure
Iran	108	119.6	1,107	1.57[b]	10.2[b]	2	30	7	9	54
Algeria	69	38.7	561	1.07	4.2	5	36	7	33	23
Venezuela	27	27.4	1,015	0.51	5.4	10	33	41	7	19
Mexico	59	26.0	441	0.18	5.1	12	46	17	12	25
Nigeria	19	14.4	758	0.17	0.9	15	26	11	16	47
Indonesia	44	14.4	327	0.23	1.1	16	41	18	16	25
Trinidad and Tobago[c]	7	6.9	983	1.35	4.5	—	57	43	—	—

— Country not ranked and projects not included in the study.

Note: Only projects costing more than $100 million are included. For this reason and for lack of data, Ecuador is excluded from the table.

a. Ranked by total investment on projects exceeding $100 million each.

b. 1977 GNP and oil windfall.

c. Gas-based industrial projects only; includes Tenneco-Midcon LNG project proposed for 1988.

Sources: Murphy (1983), table 2.5; Auty (1986a).

primary enrollment rates and had made large gains in secondary enrollment rates. The number of nursing staff available per person more than doubled, and infant mortality rates were cut by a quarter. These data suggest that part of the windfall was transformed into social consumption.

Most of the remaining investments were concentrated in a relatively small set of resource-based industries, especially oil development and refining, gas, hydrocarbon-based chemicals, and metals processing. These were the main initiatives in promoting the traded-goods sectors.

This pattern of investment proved to be a significant determinant of future events. The high proportion of infrastructural spending implied that the payoff to much of the public capital stock *depended* on the continued growth of the economy; the investment itself did not lead directly to income-generating activity. It also meant that in most countries a few key projects serving a few critical markets would determine the returns to that component of investment capable of directly generating net foreign exchange and fiscal revenue. If oil incomes should decline and these projects should fail to return profits (or worse still, fail to generate sufficient revenue to service their debts), fiscal revenue would suffer and the demand-led engine of growth would slow down. This would reduce the value of much infrastructural investment and have serious consequences for the rest of the non-oil economy.

Resource-Based Industry and Other Large Projects

As investment rates rose in the developing countries between the 1960s and 1970s (see table 3-1), so did the number, size, and complexity of "macroprojects," defined by Murphy (1983) as projects with capital costs greater than $100 million. Although some large oil-importing countries (such as Brazil) undertook many such projects, of the nineteen developing countries that invested the most in projects exceeding $100 million each, all but five were oil exporters. The number and cost of large projects in five of the sample countries plus Iran and Mexico are shown in table 7-4; total cost is also compared with 1980 GNP and with the oil windfall in 1980. Ecuador, whose public industrial programs were far more modest than those of the other countries, is excluded. Only actual and some projected investments in gas-based industry are included for Trinidad and Tobago.

The table shows that Iran (occupying second place worldwide after Saudi Arabia) initiated or planned 108 projects averaging more than $1 billion each, with a total capital cost ten times its 1977 oil windfall. The large projects identified in Algeria, Venezuela, Mexico, and Trinidad and Tobago represented four or five times the 1980 oil windfall of these countries. The poorest producers, Indonesia and Nigeria, were somewhat less inclined to mortgage oil for large projects and slower to start, but their investments of this type were still considerable. The large projects identified in table 7-4 represent roughly four and a half years of average oil revenue during 1974–81.

For a representative country (not including Trinidad and Tobago) about 35 percent of the projects were related to hydrocarbons. Another 19 percent were in metals (more in Venezuela) so that at least 54 percent of the projects were in the area of resource-based industries (RBI). Another 16 percent was in other industry, and 32 percent in infrastructure. In terms of numbers of large projects, there was therefore quite heavy emphasis on the traded sectors and RBI, though some of the infrastructural projects were very large.

Data compiled by Murphy (1983) suggest that the larger projects, which were also the more complex and technically demanding, had a greater tendency to overrun initial cost and time budgets than did smaller projects. By 1980 one-third of the largest projects had experienced cost overruns averaging 109 percent. Overruns on the smaller projects were less frequent and more modest, averaging 30 percent. Delays of between one and two years plagued half the troubled projects; a further 25 percent experienced delays of three to four years. Yet these estimates greatly understate the true extent of cost and time overruns. Many projects were not completed by 1980, and a number may never reach completion because of the effects of the oil glut and world recession. Unfortunately no later survey of the experience of such large projects is available so that the robustness of Murphy's conclusions (such as the relationship between scale and overruns) is open to question.

As is clear from table 7-4, resource-based industrialization was a key element in the growth plans of the oil exporters. Auty (1986a, b) has studied the RBI strategies of eight oil-exporting countries and their outcomes. His sample includes four of the countries in this study: Trinidad and Tobago, Venezuela, Indonesia, and Nigeria.[7] The following discussion draws heavily on his analysis.

Resource-based industry was a dominant part of the development strategy of Trinidad and Tobago and Venezuela, which were among the first developing countries to invest in RBI. Trinidad and Tobago opted for a portfolio of gas-based investments that was fairly diversified, especially in view of the small size of the country. Venezuela's portfolio, in contrast, was more heavily concentrated in the steel and aluminum industries. RBI investments in Indonesia and Nigeria were more spread out over time. As noted previously, many Indonesian RBI projects (encompassing a variety of sectors) were fortuitously delayed by the Pertamina crisis, which meant that they could be canceled or rescheduled when the second oil boom ended. Nigeria's main RBI effort, its steel complex, was not initiated until the end of the 1970s.

Why was RBI stressed so heavily? In the eyes of its promoters it promised two important economic benefits: (a) public revenues from taxes on natural resource rents and returns on public equity, and (b) foreign exchange earnings and access to foreign suppliers' credits at attractive interest rates to finance investments. RBI was also believed to offer (c) economic diversification, (d) an opportunity to enhance the skills of nationals, and (e) production linkages to more labor-intensive downstream activities, which, it was held, would compensate for the capital-intensive nature of RBI. On the political side it offered (f) high visibility, (g) a focus for patronage (employment for supporters, sometimes kickbacks from contractors), (h) gains from regional development, (i) the ability to absorb windfalls rapidly in projects with a high import content, (j) reduced dependence on multinational firms, and (k) a shift in status from raw-material exporter to industrial power. With regard to the last benefit, RBI satisfied the urge to create an exporting industrial sector without the need to take the politically difficult steps required to reform existing import-substituting, protected industry.

Although it has not been possible to make a detailed quantitative assessment of rates of return, the overall performance of the RBI projects using this measure seems to have been very poor. True, some projects (such as Indonesia's fertilizer plants) have been successful. But some public manufacturing projects have been unable to cover even their *wage* bills, let alone the costs of other inputs and a market return to investment. Many plants have survived only through the imposition of taxes, in the form of import barriers, on domestic users of their output. Loss-making public investments have left governments facing a difficult choice—to subsidize directly, to protect and so shift costs to other sectors, or to close plants and write off the losses.[8]

Reasons for Poor Performance

In considering this disappointing outcome, the first issue which arises is the *process* by which projects were evaluated and selected.

Project Selection

It is sometimes alleged that many projects were implemented without an assessment of their returns or in spite of assessments which indicated low returns, but this is an oversimplified and misleading view of what actually occurred. It is true that, in some cases, governments proceeded against the recommendations of feasibility studies. But according to Auty (1986a), much of the problem stemmed from the assessments themselves. Three general shortcomings may be noted.

1. *Overemphasis on natural resources.* Proponents of RBI usually assume that access to cheap raw materials or energy is the major factor in global competitiveness. The weight given to this factor in project assessments is far too great relative to the weights given to capital and recurrent costs, product prices, and likely capacity use. Energy costs, for example, constitute only about 22 percent of the total cost of producing steel in the United States and Japan. Power accounted for only 23 percent of total costs in a 1982 hydroelectric aluminum smelter in the United States.[9] Figure 7-1 summarizes sensitivity analyses carried out for two plants, one producing olefins and the other low-density polyethylene. Internal-rate-of-return lines are shown for plant size, cost of raw materials, capacity use, product price, and construction cost. For plants of a given production capacity, these lines indicate that the midpoint elasticities of rates of return with respect to price, capacity use, and construction cost are at least three times those with respect to the cost of raw materials. Cost overruns, increases in interest rates, or deterioration in product markets could therefore cut severely into rents and profits expected from the plants. For reasons outlined below, adequate account was not taken of the possibility of large variations in these dimensions in the feasibility studies.

2. *Consensus and moral hazard in appraisal.* Auty argues that consulting firms appraising projects are of two types. The first type has no apparent financial interest in the project (though other observers argue that there are few truly independent project appraisers). Such a firm has little incentive when assessing project performance to depart from the "range of consensus" that prevails regarding the outlook for the product, energy costs, interest rates, and other variables. If events turn out to be very different and the consensus changes, the firm can justify its assessment with the argument that "everyone else was wrong too." Risk is therefore not properly taken into account in the appraisal, and sensitivity analyses typically do not address the performance of the project under radically different market conditions.

The implication is that appraisals do not evaluate what the acceptable rate of return needs to be—*if* the project and its markets evolve as projected—to compensate for the probability of a major down-

**Figure 7-1. Sensitivity Analysis: Indonesian Olefins Complex
and Low-Density Polyethylene Plant**

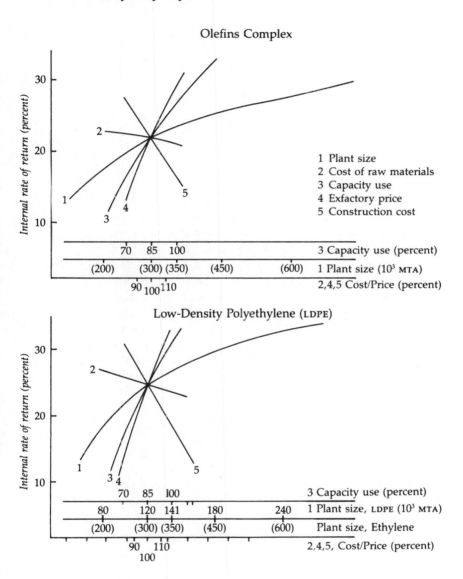

MTA = metric tons per annum

Source: UNICO International Corp., "Republic of Indonesia Survey Report
on Petrochemical Industry Development," vols. 1-6 (Tokyo, 1974), as cited in Auty
(1986a).

turn in markets (involving price cuts or protection abroad) or a large cost or time overrun.

The second type of appraising firm has a substantial potential interest in the project, possibly as a manager or a supplier of equipment. It may be prepared to take a small equity stake to encourage the project to go forward. This it can easily recoup through fees and sales—especially in the event of cost overruns, when it declines to put in more equity so that its stake shrinks while its sales to the plant increase.

This situation introduces a double element of moral hazard into both project selection and implementation. The appraiser-supplier has a strong stake in having the project go forward, whether or not it is economically justified, and little interest in containing costs once it has started.

3. *Sizing up the competition.* Project appraisals rarely considered the cost structures of *current* competitors. Some older plants, although perhaps less efficient, are fully depreciated and therefore potentially very competitive with new plants. But, because of overoptimistic scenarios concerning market growth, appraisals have assumed that product prices would be set by the costs of new capacity, that is, of *future* plants. Old, depreciated plants presumably would then earn abnormal profits. In the first spurt of industrial investment in 1974–76, it was argued that new plants would be far more expensive because of rapid inflation in plant costs and negative real interest rates. And in the second spurt of industrial investment in 1980–81, overoptimistic projections of energy prices swamped all other considerations.

As a result of these three factors, sensitivity analyses typically included only minor variations in market and cost variables, so that the risk inherent in devoting substantial resources to large, inflexible investment projects was downplayed. Once a decision had been made in principle to go ahead with a project, it was not always easy to find foreign partners prepared to share risk by taking a substantial equity position or, equally important, by contracting to purchase part of the output. And in the cases of more doubtful feasibility studies, supporters of the projects could always appeal to the less tangible of the expected benefits to support what was generally, in the last analysis, a political judgment.

Market Trends

The most important factor in the performance of the large RBI investments has been the unexpected severity of the downturn in world markets for many of their products after 1980. By the early 1980s, world demand for copper, lead, zinc, aluminum, and nickel was between 30 and 50 percent lower than what extrapolating the trend of the 1970s suggested. The relation between output and energy use in developed countries changed from an elasticity of unity to an elasticity of less than 0.7. In 1980 the Organization for Economic Cooperation and Development (OECD) forecast a doubling of world steel demand to 1,400 million tons by the year 2000; later forecasts projected only a 20 percent rise to 900 million tons. Price projections were revised downward, sometimes by 30 to 40 percent in real terms. In table 7-5 projections made in 1980 for oil, urea, and aluminum prices for 1985 and 1990 are compared with similar projections made in 1984.

In addition to their effects on price, adverse market developments affected rates of capacity use, since the domestic markets of even the larger countries in the sample were insufficient to absorb the full output of world-scale plants in sectors such as aluminum and steel. In 1979–81, for example, Venezuela's steel industry operated at less than 50 percent of capacity, while its aluminum industry operated at 40 percent of capacity. Even at the peak of the second oil boom domestic steel demand in Indonesia, Nigeria, and Venezuela averaged only 3.5 million tons a year, which is about the output of one world-scale integrated steel complex. Further, part of this demand was for steel that had to be imported, and part was for specialized steel products that had to be fabricated abroad. Such a plant would still have needed to export to achieve full-capacity operation. The domestic markets for aluminum in Indonesia and Venezuela were similar in size and averaged only 78,000 metric tons a year. This was far less than one world-scale smelter's output of 300,000 metric tons. Domestic demand for metals then contracted sharply with the end of the second boom, falling further below the output of efficient plants.[10]

But marketing was a problem for many countries that built RBI plants far in excess of domestic demand. With the slowdown in world demand, many countries protected their own producers. Lacking foreign partners and long-term marketing arrangements, plants in the oil-exporting countries were forced to sell on residual world markets, where price was set by the globally most efficient or most heavily subsidized competitors. In some cases they faced trade barriers when they attempted to export to major markets in the developed countries. For example, ISCOTT, the steel company of Trinidad and Tobago, had production costs 50 percent higher than those of the efficient U.S. minimills, and antidumping charges were successfully brought against the company when it tried to export to the vital U.S. market. The involvement of foreign partners sometimes

Table 7-5. Commodity Price Trends and Projections
(constant 1980 U.S. dollars)

Commodity	1975	1976	1977	1978	1979	1980	1985	1990
Petroleum (dollars per barrel)	17.3	18.3	18.6	16.1	22.1	30.5		
1980 projections							33.0	38.4
1984 projections							23.7	27.0
Urea (dollars per metric ton)	315	175	184	181	191	222		
1980 projections							256	270
1984 projections							155	229
Aluminum (dollars per metric ton)	1,394	1,528	1,641	1,453	1,446	1,730		
1980 projections							1,795	1,851
1984 projections							1,268	1,361

Source: World Bank data.

helped to secure markets; thus Indonesia's LNG plants, constructed with heavy foreign financial and technical involvement, benefited from marketing linkages abroad. In contrast, Algeria's larger LNG installations, which are wholly state-owned, ran at less than half of capacity for lack of markets, so that Algeria's LNG exports in the mid-1980s fell below those of Indonesia.

Plant Costs

Plant costs were typically higher in the oil exporters than in developed countries. For chemical plants built on new sites (greenfields), it was estimated that construction costs in Mexico, Saudi Arabia, and the Gulf exceeded those in the United States by 25 percent, 50 percent, and 100 percent respectively.[11] The cost of steel capacity in some of the oil exporters has been estimated at $2,000 per metric ton, compared with $800 per metric ton for integrated mills in the Republic of Korea. Venezuela's aluminum smelters experienced cost overruns of more than 70 percent, its refinery of 100 percent.

Costs were boosted by the necessary infrastructural requirements, by congestion in domestic construction industries, and by the overloading of suppliers in developed countries during the two intensive investment periods, 1974–75 and 1980–81. The sensitivity of plant costs to the timing of investments is indicated in figure 7-2. The first period represents the speculative real asset boom noted in chapter 6. The second represents the investment boom that resulted largely from widespread projections of secularly rising real energy prices, which in turn translated into large expected profits on RBI investments.

Operating Costs

In addition to high capital costs, high operating costs often contributed to lower returns. Some industries were overmanned; Nigeria's steel plants were estimated to have three times the necessary number of operatives before production even started. In some cases, operating costs were raised by technical errors caused by limited links with foreign suppliers. Such errors were costly in the early phases of the Venezuelan aluminum industry. Some degree of technical error may be considered to be part of the learning process of establishing new industries. But the public bodies in overall charge of the investment program often had little expertise in the particular industry concerned. They were therefore slow to recognize and correct emerging technical and management problems, which increased the costliness of such problems.

Figure 7-2. Plant Cost Index for a Japanese Hydrocarbon Process Plant Supplier

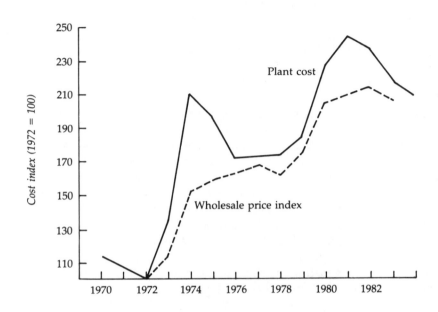

Source: H. Tanaka, "An Analysis of Elements Affecting Project Profitability Related to Contract Marketing and Contracting," paper presented to Pertamina Symposium, Jakarta, February-March 1985, as cited in Auty (1986a).

The worst performers among the RBI projects have probably been the metals projects. Very few, if any, of these appear to have been profitable. The gas-based chemical and fertilizer industries seem to have done better, though their returns have been lower than originally projected. Such plants could operate efficiently on a smaller scale and respond better to the needs of the domestic market. Oil refineries producing for export did less well, partly because transport costs for small batches of refined products are higher than for large volumes of crude oil. For the same reason, a refining industry serving the domestic market was a more attractive investment. But a chronic surplus of capacity worldwide had squeezed margins by the 1980s, with refineries in many OECD countries operating at less than 60 percent of capacity. And some domestic markets were too small, given the need for a variety of products, to support world-scale refineries.

The poor returns of many RBI plants, then, reflected a variety of factors. None was peculiar to oil-exporting countries, but all were accentuated by the scope and pace of their investment growth and rendered more important by the weight of RBI in their development strategies.[12] The exporters chose to convert enormous investable surpluses into fixed assets in a period when the range of uncertainty over key global economic variables and structural relationships was unusually large. Their strategies for developing the traded goods sectors emphasized large-scale projects in a limited set of industries. This emphasis reduced their economic flexibility at a time when just the opposite was needed. Risk was downplayed in project assessments. Projects were hastily and in some cases inadequately prepared. Foreign partners with large equity stakes were sometimes avoided for reasons of nationalism. In other cases they were sought but, being more sensitive to risk, could not be attracted on terms considered acceptable by producer governments.

Despite these difficulties, such large projects were probably the only domestic investments capable of satisfying the political urge to absorb the windfalls so rapidly; other potential options, such as land reform, labor-intensive industry, or smallholder agriculture faced administrative barriers and posed political and other problems which could not be addressed speedily, if at all. For all these reasons, the acceleration of public investments lowered the quality of public capital formation and increased risk. Many of the RBI investments made in the sample countries were internationally uncompetitive, and some were doomed from the start to make negative rates of economic return.

At the same time, it is hard to avoid the conclusion that the poor performance of other key RBI investments has been *mainly* caused by the unexpected evolution of world markets and interest rates, which has also had a serious impact on the same types of industries in other developing and in developed countries. In this sense, factors external to any individual country, but closely related to the oil price shocks by their impact on the global economy, have reduced the returns from the oil windfalls. Some projects that now show a loss may become profitable as losses are written off with restructuring (most projects have a heavily front-loaded capital structure), especially if world markets for their products improve. Even so, their unlucky timing makes it unlikely that the overall returns to invested capital will be satisfactory. The outlook is bleaker still if one accepts the proposition that a substantial part of the natural resource endowment of some countries is committed to specific product mixes, which curtails flexibility in the future use of resources.

The Drift toward Subsidies

An additional claim on public purses came from rapidly growing programs of subsidies and transfers. Consumer subsidies were usually directed to holding down the rate of inflation, producer subsidies to supporting loss-making firms. Between 1970–72 and 1974–78 fiscal subsidies and transfers expanded, on average, twice as rapidly as nonmining GDP; between 1974–78 and 1980–81 they rose 1.6 times as rapidly. Recorded fiscal subsidies rose sharply in Trinidad and Tobago to 7 percent of total GDP or 11 percent of nonmining GDP by 1981. By 1983 it was estimated that the production costs of Caroni Sugar in Trinidad were five times those of efficient producers, despite the fact that some of the latter had unit labor costs several times higher. The state enterprise deficit in Venezuela reached 8.3 percent of GDP in 1982.

For several reasons, the fiscal accounts of the sample countries greatly understate the true magnitude of the subsidies. Producer governments were reluctant to raise domestic oil prices to world levels in 1974 and 1979 and chose to pass on this part of the windfall directly to domestic consumers. In at least three countries domestic oil prices were set at the cost of production, so the governments derived no revenue from oil consumed at home. Some producers, notably Ecuador and Indonesia, raised domestic prices of oil derivatives in the early 1980s, but on the whole their prices still remained well below world levels. As their domestic oil consumption (which sometimes included illicit exports) grew more rapidly than their non-oil economies, the implicit fiscal burden on the state increased. In 1980 energy subsidies were estimated to be equivalent to almost 10 percent of household income in Ecuador, where electricity was also very heavily subsidized. Subsidies amounted to 4–6 percent of GDP in some of the other countries. Studies of their distributional impact have been limited, but there is no indication that they were targeted to the poorest groups.

Fiscal data also do not include the subsidies implicit in loans made to loss-making (usually public) firms, nominally to finance investment, and in the government guarantees which enabled them to obtain commercial loans. It is difficult to estimate these subsidies (since many such firms would probably have been unable to borrow at any interest rate without a government guarantee), but they must have been considerable since they were accorded to some extremely unprofitable firms. The RBI industries in particular were heavily subsidized. In the steel industry, for example, losses of $400 million by P. T. Krakatau in 1977–80 and $1.8 billion by SIDOR in Venezuela had to be covered by the state. Despite subsidies of $59 million in 1982–83, ISCOTT in Trinidad and Tobago recorded losses of $201 million.

Some governments stimulated employment directly through public works programs. In certain cases these programs made a useful contribution to capital formation; in others, they represented a disguised subsidy to labor. Consider the contrast between the INPRES and Bantuan Desa (village-level) rural construction programs in Indonesia and the Special Works (DEWD) infrastructure programs in Trinidad and Tobago. Each is estimated to have provided at least part-time work to some 2.5 percent of the country's labor force. INPRES created slack-season jobs at wages generally not above what was available in agriculture. Projects had to demonstrate results (periodic photographs of work in progress were one requirement) and to be completed within one year. The Bantuan Desa projects financed only materials and were conditional on local self-help in the form of unpaid labor inputs. The effect of such programs in labor-surplus Java appears to have been positive. In contrast, the Trinidad programs offered daily pay at least twice that available in agriculture. Since the average workday was light—about two hours— these programs really represented a method of transferring oil rents to the poorer sections of society. It is not clear that the programs had a major impact on infrastructure. But they accelerated the shift of labor off the land, which exacerbated the drop in agricultural output.

An indistinct yet interesting pattern emerges across countries concerning the use of oil rents to fund consumer subsidies and support price controls on consumer goods. Such measures to distribute oil income to consumers seem to have been more pronounced in the higher-income countries in the sample than in the poorest ones. This may have been because political life was marked by more electoral competition in Trinidad and Tobago and Venezuela than in Indonesia and Nigeria. It may also have reflected greater administrative reach in the richer countries. Yet another important factor may have been the more pressing need for basic infrastructural investments in the poorer countries, which argued for having public rather than private agents spend the first round of oil income.

The apparently low returns to much public investment raises a key distributional issue. Are subsidies and direct transfers of oil income from the state to private citizens irresponsible or are they sound policy? Some high-income oil-rich regions, such as Alaska and Alberta, have made direct distributions of oil wealth to their residents, but this option appears not to have been considered in the capital-importing developing producers. Yet, from the perspective of second best, such an approach may be preferable to a program of public investments which yields little or no benefit on the supply side, and is even more preferable to investments with a *negative* rate of economic return—such as steel plants requiring indefinite protection (or taxes on users) to cover costs. Simulations with a gen-

Table 7-6. Growth Trends in the Oil Exporters, 1967–81
(percent)

Country	Nonmining GDP		Domestic investment		Goods and nonfactor service			
					Exports		Imports	
	1967–72	1972–81	1967–72	1972–81	1967–72	1972–81	1967–72	1972–81
Algeria	9.5	8.6	16.7	10.8	5.7	−1.0	11.6	10.8
Ecuador	4.7	7.6	3.2	10.2	15.9	6.0	6.0	9.7
Indonesia	8.5	8.2	24.3	13.0	15.7	4.3	16.7	19.1
Iran[a]	10.1	13.3	10.2	21.1	12.9	−0.3	17.7	23.7
Nigeria	9.2	5.3	—[b]	8.7	—[b]	−4.2	—[b]	15.3
Trinidad and Tobago	5.3	5.4	6.1	9.3	2.5	−6.5	6.6	8.4
Venezuela	6.5	5.1	11.9	3.5	−1.3	−8.7	7.7	12.8
Unweighted mean (excluding Iran)	7.3	6.7	12.4	9.3	7.7	−1.7	9.7	12.7
Middle-income oil importers[c]	5.8[d]	5.1[d]	8.2	5.6	6.7	4.0	7.4	1.5

a. 1967–72 and 1972–77.
b. Deflated data unreliable before 1970.
c. 1960–70 and 1970–82.
d. GDP.
Source: World Bank data.

eral equilibrium model suggest that, without a supply-side impact, only about one-third of investment expenditures will be reflected in private consumption through the induced relative price and demand-multiplier effects (see Gelb 1985b). Low-return public investments are therefore a very inefficient way to distribute oil wealth to the citizens of a producing country. Subsidies tend to become institutionalized, however (see, for example, chapter 14), and this can also be shown to have a detrimental effect on efficiency and growth should oil revenue fall.

The Growth Impact: Models and Performance through 1981

Most theories of economic growth are based on stable relationships between factor inputs and output; they would therefore predict a substantial acceleration of growth following an investment program on the scale of those implemented by the oil exporters after 1974. Consider the simplest aggregate neoclassical production function:

$$y = A \, K^a L^{(1 - a)}$$

where y is output, K is the capital stock, L is labor, and a is the share of capital in output. The corresponding growth model is:

$$\hat{y} = \hat{A} + a\hat{K} + (1 - \hat{a})L$$

where $\hat{y}$ represents the GDP growth rate, $\hat{A}$ is the rate of (Hicks-neutral) technical change, $\hat{K}$ is the rate of capital growth, and $\hat{L}$ is the rate of growth of labor. Suppose that, for a typical country, $\hat{A} = 0.02$, $a = 0.30$, $\hat{K} = 0.10$, $\hat{L} = 0.03$, the depreciation rate is 5 percent a year, and the capital-output ratio is 2.0. This is compatible with a gross savings rate of 30 percent, a growth rate of 7.1 percent, and a growth of income per capita of 4.1 percent a year.[13]

In such a stylized economy, with a constant quality of capital formation, an extra investment effort on the scale of the real investment effect of tables 5-2 and 5-3 would add 1.4 percentage points to the growth rate, even if it is assumed that (a) no immigration occurred to increase the labor supply (in fact, immigration was considerable in Venezuela and Nigeria over the boom years) and (b) technical change was totally disembodied. If growth was theorized to be constrained by the capital stock only, or by the availability of foreign exchange or fiscal revenues, the expected impact of the windfalls would be far larger. The projected addition to growth is therefore quite conservative.[14]

Table 7-6 summarizes growth trends in the six oil exporters during 1967–72 and 1972-81 and compares these with the growth rates of middle-income oil-importing developing countries in the same periods. The cutoff date, 1981, is chosen so that the period of the emerging oil glut does not affect results. Despite this, the impact of investment on growth was at first sight very disappointing. Only Ecuador significantly accelerated the growth of its nonmining economy in 1972–81 relative to its low level in 1967–72.[15] On average, in 1974–78 non-oil economies were almost exactly the size they would have been had they maintained their 1967–72 growth trends, and in 1979–81 they were 4.1 percent *smaller* than along this trend.

These comparisons yield the real growth terms in tables 5-2 and 5-3. Combining the real allocation and the growth terms in these tables shows how the components of absorption have deviated from a scenario which combines (a) nonmining growth at the rates of 1967–72 and (b) the hypothesized structures of relative prices and composition of demand. On average, real private and public consumption and public investment were considerably larger than these scenario values during 1974–78. The averages in table 5-3 suggest a further rise in consumption (except in Nigeria) but a substantial shortfall in investment in 1979–81 relative to the first boom period, on the basis of the new hypothetical scenario.

On closer examination, the growth record through 1981, though still disappointing, is less adverse. Before 1972 Indonesia, Nigeria, and Algeria had all been in recovery phases, the first two from severe internal disturbances and the third from a protracted war of independence. The economies of Ecuador and Trinidad and Tobago had been stimulated by spending on the oil industry. The sample's non-oil growth rate of 7.3 percent in 1967–72 was exceptionally high, 1.5 percent above the average growth rate of middle-income developing countries in the 1960s.

Average non-oil growth after 1972 was still 0.9 percent above this level. However, growth in the sample countries was demand-led rather than supply-driven. As is clear from the growth effects of tables 5-2 and 5-3, growth responded to increased absorption after 1974 but slowed after 1978 despite the expectation that large investments undertaken in 1975–78 would begin to contribute to output. An outstanding case is Venezuela, which simply stopped growing in 1979 despite the largest investment program in its history. Although the spending boom of 1974–77 raised the growth rate above its previous trend, by 1983 the nonmining Venezuelan economy was one-third smaller than it would have been had it continued to grow at the pre-1973 rate.

The poor growth response is important in assessing the benefits of the windfalls. Growth was a major priority for all of the countries, and as noted in chapter 5 it cannot be argued that the exporters *directly* consumed an excessively large share of their windfalls relative to the predictions of a "permanent income" model. The widespread ineffectiveness of fiscal linkages, and especially of public investment programs, has thus been a major feature in the evolution of the sample countries.

Notes

1. Tugwell (1975), Bigler (1980), and Karl (1982) analyze the role of the Venezuelan state and the "third sector" in the economy.

2. In this study, fertilizer subsidies are included in development spending but excluded from measures of public investment.

3. Katouzian (1978) describes a similar agricultural investment policy in Iran and its similar results.

4. It is not possible to form a picture of the expenditure patterns of the states. The general lack of data raises some doubts, however, about the efficiency of state investments.

5. In 1987 the population of Abuja was estimated at 30,000 following a 2 billion naira investment. The original target was for a population of 3.1 million by the turn of the century.

6. The Caracas metro system was reputed to be the most costly, per meter, in the world.

7. Other countries considered by Auty are Saudi Arabia, Bahrain, Cameroon, and Malaysia. See Auty (1986a), (1987), and related works for a more detailed analysis.

8. Recent unpublished estimates by Auty suggest capital/output ratios of over 10 for most RBI projects.

9. Auty (1986a), tables 10 and 5. For a 1972 Japanese oil-powered plant, however, power represented 52 percent of total costs.

10. In the mid 1980s steel demand in Indonesia, Nigeria, and Venezuela averaged only about 1.5 million tons. Aluminum demand was also about half of its boom-year levels.

11. United Nations Industrial Development Organization (UNIDO) estimates as cited in Auty (1986a).

12. As shown by the $8 billion cost of the trans-Alaskan oil pipeline versus its $900 million original budget, cost overruns can be large in developed countries also. Their peculiar significance for the oil exporters is due to the weight of large projects relative to the size of their economies.

13. With gross savings of 30 percent and a capital/output ratio of 2, gross investment is 15 percent of the capital stock so that net investment is 10 percent of capital. The gross incremental output/capital ratio on such a growth path is 0.24. This is slightly below average for developing countries before 1971 (see table 3-1).

14. Embodied technical change would also cause the impact of new investment to be greater.

15. Data are limited for Iran.

Chapter 8

From Boom to Bust: The Downside of the Cycle and Asymmetric Macroeconomic Response

As world oil markets turned downward after 1981, a combination of slumping prices and cuts in sales reduced the windfall gains of the oil exporters. With 1981 taken as a new base period, the windfall effect for the six countries in 1982–84 averaged −8.1 percent of nonmining GDP, as shown in table 8-1. Only Ecuador, which managed to raise oil output considerably and so compensate for falling prices, avoided a substantial reduction in windfall gains.

Adjustment Patterns

The exporters reacted to this adverse shift in a variety of ways but typically with a lag of at least a year. They had previously found that the momentum of public spending was hard to curb as revenues fell, particularly since an increasing proportion consisted of recurrent expenditures to service the capital investments of earlier years and of subsidies to keep loss-making ventures in operation. In 1978, at the close of the first boom, government deficits had averaged 4.1 percent of nonmining GDP; current account deficits had averaged 11.8 percent of nonmining GDP (excluding Trinidad and Tobago where expenditure was more cautious in this period). Some countries had taken steps to slow the absorption of goods and services, and Indonesia had devalued by 30 percent in November 1978. These contractionary moves were interrupted by the second oil shock, which resulted in a current account surplus of $11.8 billion for the six countries in 1980, a year widely regarded as signaling the start of an era of scarce and costly energy.

But the second windfall fell off more abruptly than the first. In 1980–82 commodity exports, in current dollars, shrank by 21.6 percent as imports rose by 22.3 percent, so that current account balances shifted to a deficit of $19.6 billion by 1982. More than half the current account deterioration was due to the unexpected fall in export revenues. In 1983 the deficit dropped to $7 billion as contractionary policies were implemented. These policies included sharp reductions in public spending and cuts in subsidies. Some exporters took steps to raise domestic energy prices closer to world levels. In addition, countries postponed or canceled projects in their pipeline; Indonesia, for example, delayed or cut over half its planned heavy industrial spending, for an estimated import saving of $11 billion.

The adjustment patterns of the oil exporters in 1981–84 are presented in table 8-1, which uses the methodology developed in chapter 4 but indicates only the value effects.[1] About two-thirds of the necessary decrease in absorption relative to nonmining output was borne by investment—more in Nigeria and Venezuela and less in Indonesia, where private consumption adjusted to offset the relative fall in oil revenue. Ecuador's continuing windfall gains went to increase the share of consumption, not investment.

In assessing these responses one should bear in mind that, when the second oil boom ended in 1981, the sample countries found themselves in quite different situations. Trinidad and Tobago and Venezuela had run up large trade and nonfactor surpluses (in Venezuela this surplus was partly offset by capital outflow), whereas Nigeria had run up a large trade and nonfactor service deficit. Nigeria's investment was therefore cut sharply to achieve external balance in the face of a substantial worsening of its terms of trade rather than to attain a surplus position. Indonesia's conservative fiscal policy during the second oil boom had allowed it to build a reserve cushion to smooth adjustment. This made possible a negative trade and nonfactor service effect of −3.4 percent of nonmining GDP in 1982–84.

Economic management through booms and slumps was rendered more difficult because access to foreign savings tended to be cyclical, increasing with the actual levels of world oil prices, since these were strongly related to future price expectations and perceived creditworthiness, but reducing when oil prices fall. Until world oil markets deteriorated, countries such as Mexico and Venezuela were able to cushion the impact of growing outflows of private capital by public borrowing abroad. When it became obvious that exchange rates could not be sustained, capital outflows accelerated, especially in countries such as Venezuela with open capital accounts and interest rate controls. In 1982 that country may have experienced an outflow as large as 10 percent of GDP.

The reasons for this outflow included interest rate ceilings in the face of rising foreign rates, a reluctance to adjust the exchange rate

Table 8-1. Adjustment and Growth, 1981–84

Measure	Algeria	Ecuador	Indonesia	Nigeria	Trinidad and Tobago	Venezuela	Mean
Windfall effect[a]	−10.4	2.8	−8.7	−10.2	−13.6	−8.3	−8.1
Trade and nonfactor service effect[a]	−1.2	0.5	−3.4	10.7	n.a.	1.0	1.5[b]
Consumption effect[a]	−3.8	4.5	−9.2	−4.2	n.a.	−1.1	−2.8[b]
Private	−4.6	5.9	−8.6	−2.4	n.a.	1.9	−1.6[b]
Public	0.8	−1.4	−0.6	−1.8	n.a.	−2.6	−1.1[b]
Investment effect[a]	−5.4	−2.2	3.9	−16.7	n.a.	−8.2	−5.7[b]
Non-oil growth rate for 1981–84	7.0	−1.0	4.8	−5.6	−2.9	−2.0	0.0
Ratio of trade and nonfactor service surplus to nonmining GDP in 1981	1.4	1.1	2.8	−10.6	23.4	7.8	4.3

n.a. Not available.

a. Effect, measured as percentage of nonmining GDP, is the average for 1982–84, with 1981 as the base year.

b. Mean for five countries.

to widely perceived trends in the oil market, and contradictory policies initiated by the Venezuelan administration and its opposing legislature, which squeezed domestic profit rates while opening industry to greater foreign competition (see chapter 14). The capital outflow resulted in a prolonged decline in private investment, which was the main contributor to the large negative investment effect recorded in table 8-1. The investment slowdown caused negative growth in the period after 1978, which in turn contributed to the slowdown through the "negative accelerator" effect of depressed yields on the domestic capital stock. Increases in Venezuela's labor force and capital stock should have ensured growth of at least 4 percent a year even with zero productivity gains.

In fact, the average country experienced virtually no non-oil growth at all in 1981–84, as shown in table 8-1. Only Algeria and Indonesia managed to maintain positive growth rates in this period. Algeria was aided by growing exports of natural gas, LNG, and condensate (a liquid by-product of gas extraction) and by the implementation of an effective expenditure-switching policy, which shifted the composition of public investments from import-intensive manufacturing to social capital, notably housing. Indonesia, once again, was quick to devalue as oil income fell and was able to prevent the real effective exchange rate from appreciating for extended periods. That country's recovery was helped by a strong performance in agriculture and in miscellaneous (mostly manufactured) exports, which compensated for the depressed markets facing non-oil primary commodities.

The average growth and inflation rates of the oil exporters from 1976 to 1984 are summarized in figure 8-1. The period may be divided into five phases:

- 1970–72 marked the end of recovery from the domestic turbulence of the 1960s in Algeria, Nigeria, and Indonesia and of intensive oil development phases in Ecuador and Trinidad and Tobago. The average nonmining GDP growth rate fell from more than 10 percent in 1970 to 5.3 percent in 1971 and 1972.
- 1972–77 was the upswing of the first oil boom. Domestic prices rose sharply as real exchange rates appreciated and import costs rose. As resources were reallocated to the construction and service sectors, growth peaked in 1976 and 1977. In this period, construction sectors grew an average of 13.9 percent a year.
- 1977–79 was the downside of the first boom. As income and spending slackened, growth rates of real output fell sharply but inflation actually accelerated slightly. This period provides

Figure 8-1. Boom and Stagflation during the Oil Cycle, 1970–84

(unweighted averages, six countries)

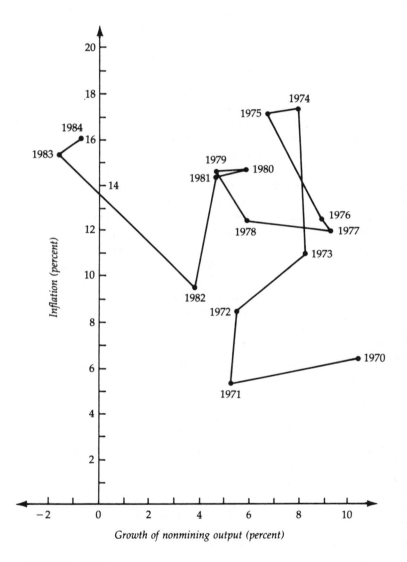

Source: World Bank data.

the first experience of asymmetric macroeconomic adjustment; by the start of the second boom in 1979 inflation was higher and growth lower than in 1972 and 1973.

- 1979–81 was the second boom. It was smaller and more abrupt than the first one. Average inflation and growth rates varied only slightly in these years.

- 1981–84 marked the downturn of the second boom. Both inflation and non-oil output growth fell sharply in 1982, but the large current account deficits were not sustainable. Governments therefore turned to domestic markets for financing, reduced subsidies, and scaled back other measures which had held down domestic prices. Rather like the oil importers in the upswing of the cycle, the exporters moved into stagflation on the downside, with negative growth in 1983 and 1984.[2]

- Ecuador, Nigeria, and Venezuela experienced foreign exchange crises. Indonesia and Algeria, as noted above, adjusted more smoothly, although their policies were very different. Trinidad and Tobago's ample reserves enabled it to postpone adjustment until 1985, although poor agricultural performance and a decline in the oil-refining industry resulted in negative growth in 1981–84.

Inclusion of the fifth period reduces average non-oil growth rates to only 4.7 percent during 1974–84. This is 1.1 percent *below* the average growth rate for developing countries in the 1960s. Despite the emerging oil glut, adverse terms of trade for oil were not responsible; even in 1984 the purchasing power of oil exports was far *larger* than it had been before 1974. The massive investment programs of the previous decade were failing to stimulate output.

Modeling Growth and Adjustment during the Cycle

To obtain a better quantitative picture of gains and losses during oil cycles and of the effects of policies and macroeconomic responses, Gelb (1985a, 1985b) investigates the impact of suboptimal and optimal policies using a general equilibrium model. The rest of this chapter outlines the model, its results, and the implications of those results for the sample countries. The exercises use the model to compare the evolution of an economy under alternative conditions: an oil price cycle and constant real world oil prices. This enables the impact of the cycle to be assessed under various policy and macroeconomic assumptions.

The model itself is a dualistic six-sector computable general equilibrium (CGE) representation of an economy similar to that of Indonesia, with oil, manufacturing, construction, services, export, and food agriculture.[3] "Modern" and "traditional" sectors are distinguished (in the latter, labor may be paid its average, rather than marginal, product), and manufacturing and service sectors are split into modern and traditional components. There are two economic agents, government and the private sector. The latter is treated from the demand side as a single household whose reaction functions are taken into account in setting policy. The model is simulated or optimized over a run of ten periods, each representing two years. The outcomes are then assessed according to a welfare function in two parts: the discounted sum of the logarithms of consumption per capita during the twenty-year period times population, and a terminal condition on the output of year 20 to represent the discounted value of the posthorizon steady-state consumption stream. The base-year social accounting matrix of the model is for 1975 and is based on Downey and Keuning (1983). Oil output, world prices, and interest rates are exogenous sequences of variables.

The model includes a richer set of interperiod links than most CGES. In addition to the conventional updating of capital stocks and labor force through investment, population growth, and migration, government consumption levels are set by the need to service public capital. This introduces a ratchet effect of investment booms on public spending. Public infrastructural investment raises productivity and output, rather than adding to capital stocks in production functions as does private investment. Rapid acceleration or deceleration in the rate of investment lowers the quality of capital formation, so that unstable investment paths are less productive than stable ones.

In the basic version of the model, prices and wages adjust smoothly to equilibrate demands and supplies, and private domestic investment is determined by private savings. But the model also includes three optional variants, which allow simulations to incorporate other important interactions during the cycle. One option is to introduce downward wage rigidity in the modern sector. The result is unemployment rather than real wage cuts to clear the modern labor market when labor demand falls. A second option is that of "sticky prices"; faced with falling demand, firms move off their long-run supply curves and cut output to slow the rate of price decline. This results in a phase of operating at less than full capacity in response to sharply falling demand. Third, private agents may be given the option of exporting their savings in addition to investing domestically. The capital-flight decision is modeled as sensitive to sharp depreciations in the real effective exchange rate, which in the real world would require large nominal devaluations.[4]

Certain features of this model, such as the treatment of labor markets, are rather specific to Indonesia. But for the most part its dynamic behavior reflects more common characteristics. The exercises described below should be interpreted as delineating oil exporters in general rather than any single country.

A first base run for steady world oil prices is constructed, and then a second base run for a windfall scenario such as that of 1978–84. In these base model runs, government is constrained; it neither lends abroad nor borrows in the windfall period—a policy representative of average behavior for the sample of exporters. Windfall gains feed public investment, and the real exchange rate appreciates with the spending effect. Private demand rises to absorb about 30 percent of the windfall during the boom because of the demand-led effects of public spending on relative prices and activity levels.

The base value of the windfall—denoted here by V_1—is given by the difference between the valuation functions of the two simulation runs. V_1 is the windfall's value under empirically representative, not optimal, policies and with flexible wages and prices in the economy.

The next step is to optimize the time profiles of public absorption, both with and without the windfall, to determine the optimal path of saving and borrowing abroad. With perfect foresight, about 70 percent of the windfall is optimally saved abroad during the boom, to be used up gradually as oil prices fall. This raises the value of the windfall by over 60 percent from its base level V_1. The optimized value of the windfall is denoted by V_2.

The gains from cautious spending are far larger, however, if the producing economy cannot adjust smoothly in the downturn through flexible prices and wages. Under the fiscal assumptions of the base run, sticky prices and wages reduce the value of the windfall by between 20 and 40 percent of V_1 (to a value denoted by V_3) because of unemployment of labor and capital on the downside of the cycle. In optimized runs with perfect foresight, the model economy never runs into such a recession because rigidities in factor and product markets are very costly in terms of lost output, investment, and growth. The value of the windfall in the optimized run, V_2, is therefore more than twice that in the base run if the economy cannot adjust smoothly; that is, V_2 is more then twice V_3.[5]

The simulations also show that capital flight is extremely costly. Because it accelerates on the downside of the cycle, it exacerbates the problems caused by falling levels of public spending and deepens the recession by cutting investment further. The economy may now be considered to have two private agents. "Speculators" own financial assets, the more internationally mobile factor of production.

By moving funds abroad as the oil market weakens, they throw the burden of adjustment onto "workers" who respond by defending real wages at the high cost of unemployment. Optimized runs with perfect foresight always avoid situations likely to trigger such capital flight.

Finally, the model is used to analyze the impact of imperfect foresight. How important has poor prediction been in determining the macroeconomic outcome of the oil shocks? Incorporating errors in predicting oil prices requires a two-stage process. First, the model is optimized subject to a path of oil prices which is predicted to rise at 6 percent in real terms after the peak of the boom. Second, the solution to that problem is used to create a new starting point for the model at the peak of the boom, for a reoptimization subject to the "correct" price expectations for the rest of the period. This process simulates the sharp downward revisions in oil market projections which took place at the peak of the second oil boom in 1981.

The results of this exercise suggest that the costs of such prediction errors are likely to be enormous. The model economy borrows against expected future oil income to increase absorption by a *further* 60 percent of the windfall during the boom.[6] The peak of the boom finds the economy with a strongly appreciated real exchange rate, unsustainable wage levels, and large debts (which must be repaid by the end of the twenty-year horizon). Under a wide range of parametric assumptions, the windfall value is *negative* because of the severity of subsequent recession and stagnation. In absolute magnitude the "cost" of the windfall, V_4, is often more than three times its "benefit" V_1 in the base run or more than four times its "benefit" V_3 with the base fiscal assumptions and sticky downward adjustment of wages and prices.

One major implication of these simulations is that the oil exporters should have saved a far higher proportion of the windfall abroad than they actually did. Another is that the increase in global volatility and uncertainty after 1973 was a very important aspect of the oil shocks. Given the magnitude of the resulting prediction errors, the shocks could certainly have left producing economies worse off than before the windfalls. This is because downside macroeconomic costs are potentially far larger than upside absorption benefits.

Notes

1. Deflators are not sufficiently reliable for enough countries to warrant presenting real and price effects. The value effects compare value shares and projected value shares and therefore combine real and price effects.

2. If the exporters had held domestic oil prices at world levels, they would have experienced the supply shock on the upside of the cycle as the oil importers did. But because domestic oil prices were raised on the downside to increase fiscal revenues, the pattern of spending and supply shocks was the mirror image of that in the oil importers.

3. CGE models are described extensively in Dervis, de Melo, and Robinson (1982). They capture the economy on the production side and on the demand side through production and demand functions and represent the whole as a set of interrelated markets which (usually) clear by adjustments in relative factor and product prices.

4. This model, like other CGEs, does not have a nominal price level; the price of imported manufactured goods is taken as the numeraire.

5. As noted in chapter 2, adjustment costs on the upswing and the downside of the cycle are largely external to individuals. The optimized run therefore cannot be identified with the outcome of a policy of distributing the windfall to private agents. This is one of the main reasons why the private sector is not modeled as an optimizing agent.

6. Mexican projections were for real oil prices to rise by 6 percent a year, and the increased borrowing of the model corresponds exactly to the extent of increased Mexican borrowing during 1979–81; see table 5-3. This is a pure, yet interesting, coincidence.

Chapter 9

Summary of Findings

Although commodity price fluctuations have long been common-place, in a number of respects the oil shocks were unprecedented. Oil is a key input into production and distribution. Even before 1973 it was the commodity with the largest value in international trade. The periodicity of the oil cycle—or cycles, if considered as two events—was far longer than that characteristic of fluctuations in most commodity prices, and the amplitudes of the oil cycles were larger. Also, no other commodity has embodied so great a share of national rent in its price.

The shocks therefore had a large impact on the global economy. They affected trade flows and capital balances between importing and exporting countries and changed the incentives for activities that consume and produce energy. In energy-importing countries, the shocks had profound regional effects. For example, the crisis of financial institutions in Texas in the mid-1980s highlights the disequilibriums and investment losses induced by oil price swings. In the producing countries, cumulated rent flows concentrated the surplus in the hands of relatively few economic decisionmakers. Oil price trends and the policy responses of major industrial countries to the shocks were poorly predicted. Consequently, so were real interest rates, inflation, exchange rates, and the evolution of world markets for other important commodities after 1973. One result of the shocks has therefore been greater global volatility and uncertainty.

This book considers the impact of these events on a set of apparent winners in the global equation—the capital-deficit, developing oil exporters. The six countries studied differ along many political and economic dimensions, and this raises difficulties for comparative study because of the small sample. But the countries share some common characteristics as well. The sizes of their oil sectors relative to their non-oil economies were similar during the windfall decade; so were the proportions of their total wealth made up of proven oil reserves. All desired to use their oil revenue to spur growth, modernization, and economic diversification and to increase the degree of national control over key economic sectors. None overtly sought to consume most of the windfall gains or to move toward a rentier state through prolonged savings abroad. These priorities account for the perspective of this study. The effects of the oil booms on income distribution, for example, have not been given greater emphasis here not only because of severe data problems but also because this was not the main thrust of policy in these countries.

It is important to recognize the extent to which continuity shaped the use of the oil windfalls. Social and political institutions changed more slowly than the availability of resources. Indeed, in some cases the abundance of oil revenues may have reduced pressure for institutional change by funding the inefficiency of existing institutions. Although in principle the windfalls represented uncommitted income which could be allocated to those activities deemed to have the greatest social value, in practice they tended to fund fairly conventional, though disparate, activities reflecting priorities and administrative capabilities that had evolved before 1973.

At the broadest level, continuity of policy dictated that the rents be translated into domestic investments, the traditional use of surplus funds. The proportion of the windfalls invested domestically was indeed large. On average, it was roughly what an economist would have recommended in 1975 on the basis of a "permanent income" model, allowing for depletion of reserves and projecting constant real prices, but abstracting from two important features: constraints on absorption capacity and uncertainty. It was above the levels which might have followed from assuming that real resource rents would increase at or above a reasonable rate of discount—an assumption which would have argued for still higher consumption. Increased investment was overwhelmingly public; for a variety of reasons private investment was unresponsive in most of the countries.

The six countries in this study all took significant steps to bring their oil and hydrocarbon sectors under national control. Some also took wide-ranging steps toward indigenization in other sectors. The oil windfalls were not responsible for such policies, which predated the shocks—often by many years. But the windfalls did accelerate the process by providing producer governments with the financial resources that helped them to buy out foreign interests and to compensate for any adverse effects on output. Progress toward the objective of increasing national control over key economic sectors was therefore quite strong.

Progress toward achieving economic diversification was far less impressive, however. Only Indonesia and possibly Ecuador managed to strengthen and diversify the nonhydrocarbon traded sectors during the windfall decade. The other producers either began and ended the period with uncompetitive manufacturing and agricultural sectors, which contributed, in total, a smaller than "normal" share to nonmining GDP (Venezuela and, especially in agriculture, Algeria), or they experienced a dramatic relative or absolute decline in these activities (Nigeria, Trinidad and Tobago) and moved to still greater dependence on oil.

As for growth, the only favorable impact of the windfalls on average performance has been the powerful demand-led expansion of 1974–77. From 1974 to 1981 average growth rates were well below what would have been predicted by a simple neoclassical model, given the size of the investment boom in relation to either the past experience of the individual countries or the performance of developing countries in the 1960s. Growth rates were even further below what would have been predicted by theories of capital- or foreign-exchange-constrained growth. Extending the period through 1984 lowers the average growth rate of the non-oil economies of the sample countries to only 4.7 percent, considerably below the growth rates registered by developing countries in the 1960s. Terms of trade were still far more favorable for oil exporters in 1984 than in 1972, so the oil glut cannot be blamed.

The theories reviewed in chapter 2 may be grouped into two sets. Booming-sector and neoclassical growth theories emphasize the *allocative consequences* of windfall gains. They highlight the spending effects on the relative prices of traded and nontraded goods and consequently on factor allocation, and they also highlight changes in growth rates caused by an increase in the quantity of capital funded by oil income. Both theories characterize the economy as being on the frontier of a production set. Although the declining efficiency of accelerating investment (and similar effects) can be incorporated, this involves adding exogenous assumptions rather than attempting to explain such a fall in efficiency.

The linkage and macro-instability theories, in contrast, emphasize more the *quality*, *nature*, and *degree of use* of windfall gains and of domestic factors of production during the oil cycle. By analogy to the theory of the firm, they could be considered as X-efficiency approaches since they do not suppose that economies are on the boundary of a conventional production set.

Both types of theory are important in accounting for the lack of economic diversification and the poor growth in the sample countries. As spending accelerated after the first oil price rise, real exchange rates appreciated. So did real effective exchange rates, except initially in Venezuela and Algeria, which liberalized trade or applied price controls. Domestic factors of production shifted toward the nontraded sectors—particularly construction, which boomed with the rise in public investment, especially in 1974–77. As real effective exchange rates appreciated, returns on foreign financial investments fell further below increases in the prices of domestic investment goods, an effect which was exacerbated by the impact of the investment boom on foreign suppliers of capital goods. This fed the speculative boom in real capital formation in the oil exporters; the more rapidly they spent, the higher domestic costs rose and the greater seemed the need for investment to make projects inflation-proof and render plants more competitive than later market entrants. This cycle was briefly punctured by the fall in revenues in 1978 and by the adoption of tight monetary policies in oil-consuming countries, which caused the dollar to appreciate after 1979 and raised interest rates relative to the price of capital goods. But predictions of rising real energy prices in 1979 and 1980 caused a resurgence of the investment boom since they promised ever growing revenues and increased the anticipated returns to energy-based industrial projects.

Because of the desire to spend rapidly, public investment favored large projects that minimized decision time and did not require laborious and controversial institutional and political changes. In the representative oil-producing developing country, about two-thirds of investment was directed toward either infrastructure or human capital formation. This part of investment therefore went to strengthen the nontraded sectors. The impact on transport, communications, and housing was in most cases considerable, and education and health indicators rose markedly—although they also improved considerably in non-oil developing countries in this period. Most of the remaining third of public investment went to the hydrocarbon sectors and to other large RBI projects, the major initiatives in the traded sectors.

In many cases these projects were inadequately planned and encountered substantial cost and time overruns; sometimes decisions did not properly allow for comparative advantage. But more generally, feasibility studies did not account properly for uncertainty. Risk was high because of the very specific nature of investments; the scale of plants, which was far larger than warranted by the size of guaranteed domestic markets; and the correlation of returns to a wide set of plants similarly affected by the level of global activity.

Therefore, when oil, petrochemical, and metals markets slumped after 1981 and interest rates simultaneously rose, the oil exporters were vulnerable. Their non-oil traded sectors were weakened, they had become more dependent on imported intermediates to sustain industrial production, and in most cases they had sizable gross international debts. Falling oil revenues and poor returns from resource-based industrial projects reduced income flows. Inflation surged as governments were forced to raise administered prices, notably of oil derivatives, and to devalue in an attempt to maintain fiscal balance by boosting the domestic buying power of oil income. Rather like the oil-consuming countries in the upswing of the oil cycles, the producers entered a phase of stagflation on the downside. Slow, and in four out of six cases negative, growth reduced the benefits of much infrastructural spending. As revenues fell, partially completed projects were postponed or canceled, and the result was that returns on the investment program were further reduced. To date, the overall payoff to most public investment programs appears to have been very low when judged by incremental output and financial results.

In most countries, labor seems to have shared in the windfalls to a considerable extent. The spending effect tightened labor markets and raised employment. The combination of price controls and construction's weight in the nontraded sectors caused consumer prices to fall relative to overall domestic prices and production costs. This allowed a considerable rise in real wages, and consumption increased as a share of non-oil GDP by about one-fourth of the windfall. Nigeria may have been an exception because a chronic shortage of wage goods followed the movement of labor out of agriculture. The poor growth performance of the sample suggests, however, that labor's gains were only temporary. Indeed, by the early 1980s there was evidence in several countries of a fall in real wages at the end of the boom.

Given the diversity of the countries, there was naturally considerable divergence from this representative picture. Some of the country-specific effects have been noted in earlier chapters, and they are discussed at greater length in the chapters that follow, so only a concise overview is offered here.

It is not easy to discern a relationship between the type of political system and the efficiency with which oil income was used. Nevertheless, two broad conclusions about the interaction between political structure and oil seem to emerge. First, the higher-income countries, whose political systems were more subject to electoral competition throughout the period, had a greater tendency to use oil income for subsidies than did the poorest countries. This may also have been due to the more obvious infrastructural needs of the latter, which strengthened the case for initial spending of the windfalls by the public rather than the private sector.

Second, the time frame of governments and the degree to which political power is centralized seem to be important determinants of the outcome of a windfall cycle. In all three countries with either frequent and discontinuous changes in government or (as in the case of Venezuela) divergent executive and legislative policies, there were foreign exchange crises when oil revenues declined. Indonesia and Algeria, which had the most centralized and continuous policy-making structure in the sample, managed to turn in the highest growth rates, especially later in the period. They responded cautiously to the second oil boom and adjusted relatively smoothly (though not painlessly) when it ended. Trinidad and Tobago also had a centralized, continuous government during the period. But its experience shows how hard it is to handle oil rents cautiously for a sustained period in the face of powerful interest groups. Organized along sectoral lines, these groups generated irresistible pressure for raising subsidies.

A fragmented or decentralized decisionmaking structure reduces the ability to spend windfall gains cautiously. First, as noted in earlier chapters and again below, some of the costs of a volatile spending sequence, both on the upswing and on the downside, are external to individual agents or small groups. If each group assumes that its actions will not influence those of other groups, spending pressure will not be adequately contained. Second, the windfall itself reduces incentives to maintain a system of checks and balances among agents. The costs to an individual agent of such a system are normally balanced by the benefits, in the form of resources made available by constraining the spending of others. Windfall gains reduce these benefits, making the task of monitoring others less attractive and shifting incentives toward obtaining as large a share of the gains as possible for the use of one's own constituency. Highly centralized decisionmaking can, however, also reduce the efficiency of investment.

What should the oil exporters have done differently? This is not an easy question to answer, partly because a final judgment about the consequences of their actual choices will not be possible for many years. From the perspective of the individual countries, however, *the most important recommendation to emerge from this study is that spending levels should have been adjusted to sharp rises in oil income far more cautiously than they actually were.* The general equilibrium modeling exercise described in chapter 8 suggests that about two-thirds of a windfall comparable in size and duration to that received by the oil exporters should be saved abroad. This would maintain the quality of capital formation and avoid a severe recession as well as losses in output and growth because of below-capacity production at the end of the boom.

But the optimal degree of saving—or dissaving—abroad appears to be very sensitive to projections of oil prices after the peak of the boom. If oil prices are firmly expected to keep rising in real terms—contrary to the historical record that commodity price trends reverse themselves—it may indeed make more sense to borrow against future revenues and run larger current account deficits than to save abroad. Even if public investment is increased to the point at which marginal expenditures have zero or negative supply-side impact, the (demand-side) spending effect raises private income, imports, and consumption and so advances the enjoyment of future oil income, even if very inefficiently.

This may create a dilemma for oil exporters. Producers have usually justified higher oil prices by citing the depletion of resources even when the immediate reasons for large price jumps lay elsewhere. It may be difficult to persuade a domestic constituency to accept a spending policy based on the likelihood of *lower* prices and demand in the future, while at the same time arguing for high current prices in international fora by referring to the inevitability of still *higher* prices in the future. The solution to this problem is to recognize that *the costs of overoptimistic projections are far greater than the costs of overcautious ones, so that a spending policy based on less than the expected price trend is to be preferred.*[1]

At the global level the recommendation to spend more slowly raises, of course, the recycling problem: how to channel large surpluses to oil-importing countries. The sample countries were not net borrowers during the booms, but they did recycle their own surpluses and, through their residents' considerable degree of asset diversification, they enabled portfolios in other countries to be diversified. (For example, some Venezuelans may have financed Brazil while Saudi Arabia may have lent to Venezuela through financial intermediaries.) Slower spending would have made the recycling problem more prounounced, although it might have eased debt problems of the mid-1980s by reducing the indebtedness of oil exporters.

Had the urge to spend rapidly not been so great, *public projects might have been subject to more rigorous appraisals that took risk more fully into account.* The experience of the sample countries suggests three important roles for nonresident equity participation in resource-based, export-oriented projects: (a) to check on the realism of feasibility studies by scrutinizing the assessment of rate of return and risk; (b) to facilitate construction, start up, and operation; and (c) to reduce risk by securing markets and lowering the government's stake. To obtain such benefits, foreign equity participation should be considerable—at least, say, about 30 percent.

The inefficiency of low-yielding public investments as a conduit for oil revenue raises another question: should the exporters have made a greater attempt to disburse revenues directly to their populations? Such payments did take place in Alaska and Alberta. Had the countries in the sample emphasized the direct distribution of oil income (as Ecuador did in part through credit policy and lower non-oil taxes), spending booms might have taken place out of private income, especially with imperfect capital markets. The composition of demand would have differed from actual patterns. But some of the costs of a spending boom—notably congestion effects when demand rises and surplus capacity when it falls—are external to individual agents and are not adequately taken into account when individuals make spending and saving decisions. It is not certain, therefore, that direct distribution would have resulted in a much better macroeconomic outcome. The scale of loss-making investments would surely have been smaller; spending cuts on the downside might have been made more promptly (or might not, if transfer programs had become institutionalized); and transient consumption gains would have been larger.

The use of oil income to fund improvements in public administration does seem to be a good option. For example, it can facilitate tax reform to broaden the basis of non-oil tax collection by permitting a period of low tax rates. Such options were not taken up by the sample countries except, to an extent, by Indonesia.

Because the costs of a volatile spending path are largely external to individual agents, there is an argument for centralizing control of the oil windfall in order to moderate spending, and also possibly for limiting foreign borrowing by public enterprises and private agents who desire to anticipate future windfall income. *The main problem is then to render longer-run saving abroad politically acceptable.* This may not be easy; indeed, it may be impossible for a country whose government faces (or consists of) powerful groups competing for a share of the rent. The experience of Indonesia and Algeria in the second boom period and of Trinidad and Tobago in the first suggests that sterilization might be possible for some countries for a number of years. But for countries such as Ecuador and Nigeria with short-lived governments and regionally disparate power groups, restraint will always be very difficult.

Whether the "Dutch disease," as manifested by poorly performing non-oil traded sectors, is inevitable in the longer run will be determined by (a) static effects—that is, the impact of the spending boom on the non-oil traded sectors through its effect on factor and product markets; and (b) dynamic effects—that is, the possible uses of oil revenue to raise productivity growth in the non-oil traded sectors. A particularly interesting contrast is the strong performance of the agricultural sector in Indonesia, which was far above world averages, and the poor performance in Nigeria and Trinidad and Tobago, which was far below world averages. Indonesia had a far lower ratio of oil income per capita than the other two countries, and a large reservoir of labor in its traditional agriculture and service sectors. The labor pull out of agriculture caused by oil income was therefore less, especially as a large share of public spending went to rural areas where it could fund the slack-season use of labor. In addition, a combination of new crop varieties, investments in irrigation and infrastructure, and the production, subsidization, and distribution of fertilizer seems to have been effective in raising productivity, especially in rice. In contrast, productivity fell in Trinidadian agriculture, especially in the nationalized sugar industry, which was increasingly subsidized. In Nigeria, smallholder production technology stood still and large-scale public projects had disappointing results. In both countries, public programs drew significant amounts of labor from the farm sector.

In addition to the static and dynamic differences, the greater willingness of Indonesia to devalue the nominal exchange rate may have affected agricultural performance and that of non-oil exports in general. Devaluation enabled the real exchange rate to depreciate rapidly as the spending effect fell off, and so non-oil exports were protected. The contrast with Nigerian exchange rate policy is notable. Although the results of the decomposition in chapter 4 do not prove the case, they do support the thesis that tightening foreign exchange controls in Nigeria led to a progressive fall in the efficiency of the non-oil economy, which largely offset the benefits of the oil windfalls. Initial conditions and policies are important determinants of the impact of windfall gains on the structure of the non-oil economy and can modify the predictions of simple models.

In some respects the empirical results suggest the need to reassess simple stereotypes. For example, the poor agricultural performance in most of the sample countries resulted from agriculture's sensitivity to labor market pulls rather than simply from its status as a traded sector. Instead of becoming relatively cheaper, therefore, food tended to become more costly during the boom period in most of the countries despite rising imports. This, in turn, may have helped to distribute at least a part of the windfall gains to rural sectors.

Because of the association of the windfalls with greater global uncertainty (which also affected importing countries), it is indeed possible to make the case that oil exporters ended the period worse off than they would have been with a far lower, more predictable rate of increase in oil prices or, indeed, with constant real oil prices. The simulation results of chapter 8 suggest that such an outcome is not unlikely. Volatility plus poor prediction translates, on average, into a poorer use of resources during the cycle, which may more than offset the increment to resources from the windfall. This conclusion may not apply to all the countries because of real consumption gains during the windfalls in most countries, because of the possible long-run impact on growth of infrastructural and educational investments in some countries, and because some residents of some countries have built up sizable foreign assets. It is possible to conclude, however, that a great proportion of the potential gains to the exporters in this study was nullified by a combination of the changes induced in the global economy by the oil shocks and the poor economic policies of the exporters themselves during the period. Together, these seriously reduced the efficiency with which the countries used their resources, as judged by their own criteria of diversification and growth. To some extent, policy errors reflect a generally incautious approach to greater global uncertainty, but the abundance of oil wealth seems to have encouraged a deterioration over and above this.

How much of the deterioration in the investment-growth relationship (shown for *all* groups of developing countries in chapter 3) can be attributed to the direct and indirect effects of the oil shocks is not clear. If none, then the only cost to the oil importers would have been the real resources transferred to the exporters. If it is supposed that the extra capital formation in the exporters was, say, one-third as efficient as "normal" (as suggested by table 3-1), the deadweight global loss on this account would have been about one-third of the transfer, which is considerable. But if even a minor part of the deterioration in economic performance of oil importers may be attributed to the oil shocks and their associated effects (as suggested by other studies), these shocks would have constituted a far more serious loss. The windfall transfers could then have involved a cost much greater than the transfers themselves while providing uncertain and small benefits, and the global deadweight loss could have far exceeded the transfer. But even without such an effect, the conclusions of this study indeed support the view that the decade of the oil windfalls has involved the global economy in a massive, negative-sum game.

Note

1. For such reasons the state of Alaska instituted a rule of budgeting on the 30th percentile of the distribution of future revenue rather than on its expected value.

PART III

Country Studies

Chapter 10

Algeria: Windfalls in a Socialist Economy

with Patrick Conway

Algeria is unique in this study of oil exporters. Whereas the other five economies relied mainly on the price system to clear markets, Algeria is a socialist economy in which product, factor, and foreign exchange markets are heavily controlled. Alone among the sample countries, Algeria responded to the first oil windfall by strongly increasing its foreign borrowing, although its response to the second windfall was far more cautious. Its patterns of relative price changes and sectoral evolution were also unusual.

How has Algeria's strategy for using its oil revenues differed from the strategies of more market-oriented economies? How has the non-oil economy adjusted, in the absence of price flexibility, to changing levels of public spending? Have controls helped it to avoid the so-called Dutch disease with its symptoms of appreciating real exchange rates, contracting non-oil tradable sectors, large shifts of resources toward construction and services, and unsustainable consumption? If so, at what cost in efficiency? And have controls helped to avert an economic crisis in the downturn of the oil cycle?

Since independence in 1962, Algeria has taken an approach to development that has been both firm and consistent. The first section below outlines this approach, as well as the structure of the economy before the first oil price increase. The distinctive elements of Algeria's response to the first and second oil windfalls are explored in the following section; both the priorities adopted by the government in the 1950s and 1960s and the natural resource endowment of the country shaped that response in important ways. The section "Adjustment of the Non-Oil Economy" analyzes the evolution

Patrick Conway is assistant professor of economics at the University of North Carolina.

of the economy after the oil price increases and notes some unusual features, including the rationing of consumer goods and the accumulation of cash balances on an exceptional scale. The findings
imply that, especially in the first boom, Algeria followed a strategy
of deferred consumption, with the windfall and the foreign borrowing it facilitated going into creating a heavy industrial base, largely
in hydrocarbons. Only with the realignment of investment priorities after 1978 did consumption, as well as industries producing consumer goods and housing, receive greater attention. The next section outlines the main features of a "fix-price" equilibrium model of
the Algerian economy. This model is used to investigate the importance of rationing and of cash balances in explaining the Algerian pattern. The final section offers an assessment of the Algerian strategy
for absorbing windfall gains.

Economic Development and State Control

Algeria's development strategy was first enunciated during the eight-
year revolution that led to independence. Its substance was shaped
by the bitter and costly nature of that war. Despite factional disputes among Algerian political leaders, stemming in part from differences in generation and the role played in the revolutionary struggle, all groups seem to have accepted three basic principles of
development:[1]

- Stimulating growth and creating jobs are important objectives.
  But Algeria should develop from a socialist perspective and
  should promote income equalization among both regions and individuals.
- Economic policy should promote self-reliance and minimize
  long-run dependence on foreign financial and technical assistance.
- Economic planning is the responsibility of the state but should
  include some participation by workers.

The economic as well as political history of Algeria since independence can be divided into three periods. The constitution of September 1962 established Algeria as a one-party socialist republic with
Ahmed Ben Bella as president. After three years he was toppled in
a bloodless coup that placed Houari Boumédienne in the presidency. In 1978 Boumédienne died and was succeeded by Bendjedid
Chadli. Each of these presidents emphasized different aspects of
the three basic principles of development.

Development Strategy

As the first president of independent Algeria, Ben Bella took a prag-
matic approach to reconstituting the economy. In the wake of a massive exodus of French *colons* during and after the revolution, he focused on the promotion of light industry, especially consumer
goods, and on agrarian reform. Management of the abandoned industrial and agricultural firms was entrusted to workers (the
autogestion program). One assessment of Ben Bella's program suggests that economic performance was disappointing and that
Algeria's chronic problem of a rural and urban labor surplus persisted (Mallarde 1975).[2] This period marked the emergence of *la
nouvelle classe*—a middle class of public bureaucrats, technocrats,
and managers—which was to play an increasingly important role in
future years.

Boumédienne's accession in June 1965 marked an important shift
in Algerian development policy. Influenced by the prominent economists François Perroux and G. Destanne de Bernis, whose work
was in the spirit of the linkage theory of Albert Hirschman, the
new president formulated a threefold strategy of industrialization, integration of domestic industry within the nation, and rejection of foreign influences.[3] "Industrializing" industries—those with strong
backward and forward linkages—were thought to be the key to developing the economy. And of these, heavy producer-goods industries
such as steel, fertilizers, and petrochemicals were believed to promise the strongest linkages. The role of the hydrocarbon sector was
considered particularly crucial; a "premier industrializing industry," it would provide a market for capital goods, supply raw materials for downstream processing activities, and generate resource
rents to fund industrialization. Perroux's study of "growth poles"
suggested that regional integration could best be achieved by establishing new industrial centers in three locations—Arzew, Skikda,
and Annaba—which at the time had only small industrial bases. Finally, the decision to become a closed economy was heavily influenced by the work of Samir Amin. Amin identified a dependent economy as one in which export goods and luxury consumer goods
were dominant sectors, and a self-reliant economy as one in which
producer goods and necessities were dominant sectors. The implications of such a classification for the Algerian strategy were clear.

To implement this revised development policy, the government
strengthened the planning mechanism, initiated a sustained public
investment drive, and held down private consumption to finance capital accumulation. In 1967–72 investment rose from 21.7 percent to

25.5 percent of GDP, while private consumption fell from 58.9 percent to 55.2 percent. In 1970–72 parastatal investment (representing the public sector's productive role) rose by 60 percent in nominal terms, and direct Treasury investment (representing the public sector's infrastructural and social role) rose by 50 percent. In the same period, the small component of private investment—estimated as a residual—was reduced by half. The public investment drive thus began some years before the first oil price rise and accelerated after 1973.

Chadli became president in 1978 just as the first oil windfall period was ending. Under Chadli capital accumulation and central planning have been given less emphasis than earlier. This movement actually began in Boumédienne's last years, as *la nouvelle classe* of technocrats gained greater power, but Chadli's accession accelerated the process. More recent economic policy, as exemplified by the five-year plan of 1980–84, has put greater stress on developing consumer-goods industries and has introduced market prices for some agricultural products.

Some shift, then, has occurred in Algeria's development strategy during the years of the oil windfalls. But the broad lines of the strategy have been well defined and stable, more so than for any other oil exporter in this study, with the possible exception of Indonesia.

Controlled Economy

Algeria has been almost unique among developing countries because of the highly controlled nature of its socialist economic system. All prices and formal wage scales were administratively determined until a very partial liberalization in the 1980s. Treasury subsidies to public enterprises essentially removed the constraint even of administered market forces, so that firms faced a "soft" budget constraint like that in the Eastern European economies, which the Algerian economy resembled.[4] Until recently, private enterprise was marginal except in some agricultural and a few minor urban activities. The state had a virtual monopoly on the allocation of investable resources through its regulation of the (public) banking system, and the Treasury also acted as a major financial intermediary. Trade took place through official channels only, imports were controlled, and foreign exchange was tightly allocated.

An obvious question is the extent to which control has been more a facade than a reality. In Algeria the institutions of control appear to have been powerful during the period under consideration. Black markets undoubtedly existed, but by all accounts they were, and probably still are, minor. The Algerian bureaucracy appears to be conspicuously free of the corruption endemic in so many other oil-exporting countries. Despite moves after 1978 to liberalize and decentralize production and free certain markets (notably for agricultural products), Algeria is still aptly described as a socialist, centrally planned "fix-price" economy.

The fix-price economy with gradual adjustment is the analytical framework that has been adopted in this discussion. "Fix-price," in the Algerian context, means not that prices are immutably fixed, but that price changes are not an important mechanism for clearing markets.[5] Relative prices play a major equilibrating role when a market economy increases absorption in response to windfall gains. This is particularly true of the real exchange rate, which appreciates to shift factors of production to nontraded sectors and to deflect demand to non-oil exportables and imports. Such standard mechanisms cannot operate in a fix-price economy, which must instead substitute various rationing systems (on either the demand or supply side of individual markets, depending on where the scarcity is). If these systems are enforced, there is no reason to presume that the evolution of key price and resource indicators will follow the free-market paradigm. But the cost of enforcing a particular relative price structure may rise, or the effectiveness of the controls decline, as the administered price structure becomes less and less appropriate. Then, to retain control, the state will probably make some adjustments—albeit reluctantly and with a lag—in the setting of wages and prices and in the allocation of investable resources.

Even before the first oil price increase, the Algerian economy displayed distinctive structural characteristics because of the ambition of its development plan. As shown in table 5-1, total absorption of goods and services as a share of nonmining GDP was high (123 percent) by international standards. The excess was financed mainly by oil exports, but foreign assistance and remittances of Algerians working abroad also contributed significantly to the current account. Private consumption represented only 65 percent of nominal nonmining GDP, compared with a norm of 66 percent of *total* GDP for a typical developing country at Algeria's level of income per capita.[6] Public consumption at 18 percent only slightly exceeded the norm of 14 percent. The high absorption ratio, therefore, was due almost entirely to investment, which at 41 percent was twice as high as the norm. It is estimated that more than 85 percent of the total investment in the years just before the first oil shock was attributable either to the central government or to public enterprises.

In the structure of production, too, Algeria's economy was distinctive, as table 6-3 makes clear. Mining, equivalent to 18 percent of nonmining output in 1972, was of course a dominant sector. Agriculture provided only 11 percent of nonmining output (the norm being 25 percent) and manufacturing 16 percent (the norm being 20 percent). In contrast, the construction sector was much larger than the norm (13 percent compared with 5 percent) and the service sector somewhat larger. Overall, the non-oil tradable sectors (agriculture and manufacturing) were smaller by some 18 percent of nonmining output than the norm for a typical non-oil country at Algeria's level of development. This reflected the disruption of agricultural and industrial production by the exodus of the French, high investment rates in the middle of the first four-year development plan (1970–73), and the financing of imports from oil, aid, and remittances rather than from non-oil exports. In this sense, Algeria suffered severely from certain symptoms of Dutch disease before 1974—even more so than Venezuela and Nigeria, which had non-oil tradable sectors that were only 14 and 9 percentage points, respectively, below the "normal" levels for non-oil economies.

Response to Higher Oil Prices

Half of Algeria's exports in the early 1960s came from oil. Following the prolonged war of independence, which severely disrupted the non-oil economy, this proportion rose to three-quarters by the early 1970s. In 1972 oil exports were equivalent to 16 percent of GDP. The quadrupling of world oil prices in 1973–74 and their redoubling in 1979–80 conferred large windfall gains on Algeria as it did on the other oil exporters. In 1974–78 Algeria's domestic oil windfall averaged 22 percent of nonmining GDP, and in 1979–81 it averaged 30 percent. In comparison, the unweighted averages for the other five oil-exporters in this study were 21 percent and 22 percent for the first and second periods. With both price and volume changes taken into account, the windfall—as shown in figure 10-1—peaked in 1974 at the equivalent of 42 percent of nomining GDP. It fell to 26 percent in 1975 and to 18 percent in 1978 as world oil prices eased and as the volume of Algeria's hydrocarbon output grew more slowly than its non-oil economy. With the second oil price rise, the ratio of oil revenue to nonmining GDP rebounded to 34 percent.

Use of the Windfalls

Although the relative size of Algeria's first oil windfall was not atypical for a capital-importing, oil-exporting developing country, the propensity to augment that windfall by borrowing abroad was distinctive. As indicated in figure 10-1, the ratio of the trade and nonfactor service deficit to nonmining GDP increased in 1974–78, rela-

Figure 10-1. The Oil Windfall and Its Use, 1973–81

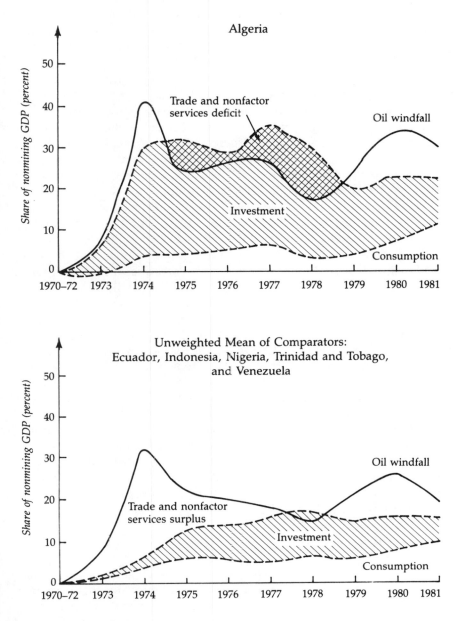

Source: World Bank data.

tive to its base in 1970–72, by the equivalent of 4.3 percentage points. The ratio of the current balance to nonmining GDP deteriorated by 9.8 percentage points, and net borrowing totaled $8.2 billion. Figure 10-1 also illustrates that the comparators reduced their ratio of trade and current deficits to nonmining GDP by 7.5 and 8.7 percentage points respectively, thereby cutting the impact of the windfall on absorption by one-third. Algeria, in effect, reacted to the first oil shock as an extremely resource-constrained economy; it took advantage of its improved creditworthiness to boost absorption almost twice as much as the average for the comparators.

Figure 10-1 reveals another unusual feature of the Algerian response. During 1974–78 only 17 percent of the increased absorption made possible by oil revenues and borrowing went to private and public consumption (5 percent to the latter). The remaining 83 percent went to raise investment further, to the remarkable level of 72 percent of nonmining GDP by 1977. Investment programs exploded in all the oil-exporting countries after 1974, but the Algerian response was extreme even by the standards of the sample.

To a considerable extent this strategy was moderated in the second windfall period, which began just after Chadli became president. Trade deficits were reduced, private and public consumption was increased, and investment was cut by the equivalent of 13 percent of nonmining GDP. As a result, the share of consumption in absorption began to rise. In 1980 and 1981, the current account was actually in surplus despite the interest burden from past borrowing. The relatively restrained response to the second oil price rise was far more in line with that of the other oil exporters. With an 8.9 percentage point fall in the ratio of absorption to nonmining GDP from the base period 1970–72, the contraction in absorption relative to the high-spending years was equivalent to 13.2 percent of nonmining GDP. The converse to the question of how the Algerian economy, without price flexibility, adjusted to the colossal rise in absorption during the first windfall is therefore: How did the economy respond to the contraction of demand—from very high levels, of course—during the second windfall?

Nature of Public Investment

Public investment in Algeria has two distinct components. The largely infrastructural component directly financed by the Treasury (on average, about one-third of the total) has remained relatively steady over time. The component going to public enterprises has been more volatile. It is financed by (a) long-term loans from the Algerian Development Bank and similar domestic financial institutions,

(b) medium-term credits from domestic commercial banks, and (c) external credits from foreign banks and suppliers with approval of the Finance Ministry. In the early 1970s, Treasury savings financed about 55 percent of the public investment program. Much of the rest was financed by the excess of domestic private savings over private investment; foreign savings also financed a small share (Conway 1982, p. 52, table 14). The increase in oil taxes permitted the Treasury to fund 65 percent of the expanded program during 1974–78. Nevertheless, between 1973 and 1979 the surplus of private savings channeled to the public investment program (estimated as a residual from the public budget and the foreign accounts) represented an unweighted average of 7.6 percent of nonmining GDP. Moreover, in this period the estimated share of public in total investment rose further, from 86 percent to 92 percent.

An indication of the composition of public investment by sector is given in tables 10-1 and 10-2. These tables indicate the remarkable extent to which investment was concentrated in the capital-intensive industrial sectors, notably in hydrocarbon exploitation. The public investment program was at least twice as large, relative to the non-oil economy, in Algeria as in the comparator countries. At the same time, the weight of the capital-intensive industrial sectors in that program was two to three times greater in Algeria than in the other countries. Relative to the non-oil economy, therefore, the Algerian investment in these sectors was at least four to six times as large as in the other countries, which themselves implemented some of the most ambitious heavy industrial programs in the world. Roughly $18 billion was invested in liquefied natural gas (LNG); this compares with Algeria's gross foreign debt (short-, medium-, and long-term) of $17.6 billion at the end of 1981. Algeria, in other words, took out a mortgage, secured by future oil revenues, to diversify its industrial base, primarily toward non-oil hydrocarbons.

With investment went moves to consolidate national control. These also had a fiscal dimension. In 1963 the share of oil company profits paid to the government was positively associated with the extent of public ownership and negatively associated with multinational ownership, with French ownership occupying an intermediate position (Mazri 1975).[7] In the same year, a public enterprise, SONATRACH, was established as a channel for state expenditures in the hydrocarbon industry. Its scope was steadily extended. By 1970 it controlled roughly half of all activity in the hydrocarbon sector and had a dominant role in exploration and domestic distribution, but only a minor role in oil, LNG, and petrochemical production. By 1980 all oil production and all but 5 percent of exploration activity

Table 10-1. Algeria: Sectoral Composition of Public Investment
(percent)

Sector	Four-year plan, 1974–77 1975	Interplan, 1978–79 1978	Five-year plan, 1980–84 1982
Agriculture	7.7	3.1	4.0
Water development	2.9	1.5	4.0
Hydrocarbons	26.4	34.9	14.8
Other industries	36.2	28.4	16.4
Housing	5.3	8.2	13.1
Construction[a]	10.3	14.3	32.7
Education and training	5.4	6.0	9.4
Services[b]	5.8	3.5	5.6

a. Includes economic, administrative, and social infrastructure, construction enterprises, commune plans, and special programs.
b. Includes tourism, transport, commerce, and distribution.
Source: World Bank data.

Table 10-2. Algeria: Structure of Industrial Investment
(percent)

Sector	Three-year plan, 1967–69	Four-year plan, 1970–73	Four-year plan, 1974–77	Interplan, 1978–79	Five-year plan Planned, 1980–84	Five-year plan Actual, 1980–82
Heavy industry	57.3	56.0	44.0	50.8	43.0	47.7
Iron and steel	43.7	30.4	21.5	21.5	16.4	27.4
Other	23.6	25.6	22.5	29.3	26.6	20.3
Light industry	42.7	44.0	56.0	49.2	57.0	52.6
Chemicals	23.1	10.1	16.0	11.8	10.4	9.5
Food and tobacco	7.3	7.0	5.1	8.8	14.5	13.2
Textiles and leather	7.9	5.7	8.2	12.6	10.6	15.4
Construction materials	1.5	12.3	20.1	9.5	11.7	5.1
Miscellaneous[a]	2.9	8.9	6.5	6.6	9.7	9.5

a. Mainly wood and paper.
Source: World Bank data.

was under the control of SONATRACH. This was a rapid transition from the 1963 situation when foreign administrators and technicians in the hydrocarbon sector had outnumbered Algerians by nearly four to one.

Between 1975 and 1980 SONATRACH was host to twenty-seven macroprojects (each with a capital cost of more than $100 million), a greater number than any other single institution in the developing world (Murphy 1983). By the early 1980s Algeria had installed the world's largest LNG export capacity, and gas began to be piped to Europe under the Mediterranean via the Straits of Messina in 1983.

Two factors account for the high priority accorded hydrocarbon investment. First, as noted above, the hydrocarbon subsector was considered a "premier industrializing industry." Second, Algeria's oil was expected to be rapidly depleted, and the proceeds were earmarked for the creation of a viable natural gas export industry.[8] Algeria's natural gas fields were estimated as the fourth largest in the world, in contrast to its limited proven oil reserves, which were expected to be exhausted by the end of the century. By 1980 proven oil reserves represented twenty-four years' output and proven natural gas reserves eighty-one years' output. Natural gas extraction also produced condensate, a liquid crude oil by-product, so that the expansion of gas output effectively increased oil production as well.

The strategy of hydrocarbon diversification began to have a real impact on exports in the early 1980s. In 1980 total hydrocarbon exports were $13.6 billion, of which crude oil—at $9.3 billion—constituted 68 percent. By 1984 crude exports had decreased to only $3.1 billion, but total hydrocarbon revenues had remained almost steady at $12.4 billion, with roughly equal shares for gas, crude, condensate, and refined products. Algeria was therefore cushioned, at least for a time, from the impact of the oil glut.

Although it is beyond the scope of this study to attempt to estimate the payoff to Algeria's hydrocarbon investments or to predict their returns in the future, the case of LNG is illustrative. In 1983–84 LNG exports averaged $2.26 billion. Before taking into account current costs such as labor, intermediate use, and depreciation, this was only a 12.5 percent return on the estimated capital costs—a figure roughly equivalent to the interest rate on foreign debt. The implication is that the payoff to such investments depends critically on the evolution of gas prices and demand relative to world interest rates.[9] It also depends on the level of capacity use; unlike Indonesia, Algeria was not able to operate its plants at full capacity because of marketing constraints (see below).

By affecting the feasibility of increasing the various components of the public investment program, past priorities shaped the use of windfalls. In general, the concentration of investment in the heavy industrial sector was facilitated by the capability of this sector to implement projects. This capability, in turn, resulted from the priority that the sector had enjoyed since 1965 in the planning process. In accordance with the development strategy, manufacturing investment initially focused on heavy industry (producer goods) at the expense of light industry (consumer goods), although the share of light industry increased with the shift in the Algerian development strategy toward greater consumption after 1978. Social and infrastructural investment also rose after that date; housing plus infrastructure accounted for only 15 percent of total public investment in 1975 but for 46 percent in 1982.

In contrast, agriculture received little emphasis in the public investment program. In the plan periods 1970–74 and 1974–77, agriculture had been budgeted for 11 percent of public investment. Actual disbursements in these two periods, however, were only an estimated 8.3 percent and 4.8 percent respectively, with a low of 3 percent in 1978. Agriculture did undergo many institutional changes in the 1970s, including land redistribution as part of the agrarian revolution of 1971. But the sector continued to perform poorly, and much food had to be imported. In 1980–83 food imports were equivalent to 80 percent of value added in agriculture.

Adjustment of the Non-Oil Economy

The size of the Algerian investment program raises three questions for the adjustment of the non-oil economy. First, how could so massive a program be reconciled with the scarcity of domestic resources relative to foreign exchange windfalls and borrowing? Second, how did the government manage to extract so large a share of domestic savings to finance public accumulation? Third, what has been the impact of the investment patterns on Algerian growth and the sectoral structure of the non-oil economy? The following section considers the first two questions; the third is taken up later.

Reconciling Aggregate Demand and Supply

The first factor that made possible the extraordinary amount of investment, especially in the first windfall period, was its high import intensity. This, in turn, followed from the sectoral distribution of investment. Roughly two-thirds of total investment in 1974 is estimated to have consisted of imported capital goods, and close to half in 1978 (Conway 1982, p. 47, table 11).[10] The high import component lessened the demand for domestic goods. This moderated pressure on the domestic economy; it also facilitated borrowing through suppliers' credits, which represented 41 percent of public outstanding and disbursed debt by 1977.

The same method of adjustment, put into reverse, was used to cushion the effect of slowing investment rates on the Algerian economy during and after the second oil boom. The reorientation of investment toward light industry and the social sectors increased the domestic content of investment. As a result, the elasticity of imports of goods and nonfactor services with respect to GDP fell from 1.4 in 1973–79 to only 0.8 in 1980–84, and the level of domestic activity was maintained.[11]

Despite the high import content of Algeria's investment program (in 1983 imports of capital goods still accounted for 19 percent of capital formation), the magnitude of the program had important domestic effects. The construction sector expanded its constant-price share in nonmining value added from 13.4 percent to 20.8 percent between 1972 and 1981. So massive a shift toward investment goods would normally be associated with substantial appreciation of the real exchange rate. This, in turn, would be mirrored in appreciation of the real effective exchange rate—unless trade policy shifted dramatically toward import liberalization. This shift did not occur in Algeria. Yet the real effective exchange rate actually *depreciated* from an index of 100 in 1970–72 to an estimated average of 96 in 1974–78. This contrasts with a real appreciation of 20–40 percent in such market-oriented economies as Ecuador, Indonesia, and Nigeria (see table 6-1). Real effective depreciation in Algeria was associated with low increases in administered prices, which—though higher than their rates in 1970–72—rarely exceeded 11 percent. Import prices thus tended to rise relative to domestic prices, and the administered domestic price structure moved rather uniformly across major categories of production and demand. By maintaining the purchasing power of oil revenues over domestic goods and services, depreciation of the real effective exchange rate facilitated the large public investment program.

The second factor that enabled the government to implement a massive investment program was an exceptional propensity for Algerians to hold cash, which also kept inflation low. In common with other developing countries, and especially with oil exporters experiencing an accelerated transformation toward a cash economy, Algeria manifested a high income elasticity of demand for money. For the period 1967–80 the elasticity of M1 stood at about 2.0 with respect to nonmining income. Even in 1970–72 an unusually high share of M1 was composed of currency circulating outside banks.

The share of currency tended to rise over time rather than to decline as is usual with deepening financial intermediation, so that between 1970 and 1981 currency holdings increased from 25 percent
to 42 percent of nonmining GDP. The bulk of these holdings is
known to have been in the hands of the private sector. This implied large seigniorage gains to the Central Bank, as shown in figure 10-2. Seigniorage averaged 7.5 percent of nonmining GDP during 1973–79, virtually equal to the internal public financing gap as
residually estimated above. The propensity to hold cash absorbed
about one-third of the domestic savings pool generated outside the
Treasury during 1974–79, almost three times the corresponding
ratio for the five other oil exporters, notwithstanding their generally higher inflation rates.[12] This caused a second leakage (after imported intermediate and capital goods) from the multiplier process
normally initiated by large increases in public investment out of oil
revenue.

Algeria's high propensity to hold money balances appears to
have resulted from rationing in markets for both private consumption and investment goods, and to have been facilitated by the moderate upward adjustment of administered prices and the low interest rates (2–4 percent) available on alternative financial assets. The
strength of the public accumulation crowded out private consumption and the accumulation of real assets. Therefore Algeria did not attempt to contain further the already moderate rise in wage rates rela-

Figure 10-2. Algeria: Currency, Inflation, and Seigniorage, 1970–81

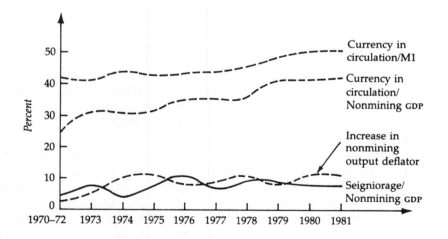

Source: IMF, *International Financial Statistics,* and World Bank data.

tive to product prices (see table 6-2) or to increase sharply the rate of non-oil taxation—which was high and buoyant by the standards of oil exporters (see tables 5-4 to 5-6; non-oil taxes represented about 25 percent of nonmining GDP). Instead, the Algerian government opted for a strategy of deferring private consumption. Private agents built up financial claims against the state, and the real unit value of these claims decreased only gradually through inflation. This strategy is captured in a fix-price macroeconomic model estimated for Algeria and outlined below.

A third factor, which limited the inflationary impact of the investment boom, was the elastic labor supply. Algeria's rate of population growth was high at nearly 3.3 percent, and its development strategy was capital-intensive. The rural population, which in 1963 was 63 percent of the resident population, continued to increase at about 1.8 percent a year despite rural-urban migration. Although the nonagricultural labor force rose by 5.0 percent a year in the decade 1973–83, Algeria therefore still had large labor reserves.

As time went on, however, it proved harder to keep consumption low and prices stable. From 1978 on, an increasing share of the windfall went to consumption (see figure 10-1). Inflation continued at just below 10 percent (measured by the Grand-Algiers consumer price index). With the nominal exchange rate pegged (causing a modest devaluation against the rising dollar after 1980) and inflation falling abroad, the real effective exchange rate began to appreciate. From a base of 100 in 1970–72 it reached an average of 104 in 1979–81, 114 in 1982–83, and 123 in 1984. The degree of rationing tended to decrease in consumer-goods markets as gradual liberalization proceeded. Though still extensively regulated, Algeria's economy was beginning to adjust more after the pattern of the other oil exporters.

Growth and Sectoral Structure

In 1972–81 Algeria attained the highest nonmining GDP growth in the sample: 8.6 percent. The investment surge did not, however, actually accelerate growth. The preceding years, 1967–72, had represented a period of recovery from the disruption of the revolution, so growth rates had been even higher—9.5 percent—before the oil boom. Incremental capital-output ratios (ICORS) were also high. Across all sectors, at constant 1974 prices, the gross ICOR was 6.8 in 1973–77, 4.4 in 1978–79, and 10.1 in 1980–82. In non-oil mining, manufacturing, and energy it was 8.5 for 1973–77, 4.7 for 1978–79, and 5.4 for 1980–82. In the hydrocarbon sector, real output remained constant between 1973 and 1977 despite the sector's receiving one-

quarter of public investment. Output expanded by 11 percent between 1977 and 1979 but contracted sharply after 1979, even
though LNG and piped gas export capacity came on stream, because
of demand constraints.

Both supply and demand constraints played a role in low capital
productivity, which was frequently associated with the existence of
surplus capacity. In 1976 Algeria's cement industry was operating
at 56 percent of capacity, the metal frame industry at 52 percent,
and the ceramic tile industry at 17 percent (World Bank estimates).
These figures reflect supply-side constraints—bureaucratization, inadequate training, and the absence of competition—rather than low
demand, since imports of building materials were high. In contrast,
the LNG industry has been operating at 40 percent of capacity in the
1980s because demand has been less than projected.

The sectoral evolution of Algeria's nonmining economy after 1972
followed a distinctive pattern. The constant-price share of construction in nonmining GDP rose by 0.82 percent a year during 1972–81.
Yet because of the rapid expansion of manufacturing, growth in the
share of the tradable sectors exceeded the norm for an economy at
Algeria's level of per capita income and rate of growth by 0.68 percent.[13] By 1981 Algeria's Dutch disease index— defined as the imbalance between nonmining tradables and nontradables relative to the
size of the nonmining economy—had almost halved, falling below
the corresponding indexes for Nigeria, Trinidad and Tobago, and Venezuela (see table 6-3). To some extent this was because the pre-
shock Algerian economy had been markedly skewed against non-
oil tradables. Although the pervasive system of state controls
contributed to the less efficient use of labor and capital, it played
some part in limiting further skewing of the economy by reducing
multiplier effects emanating from public investments.

Model: The Adjustment of a Fix-Price Economy to Oil Windfalls

To appreciate the distinctive nature of the Algerian adjustment process it is useful to consider an aggregated fix-price model of the response to windfalls of a controlled economy. The essentials of such
a model and its application to Algeria are outlined in this section.[14]

First, the labor market. Suppose that maximum non-oil value
added is a function of capital and labor, which are combined in
fixed proportions given by the development strategy selected. With
overall capital per worker in the economy below the full-em-
ployment level k^*, unemployment must occur whether or not production is at full capacity. With capital per worker greater than k^*,
labor would be in excess demand if production were near full capac-

ity; but there might still be unemployment if demand is less than at full-capacity output and if it determines actual output and labor use.

Next, the goods market. Non-oil value added is split into wages and profits (which accrue to the public sector). Households that receive wage income either spend it on consumer goods, or they build up money balances to some desired level. Thus, given output, employment, and wages, desired consumption is higher the greater is m, the level of real money balances per person. Depending on the level of demand relative to the potential availability of consumer goods, households could have their purchases rationed (that is, m is above its equilibrium), or else their demands could be insufficient to sustain full-capacity output (that is, m is below its equilibrium). The equilibrium level of m for output corresponding to full-capacity production with capital k^* is denoted by m^*.

Finally, the oil windfall. The size of the public investment program is determined by the level of oil income (assumed to be exogenous) and by the extent to which k is below k^*; the greater structural unemployment is, the more strongly investment responds to oil income and the borrowing opportunities it creates. In the medium run, therefore, an increase in oil income has two offsetting effects on the potential supply of consumer goods. On the one hand, if it stimulates a very large increase in the public investment program or other public spending, it may reduce the availability of consumer goods as factors of production are switched to producer-goods sectors.[15] On the other hand, it offers the prospect of increasing imports of consumer goods, thereby augmenting their supply.[16]

The four possible configurations for such an economy are shown in figure 10-3. At the point WAL, both the labor and goods markets are in unrationed (Walrasian) equilibrium. In region REP, the economy is in a state of repressed inflation with excess demand for goods and labor because of high k and m. In KEY the economy is in a state of Keynesian unemployment with output constrained by lack of demand. In CLA the economy is in a state of classical unemployment: the capital stock is too small, given the chosen degree of capital intensity, to employ all workers, and there is excess demand for consumer goods as indicated by high money balances. It may be shown that the boundary between CLA and REP on the one hand and KEY on the other is an upward sloping line as depicted in the figure.

Consider the impact of an oil windfall on the economy. If the capital stock is near or above k^*, the availability of labor, not capital, constrains output. There will be little urge to accumulate further, so consumption can increase by importing more consumer goods. Higher

Figure 10-3. Fix-Price and Walrasian Equilibria

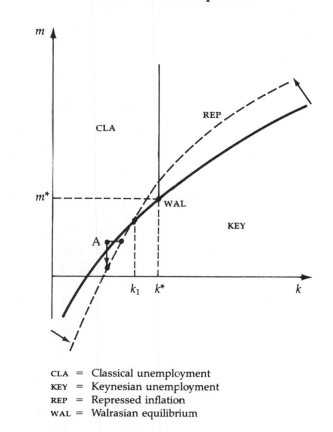

CLA = Classical unemployment
KEY = Keynesian unemployment
REP = Repressed inflation
WAL = Walrasian equilibrium

consumption requires higher m; the dividing line that brings the goods market into equilibrium therefore shifts upward, as shown in the figure. But if the rate of structural unemployment is high (that is, if k is well below some level k_1), a large investment response can crowd out private consumption demand so that the dividing line shifts downward. In such a case, the windfall will cause rationing in the goods market to increase—or it could shift a previously unrationed goods market into a state of rationing, with an involuntary accumulation of real balances.

The data are not sufficient to test econometrically which region Algeria occupied during the windfall years. But there are strong a priori grounds for believing that the Algerian economy fell within CLA—notably the persistence of the employment problem and shortages of both housing and diverse consumer goods. The fitting of alternative econometric models in Conway and Gelb (1988) provides support for this proposition.[17] The model can then be estimated, assuming that the economy is in CLA, by specifying a process of adjustment for the administered price system.

The results of estimating the model for 1967–84 suggest that the level of rationing increased considerably during the first oil windfall, from the equivalent of 3 percent of actual consumption to about 10 percent in 1973–78. Households accumulated money balances, and the economy shifted further into CLA, an indication that it had originally been at a point such as A in figure 10-3. The reduced intensity of investment and the shifts in its allocation after 1978 are reflected in a change in the response of public spending to oil income and borrowing, and in some decrease in the rationing coefficient.[18]

These results appear to confirm that the restraint on consumption and the increases in cash balances significantly affected Algeria's response to its oil windfalls, particularly during the first oil boom. Venezuela, the only other country in this study whose real effective exchange rate depreciated during the first oil boom, adjusted by controlling prices and liberalizing imports, which had been tightly constrained before the boom. As a consequence—and in contrast to Algeria—the share of Venezuela's windfall that went to increase real private consumption was high, as discussed in chapter 15.

Conclusions

The Algerian pattern of development since the early 1960s has differed from that of the other oil exporters in important ways. First, Algeria's economy has been centralized and state-controlled, with the public sector playing a crucial entrepreneurial role. Second, alone among the countries in this study but like Mexico in 1979–81, Algeria borrowed heavily against its anticipated future oil income during the first boom. It channeled both its oil revenues and its borrowed funds into investment, especially in a limited range of tradable sectors, and followed a strategy of deferring large increases in consumption.

During the second boom, the strategy shifted toward consumer, social, and infrastructural goods. This raised the domestic content of investment and permitted the momentum of growth to be maintained. In 1981–85 nonhydrocarbon GDP grew at nearly 7 percent. Large current account deficits were avoided after 1979. Total external debt, net of reserves, actually fell by $1.0 billion between 1981 and 1984. Algeria was also cushioned from the oil glut, at least through 1985, by its diversified hydrocarbon industrial base.

The remarkable investment build-up was effected without soaring inflation, without real effective exchange appreciation (for a time), and without further shrinkage in the relative size of the non-oil tradable sectors. Instead, accommodation seems to have depended on holding down consumption out of the windfall proceeds until the second boom, at which time investment was scaled back. During the period of the oil shocks, Algeria appears to have been in the classical unemployment variant of fix-price equilibrium, with excess demand for goods, excess supply of labor, and involuntary holdings of money balances resulting from rationing in the goods market.

Econometric results support this view of the Algerian adjustment process. They suggest that without rationing the Algerian price level would have had to increase in 1974–78 by some 40 percent more than its historical trend to hold consumption at pre-1973 levels, even under the favorable assumption that desired real balances were unaffected by inflation. And if desired real balances had been sensitive to inflation, the Algerian strategy of the 1970s would not have been feasible without far tighter wage controls or higher non-oil taxes; otherwise the state could not have secured so large a share of purchasing power.

Have the distinctive features of Algeria's controlled economy been an advantage or a liability in dealing with the changes in its terms of trade since 1973? On the negative side, there are indications that Algeria's investments have not been as productive as planned, either in the hydrocarbon or nonhydrocarbon sectors, and that its strategy has failed to stimulate nonhydrocarbon exports. But it is not clear how much this can be attributed to its planned economy since the same might be said for some other oil exporters as well. A serious problem, which more flexible planning might have alleviated, however, has been the capital intensity of the public investment program in the face of widespread underemployment. The strategy of deferring consumption has also had a cost in the short to medium run.

On the positive side, Algeria has avoided foreign exchange crises, partly because of the extent of control over international transactions and partly because of its more cautious approach to spending during the second oil boom. High growth has been maintained even through the oil glut. An excessive shift to nontraded goods was avoided. Moreover, major steps have been taken to diversify away from oil, a resource that is rapidly depleting, to natural gas, a resource that has a far longer expected lifetime.

It will be possible to evaluate the Algerian strategy fully only when the benefits of rapid accumulation, as well as the costs—

including forgone consumption and the accumulation of foreign debt—become clear. The outcome will depend on three factors, two external and one internal: developments in gas markets, the level of world interest rates, and the efficiency with which nonhydro-carbon investment and domestic labor can be used. If the external factors foster a high return to hydrocarbon investments (that is, if the ratio of gas price increases to interest rates is favorable) and if domestic policies encourage efficiency, the transformation of oil income and borrowing into domestic capital will permit substantial growth of real consumption in the future. If not, alternative strategies, such as saving abroad or increasing domestic consumption more directly through relaxing import restrictions and easing non-oil taxation, will appear in retrospect to have offered greater promise of improving the well-being of the Algerian population.

Notes

1. For analyses of the political differences, see Quandt (1971) and Zartman (1975). The documents enumerating the Algerian principles of development are: Program of Tripoli, May 1962; Constitution, September 1963; Charter of Algiers, April 1964; National Charter, June 1976; Constitution, November 1976; Three-Year Plan (1967–69); Four-Year Plan (1970-73); Four-Year Plan (1974–77); Five-Year Plan (1980–84).

2. Estimates made by the Ministry of Planning suggest that during Ben Bella's rule perhaps two-thirds of the rural and one-fourth of the urban labor force were either unemployed or underemployed.

3. The intellectual origins of the Algerian strategy are discussed by Raffinot and Jacquemot (1977).

4. Kornai (1978) analyzes the "soft" budget constraint of the production sector in the context of East European socialist countries. Among the developing countries only pre-reform China would seem to rival Algeria's degree of economic control.

5. The terminology is from Hicks (1965).

6. The norm is derived from regressions of Chenery and Syrquin (1975).

7. It is estimated that in 1963, whereas 44 percent of the gross profits earned by public oil companies accrued to the Treasury, only 17 percent of profits earned by privately owned companies accrued as tax or royalty (Conway 1982, p. 40, table 8).

8. This strategy was outlined in "Hydrocarbon Development Plan: 1976–2000," prepared for Algeria by the Bechtel Corporation.

9. Inclusion of condensate exports with LNG would double the gross return to gas investments as computed here. But it is not clear how to value condensate exports because their real contribution appears to have been to permit crude oil output to be reduced to levels judged more consistent with the objective of preserving the long-run production capacity of the geologically complex Algerian fields. If the cost of attempting to accelerate Alge-

rian crude oil output is indeed high, the value of condensate exports should be at least partly included in the calculation of gross return to gas investments.

10. Large hydrocarbon projects frequently have a direct import component of 80 percent, and the domestic component consists largely of construction. Value added in construction is also typically less than half of gross output. Algeria's construction sector is known to import a high proportion of intermediates. Although transport costs for such imports are often high, gross construction expenditures can overstate the direct and indirect domestic resource content of investment.

11. A similar realignment of public investment away from projects heavily dependent on foreign exchange was used to cushion adjustment in Indonesia to the downside of the second oil boom; see chapter 12.

12. Seigniorage (the rent accruing to government for its monopoly to issue fiat money) normally accounts for about 1.5–2.5 percent of GDP in developing countries. Morgan (1979a, b) has noted the tendency for money stocks to rise unusually rapidly in the oil exporters with the rapid monetization of their economies.

13. The tradable sectors—agriculture and manufacturing—would have reduced their aggregate share in the nonmining economy by 0.54 percent a year according to the Chenery-Syrquin norm. Instead, in Algeria they expanded their share by 0.14 percent a year.

14. For a complete description of the model and its estimation, see Conway and Gelb (1988).

15. Such an effect can also dominate in a flexible-price economy in which public investment draws resources from wage-goods sectors where importing is constrained; see chapter 13 on Nigeria.

16. In the long run, the domestic supply of consumer goods could of course rise, depending on the investment profile.

17. As noted above, some firms did operate at less than full capacity because of limited demand. But these were in hydrocarbons and producer goods, not in housing and consumer goods.

18. Estimates of the unrationed consumption and money demand functions imply propensities to consume and to accumulate real balances that are similar to those that have been estimated for the United States. Algeria's response is thus due more to rationing than to distinctive private preferences.

Chapter 11

Ecuador: Windfalls of a New Exporter

with Jorge Marshall-Silva

Unlike the other oil producers considered in this study, Ecuador was a new exporter at the time of the first oil price increase. Because the country's oil output during 1974–78 was only half of what had been projected, the rise in price largely compensated for the shortfall in volume, leaving a relatively small first windfall. Nevertheless, it is harder to discern a coherent strategy for absorbing oil income in Ecuador than in the other five countries. This is partly because of political instability during the period and partly because its public sector is highly decentralized. Earmarking of oil income as well as other revenues was extensive, so that the feasible range of choice was more limited than in the other countries. Perhaps as a result of this constraint, the Ecuadorian government did not use its oil revenues to implement ambitious, large-scale public industrial programs. Instead, it channeled most of the oil income received into "traditional" areas such as social and physical infrastructure. It also returned much of its potential revenue gain to the private sector through subsidies, tax rebates, and the subsidized on-lending of foreign borrowing.

In some respects this pattern of use may have turned out to be an advantage, given the performance of large-scale industrial investments in other oil-producing countries. Yet the same political and institutional conditions also weakened the government's control over public spending. In contrast to its earlier tendency (and that of the other exporters except Algeria), Ecuador ran persistent and sizable current account deficits in the 1970s and 1980s. Non-oil taxation slack-

Jorge Marshall-Silva is professor of economics at the University of Santiago, Chile.

ened. Public consumption, public investment, military expenditures, and fuel, power, and food subsidies increased. Credit policy was expansive and coupled with restrictive controls on domestic interest rates. And despite domestic inflation, the exchange rate was fixed from 1970 until the foreign exchange crisis in 1982.

Nevertheless, Ecuador's record was quite favorable compared with that of some other oil exporters. Non-oil growth increased from its past levels. Gains in infrastructure, education, and health were impressive. The country acquired considerable private industrial capacity, although primarily in protected sectors. Agricultural growth was moderately good though far less impressive than in Indonesia. But oil wealth made less of an impact on poverty than it might have because of the capital-intensive pattern of industrial development encouraged by public policies. And the mid-1980s found the country facing falling world oil prices with a far larger external debt than before the first boom and with an insufficiently diversified export portfolio. The danger, therefore, is that gains will prove to be transient since the oil windfalls were not used to correct long-standing socioeconomic problems.

The first section of this chapter outlines Ecuador's economic and political structures and the nature of its public sector before the windfall, features that influenced the country's subsequent evolution. The following sections consider the use of revenue from the first windfall of 1974–78 and then the second windfall, which ended in a foreign exchange crisis. The final section sums up with the question: How has Ecuador benefited from the windfall?

Before the Windfall

Before 1972 Ecuador was one of the poorest countries in Latin America, with great disparities among the three main geographical regions: the Coast, where plantation agriculture predominated; the Sierra, where subsistence farming predominated; and the undeveloped and sparsely populated Orient, or Amazonian region, where oil was to be found. The people of the Coast (called *montevios*) are a mixture of Indians, whites, and blacks while the people of the Sierra are 80 to 90 percent Indian or mestizo. The traditional way of life of much of the populace, the nature of social and political institutions, and great inequalities in income distribution reflected the country's economic backwardness. Vast differences between the Coast and the Sierra—in climate, pattern of landownership, type of farming, and course of economic development—were exacerbated by difficulties of communication.

Table 11-1. Ecuador: Equivalent Exchange Rates
(sucres per dollar)

Item	1971	1972	1973	1974	1975	1976	1977	1978	1979	1980
a. Imports	31.2	33.3	31.1	29.0	29.8	30.8	30.8	30.3	30.0	30.6
b. Traditional exports	23.1	22.8	21.0	21.5	23.0	21.6	23.3	22.2	22.3	23.3
c. Nontraditional exports	20.2	21.5	24.6	25.5	26.6	27.9	30.5	30.0	27.3	26.9
(a−b)/b (percent)	35.1	46.0	48.1	34.9	29.6	42.6	32.2	36.5	34.5	31.3
(a−c)/c (percent)	54.5	54.8	26.4	13.7	12.0	10.4	1.0	1.0	9.9	13.7

Note: Entries are nominal rates adjusted for tariffs and subsidies.
Source: World Bank data.

Economic Structure

Much of the political conflict between the dominant classes of the Coast and the Sierra and the consequent political instability can be traced to the socioeconomic differences that reflect regional dualism. In the Sierra output was mainly determined by domestic demand for food; industry, other than handicrafts, was almost non-existent, and economic surpluses were spent largely on imported luxuries. Foreigners dominated internal trade. The best land had long been in the hands of big landowners (*hacendados*), while small proprietors eked out a subsistence by farming their hilly and often eroded land and by working part-time for the hacendados or in nearby towns and villages.

The tropical climate of the Coast favored the cultivation of export crops. Cacao was the main engine of Ecuador's economy from the late nineteenth century until the 1920s. It led to the development of plantations and made the port city of Guayaquil a center of commerce and finance. A sharp decline in cacao production from 1920 to about 1950 thrust the country into a long period of economic stagnation. This ended with the introduction of bananas in the 1950s, which became the main export crop until superseded by oil in 1973. The banana boom of the 1950s and 1960s spurred industrial growth, which rose from a very small base at 8 percent a year in the 1950s and 10 percent a year in the 1960s.

Especially in Quito a new bourgeoisie began to emerge, the result first of industrialization and then of oil. Industrial growth proceeded within the framework of import substitution, effected by very generous concessions from the mid-1950s. By the early 1970s, duties and taxes raised the average cost of foreign exchange for imports by more than 40 percent above that received by exporters, as table 11-1 indicates. Many industrial activities added little domestic value so that effective protection rates varied widely, ranging up to 300 percent. The Ecuadorian market was small and quantitative import controls promoted oligopolistic and uncompetitive production. Meanwhile, efficient and competitive coastal agrobusiness provided nearly all of Ecuador's foreign exchange earnings until 1970.

Ecuador has produced oil in small quantities since 1911. But in 1967 Texaco made major new finds, and in the early 1970s oil development began on a large scale. From 1970 to 1976 cumulative investment in the exploration, extraction, and export of oil represented nearly half of Ecuador's average annual GDP. Current account deficits of nearly 7 percent of GDP in the early 1970s were mostly financed by direct foreign investment in the oil industry. Growth was rapid in this phase, and the ratio of total investment to GDP soared from only 6.2 percent in 1965–66 to 23.8 percent in 1970–72. By the end of 1973 foreign exchange reserves represented 70 percent of external public debt as the oil sector shifted from its extractive to its high-rent phase.

Political Structure

Ecuador's government is modeled on that of the United States. The executive branch is headed by a president who is elected for a single four-year term, and legislative power resides in a one-chamber parliament. But there is a plethora of political parties, which fall into three broad groups: conservative, centrist-popular, and marxist. Socioeconomic differences and rivalries between the dominant groups of the Coast and the Sierra help explain the country's history of political instability.

Following the cacao crisis of the 1920s, the hacendados of the Sierra and the smaller farmers of the Coast joined in unstable alliances, interrupted periodically by armed intervention. For almost forty years, political life centered around a strong populist caudillo, José Maria Velasco Ibarra, five times elected to the presidency and four times toppled by the armed forces. Most of Ibarra's Coast constituency shifted to another populist movement, headed in the late 1960s by Assad Bucaram, former mayor of Guayaquil. The likelihood of Bucaram's winning the presidency in June 1972 was the main reason for the military coup in February of that year.

During the decade of oil windfalls that followed, several more shifts in government occurred. The military dictatorship of General Rodriguez Lara that was established in 1972 was strongly nationalistic and attempted to eliminate economic dependency on foreign powers, to promote self-sufficient economic development, and to carry out a radical agrarian reform. The government gradually moderated its revolutionary stance and compromised with the dominant classes, particularly on agrarian reform. In January 1976 Lara was replaced by a military junta which was to draft a new constitution and effect a transition back to civilian rule within two years. This was finally achieved in 1979, with the election of Jaime Roldos as president. In 1981 the death of Roldos and a border conflict with Peru again precipitated political instability. Dr. Osvaldo Hurtado became president until 1984, when power passed to a conservative coalition.

These frequent shifts in government shortened the horizons of policymakers and so affected the way Ecuador used its oil windfalls.

The Ecuadorian military resembled the Peruvian military then in power, although it was less radical. Its anti-imperialistic program included defense of the country's national interests and natural resources, solidarity with Third World nations, Andean integration, active participation of workers and peasants in political life, and agrarian reform. The Lara government moved gradually to a more centrist stance. The junta (1976–79) was more conservative, although its transitional character, its collective leadership, and its preoccupation with constitutional and political problems hampered economic decisionmaking. The constitutional government (1979–84) was left of center, with Roldos (1979–81) concerned more with urban issues and Hurtado (1981–84) more with rural poverty. However, the exchange crisis and the recession which beset the economy during Hurtado's administration undermined efforts to reduce poverty.

In this highly political situation, the country could implement few long-term plans for allocating its oil revenues. Political continuity was provided mainly by the public bureaucracy (which is estimated to have increased from 6.4 percent to 8.7 percent of total employment between 1975 and 1981), the *camaras* (organizations of private businessmen that wielded a good deal of political influence), and the armed forces.[1]

The Public Sector

Ecuador's public sector had grown through the establishment of autonomous institutions and public enterprises, mostly financed from specifically earmarked sources of revenue. When account is taken of other contractual payments, such as interest on debt, some three-quarters of budgetary revenues were so earmarked. This decentralized structure was another important feature that limited the government's power of fiscal control.

In the context of the oil windfalls, the most important public enterprises were CEPE (the State Petroleum Corporation) and INECEL (the Ecuadorian Electricity Institute).[2] In the early 1970s the government set up, acquired, or participated in a variety of other productive enterprises. Between 1970 and 1973, forty-two public industrial enterprises were established with an investment roughly equivalent to $160 million. This process was discontinued in later years. And although it was proposed to create a petrochemical industry with the gas of the Guayaquil Gulf, this possibility faded with the onset of the oil glut. Ecuador's government therefore played by far the smallest entrepreneurial role of any government in the sample.

Table 11-2. Ecuador: Oil Output, Consumption, and Net Exports, 1972–83
(millions of barrels)

Item	1972	1973	1974	1975	1976	1977	1978	1979	1980	1981	1982	1983
Production of crude	28.6	76.2	64.6	58.8	68.4	67.0	73.7	78.2	74.8	77.1	77.1	86.3
Consumption	9.6	10.7	12.0	14.4	14.4	19.6	22.6	25.3	27.7	29.9	30.4	27.5
Net exports	19.0	65.5	52.6	44.4	54.0	47.4	51.1	52.9	47.1	47.2	46.7	58.8
Value (millions of U.S. dollars)	45	260	702	526	648	611	629	1,194	1,571	1,589	1,344	1,623
Index of domestic use/ nonmining GDP	100	103	103	112	104	130	142	151	155	162	161	155

Source: Marshall-Silva (1984); World Bank data.

The First Windfall

This section considers the use of Ecuador's oil revenues in 1974–78, even though the discussion occasionally touches on trends over the entire period 1974–82. Because the first oil price increase coincided with the start of oil exports, the whole of the net oil earnings may be considered as a windfall. Table 11-2 summarizes oil output and use for 1972–83, and table 11-3 computes the oil bonus. Net exports in table 11-2 are the difference between production and internal consumption. Net export revenues in table 11-3 are the value of net exports less profits of the foreign oil companies and less imports by the oil industry. Two adjustments are then made. Part of the bonus accruing to Ecuador was passed on to domestic users of oil derivatives, which continued to be sold at their pre-1974 prices. As a result of this policy, domestic sales (which were used for illicit exports as well as domestic consumption) rose rapidly; their ratio to nonmining GDP increased by 62 percent during 1972–81. The first adjustment made in table 11-3 is that the value of this implicit subsidy, which peaked in 1980 at 7.3 percent of GDP, is added to the net export revenues. Second, payments for CEPE's shares in the oil production consortium are deducted. The windfall, as thus measured, averaged 12.3 percent of GDP in 1974–78 and 16.3 percent in 1979–80.

Even by the standards of oil exporters Ecuador's domestic energy prices were kept low. The subsidy to domestic users accounted for a sizable part of the total windfall, particularly after the second oil price rise in 1979. Oil for the home market was priced at or near the cost of production plus transport (estimated at $1.00 a barrel in 1973 and about $2.75 in the early 1980s). The government therefore derived almost no revenue from oil consumed at home.

Reduction in Oil Output

Annual production, as table 11-2 shows, was lower in 1974–78 than in 1973. Although the government's revenue (in real terms) per barrel of oil exported was 2.6 times that projected before 1973, output was only half of the projected 400,000 barrels a day. This can be attributed to the nationalistic orientation of the Lara government, which retroactively applied a 1971 law limiting the concessions granted to foreign oil companies, raised oil taxes and royalties, and increased the reference price for oil exports on which taxes were based. In mid-1974 conflicts between the government and oil companies paralyzed exploration activities, and in 1976 the government decided to compute CEPE's quarter share in the oil consortium on the basis of

Table 11-3. Ecuador: The Oil Windfalls, 1973–83
(millions of U.S. dollars)

Item	1973	1974	1975	1976	1977	1978	1979	1980	1981	1982	1983
Net exports	305	702	526	648	611	629	1,194	1,571	1,589	1,344	1,623
Profits of foreign companies[a]	106	157	11	25	18	15	16	20	28	46	n.a.
Inputs from abroad	60	58	57	99	83	130	183	170	240	263	n.a.
Net export revenues	139	487	458	524	510	484	995	1,399	1,321	1,035	n.a.
Subsidy to domestic oil use	26	127	129	148	198	212	519	857	625	590	290
Subsidy/GDP (percent)	1.1	3.4	3.0	2.8	3.0	2.8	5.6	7.3	4.5	4.4	2.3
Payment for CEPE's shares	43	0	0	0	82	0	35	0	0	0	0
Total windfall/GDP (percent)	4.9	16.5	13.6	12.7	9.4	9.1	15.8	19.2	14.0	12.0	n.a.

n.a. Not available.

a. Oil company profits for 1974 and perhaps for 1973 are probably overstated because the reference price for oil at which the companies had to surrender foreign exchange to the Central Bank was higher than the actual price the companies were getting for their exports.

Source: Marshall-Silva (1984).

maximum legal production rather than actual production. In 1977 Gulf withdrew, selling its share in the consortium to CEPE. One use of the windfall, therefore, was to finance national control of the oil industry and to conserve reserves.

Intention versus Outcome: The 1973–77 Plan

How did Ecuador plan to use its oil revenues? And did it follow its plan? In 1972, at the beginning of the oil era, the Planning Board (Junta de Planificación) drafted a detailed "Plan of Transformation and Development" (PIDT). The plan noted that in the past "the periods of relative bonanza [export windfalls] were translated in a short time into economic instability manifested in balance of payments problems and a fiscal deficit of even greater magnitude than prevailed prior to the period of prosperity" (PIDT, pp. 3-4). A main objective was to avoid a similar occurrence in the future.

Ecuador's oil wealth was to be used to transform its productive structure and in particular:

- To strengthen and integrate the country and reaffirm national sovereignty
- To improve living conditions, especially for the poor
- To strengthen the productive sectors so that they could absorb more labor at rising productivity.

To achieve these goals, the plan called for three basic institutional reforms. *Agrarian reform* was essential to eliminate rural poverty. *Tax reform* would provide the state with domestic resources needed for the public investment program. And *reform of public administration* would allow the state to participate effectively in transforming the economic structure.

In practice, however, these structural reforms were essentially ignored. Agrarian reform fell far short of its goals, and the land that was made available to peasants came from colonization of new areas rather than from redistribution. There was no tax reform and virtually no reform of public administration.

Growth of the public sector was even more rapid than planned. This was especially true of consumption since the recurrent expenditures required by investments in hospitals, schools, and other facilities had been underestimated. Public consumption absorbed a third of the windfall as measured in table 5-2, the highest ratio in the sample. Again, fiscal restraint failed. After 1973 and 1974, two years of surpluses, public spending outran revenue; deficits averaged 4.4 percent of nonmining GDP in 1975–78. The distribution of public expenditures in 1974–78 also differed considerably from that of the plan. In

Table 11-4. Ecuador: Nonfinancial Public Sector
(percentage of nonmining GDP)

Item	1973	1974	1975	1976	1977	1978	1979	1980	1981	1982	1974–78	1979–82	Change from 1973	
													1974–78	1979–82
Current income	29.9	35.8	31.5	29.7	29.9	27.7	33.1	32.1	31.2	29.9	30.9	31.6	1.0	1.7
Petroleum taxes	4.3	10.5	6.9	7.0	5.5	4.8	6.9	8.5	4.1	10.6	6.9	7.5	2.6	3.2
Other taxes	15.8	14.1	12.6	11.1	11.1	11.5	11.2	10.6	15.2	9.1	12.1	11.5	-3.7	-4.3
Current expenditures	18.4	22.8	23.7	22.8	23.9	22.4	23.3	25.9	26.0	27.4	23.1	25.7	4.7	7.3
Government consumption	11.4	15.2	16.4	15.7	16.4	14.9	14.6	16.5	16.3	15.7	15.7	15.8	4.3	4.4
Remuneration	9.4	10.3	11.1	10.9	10.0	9.5	9.3	11.3	11.2	11.1	10.4	10.7	1.0	1.3
Interest	0.9	1.3	1.0	1.3	1.8	1.8	2.7	2.9	2.5	5.6	1.4	3.4	0.5	2.5
Capital expenditures	8.1	12.1	10.3	10.6	12.0	10.6	10.4	11.4	11.8	11.4	11.1	11.2	3.0	3.1
Balance	3.5	1.0	-2.4	-3.7	-6.0	-5.4	-0.6	-5.1	-6.6	-9.0	-3.3	-5.3	-6.8	-8.8
Current account/ nonmining GDP (percent)	-0.5	—	—	—	—	—	—	—	—	—	-4.1	-8.5	-3.6	-8.0

Source: World Bank data.

particular, a considerably lower share was allocated to industrial development than had been projected.

These departures from the plan resulted from Ecuador's planning and decisionmaking processes. The Planning Board had only limited influence. Many decisions were made on the spur of the moment in the face of political pressures. All major state institutions participated in policy decisions related to oil. Most of the oil revenues were already earmarked for specific recipients. Notwithstanding the weakness of the Planning Board and the constraints imposed by earmarking, however, some of the goals of the 1973–77 plan—particularly those related to growth—were exceeded. This stands in stark contrast to the outcome of the second oil boom; none of the economic goals of the 1980–84 plan were achieved, although that plan laid greater stress on improving social conditions than had the previous one.

The National Income Department of the Central Bank of Ecuador has attempted to establish the destination of oil revenue by economic activity for 1974–78, but this is not easy since it requires an assessment of spending trends in the absence of such revenue. For the period as a whole, expenditures by economic sector were:

Administration, research, and planning: 20.7 percent
Agriculture and fishing: 7.0 percent
Industry, mining, and petroleum: 9.6 percent
Electricity, roads, and transportation: 20.5 percent
Education, health, and housing: 19.4 percent
Other, including defense and the public debt: 22.8 percent

This distribution of the oil windfall signified a substantial shift toward economic and social infrastructure.

Reduction in Non-Oil Tax Revenues

An alternative fiscal classification, based on the evolution of the public sector budget relative to the nonmining economy, is presented in table 11-4. (Unfortunately, comparable data are not available before 1973.) Comparing 1973 with 1974–78, the table indicates a rise in oil revenues equivalent to 2.6 percent of nonmining GDP, but this was more than offset by a fall in non-oil taxes of 3.7 percent of nonmining GDP. Current spending increased its share by 4.7 percent, and capital spending its share by 3.0 percent. The result was a swing from a surplus of 3.5 percent in 1973 to a deficit of 3.3 percent for 1974–78, an evolution which was reflected in the current account.

Almost half of Ecuador's non-oil tax revenues came from taxes

Table 11-5. Ecuador: Subsidies, Exchange Rate Effects, and the Relative Price of Consumer Goods, 1973–82
(percentage of GDP)

Item	1973	1974	1975	1976	1977	1978	1979	1980	1981	1982
Subsidy										
Internal oil use	1.1	3.4	3.0	2.8	3.0	2.8	5.6	7.3	4.5	4.4
Credit (interest)	0.5	0.5	0.5	0.5	0.5	0.5	0.6	0.6	0.7	0.7
Wheat	0.6	0.6	0.5	0.6	0.6	0.5	0.5	0.5	0.4	n.a.
Milk and other	0.3	1.0	0.4	0.2	0.1	0.0	0.2	0.2	0.2	n.a.
Electricity	n.a.	n.a.	n.a.	0.2	n.a.	0.2	0.3	0.1	0.2	0.5
Total subsidies	2.5	5.5	4.4	4.3	4.1	4.0	7.1	8.7	6.0	5.4
Effect of cheaper imports from real exchange appreciation	n.a.	1.4	3.8	3.8	4.4	4.5	4.5	3.7	5.3	2.5
Total	2.5	6.9	8.2	8.1	8.5	8.5	11.6	12.4	11.3	7.9
Consumer price index/nonmining GDP deflator (1970–72 = 100)	96	97	98	93	90	92	91	88	89	87
Consumer deflator/nonmining GDP deflator (1970–72 = 100)	98	98	99	94	91	91	93	90	93	93
Minimum real wage index (1970 = 100)										
Paid by employers	95	122	132	148	131	119	156	247	215	199[a]
Received by employees	95	126	138	153	136	124	165	254	221	201[b]

n.a. Not available.
Note: Columns may not add up to totals because of rounding.
a. For 1983 the figure was 173.
b. For 1983 the figure was 183.
Sources: Marshall-Silva (1984); World Bank data.

on international trade, about 20 percent from income taxes, and 30 to 40 percent from sales and other excise taxes. The 1973–77 plan (and later plans) envisaged fiscal reforms to increase non-oil tax revenues and to make the distribution of the tax burden more equitable. Tax concessions and exemptions were granted, mainly to industry. Average nominal tariff rates were cut and export taxes were somewhat reduced to compensate for the overvaluation of the sucre, except for taxes on coffee during the boom of 1976–78. Nontraditional exports received incentives through negotiable export tax certificates (CATS). As a result of these policies, the degree of anti-export bias implicit in the system of trade taxes was reduced sharply for nontraditional exports after 1974 (see table 11-1), although all traded sectors were affected by the real effective appreciation of the sucre in this period—from 100 in 1970–72 to 121 in 1974–78. One use of oil income, therefore, was to cut non-oil taxes. But little was achieved in terms of broadening the base and strengthening the tax system.

CURRENT SPENDING. Public consumption increased sharply relative to nonmining GDP in 1974–75, then stabilized, although because of growing interest payments the share going to recurrent spending continued to increase. Subsidization of credit, wheat, milk, and other goods boosted current spending. Electricity was also subsidized: INECEL's return to its investments was more or less zero for 1974–78 (it turned negative after 1981) even though it benefited from fuel oil provided at roughly the cost of production. Estimates of the magnitude of these subsidies are given in table 11-5.

PUBLIC INVESTMENT. Without the oil bonus, public investment would have been about 5 percent of GDP (a figure normal before 1973). In fact, it increased its share of nonmining GDP from 8.1 percent in 1973 to 11.1 percent in 1974–78 (see table 11-4). If 5 percent is taken as a base level, then roughly half of the oil windfalls (plus the net external borrowing that they facilitated) that was not used for defense went to public investment, while the other half went to current expenditures.[3]

Table 11-6 shows the distribution of public investments by economic category. Physical and social infrastructure and electrification account for the overwhelming bulk of investment after 1973. Their combined share declined from 1975 to 1978, whereas investment in the petroleum sector increased strongly. About one-fourth of public investment was used to provide drinking water, sewage facilities, hospitals, medical centers, and schools and to improve living conditions in the cities. More than two-thirds went for energy,

**Table 11-6. Ecuador: Sectoral Composition
of Public Investment, 1973–81**
(percent)

Economic category	1973	1974	1975	1976	1977	1978	1979	1980	1981
Production sectors	n.a.	n.a.	8.4	9.0	10.2	7.4	1.5	4.6	6.1
Agriculture	7.2	7.9	8.0	8.8	10.0	7.1	1.3	4.4	5.9
Other	n.a.	n.a.	0.4	0.2	0.2	0.3	0.2	0.2	0.2
Natural resources	n.a.	n.a.	12.2	20.3	22.0	24.7	34.2	34.7	30.3
Petroleum	2.3	9.7	2.8	7.0	8.6	9.2	12.2	11.3	15.4
Electricity	18.0	12.0	9.2	13.0	12.9	15.4	21.9	23.1	14.6
Other	n.a.	n.a.	0.2	0.3	0.5	0.1	0.1	0.3	0.3
Physical infrastructure	n.a.	n.a.	48.4	39.5	37.7	38.5	40.4	34.1	27.1
Roads	39.4	42.5	38.0	31.3	27.0	24.1	20.7	21.8	18.2
Other transport	n.a.	n.a.	4.2	3.8	5.9	6.5	11.3	6.3	2.8
Hydraulic	n.a.	n.a.	4.3	3.0	3.4	4.0	3.7	2.3	4.8
Other	n.a.	n.a.	1.9	1.4	1.4	3.9	4.7	3.7	1.3
Social infrastructure	n.a.	n.a.	28.3	28.6	28.2	27.6	22.2	23.9	34.5
Water supply	n.a.	n.a.	10.6	7.0	4.5	4.2	5.6	4.5	7.2
Sewage	n.a.	n.a.	1.6	3.3	2.7	2.2	1.8	2.9	4.1
Urban equipment	n.a.	n.a.	5.7	4.9	5.9	6.5	5.0	5.6	12.3
Health	4.2	2.0	5.2	6.7	7.6	8.3	5.5	3.9	3.1
Education	12.5	8.2	5.0	6.4	5.8	6.4	4.3	6.3	6.0
Other	n.a.	n.a.	0.2	0.3	1.7	n.a.	n.a.	0.7	1.8
Other investments	n.a.	n.a.	2.7	2.6	1.9	1.8	1.7	2.7	2.0

n.a. Not available.

Note: Totals do not include investments by public finance institutions.

Sources: 1973 and 1974, U.N. Economic Commission for Latin America (ECLA), Report on Ecuador (1979); 1975–81, CONADE (1983).

roads, and transport. Investment in the non-oil tradable sectors was low, with practically all of it directed to agriculture.

BORROWING AGAINST FUTURE OIL INCOME. Ecuador's external debt at the end of 1976 was only 13 percent of GDP, but from 1976 on the government started to borrow heavily from commercial banks. Access was easy because of the country's status as an oil exporter, and real interest rates appeared to be strongly negative because of real effective appreciation of the sucre.

Remarkably, public foreign borrowing financed *more* than the public sector deficit. As shown in table 11-7, loans to the private sector rose far more rapidly than deposits by the private sector, and at rates well above the growth rate of output. This was not surprising given the interest rate policy. Real rates on savings deposits averaged −7.6 percent in 1971–83, and real lending rates were also negative, especially those from official development banks. Administered interest rates had been set at levels that took account of Ecuador's tradition as a low-inflation country. They were maintained through 1982, even though inflation accelerated from its historical trend of 5 percent to 14.7 percent in 1977–78, as measured by the consumer price index. Far from crowding out the private sector, easy access to foreign savings permitted the coexistence of a growing deficit and an expansionary credit policy until 1982. Ecuador's government therefore reduced non-oil taxes, borrowed abroad against future oil income, and passed some of the proceeds on cheaply to the private sector.

The Second Oil Boom

Fortunately for Ecuador, as oil income fell in 1977–78 non-oil exports rose. The second oil boom, in contrast, was accompanied by a decline in non-oil exports—especially coffee and cacao, which fell both in price and in value. Although the rise in the oil price cushioned the drop in non-oil export earnings, it had less impact on the economy than the earlier price increase.

Use of the Windfall

The second oil boom coincided with a political transition in August 1979 from a military dictatorship to an elected government with populist leanings. Seeking to satisfy its constituency—and reassured by predictions of a sustained global energy shortage and rising real oil prices—the government used its expanding revenues to increase current expenditures further, by 2 percent of nonmining GDP. Salaries of public employees rose sharply in 1980. Although table 11-4 suggests only a moderate growth in the ratio of the public wage bill to GDP, other estimates suggest considerable growth of public employment between 1973 and 1982, with a doubling of employment in autonomous entities and in the central government during this period (World Bank 1985, p. 34). Capital expenditures rose somewhat, with the greatest increases going to petroleum and agriculture and to upgrading the living and sanitary conditions in the main cities. Spending on electrification maintained its earlier level; spending on roads and transport declined. Defense spending increased in response to the tensions with Peru, which led to a brief war early in 1981. It accounted for an estimated 21 percent of oil revenues in 1979–82.

Table 11-7. Ecuador: Consolidated Banking System

Assets and liabilities	1972	1975	1978	1981	1982
	As percentage of GDP				
Assets					
Public sector (net)	3.3	−1.9	−3.5	−6.7	−4.6
Private sector[a]	25.5	25.6	27.2	28.7	34.1
Liabilities					
Private sector[b]	30.3	24.9	27.1	24.9	27.6
	As percentage of total assets				
Assets					
Public sector (net)	9.5	−6.6	−11.4	−23.6	−14.6
Private sector	74.7	91.8	90.0	101.0	82.0
Liabilities					
Private sector	88.7	89.4	89.5	87.7	87.4

Note: All balances are at end of period.
a. Includes other assets and float.
b. Includes M1 and other liabilities.
Source: World Bank data.

The Public Deficit

Despite higher oil prices, the public budget swung further into deficit, which averaged 5.3 percent of nonmining GDP in 1979–82 (see table 11-4). Almost one-third of the deterioration after 1973 was the result of rising interest costs. The expansive credit policy was continued, and the current account deficit widened to 8.5 percent of nonmining GDP in 1979–82.

Table 11-5 suggests that subsidies were a major factor in the public deficit. They peaked in 1980 at the equivalent of 12.4 percent of GDP, then fell abruptly from 1981 to 1982, primarily because domestic oil prices tripled. The most important subsidies during this period were those on the domestic consumption of energy, both oil and electricity. The subsidy on oil derivatives for the home market peaked in 1979 and 1980; that on electricity, in 1982. Higher domestic prices for oil derivatives would have meant a smaller increase in internal sales and higher export revenues. The subsidy to oil derivatives may have appeased urban consumers, but most of the benefits accrued to the middle and upper classes.[4]

The subsidy on imports included in table 11-5 was implicitly granted to importers through real appreciation of the exchange rate. Part of the cost of the appreciated exchange rate was borne by non-oil exporters and part by the government, which saw the domestic purchasing power of its oil income and borrowing decrease. The consumption of wheat, milk, and other selected goods was also subsidized, and their prices held down by controls.

From tables 11-4 and 11-5 it is apparent that either of two options could have eliminated the public deficit during the period of the windfalls: pricing domestic oil at world levels or maintaining non-oil tax ratios and cutting subsidies to food and electricity. The buildup of Ecuador's foreign debt may therefore be attributed entirely to its domestic transfer and credit programs.

However, the policy of holding down domestic oil prices and subsidizing other goods, together with the appreciating real exchange rate—which went from a base of 100 in 1970–72 to 121 in 1974–78, 128 in 1979–81, and 132 in 1982–83—had a substantial impact on real consumption levels. From a base of 100 in 1970–72, consumer prices declined by 13 percentage points relative to the nonmining output deflator (see table 11-5). This sparked a substantial rise in consumption, in real terms, compared with the relation between consumption and nonmining GDP that is expected for a country with Ecuador's rate of per capita income growth. The large real consumption effect is notable in tables 5-2 and 5-3, as is the corresponding negative price effect.

Table 11-8. Oil and Non-Oil Export Performance

	Growth rates at 1975 prices (percent)			
Export	1970–73	1973–79	1979–82[c]	1983[c]
Bananas (tons)	3.2	0.2	–3.1	–27.9
Coffee (tons)	13.0	1.5	–20.6	83.0
Cocoa[a]	1.3	17.8	1.7	–58.1
Industrial goods[b]	33.6	16.5	19.7	–66.4
All non-oil exports	7.6	2.0	–4.8	–31.8
Crude and fuel oil	464.8	–7.4	–1.7	38.4
Total	49.3	–3.3	–3.3	4.2

a. Includes processed cocoa.
b. Excludes processed cocoa.
c. Provisional.
Source: World Bank data.

One consequence of extending incentives to nontraditional imports and of reducing tariffs and export taxes was to reduce somewhat the degree of anti-export bias, particularly for nontraditional exports, as shown in table 11-1. This did not offset the effect of real exchange rate appreciation, however, and traditional exporters were still subject to considerable tax-induced disincentives. Ecuador's non-oil export volumes stagnated during 1973–82 before plunging in 1983, as shown in table 11-8, while industrial exports, though small, grew quite rapidly until 1983. In factor markets, duty-free import of capital goods and real appreciation of the exchange rate meant a growing disincentive to absorb labor.

Debt, the Crisis, and Stabilization

From August 1970 until 1982, Ecuador maintained a fixed exchange rate of 25 sucres to the dollar. A fluctuating market rate applied to perhaps one-third of transactions, mostly invisibles and certain capital movements. The spread between the free rate and the fixed rate widened from less than 2 percent before 1975 to about 11 percent in 1976–80, before jumping to 20–33 percent in 1981. The existence of such a free market permits diversification of assets among currencies without clear indications of capital flight, so that arriving at reliable estimates of assets held abroad by Ecuadorian residents is not easy. Marshall-Silva (1984) suggests that unofficial capital movements might have amounted to about $1 billion between 1973 and 1982. The Bank for International Settlements (BIS) has estimated that reporting banks' liabilities to Ecuadorian residents were $1.3 billion at the end of 1983, although some of this may have represented reserves held with these banks (total reserves were $800 million).[5] Gross debt less reserves at the end of 1983, at $7.3 billion, was equivalent to 3.3 years' merchandise exports, or 70 percent of GDP. If the unofficial outflow of $1 billion were deducted, net debt might have been equivalent to about 2.8 years' exports, or 60 percent of GDP.

In 1982 the dollar value of oil exports fell by 16 percent, and the current account deficit reached 9 percent of nonmining GDP. In the middle of the year, foreign lending dried up. In May the sucre was devalued to 33 per dollar, the domestic price of gasoline was doubled, and measures were taken to limit imports. Then in early 1983, as the basis for an agreement with the International Monetary Fund (IMF), further steps were taken to strengthen the financial position of the public sector. Taxes and import surcharges were imposed, duty exemptions were reduced, and the domestic price of oil derivatives was increased again. Electricity, telephone, and water rates were revised upward, and control was tightened on expenditures. In March 1983 the sucre was devalued again to 42 per dollar, and a crawling peg was established by which the price of the dollar went up 0.05 sucre a day. Interest rates were also raised and their structure simplified.

The program of the IMF went into effect in July 1983 after a rescheduling arrangement had been reached with the foreign commercial banks. The main points of the program were:

- To reduce the public sector deficit to 4.2 percent of GDP in 1983 and to limit its financing by the Central Bank
- To lower inflationary pressures by imposing a limit on the expansion of net domestic assets of the Central Bank
- To continue the flexible exchange rate policy; certain export proceeds and import payments were to be transferred to the free market, and arrears in import payments were to be eliminated
- To place a limit on the outstanding public sector external debt, including the debt guaranteed by the government.

It is difficult to disentangle the impact of the stabilization program from that of El Niño, the catastrophic rains and floods during the winter of 1982–83, especially in the coastal region. The effects of El Niño included damage to property, livestock, and the transport network of about $400 million, loss of banana and cacao exports of about $115 million, and a rise in imports of about $150 million necessitated by reduced food output. Food shortages were superimposed on the elimination of subsidies, the adjustment of prices of public goods and services, and the devaluation of the currency. The consumer price index thus catapulted from an annual growth rate of 28 percent in January to 63 percent in September, while real GDP declined about 3 percent, real per capita consumption 7 percent, and real investment 28 percent. But tightened monetary and fiscal policy and an improvement in weather conditions caused the rate of inflation to fall to less than 30 percent by mid-1984. Because of increased inflation, devaluation only partly offset the real appreciation of previous years; the real effective exchange rate based on the 1970–72 index fell to 119 in 1984. All the targets of the stabilization program were fulfilled by Ecuador except the elimination of the import arrears, for which a special agreement was reached with the foreign banks.[6]

External adjustment was rapid. The current account deficit plunged from $1.2 billion in 1982 to $104 million in 1983, largely through a drastic drop in imports and a large rise in oil output. Ecuador was the only country in this study with a positive windfall effect in 1982–84 compared with 1981; see table 8-1. On the domestic front, Ecuador has no reliable statistics on employment and unemployment. But a sample survey of 282 companies showed a drop in employment in the manufacturing sector of 2.9 percent from 1981 to 1982 and an additional drop of 3.6 percent from mid-1982 to mid-1983. The limitations on public spending and the decline in construction also had a negative impact on employment. It is estimated that by mid-1983 the minimum real wage had dropped about 15 percent from its level at the end of 1982. And relative to 1980 the decline was 24 percent (see table 11-5). The non-oil growth rate in 1981–84 averaged −1 percent.

How Has Ecuador Benefited from the Windfalls?

Despite both the short political horizons of its successive governments and the bureaucratic and decentralized nature of its public sector, Ecuador appears to have benefited considerably from its windfall gains. In certain respects, these apparently adverse features turned out to be advantages. Alone among the sample, Ecuador used its oil revenues and the borrowed funds they facilitated for traditional public functions and transfers to the private sector. It is almost certainly the only country in the sample to have ended the decade of windfalls without a large, unprofitable steel industry.[7]

Economic Effects

GROWTH. The expansion of government spending, reinforced by various incentive policies, raised the rate of economic growth to a level far higher than anything Ecuador had experienced earlier in this century. Although growth slowed after 1978 and was negative after 1981, Ecuador's performance surpassed that of most other small and medium-size Latin American economies. Higher growth plus the effects of price controls, subsidies, and real appreciation resulted in a substantial rise in private consumption from projections based on past nonmining growth rates and constant relative prices. Private consumption was about 14 percent higher than such a trend would predict in 1974–78, and 22 percent higher in 1979–81; see tables 5-2 and 5-3. The danger, however, as borne out by experience in 1982–84, was that accumulated debt, the lack of an adequately diversified export portfolio, and the dependence of consumption levels on transfers out of oil income would render such gains unsustainable.

SECTORAL STRUCTURE. As shown in table 6-3, from 1972 through 1981 the sectoral structure of Ecuador's nonmining economy did not deviate too much from a "normal" evolution, although industrial growth was stronger and agricultural growth a little weaker than normal. Several factors account for Ecuador's fairly rapid industrial growth, which actually began before the oil era. Strong demand from the public sector and from the growing middle class was important, as was Ecuador's participation in the Andean Group. Industry enjoyed low interest rates, low energy prices, and ample labor available at reasonably low product wages partly because of the subsidies on fuel, food, and utilities. But the main instruments for industrial development were the Promotion Laws applied by the Ministry of Industries, Commerce, and Integration. Under these laws, industries fall into various categories of priority. Incentives differ by category, and specific exemptions and privileges are granted by the ministry case by case. Included are exemptions from part or all of taxes—for specified periods or without any limit—and exemptions from custom duties for imports of machinery, spare parts, or raw materials not produced in Ecuador. Enterprises could also claim tax deductions for new investments in fixed capital, contributions to capital, or transfers of property.

Industrial imports exempted from duties rose from 683 million sucres ($27 million) in 1971 to 8,412 million sucres ($336 million) in 1980. Industry enjoyed more than half the exemptions granted to the private sector, with most of the benefits going to the largest manufacturers. The structure of custom duties after 1971 was also an incentive to industrial development. Whereas duties on nondurables were cut by half between 1971 and 1980, and those on inputs and capital goods by 64 percent and 55 percent respectively, duties on durable consumer goods were raised by more than 40 percent. Although average nominal protection dropped sharply from 59 to 21 percent, effective protection for much of the industry increased.

The pattern of incentives was biased toward capital-intensive industries. It reinforced the effect of exchange rate appreciation, which raised labor costs relative to those of machinery imports and investment credits. It has been estimated that the ratio of the cost of imported machines to that of industrial labor fell by 78 percent during 1971–78. Almost all employment generated in the industrial sector during the first oil boom is believed to have been provided by incentive-induced projects. By 1978 the investment cost for each job had risen to $30,000 in medium- and large-scale industry and to $6,500 in small-scale industry. Consequently, manufacturing employment grew less than 4 percent a year, although output increased 9 percent a year during 1973–82.

As for the other traded sector, even in 1982 agriculture employed about half the working population and provided most of the non-oil exports. Ecuador has great agricultural potential. During the decade of the oil windfalls this sector did less well than other activities, although far better than in Algeria, Nigeria, and Trinidad and Tobago. Agriculture was doubly disadvantaged—by real effective appreciation and by trade policy. Duty exemptions on its import requirements were relatively few, and many domestic inputs had to be obtained at high protected prices. Its products were subject to export taxes and real appreciation of the sucre, while wheat and milk had to compete with subsidized imports. Government extension programs did not always reach the farm level. Public spending on agriculture declined markedly after 1977 as credit made available by the Banco Nacional de Fomento—which directs its resources mostly to the farm sector and which also provides technical assistance—represented a declining share of total credit, with its resources falling in real terms after 1974.[8] The sector's performance was not uniform: farm production lagged, but cattle raising did quite well, and forestry and fishing experienced an extraordinary expansion.

It is not possible to discuss Ecuadorian agriculture without mentioning land distribution. According to a 1968 agricultural survey, 85 percent of agricultural properties occupied only 17 percent of the farm area and averaged less than 10 hectares (about 25 acres), while 1.5 percent of properties occupied more than 47 percent of the farm area and averaged 100 hectares. Large properties had the best land, yet they often included areas that either were not exploited or were exploited inefficiently. Because of the small size and bad quality of their land and their lack of capital, technical skills, and credit, smallholders were never assured of the means of subsisting. Despite heated debate over agrarian reform at the beginning of the 1970s, the land tenure problem remains basically as it was. The intention to use oil revenues to promote land reform came to little, other than some relatively minor colonization of new lands. Strong social and political opposition was—and is—a major obstacle.

Social Effects

The effects of growth and modernization on the distribution of income, among both individuals and regions, are more difficult to ascertain. Whereas some observers believe that oil wealth increased inequalities in income and regional distribution and thereby aggravated the social problems that existed before oil was discovered, others feel that the whole country benefited from the boom of the 1970s.

Two general effects are fairly clear. First, there was a broadening and strengthening of the middle class (bureaucrats, technicians, and professionals), which had previously been quite small and weak. Second, the oil revenues did not manage to solve—and probably only slightly mitigated—the problems of poverty and marginality that affect between 30 and 40 percent of the population. Some subsidies, such as those on domestic oil products and electricity, were regressive, while those that were intended to benefit the lower income groups had little impact.

Probably the greatest social effect was that, in the expanding economy of the 1970s, employment opportunities kept up with the rapidly growing labor force, which somewhat reduced poverty. One study (cited by Marshall-Silva 1984) has compared income distribution for 1968 and 1975, as derived from national household surveys. Middle and lower-middle income groups improved their relative positions at the expense of the upper 10 percent. At the same time, the position of the poorest 20 percent deteriorated slightly and that of the richest 0.5 percent improved slightly. According to the national accounts, between 1971 and 1982 the total real wage bill per worker grew at 3 percent a year, somewhat below real GDP per capita, which rose at 6 percent. Minimum real wages increased at 5.2 percent a year between 1970 and 1983, but the peak was reached in 1980; between that year and 1983, wages declined by 24 percent (see table 11-5). The share of compensation to workers and employees represented in the national accounts fluctuated between 31.1 and 34.8 percent during the entire period. Again, the peak came in 1980—which was also the year of highest oil prices.

Social indicators show a distinct improvement, although social projects were undeniably directed less to rural areas then to the big urban centers, where the political pressures were most intense. Between 1970 and 1981 the illiteracy rate fell from 31.6 percent to 14.5 percent. In rural areas the percentage decline was greater, but the base was higher; rural illiteracy was still 25.8 percent in 1980. Secondary school enrollment rose from 22 percent in 1970 to 56 percent in 1982, from below to above the norm for middle-income countries. Despite concern over quality and wasteful duplication (by 1982 there were at least sixteen universities), this was a considerable achievement. Those with access to drinking water increased from 28.4 percent to 43.5 percent of the population between 1970 and 1980; in rural areas the increase was from 10.3 percent in 1974 to 15.6 percent in 1980. Life expectancy, which in 1970 was 54.6 years for males and 57.6 for females, in 1980 was 61.3 and 63.6 years respectively. The number of people per doctor declined from 2,200 in 1972 to 760 in 1981, while the infant mortality index fell from 108 in 1970 to 76 in 1982.

Public spending on education in rural areas increased from 23.8

percent of the total in 1975 to 37 percent in 1980. But in health it declined in the same period from 7 to 5.8 percent.

Some idea of the changes during the oil era is given by a study comparing social indicators for the province of Bolívar with those for the country as a whole. Bolívar is one of the poorest provinces of Ecuador, with considerable out-migration. In 1974 it had 3.5 percent of the country's cultivated area and 2.2 percent of agricultural production; by 1980 those percentages had increased to 5.1 percent and 5.8 percent respectively. And whereas the rural population supplied with drinking water increased countrywide from 10.3 percent in 1974 to 15.6 percent in 1980, it increased in Bolívar from 5.7 to 16.5 percent. Expenditures on public health per capita increased in Bolívar from $4.10 to $12.50 between 1976 and 1981.

To sum up, Ecuador presents a less focused, less dramatic picture than some of the other oil producers in this study. The oil windfalls relaxed resource constraints, and the government took advantage of this to increase traditional public functions and to expand subsidy and credit programs. Any radical departure from this pattern would have been politically difficult and bureaucratically impossible. On the positive side, Ecuador managed to avoid some serious investment errors, to raise growth, and to expand much-needed public services. However, Ecuador accumulated a substantial foreign debt that contributed to a foreign exchange crisis and low growth at the end of the second oil boom; moreover, the pattern of incentives funded by oil favored capital-intensive techniques. Ecuador did not take advantage of its oil wealth to establish strong export-based manufacturing industries. And since its fundamental socioeconomic problems remain, the danger is that falling oil prices coupled with external debt will bring about a reversal of some of the gains bought with the oil windfalls.

Notes

1. In 1972–78, 13 percent of oil revenues went to the armed forces, a percentage which greatly increased in later years.

2. The largest state enterprise, CEPE increased its activities until it controlled about 70 percent of oil production. Hastily formed, subject to political pressures and continuous changes in its direction and management, CEPE inevitably developed inefficiencies. Between 1975 and 1982 the estimated real cost per barrel of the oil it produced doubled. Nevertheless, it did develop technical abilities in a new field and made Ecuadorians feel masters of their main source of wealth.

3. Oil revenues accruing to the National Defense Board tripled in real terms from 1973 to 1974, then fell off slightly until 1979, when they tripled again.

4. See Marshall-Silva (1984). World Bank estimates suggested that the 16 percent of the population with the highest income received 60 percent of the oil subsidy.

5. Data do not permit the identification of the part of BIS liabilities that corresponds to official reserve holdings.

6. The target for the public sector deficit was overfulfilled; the deficit practically disappeared in 1983.

7. The caveat is due only to lack of information on the rate of return in the Algerian steel industry.

8. For a discussion of agricultural policies and prospects, see World Bank (1985), chap. 6.

Chapter 12

Indonesia: Windfalls in a Poor Rural Economy

with Bruce Glassburner

With a per capita income of only $200 in 1974, Indonesia was the poorest country in the world to receive a substantial oil windfall. With 129 million inhabitants, it was also the most populous. Its windfalls, at 16 percent of nonmining GDP in 1974–78 and 23 percent in 1979–81 (see tables 5-2 and 5-3), were comparable to those of the other exporters in this study. But on a per capita basis, they were far lower. Oil exports in 1979 were only $62 per person in Indonesia, as opposed to an unweighted average of $778 in the other five comparators.

Indonesia's oil industry is one of the worlds's oldest.[1] The quest for oil began in 1871, only twelve years after the earliest drillings in Pennsylvania. The first commercial oil was produced in 1885. Production was only 25,000 barrels a day before World War I but had grown to 160,000 barrels a day by the start of World War II. In the early 1950s Caltex began developing its giant fields in central Sumatra (notably the Minas field), but it was not until the pioneering agreement on production-sharing in 1967 and the attainment of political and economic stability that Indonesia's oil boom really began. With weak administration of the non-oil tax system, oil provided the overwhelming bulk of tax revenues before 1973. Yet it accounted for only a third of exports because of the richness of the country's resource base. The government of Indonesia therefore had less experience than the governments of most other oil exporters in managing an economy strongly dependent on oil for foreign exchange.

Despite this lack of experience, in a number of respects Indonesia's economic performance since 1973 has been unusually good. Especially noteworthy has been the strength of the non-oil trad-

Bruce Glassburner is professor of economics emeritus at University of California, Davis.

able sectors—agriculture and manufacturing—and of non-oil exports. This is in distinct contrast to both the predictions of economic models centering on the "Dutch disease" and the record of countries such as Nigeria and Trinidad and Tobago. In Indonesia high non-oil growth rates were maintained during the two oil booms. And, although evidence is sketchy and sometimes contradictory, at least some benefits from spending the oil income seem to have spread to most segments of the population, both rural and urban. Excessive accumulation of debt was avoided, and after 1981 the country showed signs of being able to adjust to the slowdown in oil and other primary export markets with smaller cost than its comparators.

How did Indonesia manage to avoid the serious problems that beset other oil exporters? Good luck (notably breakthroughs in rice technology and events which postponed overambitious plans to build resource-based industry) and an abundant supply of labor relative to oil income played a part. But so did three distinctive features of Indonesia's economic policy:

- The government accepted the need for a flexible exchange rate policy in large part because the idea that Indonesia's comparative advantage would be in oil for some time was never widely accepted.
- Macroeconomic management was prudent and adaptive. The government was prepared to use key macro instruments to spread the absorption of windfalls over time and limit the impact of the oil booms on the non-oil tradable sectors. It was also prepared to undertake major structural reforms to help adjust to the oil glut.
- The government was committed to a broad development strategy that emphasized raising rural incomes. It devised programs to achieve this and succeeded in enlisting the participation of millions of small farmers.

As in other oil exporters, so in Indonesia institutions and policies in place before 1973 were important in determining the response to the shocks of 1974 and 1979. Perhaps they were even more important in Indonesia than elsewhere because of the exceptional continuity in policymaking. The same government has been in power since 1966, and key members of its economic team served from before the first oil boom through the oil slump of the mid-1980s. This unusual stability made it possible for the government to fashion consistent, long-term economic policies in response to the oil shocks of the 1970s.

This chapter seeks to explain Indonesia's relative success in managing its oil windfalls. It begins by outlining the country's main political and economic features before 1973, first under the "Guided Democracy" of the Sukarno period and then under the "New Order" of the Suharto government. The following sections consider the macroeconomic responses to the first and second windfalls and summarize the set of measures—far more comprehensive and more speedily implemented than in the comparator countries—that were introduced to adjust to the downturn after 1981. Sectoral issues are next discussed, including the role of policy in agricultural performance (particularly of rice), the effort to avoid undue dependence on oil, and the performance of non-oil exports. What is known, or at least is thought to be known, about how oil affected income distribution is then summarized. An overall assessment of Indonesia's use of its oil windfalls concludes the chapter.

Politics and the Economy before 1973

Indonesia proclaimed its independence from the Dutch after the end of the Japanese occupation in 1945. It achieved international recognition as a sovereign state in 1949, after a four-year revolutionary struggle against the Dutch attempt to reestablish control.

From Independence through the Sukarno Period, 1949–66

As a newly independent nation, Indonesia's economic prospects were bleak. Some twenty years of depression, occupation, and revolutionary struggle had greatly disrupted trade, damaged infrastructure, and undermined the economic system. Moreover, there were few trained nationals with expertise in economics or experience in statecraft (Glassburner 1964; Kahin 1952). It is hardly surprising, therefore, that economic performance in the 1950s was very poor.

The situation was made even bleaker by the unstable political climate. The effort to emulate European parliamentary democracy led to a proliferation of political parties. Seven cabinets fell in the first six years of independence, and the first general election in 1955 failed to establish a national consensus. An atmosphere of deep disillusionment set in as accelerating inflation, capital flight, shortages of basic commodities, and increasingly open corruption grew rampant.

In the late 1950s President Sukarno, who had previously been content to play a largely symbolic role as a charismatic nation-builder, introduced his idea of Guided Democracy. He proposed to "bury the political parties" and return to the constitution of 1945, which centered a great deal of power in the hands of the president himself.

By 1959, with the support of the army, Sukarno had overcome the opposition to his plan. Presidential decrees were given the force of
law, and the role of the legislature was diminished.

The period 1959–65 was marked by continued economic decline.
Sukarno elevated political goals over economic ones and concentrated on building national pride and international prestige
rather than productive capacity.[2] Indeed, according to one ob-
server, Guided Democracy and the accompanying "guided economy" proved to be "in terms of disruption of the economy and capital consumption, worse than most wars" (Higgins 1972). The
withering of international trade reduced tax revenues. Unemployment, both open and disguised, may have been as high as 25 percent of the labor force (Glassburner 1971, p. 431). With the end in
1957 of any effective restraint on creating money, inflation accelerated and was estimated at more than 600 percent in the early
1960s. Shortages of food, especially rice, contributed to political instability. Foreign exchange reserves and domestic savings turned negative. The extent to which output and income fell will never be
known because of the demise of the statistical service. But even a
small drop in GDP was critical for the large share of the population already living at a subsistence level, especially in densely populated
Java and Bali.

The political crisis of 1965–66, precipitated by an end to the tenu-
ous balance between the army and the Communist party, culmi-
nated in a coup that stripped Sukarno of his power. Congress
named General Suharto acting president in 1967; in 1968 the "acting" was dropped. Sukarno, confined to his residence, died in
1970.

Stabilization and Rehabilitation
under Suharto's "New Order," 1966–73

The condition of the economy when Suharto came to power could
hardly have been worse. One of the new leader's first steps upon taking office was to seek help in devising a strategy to meet the economic challenge. From the Faculty of Economics of the University of
Indonesia (FEUI) a team of presidential economic advisors was
formed which was to have an unusual degree of political influence
and continuity.[3] The central role of the FEUI in designing and implementing economic policy was strengthened when other members
of the faculty were named to important government posts. In effect, FEUI's Institute for Economic and Social Research became,
and has remained, the research arm of the government. This too contributed much to the continuity of Indonesia's economic policy.

In 1966 the FEUI economists presented a major document on economic policy. Called the *Tracee Baru* ("New Line"), this document signaled a shift in priorities from international affairs to the domestic economy. The short-term objectives were stabilization and rehabilitation. Specific priorities included:

- Strengthening agriculture, infrastructure, and industry, *in that order*
- Reviving foreign trade and promoting exports
- Reorienting import policy to facilitate domestic production and meet basic needs. Import policy was to be integrated into stabilization policy, with foreign exchange practices rationalized to avoid "wasteful" uses
- Launching a wide-ranging program of military and civilian austerity, coupled with a strong effort to reduce the budget deficit rapidly by increasing internal revenues
- Reforming the "confused" banking system and reestablishing central banking powers in the Bank of Indonesia.

The details of the nation's economic priorities were to be specified each year through an integrated program of budgetary, fiscal, monetary, price, wage, and balance of payments policies.

Remarkably, given the chaos in the monetary and fiscal systems, stabilization was soon accomplished. The rate of growth of the money supply was reduced substantially each year, and interest rates were raised successively until positive real rates were reached in May 1969 (Grenville 1981). Inflation plunged from more than 600 percent in 1966 to 84 percent in 1968, 9 percent in 1970, and only 4 percent in 1971. The exchange rate, persistently overvalued since 1955 (Gillis 1984, p. 11), was devalued. And, since widespread evasion had convinced the economic team of the futility of trying to restrict foreign exchange transactions, controls were first modified and then abolished. The foreign exchange market has remained free to this day—an enduring legacy.

The government recognized, moreover, that the large budgetary deficits had to be curbed. After 1967 the budget was, in a sense, "balanced"—although foreign aid and loans for development were counted as revenue rather than financing. This balanced budget principle was to become another enduring legacy of the Sukarno period, even though it was sometimes applied quite flexibly.[4]

The economic turnaround in just a few years was impressive. Exports recovered quickly, and net foreign reserves turned positive by 1972. Both industrial and agricultural production accelerated. The growth of trade and output helped to raise revenues; taxes collected by the central government climbed from a low of 4 percent of GDP in 1965 to 10 percent in 1970.

ROLE OF THE MARKETPLACE. Despite the Suharto government's commitment to a free foreign exchange market and a balanced budget, and despite the support for the private sector expressed in the *Tracee Baru*, the economic regime of Indonesia was, and still is, far from laissez-faire.[5] At the microeconomic level, regulation was pervasive—a legacy of Dutch colonial rule as well as of the guided economy of Sukarno. Both domestic and foreign investment was controlled by the planning ministry, Bappenas. Permission to invest might be denied for a variety of reasons, such as the judgment that a particular market was "saturated." To obtain clearance for new investment, or even to add a new line of production, could take two years or more. Such measures insulated inefficient firms from domestic and foreign competition.[6] In addition, thousands of ordinances affected every aspect of production. Many were unpublished and served only to generate opportunities for side payments to rent-seeking officials.

Trade too was regulated. Effective protective rates, though not especially high on average for broad sectors, were widely dispersed and strongly favored some activities at the expense of others. Studies of Indonesia's system of trade intervention in the mid-1970s indicate that some sectors had negative value added at world prices. The effective rate for the tire and tube industry was estimated at 4,315 percent and for the motor industry 718 percent, whereas the rate for batik production, which was adversely affected, was a negative 35 percent. At one point the capital intensity of protected, import-competing sectors was four times that of exporting sectors. Regulations, protection, and subsidies sometimes influenced technical choices to the detriment of labor absorption.[7]

One objective of the plethora of regulations was to further the economic interests of the *pribumi*—autochthonous Indonesians—over the interests of those of Chinese extraction. The latter, who constitute only 3 percent of the population, had long wielded disproportionate economic power. The Chinese proved adept, however, at circumventing the regulations, sometimes by forming associations, called *cukong* relationships, with pribumi. In reality, the main effect of the regulations was to slow private investment. Whether measured by the residual of total over public investment, by permit approvals from Bappenas, or by direct capital inflows, private investment was disappointingly low in Indonesia in the 1970s and was to remain so into the 1980s.

The regulation issue should not be left without some comment on economic planning. Under the Suharto regime, four five-year plans have been formulated. Repelita I, the plan for 1969–73, was essentially a "wish list." Nevertheless, its modest goals were generally met or exceeded.[8] The second plan was obsolete before it was printed because of the unanticipated oil bonanza. The third plan period saw the favorable shock of a second windfall in 1979–80, and then the traumatic downward plunge in the price of oil and the volume of exports in 1982–83. The fourth plan was therefore initiated in unfavorable circumstances.

All these plans have been mainly exercises undertaken for public consumption. There has never been a real attempt to formulate anything comparable to the development plans of India and Pakistan, which set broad targets for a twenty-year period. The relatively casual pattern of economic planning in Indonesia reflects the pragmatism of the economic team and the government. Yet there is considerable government intervention at all levels, and in that sense the economy might appropriately be called "planned" or "regulated" (McCawley 1978).

NATIONAL PRIORITIES. Certain priorities identified by the Suharto regime well before the first oil shock were to exert a powerful influence on the way in which oil revenues were used and the speed with which they were absorbed. The drive to stabilize the economy was closely linked to the need to expand and stabilize food supplies, particularly rice. Indonesia had become the world's largest importer in a thin and volatile world market. *Food security* was therefore the main goal of the first development plan. A variety of programs to intensify rice cultivation were introduced, and they expanded rapidly. The period 1966–73 represented a learning phase in the design and replication of these rural development programs. Serious errors were made, and although agricultural output recovered from the low levels of the mid-1960s, growth through the early 1970s was slow. Rice output actually fell by 4 percent in 1972. This raised food prices sharply and increased dependence on imported rice, which totaled 3.6 million tons in 1972–74, or 8.3 percent of domestic production. Before the first oil shock, food self-sufficiency seemed a distant target.

A second goal was to restore the conditions for sustained growth through *rural reconstruction*, especially by rehabilitating roads and irrigation works neglected under Sukarno. To help achieve this goal, the central government funded labor-intensive public works projects under *Instruksi Presiden* (INPRES) and associated programs.

These programs, which were run at the county and village levels, were later to play an important role in distributing oil income widely.

A third goal was the *consolidation of national control*. The government strengthened its administrative network, which consisted of a joint civilian-military system extending to the 383 counties (*kabupaten*) and towns and down to most of the 60,000 villages (*desa*).[9] This system gave Suharto a firm power base in the bureaucracy and the military, with important consequences for political stability. It was also an essential factor in the government's success in implementing the rural programs and promoting agricultural growth.

Two additional features of pre-1973 Indonesia were to influence use of the oil windfalls. First, the institutional power base of the Sukarno government was, in addition to the army, the *Golongan Karya*, or GOLKAR. GOLKAR is not a political party in the narrow sense but rather a coalition of diverse "functional groups"—including groups of workers, women, farmers, and youths—that dominate the parliament. GOLKAR represents a broader range of interests than the usual political party. This reduced rivalry over how oil revenues were to be spent, both before and after the first shock.[10]

Second, Indonesia's population was overwhelmingly rural. In the archetypal mineral economy, the rural sector is presumed to have little political power because the urban economy gets foreign exchange from the mining sector and is therefore less dependent on domestic agriculture for food and export revenues. But in Indonesia the power of urban centers was limited; in 1970 only about 17 percent of the population lived in urban areas and most of these had close rural ties. Rural-urban migration caused by an urban bias in public spending could have swamped Indonesia's cities and towns. The rural predominance, however, helped to ensure the wide distribution of oil rents.

Macroeconomic Responses to the Oil Windfalls, 1974–81

This section begins with the Pertamina crisis because of its important influence on the government's response to the oil windfalls. Pertamina, the state oil company, was by far the largest and most autonomous of the state enterprises. Like state enterprises (and especially national oil companies) in some other countries, it had become an economic fiefdom of diversified operations.[11] In 1972 a presidential decree required state enterprises to get official approval before negotiating long-term foreign loans. To get around this,

Pertamina increased its short-term borrowing.[12] In 1974 it failed to meet its obligations. Shock waves rebounded through the economy, and the government was forced to allocate the equivalent of two-fifths of one year's oil windfall to repay Pertamina's debt.

Although the economic system managed to avoid major disruption, the Pertamina crisis was seen at the time as a national tragedy. In retrospect, however, the debacle can be considered as a fortunate event. Because of its timing, just after the first oil price increase, it triggered an immediate and noninflationary use of oil income to repay foreign debt. The crisis reinforced the natural caution of the government and its determination to avoid becoming too dependent on oil or excessively indebted. Thus it delayed the formulation of ambitious plans for capital-intensive, resource-based investments until the second oil boom. This, in turn, allowed more time in Indonesia than in other oil countries for such plans to be reviewed and scaled down with the onset of the oil glut.

The First Windfall

Indonesia's main response to the first oil shock was to increase spending on development. Table 12-1 records the dramatic change in the fiscal accounts. From 1973–74 to 1977–78 the government allocated 49 percent of the windfall in mining value added to investment—virtually all of it public—as measured by the rise in development expenditures over the 1970–72 level (see table 5-2). Although "development expenditures" are commonly taken as an indicator of public investment in Indonesia, this category excludes investments by public enterprises not financed by the central government and includes some noninvestment expenditures.[13] Another one-third of the windfall (again, using 1970–72 as the base) went to reduce the trade and nonfactor service deficit, and the remaining 18 percent was spent on consumption (half public, half private).

Inflows of project and program aid also rose, enabling total government expenditures to exceed revenues, as shown in table 12-1, without violating the balanced budget rule. This, together with favorable trends in the non-oil terms of trade, enabled international reserves (less gold) to rise from $805 million in 1973 to $2.5 billion in 1978.

Except that Indonesia spent a relatively high share on agriculture, its distribution of development spending by broad economic activity did not differ much from that of most other oil exporters in this study. During the first oil shock the agricultural sector received a substantial share of development spending (about 13 percent; see table 7-1). This estimate includes investments in irrigation works

Table 12-1. Indonesia: Central Government Budget and Financing
(billions of rupiah)

Item	1973–74	1974–75	1975–76	1976–77	1977–78	1978–79	1979–80	1980–81	1981–82	1982–83	1983–84	1984–85
Revenue	968	1,754	2,242	2,906	3,534	4,266	6,697	10,227	12,213	12,418	14,433	16,194
Corporate tax on oil	345	973[a]	1,249	1,619	1,949	2,309	4,260	7,020	8,628	8,170	9,520	10,367
Current expenditures	713	1,016	1,333	1,630	2,149	2,744	4,062	5,800	6,978	6,996	8,412	10,101
Development expenditures	451	962	1,398	2,054	2,157	2,556	4,014	5,916	6,940	7,360	9,899	10,459
Balance (project plus program aid)	−198	−224	−488	−788	−771	−1,033	−1,379	−1,489	−1,705	−1,938	−3,878	−4,411
Undisbursed development expenditures	...	...	...	...	...	...	833	1,908	572	−434	789	n.a.
	1973	1974	1975	1976	1977	1978	1979	1980	1981	1982	1983	1984
Banking system claims on central government[b]	n.a.	n.a.	−5	−339	−613	−878	1,703	−3,619	−4,179	−3,757	−5,062	−7,657
International reserves minus gold (millions of U.S. dollars)[b]	805	1,490	584	1,497	2,509	2,626	4,062	5,391	5,014	3,144	3,718	4,773

... Negligible.
n.a. Not available.
a. Exclusive underpayment of revenues, estimated at about Rp 340 billion, owed to the government by Pertamina.
b. End of period.
Source: Revenues and expenditures, Indonesia Ministry of Finance; undisbursed expenditures, World Bank; banking system claims, Bank Indonesia; reserves, IMF.

but not the heavy subsidies on fertilizer. These subsidies, shown in table 12-2, averaged 11 percent of all domestically financed development spending during the period. As usual in the sample of oil-exporting countries (see table 7-1), the largest share of development spending—in Indonesia's case, 43 percent—went for economic infrastructure. What was unique in Indonesia, however, was that such spending extended to rural as well as urban areas. Much of the spending on infrastructure was used to fund labor-intensive public works projects undertaken through INPRES and implemented at the county and village levels; see table 12-2 and discussion below. Although INPRES funding shifted in favor of sector-specific applications in 1975–76, it changed little as a share of total development spending and thus increased rapidly after the first oil shock.

Industry was not neglected in public investments. Twelve percent of domestically financed spending on development was allocated to capital participation, mostly in public industrial firms. The industrial sector as a whole is estimated to have received almost 20 percent of development spending.

Increased domestic spending out of the windfall contributed to a sharp appreciation of the real effective exchange rate, although rising inflation was actually triggered by an adverse domestic supply shock—the poor harvest of 1972, which sent food prices skyrocketing. It is difficult to specify an equilibrium real exchange rate for the years just before the first oil shock because in 1967–72 the rupiah was continuously devalued from 150 to 415 per dollar, where it remained for seven years. But relative to a 1970–72 base of 100, the average real effective exchange rate appreciation in 1974–78 was 33 percent, the highest in the sample (see table 6-1).

Warr (1986) has constructed an index of the real exchange rate (the relative price of traded to nontraded goods) by comparing components of the price index that are representative of the traded and the nontraded sectors. His results point to a major shift of about 30 percent against non-oil tradables during the first oil boom.

Table 12-3 reveals the dip in oil exports that occurred in 1978–79 —a decline of 13 percent in dollar terms from the preceding fiscal year. Both the government and analysts of the Indonesian economy concluded that the boom was about over, and the outlook was generally thought to be cloudy.[14] In November the rupiah was devalued from 415 to 625 per dollar. This was not done because of balance of payments problems; reserves, equivalent to four months' imports, were considered adequate. Rather, the objective was to assist the non-oil traded sectors, many of which—such as rubber, coffee, and the emerging export sector of manufactured crafts—were relatively labor-intensive. Another reason for devaluation was to main-

Table 12-2. Indonesia: Selected Components of Development Spending
(percentage of total less project aid)

Item	1973–74	1974–75	1975–76	1976–77	1977–78	1978–79	1979–80	1980–81	1981–82	1982–83	1983–84
INPRES program[a]											
General	13.6	13.2	13.9	11.2	11.8	10.6	8.1	7.5	8.5	9.8	8.9
Sectoral[b]	5.7	3.2	10.2	7.3	9.7	11.2	9.3	8.4	8.4	8.2	12.8
Fertilizer subsidy	9.8	29.6	14.5	8.4	2.2	5.2	4.6	6.3	8.0	7.7	7.6
Capital participation	12.1	11.9	11.7	13.0	11.8	8.2	9.4	10.6	9.1	10.8	9.8
Other	58.8	42.1	49.7	60.1	64.5	64.8	68.6	67.2	66.0	63.5	60.9

a. Labor-intensive public works projects.
b. Primary schools (about 60 percent), health, roads, afforestation, markets.
Source: Indonesia Ministry of Finance.

tain the domestic purchasing power of falling dollar-denominated oil tax receipts; in fiscal 1977–78 these made up 65 percent of central government revenues. Plans were also initiated to contain public spending in line with the perceived tightening of resources.

The expenditure-reducing measures introduced in Indonesia at the end of the first oil boom were not unusual. The governments of most oil-exporting countries began to rein in their spending as the first oil windfall subsided. But the Indonesian government was the only one to effect a major program of switching expenditures from foreign or traded goods to domestic or nontraded goods through exchange rate adjustment.[15]

The Second Windfall

In some ways the devaluation of November 1978 could not have been more poorly timed, coming as it did just before another oil price rise. This second shock raised Indonesia's mining sector windfall, as measured in table 5-3, from 15 percent of nonmining GDP in 1978 to 26 percent by 1980. And this time, unlike in the mid-1970s, a wide spectrum of opinion outside Indonesia expected oil prices to keep increasing in real terms.

A less cautious government might have encouraged greater foreign borrowing by public firms and increased its own foreign borrowing (as the government of Mexico did) or at least have maintained the balanced budget rule. But though the Indonesian government balanced its budget in an accounting sense, it ran substantial de facto surpluses in 1979–81 by slowing down the disbursement of funds allocated to various uses in the formal budget. Claims of the banking system on the central government fell sharply, and international reserves (less gold) soared from $2.6 billion in 1978 to more than $5 billion by 1980. For measures of the surplus, see table 12-1.

Tables 5-2 and 5-3 confirm a tightened macroeconomic "absorption effect" in this period. In 1979–81 (relative to the 1970–72 base period) 22 percent of the second windfall was consumed, and 36 percent was invested at home. But 42 percent of the windfall was used to reduce trade and nonfactor deficits, with the result that the current account swung from a deficit of 1.6 percent of nonmining GDP in 1974–78 to a surplus of 2.3 percent. Although spending did rise after the second oil price increase, the Indonesian government pursued a policy of restraint in that it kept absorption well below the level permitted by the availability of oil income and foreign aid. This had not been the case during the first oil boom.

Holding down spending proved to be partially effective in reducing the extent of real exchange rate appreciation and in maintaining

Table 12-3. Indonesia: Oil and Non-Oil Export Performance

Exports	1971–72	1972–73	1973–74	1974–75	1975–76	1976–77	1977–78	1978–79	1979–80	1980–81	1981–82	1982–83	1983–84
Value (millions of U.S. dollars)													
Net oil exports[a]	n.a.	n.a.	641	2,638	3,138	3,710	4,352	3,785	6,308	9,345	8,379	5,788	6,016
Net LNG exports[a]	0	0	0	0	0	0	93	225	667	1,256	1,382	1,378	1,355
Nonhydrocarbon exports	784	977	1,905	2,033	1,873	2,863	3,506	3,996	6,171	5,485	4,034	3,928	5,235
Timber	170	275	720	615	527	885	943	1,130	2,166	1,672	952	899	1,123
Rubber	215	211	483	425	381	577	608	774	1,101	1,078	770	614	962
Palm oil	45	42	89	184	142	147	202	221	257	178	79	103	83
Coffee	54	83	79	92	112	330	626	508	715	588	343	363	469
Tin	64	70	98	166	158	181	253	324	388	454	437	349	309
Miscellaneous (mainly manufactures)	56	76	77	114	144	196	245	361	636	570	613	730	1,167
Ratio of nonhydrocarbon to oil exports (percent)	n.a.	n.a.	297	77	60	77	81	105	98	60	50	68	89

Volume growth rates (percent)	1971–72 to 1980–81	1980–81 to 1983–84
Timber	3.1	−22.3
Rubber	1.8	4.2
Palm oil	6.6	−13.4
Coffee	13.9	4.9
Tin	4.6	−7.2
Miscellaneous[b]	15.8	27.9
Total nonhydrocarbon exports[b]	11.1	−0.9

n.a. Not available.

a. Exports are net of imports of goods and services.

b. Dollar values are deflated by unit values of manufactured exports from developed to developing countries to derive volume index.

Source: Bank Indonesia.

competitiveness after the devaluation. Although price increases total-
ing 42 percent in 1979 and 1980 eroded a substantial part of the real
devaluation, the nominal rate was allowed to slide against the dollar, and the real effective exchange rate was maintained in 1979–81
at an average index of 104. This was considerably closer to the
1970–72 parity (100) than were the effective rates of exchange of the
other five oil exporters in this study, which averaged 140.[16]

The profile of Indonesia's real effective exchange rate over the
two oil shocks differs, therefore, from that of most of its comparators, as figure 12-1 makes clear. In Indonesia appreciation was initially sharp but was substantially corrected rather early on. In contrast, most of the other oil exporters continued to let their exchange
rates appreciate—particularly Nigeria, which pegged its nominal exchange rate throughout the period despite high domestic inflation
and tightened import controls as export revenue fell off.

The policies pursued by the Indonesian government during the second oil shock had a satisfactory effect on growth. Helped by good
harvests, the economy rebounded after a slump in 1979 to grow at
nearly 10 percent in 1980. In 1967–72 the nonmining economy had
grown at 8.5 percent as it recovered from the stabilization period; it
came close to maintaining this high rate during the windfall periods, with a growth rate for 1972–81 of 8.2 percent. This was the sec-

**Figure 12-1. Indonesia and Comparators: Real Effective
Exchange Rates**

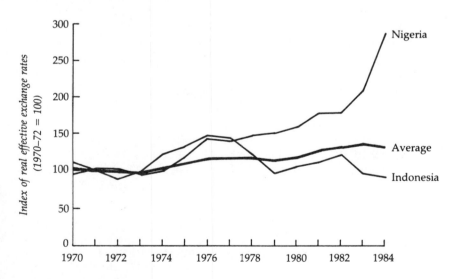

Source: World Bank data.

ond highest rate in the sample after Algeria. And because of its substantially lower population growth, Indonesia led all the comparators in the growth rate of nonmining GDP per capita.

Adjustment in the Downturn, 1982–85

Indonesia's net oil exports fell from $9.3 billion in 1980–81 to $8.3 billion in 1981–82, and the next year they plunged to $5.7 billion.[17] To make matters worse, the non-oil terms of trade deteriorated as important markets for primary products collapsed. The current account reversed abruptly; a surplus of $2.8 billion in 1980 had become a deficit of $5.3 billion, or more than 8 percent of GDP, by 1982. At the same time, growth of total GDP slowed to 2.2 percent, while growth of nonmining GDP at 3.6 percent was far below the 8 percent level of the previous decade.

What happened in Indonesia after the second plunge in oil prices again demonstrates the willingness of the government to act decisively and prudently to curb any emerging macroeconomic imbalance. The turnaround in the oil market was speedily diagnosed as not being merely short-term, and adjustments were made while reserves were still high.

In response to the adverse developments, in late 1982 and 1983 the Indonesian government introduced the most wide-ranging set of adjustment measures of any country in this study, including:

- Exchange rate adjustment. After the rupiah had drifted downward against the dollar, from 625 in November 1978 to 703 in March 1983, it was devalued to 970 per dollar.
- Tight fiscal policy. This involved, among other steps, further increases in the domestic prices of oil derivatives. These prices had traditionally been held far below world levels. The economic cost of the oil subsidy averaged some 5 percent of GDP during the two oil booms, while the budgetary subsidy peaked at 2.4 percent of GDP in 1981.[18]
- After the price increases, most subsidies were restricted to kerosene and diesel, and in 1985 the budgetary fuel subsidy was only 0.6 percent of GDP. Moreover, with the recovery of rupiah revenues in 1983 (partly as a result of devaluation) the government switched from a temporary phase of overspending in 1982–83 back to underspending in keeping with its balanced budget rule (see table 12-1).
- A drastic rephasing of the public investment program, particularly in heavy industry. By the end of 1981 industrial projects in the pipeline implied foreign exchange expenditures of $20 bil-

lion. Postponements and cancellations saved an estimated half of this figure, with negligible long-run implications for employment since the cancelled projects were highly capital-intensive.[19]

• Between Repelita III (April 1979-March 1984) and the first two years of Repelita IV (1984–85 and 1985–86) the share of development spending going to industry and mining fell by 8 percentage points, while the share to economic infrastructure rose by 2.5 points and the share to the social sectors rose by more than 6 points. In addition to reducing expenditures, this postponement of industrial programs reallocated expenditures from industry to infrastructure and social sectors and was an important expenditure-switching policy. Import coefficients were far lower, and employment coefficients higher, for the expanding than for the contracting sectors, and this cushioned the effect of falling demand. Estimates of import and employment coefficients in table 12-4 take into account direct employment and import demands as well as demands from domestic sectors supplying intermediate products. The table indicates the potentially large impact on demand that accompanies such changes in the composition of public investment.

• Financial reform and liberalization. The main objective of financial reform was to raise interest rates on deposits and so prevent the capital flight that might otherwise be provoked when people realized that devaluation would follow the deterioration

Table 12-4. Indonesia: Import and Employment Coefficients

Sector	Import requirements[a]	Employment requirements[b]
Productive sectors	0.71	0.14
Agriculture	0.45	0.22
Industry	0.87	0.09
Mines	0.91	0.06
Economic infrastructure	0.69	0.23
Irrigation	0.50	0.31
Energy	0.79	0.16
Social sectors	0.44	0.45
All sectors	0.57	0.33

Note: Aggregations are based on the plan allocations for Repelita IV.

a. Coefficients show the import requirements (in rupiah) per rupiah of development expenditures.

b. Coefficients show the labor requirements (in person-years) per million rupiah of development expenditures (in 1980 prices).

Source: World Bank data.

in the oil market. Real interest rates on term loans from state banks rose from −6 percent to 10 percent; real rates on working capital rose to 15–20 percent. These measures proved to be effective in stemming, and indeed reversing, the tendency toward capital flight that arose in 1982.[20]

• Comprehensive tax reform and simplification. Changes effected in 1983 were designed to broaden the non-oil tax base, increase its yield, and so compensate for an anticipated decline in oil taxes.

Although it is too early for a full assessment of these adjustment measures, they appear to have been successful. In 1982–83 the real effective exchange rate of 108.5 was near its previous level. But in 1984 it depreciated to 91.5 (see table 6-1), and growth, assisted by good harvests, recovered to 5 percent. Exports of manufactured goods expanded rapidly, and starting in 1979 exports of liquefied natural gas (LNG) began to be significant.

Even so, Indonesia did not escape all the adjustment costs associated with the slowdown of demand and the supply shocks of more costly energy and imported intermediates. Capacity use fell sharply in the cement and other investment goods sectors, and, although data are scant, the rate of urban unemployment appears to have increased.

Avoiding the Dutch Disease

Notwithstanding its large oil revenues, between 1972 and 1981 Indonesia was actually able to achieve a combined share of agriculture and manufacturing in its nonmining GDP that was larger than the norm for the evolution of this share with rising per capita income (see table 6-3). And this was done even though Indonesia began the decade with a "normal" sectoral distribution of economic activity, unlike Algeria and Venezuela, the other two countries that also raised their non-oil traded share.

Despite a low level of private capital formation during this period, the growth of manufacturing as a share of GDP in Indonesia outstripped "normal" growth by a considerable margin, possibly because of its continued low wages relative to other Southeast Asian countries. In contrast, agriculture lost ground quite rapidly. Its share of nonmining GDP fell by an average of 1.5 percent a year, not much less than the drop in the share of Nigerian agriculture of 1.9 percent a year. But Indonesia was a far poorer country than Nigeria, with more rapidly growing income per capita. In Indonesia, therefore, the shift of economic activity out of agriculture was relatively "normal." In Nigeria agriculture's share fell at three times the "normal" rate. It is Indonesia's unusual success in agriculture and rural development, particularly as measured by the standards typical for mineral exporters, that this section seeks to explain.

Agricultural Performance

During the two oil booms and through 1984, Indonesia's agricultural performance was on the whole impressive, especially for food crops. In particular, the output of rice grew an average of 5.7 percent a year in 1972–84, accelerating from 3.7 percent in 1972–77 to 7.2 percent in 1977–82. Table 12-5 gives the figures for rice output. Even though the output of other crops rose less dramatically, Indonesia's performance in increasing food output per capita far outpaced that of the other oil exporters as well as that of developing countries and of the world as a whole. Table 6-4 presents comparative data based on a set of uniform international price weights. By 1982–83 the index for Indonesia's food output per capita had reached 133 percent of its 1969–72 average; the corresponding ratio for the world was only 106 percent, and the unweighted average ratio for the rest of the sample was 91 percent.

Sectoral Policies

As noted above, improving the productivity of the rural economy in general and of rice cultivation in particular had been a major goal of the government since the mid-1960s. Much of its effort was directed at the most populated areas, Java and Bali. There, centuries of "agricultural involution" had resulted in tiny, highly fragmented landholdings that were cultivated with exceptionally labor-intensive techniques.[21]

In the early years of Suharto's rule, much was made of the need for Indonesia to become self-sufficient in rice. That the government was preoccupied with this goal is not surprising given the political impact of the price and availability of rice in Indonesia. Indeed, the price of rice was the focal point of anti-Sukarno sentiment in the street riots of 1965, and the availability of rice at a stable price has been the prime measure of the Suharto government's success in managing the economy. With the international market thin and volatile, increased domestic output seemed the only solution.

BIMAS AND INMAS. The cornerstone of the government's effort to raise rice production was a succession of programs known as BIMAS—an acronym for *bimbingan massal*, or mass guidance. This ap-

Table 12-5. Indonesia: Rice Output and Intensification

Year	Rice output (thousands of tons)	Average yield (tons per hectare)	Area harvested (thousands of hectares)	Area under intensification program (thousands of hectares)						Total fertilizer use (thousands of metric tons)	Ratio of rice price to fertilizer price
				BIMAS	Of which INSUS	INMAS	Of which INSUS	Total	Percentage of area covered		
1969	12,249	2.28	8,014	1,309	—	821	—	2,130	27	119.8	0.58
1970	13,140	2.41	8,135	1,248	—	845	—	2,093	26	192.4	0.66
1971	13,724	2.46	8,324	1,396	—	1,393	—	2,789	34	197.0	0.68
1972	13,183	2.46	7,987	1,203	—	1,966	—	3,169	40	244.4	0.79
1973	14,607	2.59	8,403	1,832	—	2,156	—	3,988	47	308.1	0.79
1974	15,276	2.64	8,509	2,676	—	1,048	—	3,724	44	379.2	0.76
1975	15,185	2.63	8,495	2,683	—	1,957	—	3,640	43	393.3	1.05
1976	15,845	2.78	8,368	2,424	—	1,189	—	3,613	43	422.6	0.98
1977	15,876	2.79	8,360	2,059	—	2,181	—	4,240	51	415.6	0.86
1978	17,525	2.89	8,929	1,960	—	2,888	—	4,848	54	556.8	1.01
1979	17,872	2.97	8,850	1,571	—	3,452	—	5,023	57	617.6	1.07
1980	20,163	3.29	9,005	1,374	420	4,142	640	5,516	61	698.7	1.21
1981	22,286	3.49	9,382	1,384	587	4,802	1,119	6,186	66	1012.2	1.50
1982	22,837	3.74	8,988	1,296	832	5,047	2,113	6,343	71	1240.6	1.71
1983	24,006	3.85	9,162	1,401	955	5,222	2,484	6,623	72	1364.7	1.93
1984	25,825	3.94	9,636	n.a.	n.a.	n.a.	n.a.	n.a.	n.a.	n.a.	n.a.

— Not applicable.
n.a. Not available.
Sources: Output, yield, and area from the Indonesia Bureau of Statistics Intensification Supplement to the President's Report to Participants, August 1984. Fertilizer use from Timmer (1985), table 1.

proach emerged more or less spontaneously in the early 1960s to spread the use of new high-yielding and pest-resistant varieties of rice and to intensify production. Five elements were essential to the BIMAS programs: improving water control, expanding the use of fertilizer, pesticides, and improved seeds, introducing better methods of cultivation and weed control, and strengthening village cooperatives (Mears and Moeljono 1981). The programs also granted credit on favorable terms.

BIMAS programs have undergone many changes in response to experience and circumstances since first being introduced, and they have expanded greatly. The early programs were marred by mistakes and entailed a high degree of coercion; the later ones were more successful.[22] In 1967 BIMAS was supplemented by INMAS—*intensifikasi massal*, or mass intensification—which provided credit for fertilizers, pesticides, and high-quality seeds to past participants in BIMAS. Another effort, introduced in 1968, relied heavily on European firms to supply chemical inputs on a very large scale. But the cost of these programs was higher than expected, and repayment by farmers worse than expected.

A revised program, *Bimas Nasional*, was launched in 1970; it relied more on the extension service, the national agricultural supply firm, the People's Bank, and the Logistics Board (Bulog).[23] Coercion was steadily reduced in favor of incentives, and village organization was emphasized as the way to increase local participation. Unfortunately, the expansion of the village units was much too rapid and many of them did a poor job. By 1970 more than half of the 3,800 units that had been established were reported to be insolvent (Arndt 1977a). Nevertheless, the effort to utilize local units remained a cornerstone of Indonesia's agricultural policy.

Despite their shortcomings, these programs laid the foundation for agricultural growth. At the start of the 1970s BIMAS and INMAS covered 30 percent of the harvested rice area. This proportion increased steadily until coverage reached 72 percent in 1983. Table 12-5 records the development and shows how yields have risen, especially since 1977. In that year new techniques and varieties began to defeat the *wereng* pest, which had been largely responsible for the slow growth in output during the mid-1970s.[24]

INSUS. In addition to the new wereng-resistant varieties, a coordinated planting program, called INSUS (*intesifikasi khusus*, or special intensification), was adopted. This program, initiated during the wet season of 1979–80, encourages farmers to schedule planting so that large areas of rice ripen at the same time. It had been observed that wereng damage was greater when the pest could feed on areas that ripened in succession.

PRICING OF RICE AND FERTILIZER. With the advent of Bimas Nasional in 1970 came acceptance of the principle that farmers' price incentives must be strong enough to induce them to adopt new technologies and to raise production. As Timmer (1975) has pointed out, concern with incentives to farmers was a turnabout from well-established tradition in Indonesian agricultural policy. Until the 1970s the main concern had been with the protection of the interests of consumers—and, in particular, with maintaining the real value of salaries of public servants and the military.[25]

A modest step in the direction of incentive pricing was undertaken in 1968 with the adoption of *Rumus Tani* (farmer's formula), which sought to maintain a 1:1 ratio between the price of a kilogram of rice and a kilogram of chemical fertilizer. The general instability and geographic variation of prices made it very difficult to implement this formula, however. In 1970 a policy of establishing floor and ceiling prices for rice was formally adopted. The Logistics Board, or Bulog, was to maintain a floor price that would guarantee reasonable returns to farmers in the BIMAS program. Bulog was also responsible for building a sufficient buffer stock from domestic purchases and imports to be able to prevent retail prices from rising above the farm price plus reasonable margins. The objective was to try to protect the interests of both producers and consumers by providing adequate incentives to sustain output growth while shielding consumers from price hikes in bad crop years. By reducing seasonal price variations, the policy was also expected to make rice production and trade less risky.

In the good crop years of 1970 and 1971, it was possible to meet the established price targets. But Bulog did not build up stocks large enough to meet the challenge of the next poor crop year, 1972. Rice prices doubled that year. As a result, a major program was undertaken to build storage facilities, and there was an intensified effort to diversify procurement geographically and stimulate more local participation.

By 1978 Bulog's storage capacity was sufficient to stock 1 million tons of rice in much improved facilities, with better geographical spread and rapidly improving transport—all of which contributed to Bulog's market leverage. By 1982 storage capacity had reached 2.5 million tons. These huge facilities were filled primarily by very large acquisitions of rice from international markets, both on commercial terms and through concessional food aid.[26] It was, of course, the oil bonanza that provided the foreign exchange for both the storage facilities and the stock buildup. And yet until the production spurt of 1978–81, it appeared that Indonesia's long-sought self-sufficiency in rice would remain a distant target despite quite creditable rates of growth.

One objective of the intensification programs was to encourage fertilizer use; Indonesia's huge gas reserves and investments in fertilizer plants were thus a key component of the strategy. Fertilizer use rose from 120,000 metric tons in 1969 to 1,364,700 metric tons in 1982; this represents an annual growth rate of 16 percent. The price of fertilizer was held well below the floor price of *gabah* (rough rice). Table 12-5 indicates that the relative price of fertilizer to rice was reduced to only 30 percent of its initial value from 1969 to 1983. During 1981–83 the fertilizer subsidy averaged 7.8 percent of domestically funded development expenditures, or about 1 percent of GDP.

The impact of the fertilizer subsidy on output has been assessed econometrically by Timmer (1985). He concludes that a substantial part of increased yield and output can be explained by the decrease in relative fertilizer prices. Moreover, the effect of low fertilizer prices is found to offset, by a large margin, the disincentive to production caused by holding the domestic gabah price at some 15 percent below its world level.[27] The implication of these findings is that the fertilizer subsidy has a high benefit-cost ratio, particularly if it does not result in Indonesia's becoming a net rice exporter.

Fertilizer pricing must be considered when assessing Bulog's rice pricing policy. Although at times Bulog has been criticized for attempting to suppress price increases to favor consumers, it is not apparent that Bulog has systematically depressed rice prices as opposed to trying to stabilize them. Given the goal of self-sufficiency and the thinness of the international rice market, a cheap food policy could not be sustained in the long term, at least not without offsetting input subsidies. Subsidizing fertilizer use while containing rice prices was an attempt to raise productivity in a key non-oil tradable sector while distributing some of the windfall gains to rice consumers and avoiding a greater dependence on imports.

The relative contribution of these measures remains uncertain. But it appears that the combination of the new planting patterns, the wereng-resistant varieties, improvement of infrastructure in the rural areas, sustained heavy investments in irrigation, continued subsidization of inputs (fertilizer in particular), price policy, and several years of good weather have combined to turn the rice situation around in a dramatic way.

Clark (1972) showed that virtually half the caloric intake of Indonesians came from food sources other than rice. So-called *palawija* crops (non-rice staples) were also promoted, but at a lower level, so that rice tonnage rose from 46 percent of total food crop production in 1971 to 51 percent by 1981. Yet palawija tonnage still outpaced population, growing at 2.8 percent a year.

INPRES. The rural public works programs—an important part of the strategy—also originated before the first oil shock. In 1973 INPRES absorbed 19.3 percent of domestically funded development spending. INPRES funded labor-intensive, productive investments at the county level, paying wages similar to those available in agriculture. Similar programs at the village level provided only materials, which were used by unpaid volunteer labor.[28] Although no accurate statistics are available, these programs appear to have created substantial employment. It is estimated that they generated a quarter of a million person-years of work in 1970 and about 1.5 million person-years in 1982—equivalent to 2.7 percent of the labor force. The programs also seem to have contributed positively to rural reconstruction and social developments; unlike public works programs in some other oil-exporting countries, they were not simply transfer programs. The largest of the sectoral INPRES programs was the building of primary schools. Between 1970 and 1978 the primary enrollment rate rose from 77 to 100 percent, closing the gap between Indonesia and the average middle-income country.

Growth of Non-Oil Exports

Indonesia turned in a strong non-oil export performance during the period of the oil booms as well as in the downturn after 1981. This performance, unusual for an oil exporter, indicates that between 1971 and 1981 non-oil exports grew across a wide front (see table 12-3). It also shows steady export diversification, with growth of "miscellaneous" (mainly manufactured) products at 16 percent during the boom periods and 28 percent during the slump.

Several factors, such as the reconstruction and improvement of channels of trade and transport, contributed to export growth, but macroeconomic policy played an important role too. Export growth was especially rapid in the aftermath of the two large devaluations of 1978 and 1983 (see table 12-3). In the year after the first devaluation, manufactured exports (39 six-digit categories of Brussels Tariff Nomenclature) rose by 260 percent, with many firms entering export markets for the first time. The increase in miscellaneous exports after the second devaluation was similarly dramatic.

During the 1970s agricultural and other primary exports benefited from buoyant markets. For this reason, the growth rate of the value of nonhydrocarbon exports, deflated by world manufacturers' prices, rose more than 11 percent, faster than most major non-oil export volumes. Rising world prices also compensated exporting sectors to some extent for exchange appreciation. But after 1981 commodity markets weakened, and the country experienced a deterioration in many non-oil as well as oil sectors, as shown in table 12-3. By this time manufactured exports were so large and responsive that they almost offset the decline in primary commodities. Thus they were a key component of adjustment to the world recession.

Another component in Indonesia's strategy of diversifying out of oil as a source of foreign exchange was to move into resource-based industrial (RBI) investments. The production of liquefied natural gas (LNG) began to make a positive contribution to the balance of payments and to fiscal revenues, especially after 1979; in 1983 it represented the equivalent of 23 percent of oil exports in net terms. Indonesia relied less heavily on RBI development than many other exporters, but investments in this area were still considerable. They included $4.3 billion in metal processing (steel and aluminum), $4.2 billion in refining, and $1 billion in methanol and ammonia plants.

As in other oil-exporting countries, the RBI program was to suffer from adverse world market trends and domestic markets too small to absorb full capacity output. The steel industry was protected through import restrictions; in the mid-1980s it was estimated to be selling at 30-40 percent above the cost of imported steel—a heavy burden for industrial users. Manufacturing in general was oriented toward the domestic market, frequently with high levels of protection, and this may have implications for the post-boom adjustment period. Yet Auty (1986a) considers the Indonesian RBI experience to have been less risky and more successful than that of most other oil producers. It was relatively diversified, better phased over time, and less central to the country's overall development strategy. The financing of Indonesian RBI projects was also more cautious than in other countries. For example, foreign equity in the Asahan aluminum smelter was 80 percent, compared with less than 20 percent in Venezuelan VENALUM plants. This paid off in terms of start-up and operating efficiency (Auty 1986a).

Indonesia's LNG projects were also cautiously financed, and they were protected to some extent from downturns in the world market by a combination of foreign equity and long-term contracts with Japan. Unlike Algeria's larger LNG industry, which was operating at only 40 percent of capacity in the mid-1980s, Indonesia's plants operated at full capacity. LNG exports rose from $162 million in 1977–78 to $2.40 billion by 1983–84, overtaking those of Algeria, which increased from $250 million to only $2.14 billion over the same period.

Distribution of Benefits

Wage trends and the distribution of income in Indonesia are controversial issues. Some scholars, usually those with a more microeconomic focus, have tended to the view that income inequality and perhaps absolute poverty as well have worsened during the windfall periods. Others, often those with a more aggregated perspective, have pointed to rapid per capita growth in all categories of consumption and to increasing off-farm rural employment opportunities and have argued that gains have been widely distributed. To delve extensively into such complex issues is beyond the scope of this study, but some tentative observations are offered.[29]

Indonesia's great abundance of labor in comparison with other oil exporters held both advantages and dangers. Insofar as higher spending of oil income can shift labor from extremely low-productivity to higher-productivity work or even increase the participation rate, it obviously has greater potential to stimulate growth than if the expansion of some (typically nontraded) sectors causes productive factors to move out of other (traded) sectors and so contracts their output. Unlike in Nigeria, for example, the increased demand for workers that arose from rapidly growing public programs could be met without seriously affecting the non-oil tradable sectors, in particular agriculture. There is some evidence that the Indonesian labor supply grew more rapidly in the 1970s than in the previous decade; the World Bank's (1980b) report on employment suggests that the growth rate of the labor force jumped from 1.5 percent in 1961–71 to 4.7 percent in 1971–76, although this has been disputed by other studies such as Jones (1981).

But labor demand for seasonal crops, which in 1975 provided the equivalent of 21.6 million full-time jobs out of a total of 46.3 million in the economy (Downey and Keuning 1983) was particularly susceptible to changes in production techniques and social arrangements.[30] When traditional methods are as labor-intensive as in Indonesia, any change is more likely than not to displace workers. Such changes might well be hastened by oil-funded modernization and commercialization.

Earlier research on agricultural wages in Java found no upward trend in real wages during most of the 1970s despite rising agricultural productivity.[31] Later years saw the introduction of wereng-resistant varieties of rice, the accelerated growth of rice output, and an increase in rural public spending. Some researchers, such as Collier and others (1982), began to report sizable increases in real agricultural wages and nonfarm rural employment. This trend was confirmed by a panel study of households in six villages in West Java between 1977 and 1983. The results suggest a 15 percent rise in the average real wage for hoeing, planting, and unskilled and skilled construction work in these villages (see table 6-2).

The panel study also indicates that an important source of increases in household income was the diversification of economic activity: households shifted from low-productivity cottage industries, such as the weaving of bamboo mats,[32] to higher-paying work in construction and transport. The study suggests further that the size distribution of rural income has remained roughly unchanged. In both 1976 and 1983 the poorest 40 percent received 14 percent of the total income, while the richest 20 percent received 53 percent in 1976 and 52 percent in 1983.

Other studies suggest a considerable increase in urban real wages during the windfall years.[33] As for income distribution, the situation may have been different in urban and rural areas. Certain studies (for example, Booth and Sundrum 1981) suggest a tendency for income differentials to widen, but data are far from adequate to paint a definitive picture.

Conclusion

It is sometimes suggested that Indonesia's success in managing its oil windfalls reflected the good health of its economy before 1973. But this is misleading. Other oil exporters that experienced a less favorable outcome after 1973 had also been in good economic shape before then; the non-oil growth of the sample countries in 1967–73, an unweighted average of 7.3 percent, was extremely high relative to other developing countries. A more accurate statement, therefore, might be that Indonesia's good performance during the oil booms reflected the *institutions* developed earlier to nurse the economy back to health, the *approach to policy* set in the Suharto government's formative years, and the *unusual degree of continuity*. All the main institutional components of the post-shock period—BIMAS, INPRES, the balanced budget policy, a free foreign exchange market—predated the oil shocks. So did the cautious approach to macroeconomic policy, which was reinforced by the Pertamina disaster, and the willingness to adjust the exchange rate.

These positive policy and institutional features combined with Indonesia's abundance of labor and non-oil resources as well as with technical changes in the food crop sector, which oil revenues helped to accelerate by financing the diffusion of improved techniques. Together, they resulted in a distinctive pattern of growth for the former Dutch colony. To a surprising extent, the poorest country in the sample has managed to avoid the most serious problems of the Dutch disease, and its economic performance stands out as being relatively successful.

Notes

1. The industry is described in Hunter (1971).

2. The conflict over Irian Jaya is the prime example. The Dutch continued to control this territory after 1949, and Sukarno resorted to diplomatic and military maneuvers to oust them. In 1963 Irian Jaya was finally transferred to Indonesia.

3. Of the five academics on the team, three were fairly recent Ph.D.'s from the University of California, Berkeley, who came to be called "the Berkeley Mafia." In due course, all five became cabinet members. Professor Widjojo Nitisastro, formerly dean of the FEUI and subsequently minister for economics as well as director of the Planning Commission, became— and remained in 1986—the leading figure in the nation's economic affairs.

4. Less successful were attempts to put the state enterprises on an unsubsidized basis (Glassburner 1984, p. 13).

5. The role of the government, as defined in the *Tracee Baru*, is not to control economic activity "to the greatest extent possible" but to lead the nongovernment sector and to mobilize and develop the potential of the people. The tone of the document strongly favors allowing the private sector to expand much more than was allowed under Sukarno. At the same time, the document declares that the country's resources are to be controlled for the benefit of all the people. "Free-flight liberalism" (a phrase always rendered in English) is viewed as giving rise to the exploitation of humanity. Thus, although the economic advisers clearly wanted to revive Indonesia's market system, they did not advocate anything close to laissez-faire.

6. Pitt and Lee (1981) found that technical inefficiency in the Indonesian weaving industry in the early 1970s was as high as 38 percent.

7. Hill (1980) analyzes the impact of policy on the choice of technology in the weaving industry. Finding a potentially wide range of choices, he concludes that policies such as subsidized interest rates may have been important in encouraging the use of capital-intensive methods.

8. The notable exception was self-sufficiency in rice; the actual growth in rice output was 4.5 percent a year for 1968–73, only half the targeted amount.

9. Tinker and Walker (1973) describe the Indonesian administrative system. The development of administrative capability at local levels strengthened the ability to implement and decentralize rural projects.

10. In the span of interests represented, GOLKAR resembled the PRI in Mexico. But there was no succession of presidents in Indonesia as there was in Mexico.

11. Even before the first oil shock, Pertamina had taken advantage of its position as a collector of oil taxes to build a conglomerate comprising several thousand filling stations, a fleet of tanks and trucks, several office buildings, a data processing center, a tourism complex, a fertilizer factory, an airline, and several rice plantations.

12. A similar situation in Venezuela led public enterprises to incur a heavy short-term debt burden; see chapter 15.

13. Total public investment is actually larger than development spending. Recently available information on public investment during 1974–83 (but not earlier) suggests that the public sector was responsible for the bulk of capital formation recorded in the Indonesian national accounts.

14. Arndt (1978) provides a good indication of expectations at this time.

15. Algeria did effect a switch in spending after 1978 by redirecting the public investment program toward sectors making more intensive use of domestic factors of production (chapter 10). Indonesia was to follow this strategy after the second oil shock, as described below.

16. With regard to the sectoral impact of exchange rate shifts, Warr's (1986) index of the Indonesian real exchange rate suggests a smaller shift in relative prices between traded and nontraded sectors than the movements in the real effective exchange rate would be expected to produce. This is mainly because of the failure of the so-called law of one price in the tradables sectors, where domestic prices fell below those abroad after the devaluation. This does not invalidate the resource allocation arguments for exchange rate adjustment, but it does suggest that the differential effect on relative prices will be felt more in specific trade-related activities than across broad sectors.

17. Net oil exports are gross exports less imports of goods and services attributed to the oil sector. This measure is conventionally used to express the contribution of the sector to foreign exchange earnings in Indonesia.

18. The budgetary cost of the oil subsidy was far less since it reflected mainly the explicit subsidization of refined imports from Singapore.

19. It was estimated that the capital cost per job of the more capital intensive investments would have been about $1 million.

20. With an open capital market the impact on private investment of such measures is probably less than that of controlling interest rates. The contrasting Venezuelan case (see chapter 15) suggests that interest rate ceilings may have further depressed investment by encouraging domestic savers to transfer funds abroad.

21. Geertz (1966) analyzes the process of agricultural involution, which involves progressive fragmentation of landholdings and the raising of land productivity through the intensive application of labor.

22. Heavy pressure to participate was widely acknowledged both before and after 1970; see Glassburner (1978b).

23. Originally a procurement agency for the military, Bulog was later prominent in the implementation of rice pricing policies, as discussed below.

24. The *wereng* is a hopper that carries a virus. It was controlled tolerably well in the 1960s and early 1970s by widespread use of insecticides, but

new breeds of the insect that could survive even heavy spraying evolved in the mid-1970s. Many areas of Java repeatedly suffered heavy crop losses.

25. Government employees' real incomes were hedged by partial payments in kind, that is, by a rice allocation.

26. Rice imports totaled 9.1 million tons in 1972–78 and 6.0 million tons in 1978–79 to 1983–84. Bulog's "end stock" for crop year 1983–84 was 1.3 million tons.

27. The relation between world and domestic rice prices is estimated by Timmer (1985) for 1982 only.

28. Note the contrast between these *Bantuan Desa* programs and the DEWD programs of Trinidad and Tobago (chapter 14). DEWD paid effective wages several times higher than those available in agriculture, even though agricultural workers were substantially unionized.

29. For some contrasting views on these issues, see Booth and Sundrum (1981), Palmer (1978), and World Bank (1980b).

30. It has been estimated that harvest labor was reduced 54 percent after a switch from the traditional *bawon* system to the *tebasan* system, which involves the sale of standing crops to middlemen not bound by local custom to employ other villagers (World Bank 1984).

31. These studies are discussed in World Bank (1984).

32. Hart and Sisler (1978) found such activities to pay even less than those associated with food crops.

33. Warr (1986) analyzes wage levels in seven branches of manufacturing during 1975–82. He finds two periods of rapid increase: 1975–77 and 1979–82. Overall, there is a clear upward trend.

Chapter 13

Nigeria: From Windfall Gains to Welfare Losses?

with Henry Bienen

Nigeria's oil revenues and its size—it is by far the most populous Sub-Saharan country—make it distinctive in Africa; at the same time, it shares many of the features common to African countries. Oil was discovered in Nigeria in 1956 and began to be exported in 1958. By the mid-1960s the economic and political significance of oil had become obvious, and in 1969 the state assumed a major role in the petroleum sector. By the early 1970s, with oil constituting more than half of Nigeria's commodity exports, the sectoral structure and trade patterns of the economy were beginning to show the effects of the oil income. But Nigeria was still far from being dependent on oil. Agriculture remained the dominant sector, accounting for some 40 percent of non-oil GDP and 42 percent of commodity exports, and employing roughly 70 percent of the work force.

This state of affairs, unfortunately, was to be short-lived. By the end of the decade, Nigeria was widely cited as suffering acutely from the "oil syndrome." Non-oil exports had collapsed, the relative size of the agricultural sector was declining sharply, and the real effective exchange rate was appreciating rapidly. The mineral sector's share of GDP went from about 1 percent in 1960 to more than 25 percent in the late 1970s. Petroleum exports rose to well over 90 percent of total exports in 1979, and they accounted for four-fifths of total government revenue.

This extraordinary rise in oil income not only provided the government with the financial resources to undertake new programs; it also permeated the very institutions that formulated policy and profoundly influenced the decisionmaking processes. By the mid-1980s Nigeria was the only one of the six countries in this study in which

Henry S. Bienen is James S. McDonnell Distinguished Professor and director of the Center of International Studies at Princeton University.

the overall standard of living had probably sunk *below* its pre-shock level. Whether the oil windfalls have conferred a lasting value on Nigerian society is, therefore, a particularly pertinent question.

This analysis of the impact of oil on Nigeria's economy stresses three themes. First, the specific uses to which oil income was put were conditioned by the country's distinctive social and political makeup. More so than in the other sample countries, the central government presided over a federation with strong ethnic and regional loyalties, which gave rise to great rivalry over the delivery of public services. Class and sectoral interests, in contrast, were relatively weak. The state was under intense pressure to deliver public services rapidly to large numbers of people. This pressure, which persisted through several discontinuous changes of government, was responsible for a heavy concentration of public investment in the nontraded sectors. That strategy, in turn, goes far to explain Nigeria's difficulty in accommodating to a weakening oil market after 1981.

Second, there was little pressure to use oil revenues to improve the productivity of traditional agriculture. In this respect Nigeria differed greatly from Indonesia, the other oil exporter with a large agricultural sector. In Indonesia agriculture prospered; in Nigeria it languished. Although technical factors were somewhat more favorable in Indonesia than in Nigeria, another important factor was the political and institutional differences between the two countries, which manifested themselves in different priorities and capabilities.

Third, Nigeria's macroeconomic adjustment to decelerating oil revenues differed considerably from that of most of the other exporters. Indonesia took decisive action to devalue its currency in 1978 and again after 1981, so it can be regarded as a speedy exchange rate adjuster. Ecuador, Venezuela, and Trinidad and Tobago were more reluctant adjusters, but each effected at least one large devaluation some time after 1981 as the foreign balance came under pressure. The role of the exchange rate is not apparent in Algeria's tightly controlled economy—and its inflation rate was, in any event, relatively low. In Nigeria the government made no effective move, as inflation soared, to realign the real effective exchange rate by adjusting the nominal rate. Instead, it turned more and more to various types of quantitative import restrictions. In effect, this strategy redistributed part of the oil revenue from the government to favored importers and to certain other agents and activities, and so severely aggravated the fiscal problem caused by falling oil revenues. Nigeria's prices moved more and more out of line with those of its trading partners. The result was a vicious cycle of rising distortions, declining efficiency, falling non-oil output, fiscal deficits, inflation, and disruptive cuts in public spending. Of all the countries in the sample, Nigeria experienced the most severe economic contraction after 1981.

This chapter investigates how political and institutional factors in Nigeria shaped decisions about using the oil revenues, and how these decisions affected the non-oil economy. The first section lays out the economic and political background of the pre-shock period. The second summarizes the three persistent concerns of the Nigerian leadership both before and after the first oil price rise: growth and modernization, indigenization, and income distribution. The third section discusses the time profile and the composition of public spending after 1973 and the disastrous interaction of fiscal, trade, and exchange policies. Then the impact of the spending on the non-oil economy is assessed. In an attempt to account for the policies pursued, the pressures on the government and on the administrative structure of the country are analyzed. Conclusions are drawn in the final section.

Nigeria before the Oil Boom

In the five years before the first oil boom, Nigeria's economy grew rapidly as it recovered from two military coups in 1966 and a destructive civil war in 1967–70, the causes of which were not unrelated to oil. Recovery was helped by rising oil income. In 1967–72 nonmining GDP grew at 9.2 percent, well above the population growth rate of about 2.6 percent.

Economic Background

Despite its oil, Nigeria in the early 1970s was still a poor country with an economy resembling those of many other African nations. It was heavily dependent on agriculture as a source of food, employment, investable surplus, and exports. In 1960, 71 percent of the labor force was engaged in agriculture, and this share seems to have fallen only slightly by 1970. Production was mostly rainfed and dominated by smallholders using simple techniques, unimproved varieties, and few modern inputs. Although arable land far exceeded cultivated land, extensive farming practices required that large areas lie fallow to regenerate soil fertility. It is unclear to what extent the land frontier could have been pushed back without adopting improved techniques or risking long-term ecological damage.

A high correlation has long existed in Nigeria between ethnic community and export crop: cocoa is overwhelmingly grown by Yoruba in the west, groundnuts by Hausa in the north, palm products by

Table 13-1. Nigeria: Export-Crop Producers' Potential Earnings Withheld by Marketing Board, 1947–62

Crop	Crop years	Total withholdings (millions of £)	Percentage of potential earnings
Cocoa	1947–48 to 1953–54	61.8	39.4
	1954–55 to 1961–62	53.9	26.1
	1947–48 to 1961–62	115.7	31.9
Groundnuts	1947–48 to 1953–54	39.5	40.0
	1954–55 to 1960–61	22.3	14.9
	1947–48 to 1960–61	61.9	24.9
Palm kernels	1947–54	37.0	29.2
	1955–61	31.3	27.1
	1947–61	68.3	28.1
Palm oil	1947–54	13.9	17.0
	1955–61	18.5	25.6
	1947–61	32.4	21.0
Cotton	1949–50 to 1953–54	9.7	42.3
	1954–55 to 1960–61	4.8	11.2
	1949–50 to 1960–61	14.5	22.1

Note: The mechanisms for withholding potential earnings include trading surpluses, export duties, and produce sales tax.
Source: Helleiner (1966) as cited in Bienen (1985), table 15.

Ibo in the east. This division along ethnic and regional lines—as well as geographic dispersion, repression, and a lack of resources—made it difficult for Nigeria's farmers to form cohesive producer organizations.[1] As a result, small farmers were poorly organized compared with industrial, bureaucratic, and military personnel. It is no surprise, therefore, that urban groups exerted more political pressure on policymakers than did rural groups.

The trade regime had long discriminated against agriculture. From the late 1940s until the 1960s, producers of agricultural exports were subject to heavy and discriminatory taxation through a marketing board system, introduced by the colonial government, that withheld on average about one-fourth of potential earnings. Table 13-1 tells the story. For some, notably cocoa producers, this taxation was a shift from the practice of the early and middle years of the colonial occupation, when they had retained most of their earnings. For others, it was a continuation of previous policies of colonial and local administrators. Although one intention of the marketing boards had been to stabilize producers' earnings, an important goal was to create capital assets that could be used to foster development. Indeed, the large reserves that accumulated were the direct or indirect source of about 95 percent of the funds made available to development boards and corporations in 1946–62 (Rimmer 1981).[2]

As the country moved first toward regional self-rule in the 1950s and then to independence in 1960, the marketing boards and their associated institutions became more and more politicized. Rural interests suffered doubly. Producers, besides being heavily taxed, received below-market prices for their crops and were sometimes cheated by the licensed buying agents. Yet little of the revenue thus generated was plowed back into efforts to increase agricultural productivity. Instead, the funds were channeled to development corporations, whose activities were centered on the cities, and to other urban clients of political leaders (Bienen 1985, pp. 18, 20). This flow of surplus from rural to urban areas effected by the marketing boards increased after independence and continued into the early 1970s.

Although the pattern varied somewhat among regions,[3] the net result of this policy was a relative neglect of agriculture, especially of smallholder production. Despite this, between 1960 and 1967 export crops grew in volume at an annual compound rate of 4–6 percent (Watts 1983, p. 469), while staple food production kept pace with population growth and food imports grew only moderately. As a result, little concern was voiced at the time either about food self-sufficiency or about the traditional export sector (Bienen 1985, p. 29).

It was to manufacturing rather than to agriculture that politicians and planners looked for economic autonomy in the early 1960s. These first years of independence mark the beginning of a shift in the structure of manufacturing from processing traditional primary products for export to processing imported materials for the domestic market. Import-substituting industries grew in part because of the greater protection accorded the domestic market. Protective measures included both quantitative restrictions and tariffs. Import duties represented almost 40 percent of all revenue collected by the federal government in 1969–70, or 32 percent of import value. Because domestic industrial activities with low value added were favored, effective protection rates were doubtless high in many cases, with wide sectoral variation.

The impact of government spending on the economy was quite small until oil became important. In 1965–66, for example, total revenue collected by the federal and state governments amounted to only 12.0 percent of GDP, and their combined capital spending was only 5.5 percent of GDP. Almost half of this amount was allocated to economic services (with 12 percent of this category going to agriculture). Only 14.7 percent of total capital spending, or 0.8 percent of GDP, was allocated to social and community services. Education, in particular, suffered—a situation made worse by the civil war. Primary enrollment rates remained at a virtual standstill: 36 percent in 1960 and 37 percent in 1970 (in contrast to norms of 80 percent for low-income and 88 percent for middle-income economies). And the secondary enrollment rate in 1970 was a tiny 4 percent compared with 25 percent in middle-income countries (table 7-3).

The fiscal situation began to change in the late 1960s as more and more oil was produced. Oil taxes collected by the government rose from 2.8 percent of nonmining GDP in 1970 to 8.5 percent in 1972. This permitted a rise in both current and capital spending as well as a slight fiscal surplus. Then, with the huge and unanticipated surge in oil revenues in 1974, federal government outlays skyrocketed in an unprecedented manner.

Political Background

As a part of its colonial legacy, Nigeria—like many other African countries—found itself with a set of institutions that allowed a high degree of regional autonomy. Indeed, the political history of Nigeria from 1960 until the present can be viewed as a continuous struggle between regional autonomy and central control.

In the 1950s, under a constitution granting wide powers to the three regions of the country—Northern, Eastern, and Western— elections were held for regional parliaments as well as for the Federal House of Representatives.[4] A single party came to dominate each region. Ibo, Hausa-Fulani, and Yoruba leaders ruled in the east, north, and west, respectively, although only the Western Region was ethnically homogeneous. Indeed, about half of Nigeria's population was neither Hausa-Fulani, Ibo, nor Yoruba. Even after independence, political power and economic strategies continued to be defined in regional and ethnic rather than class terms. This ethnic-regional competition led to a continuous search for a constitutional formula to hold together the Nigerian Federation, and to an ongoing battle over the regional allocation of public revenue, most of which derived from the sale of export crops.

In none of the dominating parties were farming interests well represented. Nor was there any active commitment—even among populist parties and leaders—to increasing equity. Pressures from poor farmers were blunted by ethnic cleavages and by the widespread desire to leave the agricultural sector, while pressures from the urban elites grew sharper. Not surprisingly, then, Nigeria's rulers had little inclination to invest in agriculture. Both their views on development and their political priorities led them to look elsewhere.

CIVIL WAR. By 1965 ethnic tensions in the country had intensified greatly. Electoral politics broke down because of ethnic-regional conflicts over appointments to civil service and military positions; over investment in infrastructure, plants, and social services in different parts of the country; over how revenue was allocated by the federal government to the regions; and over the interjection of northern power into the Western Region. Violence increased, and peaceful elections could not be carried out everywhere.[5]

Nigeria's civilian government was toppled by a military coup in January 1966. A second coup followed six months later. During the period between the two coups, ethnic violence broke out against Ibos in northern and western cities. When negotiations with the country's military leaders collapsed, the Ibo area constituted itself as the Republic of Biafra and tried to secede. After a devastating civil war, during which an estimated 2 million people died of famine, disease, and battle wounds, Biafra surrendered in January 1970.

Oil had played a role in precipitating the civil war. Before 1960 the governments of the Northern and Western regions had favored applying the principle of derivation to the allocation of federal revenue—arguing, in effect, that revenue collected by the federal government should be allocated to the regions in accordance with how much revenue each region had generated. At that time, groundnuts and cocoa, which were grown in the Northern and Western regions, were the main sources of export revenue. But when petroleum was found in the Eastern Region and in the delta areas of what became the Midwestern Region, the Northern and Western regions reversed their former position, while the Eastern Region became the new champion of the principle of derivation.[6]

Although the changes in revenue allocation that became effective in 1966 returned a larger share of revenue to the regions than before, they worked to the disadvantage of the Eastern Region. A relatively poor part of the country, it hoped that secession would make it financially secure. But Biafra lost control of its ports and oil facilities early in the war and was deprived of funds, blockaded, and eventually starved into submission.

OIL, WAR, AND CENTRALIZATION. Early in the civil war the military government replaced the four regions with twelve states. The purpose was to gain the support of minorities living in northern and southeastern Nigeria, who wanted to be free from the domination of large ethnic groups. Yet this step also set the stage for centralizing the government since it diluted regional power.

Rising oil revenues likewise contributed to this centralizing trend. The output of oil declined in 1967 and 1968 because of the civil war, but by 1969 it exceeded the 1966 figure of 152.4 million barrels a year, reaching 197.2 barrels in 1969 and 750.4 million barrels in 1973. The surge in revenues, which would increase far more dramatically in 1974, meant that as the power of the central government grew it had an easy way to keep the federal coffers filled.

The civil war itself hastened centralization. The military had become extremely conscious during the war of Nigeria's fragility and its vulnerability to outside powers. This stood in stark contrast to the prevalent mood in the late 1950s, when Nigeria's leaders fully expected their country to become the "giant of Africa" by virtue of its size and potential wealth. The sense of vulnerability in the late 1960s was heightened by the fact that Nigeria's oil was being developed by foreigners. Concerned about sovereignty as well as national security, the military officers were committed to a strong central government. In this they were joined by civil servants, many of whom came from minority ethnic communities and had risen in influence when Ibos fled to Biafra.

By the time Biafra was defeated, the Nigerian army had expanded from a small force of around 10,000 in 1966 to more than 200,000 in 1970. The ethnic composition of the army had altered too: Yoruba soldiers increased from relatively few to about 20 percent, whereas Ibo technical officers were gone. A significant number of high-level officers, including General Yakubu Gowon, the military head of state, came from smaller ethnic groups in the Middle Belt between the north and south. Although military spending declined somewhat from its wartime peak, this large army was to be an important claimant for resources, and its leaders were to make critical decisions about the use of the new oil revenues.

Policy Goals since Independence

Nigeria has been one of the most politically violent countries in Africa. The First Republic came to an end in 1966. Between that year and 1979 the country was led by four military leaders. General A. Ironsi inherited command after the first coup of 1966, but was assassinated in July 1966. General Y. Gowon served as head of state until July 1975, when he was replaced by General Murtala Mohammed. When General Mohammed was assassinated in an abortive coup in February 1976, his second in command, General O. Obasanjo, succeeded him. He remained in power until a new civilian regime, headed by an elected president, Shehu Shagari, took office in late 1979. But the Second Republic lasted only four years. Shagari was ousted by a coup in December 1983. And yet another military regime took over in August 1985.

Despite these frequent changes in government, certain broad economic and political concerns have persisted from before the first oil price increase until the end of the second boom. The country's leaders have, of course, embraced many different objectives at various times, but three goals stand out as consistently important:

* To grow and modernize
* To indigenize the economy, in both the oil and non-oil sectors
* To improve income distribution. But in Nigeria's case this goal must be interpreted as distribution among ethnic groups and regions rather than among socioeconomic classes or occupations.

In the late 1970s the military government committed itself to two more concrete goals which were to have a considerable fiscal impact. The first was to establish a steel industry, which can be seen as a specific manifestation of the drive for modernization and industrial self-reliance. To appease regional rivalries, steel-producing capacity was divided among several locations. The second objective, which again related to the regional factor, was to build a new capital at Abuja. This was nearer to the center of the country than Lagos, away from the coast and the domination of Yorubaland, and closer to the politically powerful north.

Growth

The first major statement on economic policy by a Nigerian military regime was made just before the second coup of July 1966. In June of that year *Guidelines for the Second National Development Plan* was published. The main objectives set forth were a high overall rate of economic growth, rapid industrialization, increased production of food for domestic consumption without relaxing efforts in the export sector, and a drastic reduction in unemployment. The *Guidelines* made clear that growth was the priority, should the objectives prove inconsistent. This emphasis on growth as the prime goal was to continue through the 1970s.

The Second National Development Plan for 1970–74, having been delayed by the civil war, was prepared in a context of economic optimism. The plan called for avoiding uncertainty and instability, for building national unity, and for exploiting the economic base provided by oil. The goals articulated included "a just and egalitarian society" and "a land of bright and full opportunities for all citizens"— but the real priority was ambitious economic growth. Nationalism was also stressed, although in practice there were many compromises with foreign interests in this period.

When the Third National Development Plan for 1975–80 was prepared, the spirit at the top of the Nigerian government was expansive. The Gowon regime felt that it had the resources both to increase welfare and to lay the groundwork for a modern and powerful Nigeria. The third plan noted that oil was a wasting asset and that the productive capacity of the non-oil economy had to be developed. At the same time, a more even distribution of income and control of inflation were high priorities. It is not clear from the plan document whether growth was intended to take precedence over all other objectives.

By the time the fourth plan began, in January 1981, concern over the wasting of the smallholder agricultural sector had mounted. This sector was therefore singled out as vital for growth.

Indigenization

Perhaps the most striking goal of the Nigerian military regimes of the early and mid-1970s was the indigenization of the economy. Heated debate took place both within and outside government about the meaning of such a policy and how it was to be carried out.

The indigenization decrees put forward by the Gowon and Obasanjo regimes in 1972 and 1977 reflected pressures that predated the first military coup and even Nigeria's independence.[7] Nigerians had long been conscious of the role of foreigners in their economy. The Tax Relief Act of 1958 required transnational corporations seeking "pioneer" status to increase Nigerian ownership and personnel and to use Nigerian materials. And immigration laws established quotas for expatriates to increase the opportunities for Nigerians to participate in management.

In the petroleum sector specifically, Nigeria's actions paralleled those of Venezuela and the Arab oil exporters. In 1959, through the Petroleum Profits Tax Ordinance, the government instituted a fifty-fifty profit-sharing arrangement with foreign concerns. In 1966 it reduced by one-half the rate at which companies were allowed to depreciate capitalized investment. In 1967 it applied OPEC terms in Nigeria. In 1969 a Petroleum Decree established the state's option to own shares in commercial oil operations. In 1971 the Nigerian National Oil Company (NNOC) was created, and between 1972 and 1975, in accordance with other indigenization measures, the state increased its share of ownership and altered the terms of compensation and buy-back arrangements in its favor.[8] NNOC's participation in foreign companies up to 1974 is estimated to have cost Nigeria $1.3 billion, but receipts to the government from NNOC's shares, along with revenues from royalties, were more than ten times that amount (von Lazar and Duerstein 1976, p. 11). In terms of direct revenue use, indigenization was not costly.[9]

Both the first and second plans stressed increased national control over the economy. But it was the Nigerian Enterprise Promotion Decree of 1972 that set out the broad objectives and the means to increase that control. During the late 1960s and early 1970s, the nations' planners were committed to acquiring and controlling productive assets, especially strategic national resources. This was to be done by the government acting either alone or in partnership with private concerns. Although the planners, along with others, were well aware of the inefficiency and corruption of Nigerian statutory corporations and state-owned companies, they nevertheless pushed for control of the oil and other mining sectors.

From the viewpoint of military and civilian policymakers as well, indigenization meant increasing Nigeria's control over its own resources. Since it was also seen as a way to expand public involvement, the intention was not merely to hand over foreign-owned equity to the private sector. Yet policymakers were not completely unresponsive to pressures from Nigerian businessmen either (Hoogvelt 1979; Biersteker 1980). Moreover, although some military officers and civil servants wanted to move ahead and nationalize large sectors of the economy, most of them—including those in the highest positions—were committed to maintaining the private sector as an important actor. Businessmen, for their part, were much more interested in participation and in windfall profits than in control over foreign enterprises.

As for indigenization in the rural sector, the colonial companies had pulled out of agricultural production and trade in the 1950s and 1960s. In the 1970s some Nigerian businessmen did push into agriculture, but not at all to the extent that they moved into services and manufacturing. Thus the indigenization programs did not stem the decline of the agricultural export sector.

Overall, indigenization has proceeded rather slowly in Nigeria, and the government has adjusted its programs from time to time. Recognizing the country's acute shortage of indigenous technical and managerial skills, those in both the public and private sectors have acted cautiously so as not to jeopardize the prime goal of economic growth.

Distribution

In Nigeria formulas for allocating revenues between the federal and state governments have an influence on public spending patterns and their distributional effects. This is because various states as well as the federal government have different responsibilities and priorities, which often reflect their different constituencies. Under the Nigerian federal system, some responsibilities are vested in the central government only, some in the states only, and some in both. Even before the constitutional changes made at the end of 1979, the relationship of the states to the federal government had been shifting. Specifically, as the states' power to raise revenue through marketing boards, taxation, and other means was reduced, the funds allocated to them by the federal government became an ever larger share of their spending. This centralizing trend has been reinforced by oil.

Almost all observers of Nigeria agree that interregional income differences have been politically more important than interpersonal ones, and that income differences per se have been less of a problem than the more visible uneven distribution of schools, roads, health services, and the like. In fact, regional disparities in per capita income have been less than most other regional disparities that have been measured.

Although the Second National Development Plan increased the emphasis on the welfare of the common man and on a more equitable distribution of income, no direct assault was launched on the size distribution of income or on sectoral or rural-urban differences. Indeed, such an assault would have been difficult to mount given the conditions of Nigerian economic and political life. There was no landed aristocracy with lands that could be expropriated, and the government, as noted above, was unwilling to risk a sharp decline in growth by taking over private businesses. Nigeria's leaders and planners in the 1970s therefore preferred to guide investment through the use of incentives, to create more entrepreneurial know-how, and to rely on indigenization to expand opportunities. The private sector, for its part, was expected to develop better habits of saving and thereby raise economic levels in the country (Onage 1975, p. 61).

At the same time, through public sector programs—including electrification, water supply, health services, cooperatives, community development in the rural areas, and housing in the urban areas— the government would seek to raise the standard of living of the poor. Universal free primary education was regarded as the main hope for bringing about equal opportunities because of the widely perceived link between education and access to the modern economy.

There is no doubt that equity became a more salient issue. General Mohammed came to power in 1975, but the Third National Development Plan, launched in April 1975, carried on the distributional strategy of the second plan. Again, no direct assault on inequity was proposed. Oil revenues were to be used to create an infrastructure for self-sustaining growth and to expand greatly the delivery of welfare benefits. True, the third plan emphasized not only an increase in income but a more even distribution, largely to be effected by delivery of public services. Yet the *Guidelines to the Third Plan*, published in September 1973, had argued that basic amenities should not be provided to communities of less than 20,000. This policy is not easy to reconcile with the desire to use social services and public utilities to relieve poverty. There could be no rapid and frontal assault on the size distribution of income or on rural-urban imbalances with such a criterion for service delivery.

Use of the Oil Windfalls, 1974–84

The price that Nigeria received for its oil increased steadily between 1971 and 1973; in nominal dollar terms the rise was about 22 percent. Then, in nine months from late 1973 to mid-1974, the government's oil revenues almost quintupled because of much higher prices, greater production, and an increase in its share of the oil revenues through greater public ownership and higher taxes and royalties. Thus the Nigerian government found itself in mid-1974 with much more revenue than it had anticipated. Its budget surplus for

Table 13-2. Nigeria: Federal Budget, 1970–84
(percentage of nonmining GDP)

Item[a]	1970	1971	1972	1973	1974	1975	1976	1977	1978	1979	1980	1981	1982[d]	1983[d]	1984[d]
Total revenue	10.7	16.0	16.2	24.0	40.6	34.3	33.9	33.0	24.9	42.2	47.2	37.2	29.7	25.7	28.2
Non-oil revenue	7.9	8.2	7.7	7.5	7.7	7.2	7.5	8.6	8.1	7.7	8.7	8.7	7.0	7.0	5.4
Current expenditure[b]	8.5	8.6	9.6	10.9	11.6	15.9	13.2	14.7	13.3	18.1	21.1	21.1	42.7	39.6	37.0
Capital expenditure[b]	3.6	4.9	5.7	7.5	17.8	27.5	29.5	28.0	20.3	26.7	26.5	29.6			
Balance[c]	−1.5	2.6	0.8	5.6	11.1	−9.1	−8.9	−9.7	−8.8	−2.6	−0.5	−13.5	−13.0	−13.9	−8.8
Claims on government by the banking system	n.a.	n.a.	n.a.	n.a.	−13.5	n.a.	2.7	n.a.	12.3	n.a.	11.0	18.0	23.4	34.2	n.a.
Loss of real income due to exchange appreciation	n.a.	n.a.	n.a.	n.a.	n.a.	3.3	5.0	3.5	4.6	7.2	10.1	5.2	3.9	3.9	8.8

n.a. Not available.

Note: To compute these estimates, the cumulative surplus of 1973–74 was equally distributed over spending out of oil income in 1975–78. For 1979–82 more detailed estimates of the domestic deficit (the excess of spending on domestic goods over domestic revenues) are available. This present method yields a slightly lower estimate of the domestic deficit; the estimates of real income losses due to real effective appreciation are correspondingly more conservative.

a. Includes all federally collected revenues.

b. Apportions statutory and nonstatutory transfers to states to current and capital expenditure according to the limited data available.

c. Federal government only.

d. Provisional.

Source: World Bank data.

1974–75 was very large, and the balance of payments surplus shot up about twenty times from the relatively small sum of 153 million naira in 1973. Nigeria's leaders suddenly found themselves with vast new resources that could be used to accomplish their economic, political, and social objectives.

The Expenditure Response

When oil prices surged the Nigerian government had just published the *Guidelines to the Third Plan*, which put forward a relatively expansionary scenario for public spending. The response of the government to the unexpected windfall, and to the expectations of further increases in oil income, is shown in table 13-2. This table includes all federally collected revenues, an increasing share of which was transferred to the states after 1974. The transferred funds have been apportioned to recurrent and investment spending based on the limited information available on the states' spending patterns.

After an initial lag in 1973 and 1974, when large surpluses were accumulated abroad, public capital spending accelerated rapidly from only 3.6 percent of nonmining GDP in 1970 to 29.5 percent by 1976. This acceleration was so strong that it alone absorbed *more* than the entire increase in oil income between 1970 and 1976. The excess, together with a considerable rise in current spending, resulted in a substantial deficit that was financed by drawing down reserves accumulated in 1973 and 1974 and by expanding the money supply.

WAGE INCREASES. Current spending rose sharply in 1975, largely because the Gowon government moved to implement the recommendations of the Public Service Review Commission, better known as the Udoji Commission. In response to intense pressure from public employees, the average pay for civil servants was doubled (retroactively to April 1974), with rises of up to 130 percent for employees in the lower grades. Other organized workers clamored to keep up, and this fueled inflation. It has been estimated that the Udoji wage accords increased the public sector wage bill by 50–60 percent.

Commentators have interpreted the Udoji accords as an attempt by General Gowon to stay in power (despite an earlier promise to withdraw in 1975) by giving a pivotal sector of the population a sizable share of the oil wealth (Oyediran and Ajibola 1976; Joseph 1978). For just as the Udoji awards were announced, General Gowon also stated that the country was not ready to return to civilian rule.[10]

In addition to wanting to build support among its immediate constituency—officials in the civilian public sector and the military—

the government was in a hurry to use its oil revenues. It wanted to avoid being accused of not spending when Nigeria was so poor. Increasing wages was one way to spend money rapidly. Investing heavily in education, transportation, and construction was another. Officials involved in formulating plans for the public sector have related how orders came down to multiply spending on education and transportation. By 1975–76 new programs were under way, and expenditures increased sixfold over the level of only three years before (Schatz 1981). Not surprisingly, committing funds hastily to new domestic investment led to waste and corruption.

As inflation accelerated after 1974 (raising domestic costs relative to oil prices) and the oil market weakened, the ratio of total revenue to nonmining GDP fell from 41 to 25 percent. Although spending pressures were moderated somewhat, the budget swung from a surplus of 11 percent of nonmining GDP in 1974 to a deficit of 9 percent in 1975–78.

THE DOWNTURN. The second oil price rise, despite its considerable effect, was not sufficient to bring the budget back into surplus even in the peak year of 1980. Expecting a quick reversal of the deteriorating oil market, the government failed to adjust adequately to falling revenues, although it cut many programs sharply. The result was the emergence of large fiscal deficits, which averaged 12.3 percent of nonmining GDP in 1981–84 and generated further inflationary pressure.

As shown in tables 5-7 and 5-8, Nigeria's foreign borrowing prior to 1981 had been relatively cautious compared with that of the other sample countries. At the end of 1980, gross external debt was only $9.0 billion (of which $3.5 billion was short-term) while reserves were $10.6 billion. But cumulative current account deficits of $17.2 billion in 1981–83 were mirrored in a rise in debt to $19.7 billion (including trade arrears of about $5 billion) and a fall in reserves to $1.3 billion. The result was a sharp deterioration of Nigeria's credibility on international capital markets. Discussions with the IMF for an Extended Fund Facility and with the World Bank for a structural adjustment loan stalled over issues of devaluation, trade liberalization, and domestic energy pricing.[11]

Patterns of Public Spending

It is not possible to present a comprehensive picture of the composition of Nigerian public spending funded by oil revenues because information is lacking on the expenditure patterns of the states. Statutory and nonstatutory allocations to the states represented about one-fourth of all federal outlays after the first oil shock.[12] Although the states employ about twice as many civil servants as the federal government, state administration is often very weak. Detailed data are scarce, but there is good reason to suspect that while the states have been at least as responsive to popular wishes as the federal government in their spending patterns, they have been less financially responsible in their overall budget and revenue processes. A reasonably good indication of the use of oil revenues, however, is provided by the available information on capital spending by the federal government (see table 13-3). For a comparison with the other countries in this study, see table 7-1.

More than in the other five countries studied, public investment in Nigeria emphasized the nontraded sectors—even though the share of general services (including defense) fell after 1976. Table 13-3 indicates a large rise in the allocation to transport and communications. Much of this went into a program of constructing trunk roads. Since rural feeder roads were neglected, however, only farmers in the most densely populated areas were within even five miles of a road that could accommodate motor vehicles by 1979. Access costs thus remained very high. This policy, like the one of providing amenities only to large communities, suggests the extent to which public spending on infrastructure was directed to the urban rather than the rural population. The contrast to Indonesia is notable.

Capital spending on education also increased sharply, from 3.9 percent of the total in 1973–74 to 18.2 percent in 1975–76. The massive universal primary education system was launched in 1975–77. It was estimated that the program would cost the government 17 million naira by 1982, but by 1978 it was already costing four times that amount. The demand was far larger than projected; primary enrollment shot up from 3.5 million in 1970 to 9.5 million in 1976 and to 13 million by 1980. The drop in federal allocations to education after 1975–76 in table 13-3 is misleading. As a result of constitutional changes, authority for primary education was shifted from federal to local government. Nonstatutory transfers to states (997 million naira by 1979, or 3 percent of non-oil GDP) went mainly to fund educational programs. Accelerated investment in building roads as well as schools caused an exceptional boom in the construction sector.

In the non-oil tradable sectors—manufacturing and agriculture—it is obvious from table 13-3 how investment was concentrated in manufacturing. The share of industrial investment (mostly in heavy manufacturing) rose especially rapidly after the decision to build up a steel industry in the late 1970s. Agriculture's share, quite minor be-

Table 13-3. Nigeria: Capital Expenditures of the Federal Government, 1973–80
(percentage of total)

Sector	1973–74	1974–75	1975–76	1976–77	1977–78	1978–79	1979–80
General services	26.0	16.6	26.3	19.9	19.0	17.8	17.4
Defense	11.9	10.4	9.4	8.5	9.5	11.3	10.1
Other	14.1	6.2	16.9	11.4	9.5	6.5	7.2
Community services	1.3	13.2	5.4	9.5	9.5	10.0	5.2
Housing	1.3	10.5	4.0	4.9	3.4	2.8	1.1
Water resources	. . .	2.6	0.7	4.2	4.6	3.9	3.1
Other	. . .	0.1	0.7	0.4	1.5	3.3	1.0
Social services	5.2	10.4	19.2	11.6	5.9	5.6	10.2
Education	3.9	9.7	18.2	10.6	5.0	4.8	8.2
Health	1.3	0.7	1.0	1.0	0.9	0.8	2.0
Economic services	36.0	36.3	37.6	50.1	58.4	56.2	56.6
Agriculture	5.3	5.6	4.2	1.7	2.4	2.1	3.2
Power	2.7	5.0	2.7	3.0	3.5	11.6	8.8
Manufacturing, mining, and quarrying	8.0	7.2	7.8	11.6	23.9	16.8	20.1
Transportation and communication	20.0	18.5	22.9	33.8	28.6	25.7	24.4
Transfers and loans on-lent to states	31.5	23.4	11.6	8.9	7.2	10.4	10.0

. . . Negligible.
Sources: Nigerian Federal Ministry of Finance and World Bank data.

244

fore the oil price rise, declined further, so that in 1975–78 the sector received only 2.6 percent of total federal capital outlays. Agriculture had been budgeted for 6.5 percent of capital spending in the third plan (1975–79), about the same level as in the second plan (1970–74). But severe problems in administering and coordinating institutions and programs limited disbursements.

The military rulers' preference was to centralize control over agriculture. In 1973 the power to set producer prices was transferred from the marketing boards, which had long been criticized for their negative effect on agricultural production, to the federal government by creating a national board for each commodity. Also in 1973 export duties and state producer sales taxes were replaced by a 10 percent federal tax, which itself was abolished the following year. The declared purpose of these reforms was to benefit producers, but an equally strong motive may well have been the desire of military leaders and civil servants to centralize their power (see Rimmer 1981).

All through the 1970s government policies affecting agriculture were contradictory. But there was consistency in that the strategy for improving production relied primarily on the public sector (Olayide 1980, pp. 159–70). Instead of funds going to existing smallholder activities or extension services, they were used largely to promote the growth of large-scale, mechanized, parastatal farms for food production. The government intervened heavily in such agribusinesses, and capital allocations to government food companies (the National Livestock Production Company, the National Grains Production Company, and the National Rootcrop Production Company) increased sharply during 1975–79. But success stories were few.[13]

In 1976 the government took over fertilizer distribution from the states and placed it in the hands of the newly created Ministry of Agriculture. Fertilizer imports by individual states had been growing rapidly since the early 1970s. The programs, politically popular with bureaucrats, provided an important vehicle for getting money into agriculture by subsidizing inputs (Idachaba 1982). Increasing the use of fertilizer became a central element in World Bank-financed agricultural development projects, although the Bank tried and eventually succeeded in reducing the subsidy given to fertilizer.[14]

Other important initiatives in the agricultural sector were the River Basin Development Authorities (RBDAS) and the integrated agricultural development projects (ADPS). Started in 1973, the RBDAS were originally seen as an attractive centralizing mechanism since irrigation works would follow river flows and thus cut across state lines. But largely for geographical reasons, many of the RBDAS were organized on a statewide basis. They became relatively strong claimants for funds; the importance of water resources in capital spending is shown in figure 13-1. At the end of the 1970s, however, the

Figure 13-1. Nigeria: Federal Government Capital Budget Allocations to Agriculture and Water Resources, 1976–77 to 1981

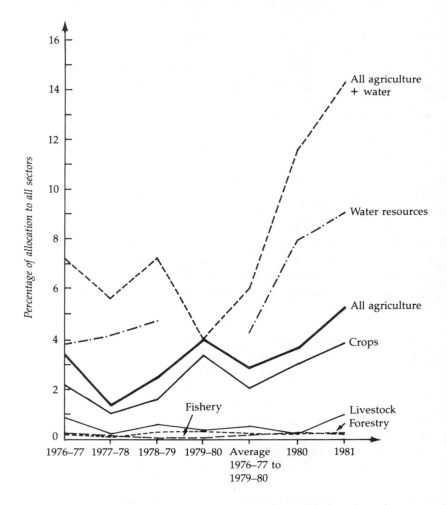

Note: 1980 and 1981 figures for agriculture include crops and rural development; 1980 figures refer to nine months (April-December) only; 1981 figures refer to the calendar year.

Source: Idachaba (1982), figure 14 as cited in Bienen (1985).

RBDAS were not providing significant increases in food output, and in 1980–82 only 40,000 tons of grain were being produced on irrigated land.[15]

Begun in 1974 to increase grain production, the purpose of the ADPS was to supply an improved package of services to the small farmer. ADPS expanded rapidly, so that by 1979 they covered 7.5 percent of the population in nine states. The impact of the ADPS is unclear, however. They have been criticized by some for poor management and for benefiting large farmers more than small ones.[16]

It might be hypothesized that decisionmaking units closer to the rural areas—that is, on the state rather than the federal level—would be more sensitive to farmers' interests. But this is not obviously the case in Nigeria. Throughout the 1970s and into the 1980s the states are believed to have had shortfalls from planned expenditures in agriculture at least as great as those of the federal government. And a 1980 government report on revenue allocation revealed that, between 1970 and 1975, the states had diverted significant funds away from agriculture even when the federal government had made specific, not matching, grants to agriculture.

Deficits, Inflation, and Exchange Rates: A Very Vicious Cycle

Like most of the other oil exporters, Nigeria experienced a sharp burst of inflation in the mid-1970s as public spending rose. The government may have thought that large wage increases would result in a similarly large increase in real private consumption. But since imports were restricted through tariffs and direct controls, and domestic food supply was inelastic, prices could be expected to rise to choke off excess demand. Efforts to reduce inflation, such as by holding down utility prices, contributed to growing public sector deficits.[17] With an exchange rate pegged to a currency basket of trading partners and inflation averaging 20 percent in 1973–78, the real naira appreciated from its 1970–72 purchasing power parity (100) to an average of 129 in 1974–78. Except for Indonesia, this was the sharpest appreciation in the sample.

Unlike most of the other exporters, however, Nigeria followed a policy of tightening import restrictions and raising tariffs, particularly when oil revenues started to decline. As early as the mid-1970s the focus of tariff policy had begun to shift from raising revenue to protecting domestic industry; table 13-4 indicates the progressive escalation in effective rates of protection. On average, the net effective rate for the industrial groups listed rose by 177 percent, assuming a constant shadow-priced exchange rate. The effect of increasing protection was to appreciate the real effective ex-

Table 13-4. Nigeria: Net Effective Rates of Protection for Selected Industrial Groups
(percent)

Industrial group	1977[a]	1979–80[a]
Consumer goods industries	55.8	124.9
Processing mainly domestic raw materials	12.7	81.7
Processing mainly imported raw materials	74.6	146.9
Intermediate and capital goods industries	1.5	37.7
Processing mainly domestic raw materials	−9.9	16.4
Processing mainly imported raw materials	24.4	65.6
Assembly industries	79.4	215.8

a. The exchange rate is shadow-priced at 65 percent.
Source: World Bank data.

change rate even more by shifting the basis of adjustment onto a smaller set of sectors (see chapter 3).

At the same time, the public deficits were financed internally to a large extent, mostly by the Central Bank. The banking system's claims on the government rose from −13.5 to 34.2 percent of nonmining GDP in 1974–83 (see table 13-2). The combination of tighter trade restrictions and money creation caused the real effective exchange rate to appreciate still further, to 163 in 1979–81, 194 in 1982–83, and 287 in 1984. By this point it had appreciated almost twice as much as the next most appreciated currency in the sample, that of Trinidad and Tobago.

As a result of this appreciation, real income should have been redistributed from the government, which suffered a sharp reduction in the purchasing power of its dollar-denominated income from oil exports, to private agents and economic activities. Let us leave aside for the moment the question of who appropriated this transfer, however, and consider only its magnitude. An accurate estimate would require knowledge of the movement in the price index of public expenditures relative to public revenues caused by exchange appreciation, and hence knowledge of the shares of oil taxes spent on domestic and foreign goods. For simplicity, suppose that all imports of plant and transport equipment are public purchases, that all other public expenditures are for domestic goods, and that the price of these goods moves in line with the general price level.

Table 13-2 shows the loss in the government's real income implied by the appreciation of the real effective exchange rate from its 1970–72 base. For the decade 1975–84, the ratio of this loss to nonmining GDP averaged 5.5 percent. For comparison, the ratio of the federal deficit to nonmining GDP averaged 8.9 percent.

Although the former estimate is rough, it indicates the magnitude of the vicious circle induced by responding to inflation and falling oil revenues by tightening import restrictions rather than by adjusting the nominal exchange rate. First, the purchasing power of oil revenues shrinks more rapidly because of rising domestic costs. Next, domestic financing of the resulting increase in the fiscal deficit places greater upward pressure on the price level. This in turn is met by tighter import restrictions and a more appreciated real effective exchange rate. This erodes the value of oil income still further, increasing the pressure on domestic financing, and so on.

As a complement to the adverse macroeconomic effect, cutbacks in public demand leave projects uncompleted and thus lower the returns to public investment. And import restrictions reduce the efficiency of the non-oil economy, as discussed below.

Some Effects of Oil Spending

Because oil wealth has had so profound an impact on Nigeria's political economy, it is possible to analyze its effects from many different perspectives. One of the main political effects, as noted above, has been the impetus given to the centralization of power. From an economic perspective, crucial to any assessment of how Nigeria managed its windfalls are the effects on growth, sectoral structure (the Dutch disease), and consumption.

Growth

Had there been no oil windfalls, in all likelihood Nigerian growth rates would have slowed substantially once the recovery from the civil war was complete. It is difficult, therefore, to project growth in the absence of the windfalls. Still, it would be very hard to argue that the overall impact of the windfalls was to stimulate growth. Nonmining GDP grew by only 5.3 percent a year during 1972–81, and it contracted by 5.6 percent a year in 1982–84. This gives a growth rate for the years 1972–84 of only 2.5 percent a year, slightly below the population growth rate of around 2.6 percent— despite by far the largest investment boom in Nigeria's history.

Poor growth appears to have been caused by a number of factors. The first is the high proportion of investment that went for physical and social infrastructure, and the supply-side failure of that investment to stimulate other economic activities. The second factor

Table 13-5. Nigeria: Oil and Non-Oil Export Performance, 1973–84

Non-oil exports	1973	1974	1975	1976	1977	1978	1979	1980	1981	1982[a]	1983[a]	1984[a]
Volume[b]												
Cocoa	214	194	175	219	168	192	218	187	108	125	232	125
Palm kernels	138	186	171	272	186	57	51	50	92	64	80	14
Rubber	49	61	61	34	28	31	34	31	24	27	29	29
Groundnuts	199	30	5	2	0	0	0	0	0	0	0	0
Total non-oil exports (millions of 1975 naira)	549	578	350	343	366	375	360	270	141	76	133	63
Petroleum/total exports (percent)	84.7	92.9	93.2	93.3	93.4	90.5	93.4	95.9	96.9	97.5	94.3	96.8

a. Estimated.
b. A constant-price measure.
Source: World Bank data.

appears to be the lowering of investment quality, which was related to the relaxation in approval procedures that accompanied the acceleration of public programs. A third factor was the disruptive effects of cutbacks in investment after the second oil boom. In 1985 it was estimated that about 14 billion naira would be needed to complete public industrial projects alone. But only about 10 billion naira was projected to be available for all public investments through 1990. Both the acceleration and the deceleration of investments therefore appear to have effectively eliminated the potential payoffs to a large part of domestic capital formation.[18]

A fourth factor, especially relevant to the decline in output after 1981 (and Nigeria's decline in nonmining output was the largest in the sample), seems to have been the the way the allocation of foreign exchange affected industrial activity. The inefficiency of the licensing system caused shortfalls in imported raw materials and spare parts that severely affected industry. According to one estimate, in 1984 the manufacturing sector operated at only 30–40 percent of capacity. One indication that the proximate cause of this was on the supply side, rather than on the demand side, is the fact that the prices of manufactured goods soared, apparently reflecting scarcity premiums. The importance of inefficiencies and supply constraints in explaining observed wage and consumption trends is further highlighted below.

The Performance of Non-Oil Tradables

As table 6-3 indicates, during 1972–81 the composition of Nigeria's nonmining economy swung substantially more to the nontradable sector relative to its "norms." The average annual decline in the share of agriculture in nonmining GDP was the largest in the sample, and it took place despite the relatively low growth of income per capita.

Nigeria's non-oil trade performance is summarized in table 13-5 and figure 13-2. Although export taxes on agricultural exports were reduced when oil income soared and were largely eliminated after 1976, this was insufficient to compensate for the initial demand-led appreciation of the exchange rate and the later antiexport bias caused by the intensification of import restrictions. By the mid-1970s non-oil exports had become insignificant, falling to one-seventh of their 1973 value (in 1975 naira) by 1982. Nigeria became a net importer of agricultural products in 1975. Imports soared, especially in 1975–78 and 1980–82 (see figure 13-2).

Estimates of agricultural production levels and trends are available from at least five different sources, but they diverge a great deal.[19] It is therefore difficult to obtain a clear picture of agricultural performance and consumption of agricultural products during the boom years and thereafter. The various time series agree in only one respect: total calorie consumption per capita declined from 1970 to 1982, even when imports are taken into account. Inasmuch as imports rose, domestic production would have fallen even further behind. For example, in terms of a bundle of commodities valued at common international prices, the U.S. Department of Agriculture (USDA) estimated that per capita food output (not availability) fell from an index of 100 in 1969–72 to 85 in 1982–83 (see table 6-4).

Despite this extremely gloomy supply picture, however, real private consumption per capita is estimated to have risen considerably

Figure 13-2. Nigeria: Agricultural Imports and Exports

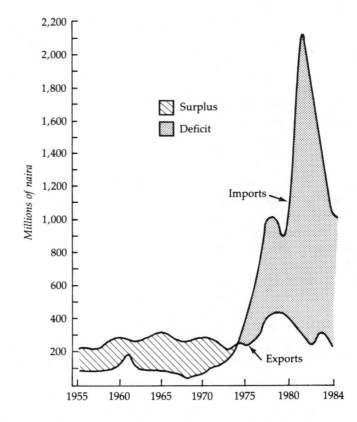

Source: Agribusiness Associates, "Agricultural Investment: The Opportunities and Realities for U.S. Agribusiness Companies," prepared for OICD/USDA, p. 51, as cited in Bienen (1983), and World Bank data.

during the boom period. Between 1970 and 1978, for example, real private consumption a head rose by about 4 percent a year according to national accounts data (a population growth rate of 2.6 percent is assumed), although by the mid-1980s real private consumption levels had declined back to about their level of 1970. Even allowing for possibly growing inequality of income distribution and for substitution effects caused by a rise in the relative price of food, such growth in private consumption would not have been possible without at least some growth in food availability per capita. The supply data are therefore not fully consistent with likely demand trends. It seems probable that agricultural performance, at least in the food sector, may have been somewhat better than the production data indicate. It is still likely that agricultural production, at best, barely kept up with population growth, and it may have fallen somewhat behind.

Nigeria's poor performance in food production was not the simple result of a drop in relative food prices caused by its massive imports. On the contrary, if 1970–72 is taken as the base, the price of food to consumers was higher in 1974–83 than the price of other components of the consumer price index (see table 6-5). It is possible that this reflected higher distribution margins rather than higher farmgate prices—the data are insufficient to judge. A more probable explanation, however, is that agriculture, the largest employer of unskilled labor, lost workers to the rapidly growing construction sector and was also adversely affected by the spread of primary education, which reduced the use of child labor on farms.[20] With stagnant levels of productivity, agriculture would not have been able to raise per capita income enough to retain sufficient workers to satisfy food demand at constant rural-urban terms of trade.[21]

One factor sometimes cited in accounting for the far better performance of Indonesia's food crop sector is the Green Revolution in rice production. As described in chapter 12, this was brought about by the development and dissemination of improved high-yielding and disease-resistant varieties and the adoption of improved farming techniques. No such dramatic advances were made in the rainfed agriculture of Nigeria, but even so, yields were low.[22] The gap was considerable between actual practice and potential improvements. The obstacles were partly technical but also infrastructural and institutional ones. The inefficiency of input distribution services (notably for fertilizer) and the lack of a good extension service were serious problems.[23] These, in turn, reflected the lack of urgency that successive governments assigned to the development of agriculture, especially among smallholders. Unlike Indonesia, Nigeria had very limited success in using oil income to raise rural productivity.

Consumption and Wages

So far the Nigerian story is relatively clear. But now we come to three related and puzzling issues. First, who appropriated the considerable transfers from the government implied by the sharp real appreciation of the naira? Second, have there been real wage gains in the Nigerian economy? Third, if real wages in urban activities did indeed fail to rise when public spending rose, how was it possible to continue to attract large numbers of workers from an agricultural sector that supposedly was not in labor surplus?

On the first issue, the expected counterpart to the transfer from the fiscal budget would be a gain in real absorption as prices of goods rose less rapidly than prices of domestic non-oil output because of the cheapening of imports. But table 5-2 indicates no such gain in 1974–78—in fact, the effect goes the other way. There is a substantial gain in consumption in 1979–81, equivalent to a transfer of 4.1 percent of nonmining GDP (see table 5-3). This is offset, however, by increases in the relative price of investment goods, so that the overall effect is eliminated. Where, then, did the transfers from the real exchange rate movement go?

Several explanations are possible. One, of course, is that the relevant data are flawed. The situation is not improved, however, if the consumer price index is substituted for the consumption deflator. A second possibility is that the increased resource cost of transport and distribution systems, strained by greatly increased import levels, could have offset the transfer. This might have been a factor, but only in the initial stages of the oil boom. A third explanation could be capital flight, effected by overinvoicing imports. Had this attained macroeconomic proportions, the transfer would have been offset by apparent non-oil terms of trade losses.

The fourth possibility, and probably the only one able to account for a transfer as large as that computed above, is the absorption of the transfer in rent-seeking activities induced by the increased resort to tariffs and quantitative restrictions. Such a loss would include not only the real resources expended by importers on obtaining licenses, but the general decrease in allocative and X-efficiency of an economy increasingly operating behind quantitative restrictions that inhibited competition. If this interpretation is correct, a substantial part of Nigeria's windfall gains were eaten up in the reduced efficiency of its non-oil economy, which resulted largely from the protectionist policies adopted in response to the falling purchasing power of oil receipts.

The question of whether real wages rose has been investigated (see, for example, Collier 1985), but here, too, are problems of interpretation. The available wage data, though incomplete and confusing (especially when juxtaposed with estimates of the evolution of income distribution and private consumption) appear to argue against a substantial real wage gain in urban activities. If anything, they argue for a real wage loss in construction and more so in the public sector. Such an evolution is quite unusual; the pattern for the other countries suggests considerable real wage gains in the windfall period (see table 6-2).

Stagnant or falling real wages are not necessarily inconsistent with a rise in private consumption per capita. Much depends on changes in the distribution of private income, and if—as in Nigeria—labor is rapidly reallocated from low-wage activities (such as farming) to higher-wage urban activities (such as construction), private income and consumption per capita can rise even with static or falling real wages for specific activities. Diejomaoh and Anusionwu (1981) concluded that there was a sharp trend toward inequality within the modern sector from 1970 to the mid-1970s, with the Gini coefficient rising from 0.55 to 0.70. For the urban sector as a whole, the bottom layer of which is the self-employed in the informal sector, the studies reported in Bienen (1983) also suggest a rise in inequality from 1970 through 1976.[24] Income inequality in the rural sector has been estimated to be low, with a Gini coefficient of about 0.3 (Bienen 1983, p. 37). According to some estimates, the trend of rural wages may have been upward. In contrast to the data of table 6-2, Collier (1985) suggests that in 1973–81 real wages in agriculture may have risen by about 50 percent, although such an estimate seems very high given the macroeconomic context.

Whatever the precise pattern of real wages, the main reasons for their failure to rise faster appear to lie in (a) the impact on the food sector of labor market pressures created by oil-financed spending, and (b) an insufficiency of permitted imports to make up the supply-demand gap. Food import policy was, indeed, erratic during the period, so that the sector is best classed as semitraded, although in principle many staple items are tradable. Increasing nominal urban incomes combined with the economy's shift toward producer goods to bid up the price of the main consumer goods; this, together with low growth and falling efficiency, reduced or eliminated real wage gains.

If urban wages were not rising, how was labor drawn out of the farm sector? Collier (1985) provides evidence of a substantial wage gap between urban and rural—or between modern and traditional—activities in the early 1970s. He estimates that unskilled wages in nonagricultural activities were about 80 percent higher than those in agriculture in 1973, essentially because of the political clout of public sector employees and the impact of public wage levels on the urban private sector through "fair wage" clauses in employment contracts. But by the early 1980s, Collier finds, the difference had all but disappeared. According to this view, the large initial gap made possible the expansion of labor use in the modern sector, and real urban wages fell because of the scarcity of key wage goods.

Accounting for the Policy Response

Nigeria's strategy for managing its extraordinary windfalls cannot be regarded as a carefully articulated one in the sense that, say, Algeria's can. Nigerian policymakers do not seem to have resolutely set out to pursue a strategy heavily biased toward infrastructure and education and away from agriculture, but they were inclined to believe that achieving productivity gains in traditional smallholder agriculture would be very difficult (see Bienen 1985, p. 11). What, then, explains the policy response? Did the choices made regarding the use of oil revenues reflect a representative balance of individual preferences? Or did they result from a combination of the political process and administrative constraints?

A useful point of departure is the observation that there has been no clear development of class-based politics in Nigeria. Neither peasant organizations nor trade unions have exerted strong pressure for income redistribution. Nor have informal urban workers constituted an effective force for radical change. The very meanings of wealth and equity differ within and among communal and occupational groups. Relationships between workers in the formal and informal sectors are complex, and they vary by city, region, and ethnic group. This weakens pressures from the urban poor.

Neither in the 1950s, nor in the 1960s, nor in the 1979 elections did political parties organize on the basis of class, income group, or occupation. Surveys help to explain why this pattern has not developed. Morrison (1981) analyzes a 1974 national survey. He argues that, although in reality social and occupational mobility may have decreased, respondents still assumed the possibility of social mobility. Views differed markedly, however, among states (and thus among ethnic groups) about whether people received a "fair share" in life and whether ordinary people were better or worse off since independence. Earlier surveys had yielded many of the same results, with communal cleavages stronger than occupational ones.[25]

Furthermore, there were strong positive associations between status and participation, between fathers' and children's levels of education, and between occupation and education. Mobility and opportunity were thus related to an individual's start in life and in particular to educational attainment. Many rural Nigerians wanted to acquire the skills needed to compete in urban labor markets, so spending on education was popular, despite widespread concern about the quality of the education provided. The personal preferences of many rural inhabitants coincided with the political preferences of Nigeria's leaders as well as with their recognition of the administrative problems inherent in any attempt to reform smallholder agriculture. Both individuals and politicians have pushed, therefore, for more funds to be spent on education at all levels.[26]

The push to spend funds on the agricultural sector was far weaker. As already noted, agricultural interests in Nigeria had never managed to surmount regional differences to form a significant pressure group, and the widespread desire of rural residents to move out of the sector further undermined any efforts in this direction. The political power of those in the agricultural sector was, as in most African countries, dispersed and unorganized. When military regimes were in power, elections did not count, so the rulers could not be called to account for the relative neglect of agriculture in government spending. Even in the 1950s and 1960s, when governments were elected and when groundnuts and cocoa were important sources of export revenue, farmers wielded neither political nor economic power. Cocoa farmers in the Yoruba areas, for example, never formed a well-organized pressure group as did planters in the Côte d'Ivoire.

The one major exception to the weakness of agricultural interests was the *Agbekoya* revolts of 1968–69 in the Western Region. Agbekoya, which means in Yoruba "farmers who reject injustice," was an agrarian populist movement and a revolt against high taxes and poor services. It centered in areas where cocoa production had been declining.[27] The revolts were put down with some loss of life. After initial relief, not much was done to benefit these areas. Military officers tended to see the movement as a plot hatched by former politicians and were insensitive to farmers' grievances (Adebayo 1969). Those in revolt could not sustain the pressure on the government. The pressures were not echoed throughout Nigeria, nor did they recur on a similar scale in the 1970s.

Policymakers were thus relatively free to focus on urban rather than rural problems and to follow their own predilections. They believed that urban inequality and urban poverty could be attacked through service delivery, whereas investments that would benefit small and medium-size farmers were difficult to make, especially investments in agricultural extension, new seeds and other inputs, marketing facilities, and so on. This abandonment of the smallholder in the 1970s, before making any major commitment to agriculture, has not been unique to Nigeria in Africa.

Nigeria also had many bottlenecks in administration. Public sector investment programs suffered because of constraints in the implementation process. This was especially true for agriculture, where expenditures increasingly fell short of projections as the 1970s progressed. The government had difficulty getting funds out to the rural areas, in part because it was hard to find good projects to fund and in part because the administrative networks to develop and implement rural projects were very weak. It was much easier to contract for the building of roads and ports and to invest in plants.

In addition, the elites of the state, both civilian and military, had interests of their own, which they were in a position to further. It has been suggested that the Udoji awards were one attempt to distribute oil income to civil servants as patronage. As noted earlier, the elites were in a hurry to spend oil income because of the patronage available from large projects and because they did not wish to be charged with not spending "the people's money" in worthwhile, usually highly visible, ways.[28] Agriculture suffered from this emphasis on rapid spending. Without lengthy institution-building efforts (such as the improvement of extension services) there was no effective way to reach the smallholder or to improve inefficient institutions.

Spending priorities were therefore shaped partly by policymakers' (correct) interpretation of widespread desires, partly by the distinctive structure of government, and partly by administrative practicality.

A final question concerns the possible reasons for Nigeria's decision to adjust to falling oil income through trade restriction rather than devaluation, despite the disastrous macroeconomic implications of such a choice. Two explanations suggest themselves. First, it is clear that by the early 1980s the exchange rate issue had come to be regarded as one of national sovereignty rather than simple economics. It was almost surely the case that Nigeria's non-oil comparative advantage still lay in the export of agricultural products. A large devaluation accompanied by a substantial liberalization of trade could therefore have seemed threatening to the modern industrial sector, thought to be so essential to making Nigeria the "giant of Africa." Second, it may be that the scarcity rents generated by restrictions had given rise to a pressure group sufficiently powerful to influence policy.

Summing Up: Have the Windfalls Benefited Nigeria?

As is apparent from this analysis, it is not easy to judge how much the oil windfalls have benefited the Nigerian economy—or, indeed, whether they have benefited the Nigerian people at all. Yet some conclusions are obvious. Unlike Ecuador, Venezuela, and Trinidad and Tobago, the other countries in this study that registered substantial declines in their nonmining economies after 1981, Nigeria apparently did not translate its oil wealth into substantial gains in real per capita private consumption (relative to the hypothetical scenarios without windfalls in chapter 5) during the boom years. Unlike Indonesia, it did not emerge from the windfall era with a strengthened agricultural sector. Unlike Algeria, it did not invest in industrial sectors with the potential (even if not fully realized) of generating appreciable non-oil exports. Nigeria's non-oil tradable sectors almost certainly weakened during the decade of windfalls. And certain of its import substitution ventures, notably in steel, will probably involve a net economic loss through debt service and high production costs.

In the context of the present sample of countries, the growth stimulus of Nigeria's oil income took mainly the indirect route of strengthening key infrastructure and social sectors. Nigeria did improve its physical infrastructure significantly, even though it failed to extend key services to rural areas. But perhaps its major achievement has been the use of oil income to fund almost universal primary education. Without this, it can be argued, a long-run transformation of agriculture would be far more difficult. Enrollment in secondary and higher education also increased. By 1980 Nigeria had virtually closed the education gap between itself and the other developing oil exporters, at least in quantitative terms. How Nigeria can translate such improvements into future growth will largely determine the long run value of the oil windfalls.

Notes

1. For a discussion of the difficulty of forming rural interest groups, see Bates (1981).
2. The literature on the marketing boards is very large. See Helleiner (1966), Wells (1974), and Rimmer (1981).
3. See Bienen (1985, pp. 20–23) for a discussion of regional variations in public spending on agriculture.
4. A fourth, Midwestern, region was later created.
5. The history of this period is treated in Coleman (1964), Mackintosh (1966), Sklar (1966), Panter-Brick (1970), Dudley (1973), and Oyediran (1979).

6. For a discussion of revenue-sharing in Nigeria, see Rupley (1981) and Rimmer (1981).

7. For a discussion of Nigeria's indigenization policy, see Biersteker (1978, 1980) and Akinsanya (1981).

8. For the early years of the Nigerian oil industry, see Schatzl (1969) and Pearson (1970). For accounts of the early 1970s, see Meyer and Pearson (1974) and von Lazar and Duerstein (1976).

9. It was not Nigeria's imposition of OPEC terms on foreign companies that affected their willingness to invest in Nigeria's oil potential in the late 1970s and early 1980s, but the fact that Nigeria was consistently a price hawk in OPEC. Indigenization may well have slowed capital flows, however, especially after 1977. And there may have been indirect costs associated with restrictions on foreign managers and technical personnel. Some companies whose shares were bought by the states—particularly textile firms—probably were poor purchases and costly to public purses.

10. The Udoji wage increases and the burden of inflation triggered a backlash against General Gowon, who was already unpopular because of his announced intention to stay in power beyond 1975. In July 1975 he was replaced by General Mohammed, who advocated "clean government" and used the rhetoric of populism to build support.

11. As in other countries in the sample, domestic oil prices had not been raised to world levels, although the average divergence and the implicit subsidy seem to have been lower in Nigeria than in some of the other exporters.

12. Loans and nonstatutory allocations became important to the states after 1976. Between 1969 and 1977 federal lending to the states rose well over 1,000 percent; federal development in the states also rose markedly, from 91.6 million naira to more than 5 billion naira.

13. For further discussion, see Bienen (1985, p. 63).

14. The use of fertilizers in the late 1970s was subsidized up to a rate of 85 percent (Norton 1983, p. 41).

15. For a summary of the results achieved by the RBDAS, see Bienen (1985, pp. 67–69).

16. For a summary of (sometimes divergent) views on the ADPS, see Bienen (1985, pp. 69–75).

17. Utility prices rose by only 5 percent between 1973–74 and 1979–80. In this period the corporate consumer price index for rural and urban centers increased by 176 percent; see Bienen (1983, tables 13 and 18).

18. A critical view of spending on the new federal capital at Abuja illustrates the losses from both acceleration and deceleration of investment. It points out the waste involved both in unfinished construction and in its poor quality (*Washington Post*, 20 January 1984, pp. A23–28).

19. The five sources are Nigerian Federal Office of Statistics (FOS), Central Bank of Nigeria, Nigerian Federal Department of Agriculture, the Food and Agriculture Organization (FAO), and the U.S. Department of Agriculture (USDA). To give some idea of the larger divergences, in 1981 the FOS estimated cassava production at 580,000 tons and the USDA estimated it at 11.8 million tons.

20. The share of Nigeria's work force actively engaged in agriculture fell from about 70 percent throughout the 1960s to 55 percent in 1980.

21. If real agricultural wages did rise as suggested by Collier (1985), the sector would have been squeezed with labor costs rising faster than prices.

22. Cotton yields in Nigeria, for example, were just over half those in Mali.

23. The ratio of extension workers to farmers was estimated to be 1 to 2,500 in Nigeria in the late 1970s, compared with 1 to 200 in India and 1 to 250 in Kenya (*Guidelines for the Fourth National Development Plan, 1981–85*, p. 26). Some observers believe that the extension service was in worse shape in the late 1970s than a decade earlier.

24. As noted by Bienen (1983, p. 36), there are severe problems with Nigerian data on income distribution, especially after 1975. Bienen's study surveys research on income distribution covering the period to 1976.

25. See Verba, Nie, and Kim (1978, p. 103, table 6-1). Fieldwork for this study was carried out in 1966.

26. By the time of the 1981 budget, the planned capital expenditure for universities amounted to more than half the total capital allocated to education.

27. The most important accounts of the Agbekoya revolts are in Beer (1976) and Beer and Williams (1976).

28. In countries with an extensive history of public corruption, it may be difficult for governments to save abroad openly since they are vulnerable to accusations that money is being siphoned into officials' pockets. This point has been made several times in discussion with officials from countries included in this study.

Chapter 14

Trinidad and Tobago: Windfalls in a Small Parliamentary Democracy

with Richard Auty

The smallest of the oil-exporting developing countries in this study, Trinidad and Tobago has a slow-growing population of a little more than one million and an area only one-fiftieth that of Ecuador, the next smallest country. It is also the most densely populated, with three times as many people per square mile as Indonesia or Nigeria. Although its 1974 per capita income was slightly less than Venezuela's, its 1982 per capita income of US$6,840 placed it at the top of the group of all middle-income developing countries.

Trinidad and Tobago is a democracy. Unlike Venezuela—the only other comparator with an elected government throughout the windfall period—its government is modeled on the British rather than the American system and is therefore less prone to disagreements between the executive and the legislature over how to manage oil revenues. Also unlike Venezuela, the same political party dominated the government during and after the entire windfall period.

Another distinctive feature of the country is that before the first windfall the gradual decline in oil output from established fields had precipitated a period of austerity. By 1974 it was widely understood that the new offshore finds developed in the early 1970s were limited. The public was therefore aware of the need to proceed with caution in using the income from the country's finite oil resources.

Except for its size—which, as this study confirms, reduced the effectiveness of certain strategies for absorbing oil rents—these features enhanced the chances for Trinidad and Tobago to put its windfalls to good use. In relation to the comparator countries, it began with some important advantages.

Other features, however, made it more difficult for the govern-

Richard M. Auty is lecturer in geography at the University of Lancaster, United Kingdom.

ment to use oil income to increase the productivity of the non-oil economy. These included a society strongly divided along ethnic, political, and economic lines and an economy that has been described as the most regulated in the Caribbean except for Cuba's (Black and others 1976, p. 209). Faced with the demands of powerful interest groups, the government has traditionally accepted a great deal of the responsibility for maintaining employment and income. These factors created strong pressures to distribute windfall gains widely. Political pressure to raise and sustain consumption was to be one serious weakness in the development strategy.

At the same time, the above features, combined with windfall gains, relaxed efforts to raise productivity in the non-oil economy, to arrest agriculture's decline, and to improve manufacturing's competitiveness. Trinidad and Tobago lacked effective means to make productive investments in agriculture and competitive light industry, particularly as the windfalls pushed up wages. Investments either were not effective or suffered from lack of demand, and in its eagerness to use oil revenues for large projects the government downplayed the risks and decided to go ahead on its own. Consequently, the country ended the second boom far more dependent on oil than before, even though it had accumulated a cushion of foreign assets.

This chapter assesses the impact of the development strategy implemented in Trinidad and Tobago during the decade of the oil windfalls. It first outlines the conditions of the political system and of the economy before the first oil shock. The response to the boom of 1974–78 is then described. In absorbing its windfall gains, the country did, in fact, proceed much more cautiously than the other five oil exporters. Nevertheless, many of the policies adopted during these years—notably to extend state ownership of enterprises, to increase subsidies to consumers and failing firms, and to promote gas-based industrial development—adversely affected the economy later on. The discussion of the second boom, 1979–81, therefore emphasizes state ownership, subsidies, and the performance of the non-hydrocarbon-based tradable sectors. As in Algeria, gas-based industrial development played a central part in the Trinidadian strategy of "sowing the oil." This strategy is the subject of a separate section because of its crucial importance in the 1980s and beyond. Conclusions follow in the final section.

Before the First Boom

Trinidad and Tobago evolved into a parliamentary democracy after World War II, and by 1956 its two-party structure was set. The political process, however, had to contend with ethnic cleavage. In 1970 blacks constituted 43 percent of the population, East Indians 40 percent, and people of mixed race 14 percent. The island's black population was strongly represented in government and predominant in industry. The East Indian population, descendants of indentured laborers imported to work on the plantations after slavery was abolished in the 1830s, was generally poor, largely rural, and heavily dependent on sugar production for a livelihood (Black and others 1976).

Political Structure

The People's National Movement (PNM), which held power from 1956 to 1986, has a primarily black constituency. The party was led by the increasingly autocratic Dr. Eric Williams until his death in 1981, and then by George Chambers. The Democratic Labour Party (DPL), the leading opposition, has drawn its support more from the East Indians.[1]

Influenced by the views of Lewis (1950), the PNM, upon coming to power, made industrialization its main goal, initially with heavy reliance on foreign capital, technology, and management. Unlike Lewis (1950, 1972), however, it did not emphasize competitive, labor-intensive exports as an essential part of its strategy. The DPL attacked the government for depending too much on "exploitative foreign capital." But because it represented an unwieldy coalition of rural East Indians, urban poor, and a small European elite, the party never cohered, despite receiving almost half the votes in the 1956 election. The DPL's weakness allowed the PNM to emerge as a strong, unified government largely free of competition within its ranks. In the mid-1970s this lack of opposition enabled the government to keep public spending more disciplined in Trinidad and Tobago than in most of the other oil exporters.

The lack of an effective opposition, however, also encouraged extra-parliamentary attempts to influence government policy. Early in 1970 street demonstrations and a mutiny in the army gave voice to widespread dissatisfaction over growing economic problems caused, indirectly, by declining oil revenues. Despite a sweeping electoral victory in 1971 (the DPL boycotted the elections and the PNM won every seat in Parliament), the PNM recognized that there was enough discontent in the country to challenge its power. So it reluctantly shifted to a populist program with three main goals:

- To extend public ownership in both the oil and non-oil sectors
- To redistribute income more equitably
- To accelerate industrial diversification out of oil.

Economic Structure

OIL SECTOR. Trinidad and Tobago is a long-established oil producer. Oil was discovered in 1857, and Shell became the first producer in 1913. By the 1950s British Petroleum, Royal Dutch Shell, and Texaco operated oil refineries and augmented domestic crude with imports from Venezuela. By the early 1970s petroleum extraction and refining accounted for almost three-quarters of exports, one-fifth of government revenue, and one-fifth of GDP.

The fortunes of the oil industry had long determined the rhythm of the overall economy. In the late 1960s both oil production and refined exports began to fall as traditional fields were exhausted. Public spending dropped from 23 to 20 percent of GDP in 1971–73, and a modest budget deficit of 4.7 percent of GDP was financed half from foreign and half from domestic sources. Between 1970 and 1973, GDP growth slowed from an annual average of almost 5.5 percent over the preceding fifteen years to 3.6 percent a year (4.5 percent for nonmining GDP). Inflation rose from an average of 2.5 percent a year in the 1960s to more than 10 percent in the early 1970s.

Marine exploration between 1969 and 1971 revealed substantial new sources of recoverable oil and gas. Oil production rose from a low of 129,000 barrels a day in 1971 to 191,000 in 1973, exceeding the previous peak in 1969. Although oil reserves were expected to last only about ten years, the new finds reduced the immediate pressure for politically difficult structural change. Their anticipated earnings permitted the economy to tide itself over the interim period by borrowing abroad.

Even before the disturbances of 1970, the government had taken a small step toward nationalizing the oil industry when it bought British Petroleum's refinery and field facilities (Sandoval 1983). Then the discovery of natural gas spurred a growing debate on how best to use it. Amoco, which had made the critical discoveries on the east coast, proposed in 1971 to ship gas to the United States as liquefied natural gas (LNG). This drew criticism from a younger generation of economists, who were influenced by dependency theory. They argued for using gas as a fuel or a feedstock for local industry under national (rather than foreign) control instead of continuing to export raw materials (Girvan 1970; Parsan 1981).

NON-OIL SECTORS. The non-oil sectors of Trinidad and Tobago's economy had long relied on protection from foreign competition (Seers 1964; Brewster 1972). In the early 1970s manufacturing—though heavily protected by a "negative list" of prohibited imports and by other measures, which in many cases doubled prices relative to those of imports—accounted for only 22 percent of nonmining GDP, with half of this from refining. Agriculture, dominated by sugar, accounted for only about 6 percent. In 1971 the government had moved into non-oil entrepreneurial activity by buying a majority holding in Caroni, the largest sugar company. Food imports represented 226 percent of value added in all nonsugar, nonexport agriculture. Unlike many Caribbean islands, Trinidad and Tobago enjoyed little tourist trade.

The economy, therefore, was heavily dependent on oil earnings on the eve of the first oil shock. Non-oil tradables—manufacturing and agriculture—accounted for just under 28 percent of nonmining GDP, in contrast to the Chenery-Sryquin "norm" of 42 percent for countries with a comparable per capita income.[2] This was despite the fact that economic diversification had been a major goal of the third five-year plan (1969–73).

Income was unevenly distributed, the result of a pronounced dualism in the economy between high-technology oil and manufacturing sectors on the one hand and a low-skill agricultural sector on the other. In 1973 agriculture generated one-sixteenth of the value added per worker in oil refining and one-fifth of that in chemicals. Agriculture itself was dualistic: value added per worker in sugar was almost four times value added in the rest of the sector. The elite oil workers (less than 4 percent of the country's labor force) earned US$5,000 a year, compared with US$750 for all other workers and US$325 for agricultural workers (Black and others 1976). The effects of this uneven income distribution were accentuated by high and rising unemployment, which topped 14 percent in the early 1970s. These disparities provided labor with a powerful impetus to organize; 70 percent of all workers were unionized, a figure exceeded in only a few small European countries.

The First Oil Shock, 1974–78

As shown in figure 14-1 and table 5-2, the 1974–78 windfall of Trinidad and Tobago was unusually large compared with that of other capital-importing oil exporters—equivalent to 39 percent of nonmining GDP.[3] This was because new oil fields began to produce in substantial quantities just as the embargo of 1973 caused the worldwide price of oil to quadruple. Corporate and other taxes (Trinidad and Tobago does not follow the common OPEC system) were rapidly adjusted to siphon off five-sixths of increased revenues. Oil taxes, charted in figure 14-2, jumped from 20 percent of government revenues before the boom to 60 percent in 1974–78.

Figure 14-1. Trinidad and Tobago: The Oil Windfall and Its Use, 1973–81

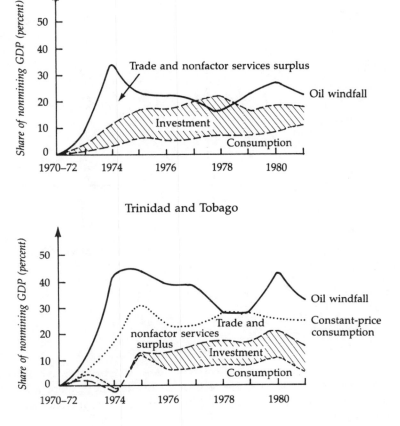

Unweighted Average of Algeria, Ecuador, Indonesia, Nigeria, Trinidad and Tobago, and Venezuela

Trinidad and Tobago

Source: World Bank data.

Uses of the Windfall

Fiscal policy was initially very cautious for several reasons. The country had just emerged from a period of austerity. Unlike Ecuador and Nigeria, it had a centralized government, which reduced competition for revenues within the public sector. There were no powerful regional governments with claims to a portion of the windfall. Fur-

Figure 14-2. Trinidad and Tobago: Fiscal Evolution

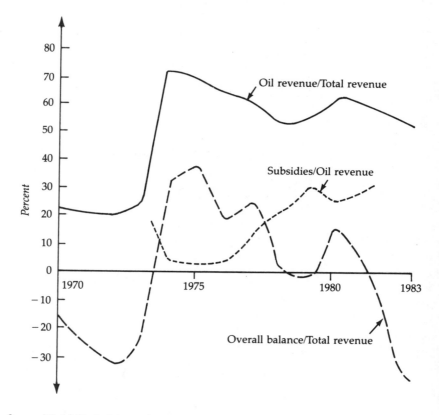

Source: World Bank data.

ther, to limit dependence on oil revenues, the progressive non-oil tax system was kept in place, although tax brackets were adjusted for inflation to prevent a sharp rise in yields. Oil revenue therefore exceeded recurrent spending by 40 percent.

In 1973 the government had just completed drafting its fourth five-year plan for 1974–78. Most unusually for an oil exporter, existing public investment programs were not scaled up in line with revenues. Nor did the government immediately revise the plan. A nationwide debate on how to deploy the new wealth extended into 1976 and delayed domestic investment. Almost half of the 1974–78 windfall was invested abroad in special funds for long-term development, which were gradually drawn down to finance domestic projects.

As a percentage of nonmining GDP, total absorption had been high in 1970–72 because foreign-financed investment to tap the new offshore finds had permitted a current deficit averaging 14.5 percent of nonmining GDP. Two-thirds of this, however, had been financed by direct investment—a flow far higher in Trinidad and Tobago, relative to the size of its economy, than in any of the other countries in this study. Absorption rose further after 1975 as spending from the windfall accelerated (see figure 14-1). During 1974–78 the extra revenues were used in three ways:

- 70 percent was saved abroad, transforming current deficits into surpluses that averaged 10 percent of 1976 nonmining GDP during 1974–78.
- 12 percent was invested domestically.
- 18 percent was consumed.

As is apparent from figure 14-1, Trinidad and Tobago's savings abroad were extremely large compared with the five other exporters. Domestic investment was initially modest, and consumption out of windfall gains was fairly high after 1975.

SAVINGS ABROAD. By 1978 savings abroad had boosted international reserves to US$1.8 billion, up from US$47 million in 1973, and equivalent to twenty months of imports. Reserves were used to establish a high international credit rating, and loans of US$157 million and US$112 million were negotiated in 1977 and 1978. Strict capital controls limited outflows; medium- and long-term debt was US$417 million at the end of 1978 and short-term debt only US$117 million.

DOMESTIC INVESTMENT. The largest allocations to domestic investment were for economic and social infrastructure, for gas-based industrial development, and for nationalizing and bailing out existing industries. Only half of the TT$4 billion earmarked as funds for long-term development had been spent by the close of 1978. Of the funds actually used, about half went into economic infrastructure—transport, power, and water—and one-fifth went into social infrastructure—education and housing. Such investment was intended to provide employment and to eliminate the shortage of infrastructure that had developed in the late 1960s.

Instead of accepting Amoco's proposal to export LNG to the United States, the government created a task force in 1975 to plan gas-based industrialization. It experimented with different forms of ownership, refusing joint ownership proposed by Shell when Shell's oil refinery was bought out but accepting it for two fertilizer plants with 51 percent equity. Foreign partners were responsible for technology, management, and marketing. Attempts to negotiate other joint ventures collapsed because the desire to spend oil revenues led the government to downplay risk more than its potential private partners. In 1976, for example, the government planned a joint steel venture in which the state was to own 67 percent and Hoesch-Estel, Kawasaki, and Mitsui the balance. Later the same year, however, it canceled the agreement on the grounds that the private investors were offering poor terms, that their demands for fiscal incentives were unreasonable, and that their sales strategy excluded North American markets. The state went ahead on its own, relying on four international companies to develop the plant on contract, despite warnings of a low rate of return and problems in accessing the market. By the end of 1978, TT$240 million had been spent on the project. In another case the government, impatient with slow progress, abandoned plans to build a gas-based aluminum smelter with Guyana and Jamaica. Another partner was found, National Southwire, which committed itself to provide only 10 percent of the equity and undertook feasibility studies.

But the goal of creating new industries was increasingly sidetracked by the need to take over declining industries to save jobs. In 1974–78, TT$1.67 billion (equal to one year's oil revenues) was spent in acquiring forty companies. This sum included funds to purchase remaining control in Caroni, the dominant sugar company, and to buy out—for TT$93.6 million—Royal Dutch Shell's refinery (renamed the Trintoc refinery), the second largest in the country. The latter move was popular, especially with the militant oil workers' union, which saw it as a step toward nationalizing the larger, more complex Texaco refinery. That refinery employed 4,000 workers (several times the necessary number) and had an average net annual income of only 1.3 percent of book value in 1971–77.

DOMESTIC CONSUMPTION. Rising subsidies for food, fuel, and utilities absorbed TT$760 million in 1974–78. Prices were controlled for a variety of foodstuffs, and domestic oil prices were held to half of international prices. Utility companies began to run large operating deficits, not having been allowed to raise rates since the late 1960s and in one case since 1937. Consumer prices therefore rose less rapidly than other prices, as shown in figure 14-3. Deflated consumption—as measured in the national accounts—rose sharply relative to nominal consumption (see table 5-2). By 1978 subsidies were estimated to account for more than 7 percent of GDP, and subsidies recorded in the fiscal budget accounted for 22 percent of oil revenues (see figure 14-2).

Figure 14-3. Trinidad and Tobago: Relative Prices and Wages

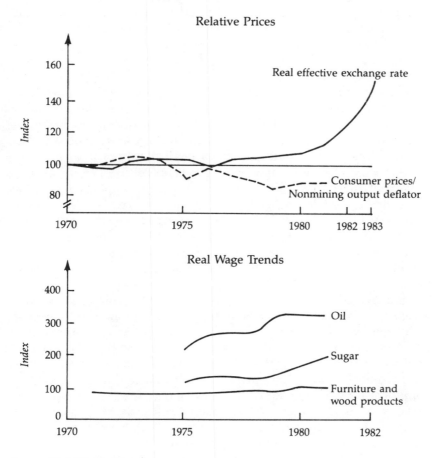

Source: World Bank data.

Labor was also subsidized directly through the state public works program (DEWD) described below. Overall, public sector employment expanded from 86,000 to 158,000, or from less than one-quarter to more than one-third of all workers. Unemployment fell from 15 percent in 1974 to about 12 percent in 1978—not, however, because of labor demand from the private sector.

Response of the Economy

Because of the government's cautious approach, the main consequences of the policies initiated during the first oil boom did not appear until later. Although a large reserve had been built up, and interest payments on foreign assets reached US$100 million in 1978, recurrent expenditures began to rise and generated small fiscal and current balance deficits in 1979. Investing in declining industries diverted revenues from more productive uses; in the case of the sugar industry, for example, the government had to cover operating losses of TT$247 million in 1977–78.

Management difficulties added to political expediency made it impossible to reverse a growing structural shift in favor of nontradables. This shift is shown as the Dutch disease index in figure 14-4. Programs to expand domestic food production were poorly conceived. Despite a plentiful supply of land, inappropriate sites and farmers were chosen for new rural projects (Pollard 1981b). Only a quarter of the outlays for food subsidies went to producer incentives; the remainder held down consumer prices. Price controls squeezed profit margins, and food imports rose sharply from TT$161 million in 1973 to TT$458 million in 1978. The even more dramatic decline of agricultural exports, which has also been analyzed by Pollard (1985), is dealt with in the discussion of the second windfall.

Manufacturing continued to be oriented to the domestic market, which was too small to benefit from competition, economies of scale, and vertical linkages. Two-thirds of all manufacturing consisted of final assembly of imported products, notably car kits and food to be processed, with low added value. Import controls further reduced competitive pressure to produce quality products (Sandoval 1983; Wright 1982). Refinery activity fell by 40 percent because Venezuela, which had supplied two-thirds of Trinidad and Tobago's crude, cut back output and internalized its refining, and because legislation in the United States increasingly favored domestic refineries. The high growth rate of nonmining output—7.0 percent during 1974–78—was therefore based on activities that did not need to compete with efficient world producers. As may be inferred from figure 14-4, by 1978 construction and services accounted for 79 percent of nonmining GDP. In an average country with Trinidad and Tobago's per capita income, these sectors would account for only 40 percent of nonmining GDP. The dollar value of non-oil exports contracted by 30 percent during 1974–78. With respect to both sectoral output and trade, Trinidad and Tobago was steadily increasing its dependence on oil.

In addition, a shift away from the use of heavy oil in the United States reduced the demand for oil imports from the Caribbean. In constant 1970 dollars, the mining sector's share in total GDP declined from 9 percent in 1974 to only 7 percent in 1978. Thus Trini-

Figure 14-4. Trinidad and Tobago: Structural Change in the Economy (the Dutch Disease)

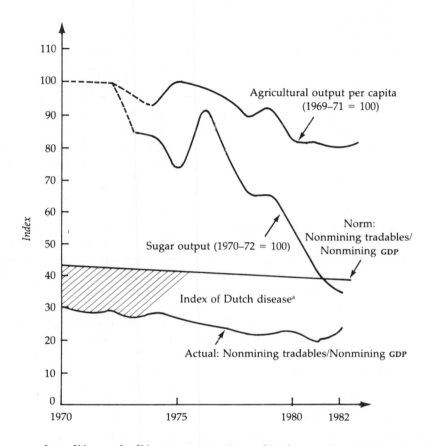

a. Let SN_{ag} and SN_{ma} represent "normal" shares of agriculture and manufacturing in nonmining GDP for a country at Trinidad and Tobago's level of income per capita, as derived from Chenery and Syrquin (1975), and let S_{ag} and S_{ma} be the actual shares. The Dutch disease index is defined as $(SN_{ag} + SN_{ma}) - (S_{ag} + S_{ma})$. It therefore measures the shortfall in the share of tradable nonmining sectors relative to its norm.

Source: Table 6-3, U.S. Department of Agriculture, and World Bank data.

dad and Tobago was steadily increasing its dependence on an oil sector that was *contracting* in relative terms.

Nevertheless, this period was in other respects a favorable one. Inflation was moderated by price controls and the openness of the economy: the inflation rate jumped to 22 percent in 1974 but fell back to 17 percent and then to 10 percent in the following years. The country devalued its currency by 22 percent against the weak U.S. dollar in 1975–77. Thereafter, it maintained a fixed parity of TT$2.40 to the dollar. The average trade-weighted real effective exchange rate in 1974–78 appreciated only 5.6 percent relative to its 1970–72 level, as shown in table 6-1. Further, between 1975 and 1978 employment increased by 4.7 percent, while unemployment decreased from 15.2 percent at the start of the boom to just over 12 percent. As already noted, however, this decrease was due to government-subsidized work programs and an increase in public sector employment; private sector employment was actually dropping.

By 1978 there was growing concern that the oil sector might not be able to sustain the current levels of public investment and consumption. At that year's rate of production, the remaining oil reserves of 700 million barrels would last only nine years. Production peaked in 1978; it was then expected to fall by one-fourth, to 167,000 barrels a day by 1983, with an implied drop of TT$0.5 billion a year in revenue. A government committee on public expenditure forecast nominal revenue growth of no more than 6 or 7 percent a year through 1983, compared with 54 percent a year during the first boom (Bobb 1978). It also projected that welfare programs alone would absorb a quarter of current revenues, or 12 percent of nonmining GDP.

Thus by 1978 the government was aware of its looming economic problems. Unlike some other oil-exporting nations, it planned to address them. But new natural gas finds in 1978—7.8 trillion cubic feet in proven reserves and 17 trillion cubic feet in estimated recoverable reserves—were considered sufficient to permit both an LNG plant and industrial uses (Niering 1982). These finds promised to offset the projected decline in oil revenues and reduced the urgency of making politically difficult choices. The second oil shock, coming soon after, removed any remaining bias toward caution.

The Second Oil Shock, 1979–81, and Its Aftermath

The second windfall—briefer than the first—was equivalent to 34.7 percent of nonmining GDP during 1979–81 and to half that during 1981–84.

Uses of the Windfall

The absorption patterns associated with the first oil boom gained momentum. Approximately one-fourth of the second windfall went to domestic investment and one-fourth to consumption; slightly less than one-half was saved abroad (relative to the base period

1970–72; see figure 14-1). The current account surplus was sharply reduced from 12.7 percent of nonmining GDP in the first boom to only 4.7 percent in the second.

The country ended the second boom in a sound financial position: by the end of 1981 reserves were US$3.4 billion and medium- and long-term debt only US$925 million. But absorption was on a rising trend, while oil revenues were falling rapidly. After 1982 demands for revenue to finance investment, public consumption, subsidies, and transfers threatened to eliminate the large international surplus accumulated since 1973. In 1982–83 fiscal deficits equaled 67 percent of oil revenues, current account deficits totaled US$1.9 billion (averaging 15.5 percent of nonmining GDP), and reserves fell to US$2.1 billion. In both 1984 and 1985 the government made substantial cutbacks in capital spending and subsidies, so that the current account deficits totaled only US$750 million, but reserves fell by a further US$1 billion. At the end of 1985 the Trinidadian dollar was devalued by half against the U.S. dollar.

Three chronic problems—low investment quality, high consumption levels, and a seriously weakened nonmining economic structure —became apparent during the second oil boom. Each resulted in greater dependence on the shrinking oil sector (Dutch disease) and made the gas-based industries all the more crucial to the economy, as described below.

Public Investment: The Overextension of State Ownership

Public investment accelerated sharply during 1979–81, putting Trinidad and Tobago more in line with the public investment intensity of other capital-scarce, oil-exporting countries. As figure 14-1 shows, nominal domestic investment rose relative to nonmining output by 9.3 percentage points over its 1970–72 value. Forty-six percent of government expenditures during the second boom went to capital outlays (up from 43 percent in the first). Roughly half was allocated to economic infrastructure, mainly transport and power, and one-fifth to social infrastructure. Much of the rest was earmarked for the gas-based industrial complex taking shape at Point Lisas.

The acceleration of investment appears to have reduced the quality of capital formation rather severely. Few projects were rigorously appraised or comparatively evaluated, and interactions among investment decisions were not adequately considered. For example, the large volume of public construction boosted unit costs of social infrastructure and caused delays that adversely affected the viability of the steel and fertilizer projects. Despite heavy spending on roads and transport, congestion remained serious in the early 1980s, and the woeful deficiencies of public transportation forced many to use costly private taxis.⁴ Some capital, in contrast, was seriously overbuilt. Because the demand for electricity failed to keep growing at its 14 percent rate of 1975–82, total generating capacity was twice as much as peak demand by the mid-1980s.

The proportion of funds allocated to acquiring existing firms, to financing new construction, and to making loans and advances to existing firms differed from that in the first boom. Outlays for acquisitions shrank to a small fraction of total public investment as loans and advances grew from approximately one-quarter to one-half of total outlays. This was partly to meet the start-up requirements of the largest capital projects and partly to cope with the increasing cash-flow problems of state-owned enterprises.

Severe difficulties developed in the state airline (BWIA) and in three large acquisitions from the first boom—sugar (Caroni), cement (Trinidad Cement), and oil refining (Trintoc). BWIA required TT$630 million in government loans from 1979 to 1981 to cover losses. Caroni lost TT$450 million; sugar production dropped from 143,000 tons in 1979 to 93,000 in 1981, and 1979–81 production averaged only half of installed capacity. Trinidad Cement's output dropped to less than half of capacity by 1981, and it could meet only one-third of domestic demand. The twenty-two-year-old plant used twice the energy of an efficient dry-process plant and had one-quarter the labor productivity. Its average production costs were almost twice those of a typical North African gas-based cement plant and half again those of a typical European plant, despite far lower energy charges. The cement subsidy rose steadily to TT$53 million by 1981. The government rejected the previous owners' proposal to replace the facility with a new one and planned instead to refurbish the plant and construct a second one. The Trintoc refinery suffered a small loss in 1980 as demand weakened and a TT$114 million loss in 1981. The government was faced with the choice of either closing the refinery at the cost of 1,000 jobs or investing more than US$400 million to upgrade it to produce lighter products. If it chose the second alternative, Trintoc would then rival the larger, unprofitable Texaco refinery employing 4,000 people, and pressure for its nationalization would increase. The total of all these losses, cumulated over 1979–81, represented the equivalent of 55 percent of 1979 oil revenues.

The new gas-based industries discussed at greater length below required greater capital infusions than had been expected. The ISCOTT DRI (direct reduced iron) steel plant and the Fertrin ammonia plant experienced significant construction delays and start-up difficulties. Construction of a urea factory and a methanol facility began in 1981, but by then their markets were turning down in the face of international recession.

Public Consumption and Unsustainable Subsidies

Constant-price consumption increased by 27 percent of nonmining output over 1970–72, as shown by the dotted line in figure 14-1. So measured, it accounted for much of the second windfall. The effect is less if the consumer price index is used to deflate consumption, but it is still large.

Subsidies for gasoline, cement, food, and public utilities rose from 3 percent of GDP in 1978 to 5 percent of GDP in 1981. Using a wider definition of subsidies, the new prime minister estimated them at 7 percent of GDP, or one-third of oil revenues in 1981 (Chambers 1982; see figure 14-2). In 1982 gasoline sold in Trinidad and Tobago for US$0.52 an imperial gallon, although the ex-refinery cost was twice that and the production cost at the pump was US$1.64 (Minister of State Enterprises 1982). With little incentive to economize, domestic gasoline sales increased from 0.75 million barrels in 1972 to 2.7 million barrels in 1981.

Despite controls, inflation rose to 14.7 percent in 1979 and 17.5 percent in 1980, then fell back to 14.2 percent in 1981. This was a sharp jump from the plateau of 11 percent in 1976–78.

The Dutch Disease: Weakening of Non-Oil Tradables

During the second oil boom, real output of the mining sector at 1970 prices fell by 4 percent, that of agriculture by 10 percent, and that of manufacturing by 5 percent. The share of nonmining tradables in nonmining GDP slipped further behind its Chenery-Syrquin norm, as shown in figure 14-4; agriculture's share fell to 3.3 percent and manufacturing's (including refining) to 17.7 percent. The extent to which Trinidad and Tobago's non-oil traded sectors lost ground to construction and services, relative to the "normal" pattern, was greater than in any of the other comparator countries (see table 6-3). Industrial production faltered as high domestic inflation plus the link to the appreciating U.S. dollar eroded competitiveness and appreciated the real exchange rate. Several large manufacturing firms went out of business in 1981 (Central Bank 1981). The real effective exchange rate averaged 116 in 1979–81, 140 in 1982–83, and 170 in 1984 (see figure 14-3), making it the second most appreciated rate in the sample after Nigeria's.

WAGES AND INFLATION. Wage trends and labor subsidies effected through public employment were important contributors to the decline of non-oil tradables. The special public works program (DEWD) spent an estimated TT$110 million to employ 50,000 people in 1980 (about 10,000 people at any given time). Work was light (typically two hours a day), and effective wages were therefore high at TT$20 an hour. This attracted workers particularly from agriculture (Inter-American Development Bank 1983; Pollard 1985). There is little evidence that DEWD's work was well conceived or that it made a significant supply-side contribution to output.

Wage increases were increasingly divorced from productivity and the ability of employers to pay. The Industrial Court lacked competence to determine the financial viability of settlements, so that wage agreements outstripped productivity. In 1977–81 labor productivity in industry, excluding oil and sugar, grew by 2.4 percent as real wages rose by 5 percent a year. During the same period, labor productivity decreased 10 percent a year in sugar, 4.3 percent in oil refining, and 2.1 percent in chemicals.

The public sector wage bill was TT$3.1 billion in 1982, almost twice that of 1981 and four times that of 1978, even though revenues were projected to drop and a budget deficit of TT$3.3 billion (almost 14 percent of GDP) was forecast. The fiscal deficit averaged 67 percent of oil revenues in 1982–83. Across the economy, pay negotiations in 1983 were heavily influenced by the inflationary spurt from the second oil boom. Three-year settlements called for an increase in wages of at least 42 percent in two oil companies, 50 percent in the Water and Sewerage Authority, 65 percent in the public telephone company, 62–80 percent in the government, and 94 percent in the sugar industry (Central Bank 1982b). Figure 14-3 shows the trend of increasing real wages, particularly in sugar.

Real exchange rate appreciation in 1983 and 1984 also reflected a new factor. Trinidad and Tobago, like Venezuela, had been able to avoid excessive inflation and appreciation of its real effective exchange rate in the mid-1970s. One reason was that both economies, unlike those of many of their trading partners, had been insulated from the supply shock of higher energy prices by explicit or implicit subsidies. This relationship reversed as declining oil revenues forced the rapid curtailment of a number of subsidies in 1983 and 1984. Between 1981 and 1984 regular gasoline prices in Trinidad and Tobago rose by 344 percent to approximately world levels, as did prices of other petroleum products. In 1984 inflation jumped to 16.8 percent and growth slowed—non-oil GDP is estimated to have contracted by 22 percent between 1982 and 1985. Unemployment climbed back up to an estimated 15 percent by 1985, and real wage increases began to fall below the rate of increase in labor productivity. The period of booming consumption was over.

THE COLLAPSE OF AGRICULTURE. In the early 1970s sugar had accounted for half of agricultural value added, other export crops for about 12 percent, and food crops for the rest. Even before the state began to acquire sugar operations, strong unions had captured much of the benefits from economies of scale in the large foreign-owned plantations. The resulting low profitability discouraged further investment (Auty 1976). In 1970 Tate and Lyle, the company responsible for nine-tenths of Trinidad's sugar capacity, partially withdrew, and the government acquired majority ownership. At that time severe strikes forced the declaration of a three-year state of emergency. In 1975 the state took over the company completely. Public ownership greatly reduced the threat of closing, and high profits in the 1974–75 sugar boom made the strong sugar trade unions more demanding. When the government completed its purchase of Tate and Lyle in 1975, it conceded a 100 percent pay raise to sugar workers, lest history repeat itself.

After the first oil boom, sugar production fell increasingly short of the industry's 220,000-ton capacity. By 1979 it had fallen to two-thirds and by 1981 to almost one-third of capacity (see figure 14-4). Real wage rates, however, rose by 80 percent between 1975 and 1981. In 1979 the actual cost of sugar production was about US$800 a ton, compared with US$240 in Australia. By the early 1980s yields had fallen to 3.7 tons of sugar per hectare, one-third of the yield in Australia and one-half the yield of two decades earlier in Trinidad and Tobago. By 1983 Caroni sugar was receiving subsidies worth an estimated TT$300 million a year (9 percent of oil revenues) while its average costs were five times those of a globally efficient producer. Rationalization by cutting capacity to 70,000 tons was considered in 1981. But this was politically difficult because most of the 20,000 workers dependent on sugar were highly organized.

Sugar was not the only export crop which performed poorly. Others, notably citrus, also declined substantially during the oil booms (Pollard 1985).

Imports increased their share of domestic food supplies from 70 percent to 90 percent between 1976 and 1980 (Ministry of Agriculture 1983). The government had long planned to shift resources from export to domestic crop production, but more than a decade after that decision, 70 percent of the arable land remained in export crop production, and the poorly performing export sector received most of the subsidized farm inputs. In 1983 Trinidad and Tobago produced one-fifth of its rice needs from farms that averaged 0.5 hectares, yielded about two tons of rice per hectare, and grew only one crop annually. In that year the domestic selling price for rice was US$417 a ton; the subsidized price guaranteed to farmers was US$825, which was said to be insufficient to cover costs. In contrast, mechanized rice farms in Suriname could provide an income of over US$6,000 per hectare at internationally competitive prices with one-third the labor required in Trinidad and Tobago and at lower unit labor costs.

In terms of financial allocations, it cannot be said that agriculture was neglected. Including sums made available for special lending to farmers, fiscal resources going to agriculture rose from TT$73 million in 1975 to TT$600 million in 1981 (*Trinidad Guardian* January 19, 1982). During this period, value added in the sector increased from TT$280 million to only TT$440 million, so that public spending exceeded income by a considerable margin. Yet severe infrastructural problems persisted. The cost of providing access roads was estimated to be twice as high as in Europe, and the poor quality led to rapid deterioration. In addition, because there was little pressure to raise productivity, spending in the rural areas has probably undermined rather than strengthened the sector.

Reversing Oil Dependence: The Role of Gas

By 1981 proven recoverable oil reserves were estimated at 600 million barrels, or a ten-year supply, and oil prices were falling. As late as the middle of 1981, gas-based industries were projected to yield enough revenue to offset the decline in oil until LNG exports and downstream industries could be developed in the late 1980s (Rampersad 1981b). At 1983 levels of production, proven gas reserves represented a fifty-four-year supply and probable reserves could extend this to seventy years. The proposed large Tenneco-Midcon LNG export project, even if feasible, had a lead time of five to six years, so that much depended on the performance of the first round of Point Lisas gas-based projects coming on stream.

The Appeal of Gas-Based Industry

In common with other oil-exporting governments, the first PNM government had encouraged capital-intensive, resource-based export projects while protecting other, import-substituting industries. The first gas-based factory, built in the late 1950s near Point Lisas produced, fertilizer for export. In 1966 the Point Lisas Industrial Development Corporation was formed to promote gas-based industry, but major development did not come until the first oil boom.

In 1974 the governments of Trinidad and Tobago, Jamaica, and Guyana agreed to conduct feasibility studies of a jointly owned smelter at Point Lisas. Amoco had put forth an alternative proposal for an LNG plant that would have absorbed the greater part of gas reserves while yielding US$15 million in tax revenues—less than one-quarter of oil revenues at the time (Ministry of Petroleum 1971). The Amoco proposal was rejected in favor of a gas-based industry, but there is no evidence that the alternatives were systematically compared. Though the government did envisage fifty labor-intensive downstream processing plants, capital-intensive heavy industry was to dominate the first decade of Point Lisas's development.

Advocates justified gas-based projects on at least three grounds. They could attract outside financing at favorable interest rates, leaving oil revenues for other uses. (The government financed only one-third of the average venture and borrowed most of the rest.) They could generate net foreign exchange earnings. And they could provide substantial revenues through taxes and returns on state equity. Although the projects promised few permanent jobs, they would generate construction jobs, give rise to a demand for labor when the projected downstream factories were built, and create a permanent pool of skilled nationals—all of which were seen as benefits (National Energy Corporation 1981). Also important was the strongly nationalistic appeal of leaping from a plantation economy to a technologically sophisticated one.

But gas-based industrial development had some serious disadvantages as well, particularly for a state as small as Trinidad and Tobago. First, it projected the problems of a mineral economy (such as dualism) into the drive for industrial diversification. Second, it postponed reform and attempts to raise efficiency in the nonhydrocarbon sectors. And third, it was risky since it involved a small number of plants that were highly leveraged and dependent on volatile external markets whose accessibility could not, in most cases, be guaranteed.

To reduce the risk, the government chose a fairly diversified portfolio, especially given the size of the country. In 1975 it concluded agreements with W. R. Grace to build a large ammonia plant and with three steel firms to construct a DRI steel unit. In 1976 it agreed to a joint Amoco fertilizer plant. Later it explored proposals for an aluminum smelter with National Southwire, for an LNG terminal with Tenneco and Midcon, for a urea plant with Agrico-Chemicals, and for a methanol facility with Borden. Not all the schemes were implemented before the second oil boom collapsed; aluminum and LNG plants were two particularly large projects that were never carried out.

As noted in chapter 7 and in Auty (1986a), the motivation for accelerating the construction of resource-based industrial plants shifted during the 1970s. Because resource-based projects are highly capital-intensive, pressure for premature entry increases when inflation is expected to be high and real interest rates low, as in the mid-1970s. A typical venture, such as a methanol plant, might take three years to construct and be two-thirds loan-financed. Repayment would be over eight years, during which time the plant would be depreciated. Thereafter, the government would own outright a plant that could be expected to last for at least another ten to twenty years. It would be able to undercut the production costs of new plants built at higher prices and facing higher capital costs, and it would therefore be profitable—provided that demand expanded rapidly enough for prices to be set by the costs of the marginal, newest plant. Real interest rates had, of course, risen to substantially positive levels by the second windfall period, but energy prices were projected to keep on rising in real terms, and this expectation had a major impact on feasibility studies. The risks that demand would falter, that markets would turn down, and that access would dry up were especially serious for a small country such as Trinidad and Tobago, whose domestic market is far smaller than the capacity of an efficient plant in a resource-based industry. There risks, however, were never seriously taken into account.

Problems of Entry: The Case of Steel

In 1977, after withdrawing from the planned joint steel venture with three multinational partners, the government began its own venture through ISCOTT. This called for a plant with 750,000 tons of billet and a 450,000-ton DRI unit with a scrap complement. But anticipations of scrap shortages prompted the addition of a second DRI unit, which added 25 percent to costs and unbalanced the production chain. The second DRI unit and a construction cost overrun of 30 percent resulted in a final capital cost of US$500 million, which required substantial new financing at high interest rates.

Since the domestic market was only 60,000 tons, two-thirds of production was targeted to the southeastern United States, where efficient minimills are among the most competitive in the world (Barnett and Schorsch 1983). ISCOTT's unit costs—on the assumption of full capacity for the first DRI unit and 80 percent capacity for the billet plant—were US$410 per metric ton compared with US$270 per metric ton for the minimills. A marketing survey had warned that ISCOTT would need to undercut its U.S. competitors by 15 percent, but a successful U.S. anti-dumping suit in 1982 imposed a 14 percent penalty on ISCOTT (Chambers 1984). This left the plant with woefully inadequate markets and annual capital charges of more than US$100 million. The worst-case projection for ISCOTT quickly became overly optimistic; cumulative losses to April 1982 were almost TT$400 million, equal to one-fifth of 1979 oil revenue (*Caribbean Contact* 1982).

The unexpectedly severe world recession that began in 1981 invalidated all projections of real interest rate, relative price, and demand. As late as 1980 the OECD was forecasting that global steel consumption would almost double to 1,400 million tons by the year 2000. More recent projections indicate a rise of only 20 percent, to 900 million tons, with almost all the reduction in consumption from industrial countries (Barnett and Schorsch 1983). Marginal, export-oriented new plants such as ISCOTT's were the most seriously affected by the altered trend.

Trinidad and Tobago would have had a second crippling investment had it proceeded with plans for the 150,000-ton aluminum smelter. Ironically, the principal reason for abandoning the project was the government's impatience with the lack of progress; it wanted to enter the market in time to capture the widely anticipated boom in aluminum prices. By 1980 the government was close to agreement on a joint venture with National Southwire for a US$500 million smelter to start up in 1984. To be profitable, it required an estimated metal price of US$0.92 a pound in 1982 dollars, but in 1982 the price of aluminum collapsed to US$0.43 a pound (Vais 1982). The prudent decision not to proceed confirms the important role of private equity partners in heightening the sensitivity of state corporations to risk.

Ranking the Options: Rent and Risk in Gas-Based Industry

Did Trinidad and Tobago have good reason to expect gas to replace oil as a source of economic rent? To answer this, it is necessary to review some actual and proposed projects. Table 14-1 lists the seven gas-based projects built, under construction, or proposed for Point Lisas by the end of the second oil boom. All costs are based on industry estimates for the operating characteristics of the Point Lisas plants. These costs, expressed in 1982 U.S. dollars, total four and a half times the 1980 oil windfall. Estimates assume that the projects operate at designed capacity. The comparison therefore abstracts from the problem of access to foreign markets, which became so critical with the slowdown in world demand.

The netbacks on gas inputs for each project are calculated by assuming a 20 percent pretax accounting rate of return on equity.

Table 14-1. Trinidad and Tobago: Actual and Potential Gas Netbacks for Gas-Based Industry, 1982

Gas-based industry	Gas input (MCF per ton)	Investment[a] (U.S. dollars per MCF per year)	Gas netback[b] (1982 U.S. dollars per MCF)	
			1982 prices	Long-run prices
Metals				
DRI	12.5	12.68	0.41	0.07
Steel	19.9	26.98	3.61	0.85
Aluminum[c]	128.0	16.24	6.25	1.30
Chemicals				
Ammonia	33.0	13.37	0.27	1.76
Urea	23.8	1.47	0.85	2.76
Methanol	29.3	14.09	1.88	0.85
Gas export				
LNG[c]	59.0	8.69	2.11	3.51

MCF = thousand cubic feet.

a. Total investment divided by total MCF consumed per year.

b. Gas netback = residual payment to gas at wellhead after deducting a 20 percent pretax return on equity and all other costs exclusive of gas input. Price assumptions (U.S. dollars per ton) are:

	1982 prices	Long-run prices
DRI	100	130
Steel	275	330
Aluminum	1,102	1,989
Ammonia	145	231
Urea	145	231
Methanol	160	240
Gas	4.5 (per MCF)	5.9 (per MCF)

c. Proposed project.

Source: Auty (1983).

Two hypothetical sets of product prices are assumed, 1982 prices and long-run prices, as they might have appeared in the optimistic period of the second boom.[5] The netbacks indicate the price that could have been paid for natural gas by the industry, under the given assumptions.

The table suggests that the metals projects could not afford to make any positive payment for gas at 1982 prices, and that only the aluminum project might have afforded it at long-run prices. However, long-run aluminum price projections have since been revised downward by about 25 percent, as have those of many other resource-based products (see table 7-5) so that none of the metals projects seems viable. The chemical plants looked somewhat better at the hypothetical prices, although price trends for gas-based chemical products have also been revised downward substantially.

The table indicates, further, that the only way to be able to afford a sizable gas payment (or netback) would be to export LNG at prices high enough to accommodate the very high capital costs of such a project. But the costs of extracting and gathering gas must still be deducted in order to arrive at an estimate of the residual rent on gas. Natural gas production and gathering costs vary greatly by field and scale. For large Middle Eastern and North African fields, they may be US$0.25 per thousand cubic feet (MCF) and may even be negative if the return from condensate by-products is able to offset the cost of development. For Trinidad and Tobago, gas costs are more difficult to determine because of geological differences among gas fields and variations in the timing of sunk investments. In 1982 dollars, and allowing for probable condensate by-products, gas from Trinidad and Tobago's southeast coastal fields would cost in the region of US$0.50 per MCF. But estimates for the costlier north coast fields in deeper waters and in more dispersed reservoirs range up to US$3.00 per MCF. Such development, together with its dedicated transmission system, would be necessary to support a major LNG plant. The Ricardian rent on gas even at the long-run product prices underlying the table (which by the mid-1980s looked very high indeed!) would have been very low relative to oil.

Despite reservations about gas-based industrialization, Turner and Bedare (1979) have argued in its favor. They point to externalities of such projects in triggering more broadly based industrialization and expanding domestic skills. Stauffer (1975) considers the case for gas-based industrialization to be strongest where—as in Trinidad and Tobago—oil reserves are small and gas is mostly nonassociated. Indeed, although the projects listed in table 14-1 promised little natural resource rent from their gas inputs even at optimistic prices, their total gross exports were projected to be three-quarters of 1982 oil exports, and taxes plus returns to public equity were projected at one-third of the fiscal revenue derived from oil in 1982. Two-thirds of projected sales and revenues were to come from the proposed LNG project, however—a calculation that warrants a more critical look.

For a small country, an LNG project is a major gamble. Whereas ISCOTT involved a total capital investment equal to less than 10 percent of Trinidad and Tobago's 1982 GDP, the cost of the LNG proposal may be about eight times that figure. By mixing cheap and more expensive gas, the average investment cost could have been kept down to about US$2.25 per MCF, not far above the netback from 1982 LNG prices in table 14-1. But only if the price of LNG were above that assumed in the table, or if the costs of extraction were lower, would any true rent accrue to the government. Lower LNG prices would seriously erode the government's tax and returns on investment.[6] The conclusion is clear: only if the timing of an LNG plant had enabled a long-term contract to be locked in at particularly advantageous terms, or if the plant had used gas from the older and cheaper fields, might it have generated sizable tax and investment revenues, let alone a large rent component. By the mid-1980s LNG was clearly not a viable option.

Assessment

The experience of Trinidad and Tobago illustrates the political and economic obstacles to avoiding an increased dependence on natural resource rents in the face of substantial windfalls. As might have been expected from its recent history, the country's fiscal policy was initially cautious. Domestic investments rose more slowly than in other oil-exporting countries, and savings abroad were much greater. But at the same time, the political need to distribute rent widely across the economy led to the rapid growth of subsidies to consumers, workers, and failing firms. These subsidies were higher in Trinidad and Tobago than in the comparators—especially the poorest ones—because of its democratic political system and the vulnerability of its government to organized protest after 1970.

Real consumption gains were greater than in most of the comparators—relative, of course, to nonmining income. One important reason for this was that in Trinidad and Tobago declining non-oil tradable sectors were better able to preserve, and even augment, their incomes.

Political pressure to raise and sustain consumption has been an Achilles' heel in Trinidad and Tobago's strategy. Subsidies and price controls, together with wage increases, real exchange appreciation, and the extension of public ownership undermined agriculture and manufacturing industry. Windfalls also financed the postponement of fundamental change needed to arrest agricultural decline and improve manufacturing's competitiveness. As a result, between 1972 and 1981 the share of nonmining tradables in nonmining GDP relative to the norm contracted more in Trinidad and Tobago than in any other country in the sample. Thus, although Trinidad and Tobago ended the second boom with US$2.6 billion in net assets abroad, its economy was far more dependent on oil than ever before, as revealed by the magnitude of later fiscal and current account deficits and the severity of economic contraction after 1982. By the mid 1980s reserves had fallen sharply.

Why has the country's growth performance not been better, given the volume of investment in its economy since 1974? For one thing, it lacked effective means to make productive investments in agriculture or competitive light industry, particularly given the wage push engendered by the windfalls. Furthermore, investments in infrastructure either were not cost-effective (as in transport) or suffered from lack of demand as the economy ceased to grow (as in electricity) and therefore yielded low economic returns. Attempts to diversify had emphasized gas-based industry, much of which, especially steel (another Achilles' heel), promised low returns. Eagerness to use oil revenues in this way led the government to downplay the risk involved in such large projects and to "go it alone." The lack of downstream foreign partners compounded marketing problems when demand forecasts proved to be overoptimistic. One lesson from Trinidad and Tobago's experience, therefore, is that foreign investors are important in screening projects, diversifying risk, and securing market access for large export-oriented, resource-based industries.

How to limit the effects of rising wage and employment pressures on the non-oil economy, given political and social institutions, is more problematic. Direct income transfers (as in Alaska) or transfers that encouraged retraining rather than subsidies to declining sectors might have helped to move workers to potentially more productive activities. And greater incentives to direct foreign investment might have attracted new industries. It is important to recognize, however, that the composition of groups seeking shares of the oil rent mirrored the existing economic structure quite closely. This would have made such policies difficult to implement.

To sum up, Trinidad and Tobago's experience during the oil boom years had some positive features. Its citizens reaped large consumption gains; and when the boom ended and oil revenues fell, the country had a sufficient reserve to avoid an immediate foreign exchange crisis. In view of the caution with which the government set out to manage the windfalls, it is a pity that these gains may well prove to be transitory because of the inability to effect structural improvements in the non-oil economy.

Notes

1. For further discussion see Renwick (1982). Lowenthal (1972) defines the social structure as "cultural pluralism," in which groups interact for economic purposes but adhere to religious or ethnic groupings in social matters.

2. Norm estimates are based on Chenery and Syrquin (1975), with nonmining per capita GDP taken as the indicator of per capita income.

3. As in chapter 5, the windfall and its uses are estimated by comparing actual figures with a hypothetical projection of what would have transpired without the windfall based on four assumptions: (a) relative price deflators are constant at their average 1970–72 level, (b) the ratio of real mining output to nonmining GDP is constant, (c) the ratio of total absorption to output is constant, and (d) consumption and investment change their share of absorption in line with the norms given in Chenery and Syrquin (1975).

4. Public buses could handle only 4.5 percent of passenger trips. The 55 percent of households that did not own a private car spent, on average, an estimated 27 percent of their household income on transportation, mostly on private taxis (Trinidad and Tobago 1984).

5. This method of comparison builds on a study of gas-based industry in the Persian/Arabian Gulf (Stauffer 1975).

6. The LNG prices in table 14-1 can be compared with the US$4.50 border price for Mexican and Canadian gas in 1982, the US$2.80-US$3.40 price for new wells in the United States, and the US$7.30 price for deep gas in the United States.

Chapter 15

Venezuela: Absorption without Growth

with François Bourguignon

The increases in world oil prices in 1973–74 and in 1979–80 dramatically raised expectations of accelerated development in Venezuela. The democratically elected government had the opportunity to use the surging fiscal revenue to increase the country's economic growth and improve the welfare of its people. And for a time, the Venezuelan economy did boom: between 1972 and 1978 non-oil GDP rose at an average annual rate of 8.4 percent, private consumption rose at 12 percent, and gross investment rose at almost 15 percent. Curiously, however, the boom ended with the redoubling of oil prices in 1979, which coincided with a political transition. GDP has been stagnating since 1979, and the government had to turn to the IMF for help in financing a $20 billion debt. Ten years after the first oil price increase, Venezuela faced its worst economic crisis since World War II—although world oil prices were still far higher in real terms than they had been before 1973.

This chapter seeks to understand the reasons for this paradox in the evolution of Venezuela's economy since 1973. More precisely, the objective is to determine how large the windfalls were, how they were used by those who benefited directly (the government and the oil companies), how some of the extra revenue was transferred to other economic agents, and what the overall effects were on the non-oil economy.

The analysis addresses two central questions. What have the windfalls contributed to Venezuela's development? And did the Venezuelan government, faced suddenly with greatly improved terms of trade, make the best possible policy choices? As will become apparent, the policies followed were far from optimal. The stagnation of

François Bourguignon is professor of economics at the Ecole Normale Supérieure, Paris.

the economy after 1979 and the ensuing crisis were heavily influenced by choices made at the outset of the oil boom, as well as by macroeconomic policies adopted after 1979. But the government was not entirely free in making choices and setting policies. Social pressures triggered by the dramatic change in the country's terms of trade expressed themselves through the political system. Public choice was further constrained—indeed, rendered inconsistent—by the country's institutions, which gave rise to conflicting policies after 1978.

The first section describes the economic and political outlook in Venezuela in the early 1970s. The next section analyzes and appraises the first oil boom, a period of rapid growth. A discussion of the second boom, a period of economic stagnation, follows, together with a summation of Venezuela's use of the windfalls for the full period. The financial crisis of 1983 is then outlined, and the final section draws some general lessons from the Venezuelan experience.

Economic and Political Background

Oil has had a pervasive influence on Venezuela's economic and political evolution since the country made the transition to a mineral economy in the 1920s. By 1930 oil accounted for 83 percent of exports, and it was responsible for the relatively high and rapidly rising rate of urbanization (Karl 1982, table II-2). Hit by the combination of an appreciating exchange rate and worldwide depression, agriculture's share of GDP dwindled. Meanwhile, the oil mining camps provided a natural setting for labor to organize and to develop a strong national political party.

After the overthrow of the dictator Pérez Jiménez in 1958, the country became a constitutional democracy modeled on the U.S. system—the only one of the countries in this study with such a government throughout the period of the windfalls. The political climate, moreover, has been unusually competitive. Two parties dominate: Acción Democrática or AD (equivalent to the Social Democrats in other Latin American countries) and COPEI (equivalent to Christian Democrats). But there are also many smaller parties, and they steadily increased their share of the vote in the 1950s and 1960s to 46 percent by 1968 (Karl 1982, table II-20).

Oil had made possible continuous economic growth since the 1930s. By the early 1970s Venezuela's per capita income was just below that of the least developed European countries (Ireland, Portugal, and Spain). The structure of GDP had changed dramatically since the 1950s. Between 1958 and 1972 non-oil GDP grew at an average annual rate of 6.8 percent. The share of the petroleum sector (including oil refining) in total GDP at 1968 prices dropped from 31 percent to 20 percent. Manufacturing (excluding oil refining) was the fastest growing sector, expanding at 7.8 percent a year. This was the result of a dynamic import substitution process, helped by foreign investments, which brought down the share of imports in final private consumption from 30 percent at the end of the 1950s to 3 percent in 1970. Agriculture lagged; its share in GDP was only 6 percent in 1972. Despite substantial investments and relatively high tariffs, food output could not satisfy domestic demand. Imports made up 15 percent of all food consumed.[1]

The rate of investment was high, exceeding 23 percent of GDP between 1968 and 1972. (It had probably been slightly higher in the early 1960s, but no comparable figure is available before 1968 because of a change in definitions in the national accounts.) The high rate of investment was the result of the considerable fiscal revenue from oil exports, as well as public choices about how to use that revenue. Oil was also responsible for the unusual size of the public sector. By 1972 public savings represented just over 40 percent of total national savings. But the government did not transfer its savings to the private sector. Instead, very early, it established state-owned companies in various fields: electricity, transport, communications, aluminum, iron ore, steel (with the ambitious Orinoco steel company), and finally oil.[2] Value added by the entire public sector exceeded 16 percent of GDP in 1972, of which 11 percent was added by the government itself. Between 1968 and 1972, 30 percent of gross investment was public, half of it made by state enterprises.

Two other aspects of Venezuela's pre-1973 economy are notable. First, inflation was exceptionally low. Between 1958 and 1972 the rise in the consumer price index averaged only 1.8 percent a year.[3] Second, in 1972 public foreign debt was less than $1 billion. Most of it had been accumulated over the preceding five years, when the terms of trade had been at their worst since 1950. However, because foreign reserves increased by $800 million between 1970 and 1972 as oil prices recovered and sales rose, the net position was more or less balanced. Yet industrialization, especially in the petroleum sector, had relied heavily on foreign investment. Profit repatriation amounted to $1 billion in 1972, approximately 30 percent of export revenue. Since $800 million of this came from the oil sector, Venezuela's balance of payments would be greatly improved by the total nationalization of the oil industry in 1975.

The most negative aspects of Venezuela's economy in the early 1970s were high unemployment, inequitable income distribution, and inadequate public services. Karl (1982) attributes the loss of voting strength by AD and COPEI to a "crisis of legitimacy" gradually brought about by the extent of economic inequality. Data are scarce, but there is wide agreement on several points. Open unemployment, estimated at 8 percent in 1971, was almost certainly higher (underemployment was not measured). Income distribution was among the most inegalitarian in the world.[4] The sketchy evidence suggests that little change in the distribution of income had occurred between 1968 and 1972. Wages might have grown a little faster than non-oil GDP per capita. But private consumption grew more slowly, with an elasticity of about 0.80, which may indicate a slight worsening of income distribution (Bourguignon 1980a,b).

The failure of the extremely high growth of non-oil GDP to reduce unemployment and equalize income may be attributed to a strong policy bias toward capital-intensive and monopolistic manufacturing. There were virtually no non-oil exports, and heavy regulation rendered most of the non-oil economy nontraded in the sense that there was little effective competition with imports. Import-substituting industries relied on protection and on implicit subsidies to large public and private companies. Although the small size of the domestic market precluded economies of scale, in heavily protected subsectors such as automobiles profit rates were estimated to be twice those for comparable industries in the United States.

The concentration of income may also explain the temporary slowdown of industrialization that occurred in the late 1960s. Once most imported consumer goods had been substituted by domestic products, domestic markets were saturated and producers were left with excess capacity. Manufacturing growth (excluding oil refining), which had averaged 8.4 percent between 1958 and 1965, dropped to 4.7 percent between 1965 and 1969. Unused capacity was an estimated 40 percent by 1969, while the trade balance swung into deficit in 1968 and 1969. Policymakers recognized these problems but attributed them solely to the fact that the first phase of import substitution was nearing completion. Consequently, the COPEI administration of President Rafael Caldera (1968–73) took steps to reorient the development strategy toward nontraditional exports. Ambitious resource-based industrial projects were launched, especially in steel and aluminum—subsectors in which estimates of low effective protection confirmed a general belief that Venezuela had some comparative advantage, at least in relation to its other non-oil sectors.

The administration also took steps that would eventually lead to the nationalization of the oil industry. They included a unilateral increase in export tax rates, nationalization of natural gas production, and a revision of contracts between foreign oil companies and the national oil company. These measures, along with improved terms of trade, enabled the administration to compensate for slower domestic growth by expanding public spending out of increased oil revenue. Perhaps because of the new prosperity, however, it put little emphasis on resolving the crucial problems of unemployment and poverty.

The 1973 presidential campaign focused, uncharacteristically for Venezuela, on social issues. The AD candidate, Carlos Andrés Pérez, stressed the need to fight poverty. When the price of oil skyrocketed less than two months before the election, Pérez's program suddenly became affordable. Pérez was elected with a solid majority, and his party also won the legislative elections.[5] In his inaugural speech, the new president reaffirmed his commitment to solving the country's social problems:

> This period must be the beginning of an era of authentic popular achievements . . . The economic and social democracy to which my government is committed requires that the wealth of this nation reaches all social classes. The concentration of oil revenue in the hands of a minority would mean opulence without democratic vocation. (Carlos Andrés Pérez, March 1974, as quoted in Bourguignon 1985, p. 13.)

The First Oil Windfall, 1973–78

Between 1972 and 1974 the average price of Venezuelan crude oil climbed from $2.50 to $10.50 a barrel. It was widely expected that the resulting dramatic—and seemingly permanent—increase in national income would accelerate economic development and enable Venezuela to catch up with the industrialized democracies. Pérez envisioned a great future for his country:

> You are actors in the great national transformation that is going to make Venezuela one of the great countries of the world . . . A Great Venezuela because all Venezuelans can have work . . . A Great Venezuela because we know how to utilise . . . science and technology to transform our natural resources so that we may be incorporated . . . into the concert of the great nations of the world. (Carlos Andrés Pérez, 11 September 1974, as quoted in Karl 1982, p. 65.)

Size of the Windfall

To estimate the size of Venezuela's first oil windfall, it is necessary to project what the economy would have been like had the price of

Table 15-1. Venezuela: The First Oil Windfall, 1973–78
(billions of bolivares)

Measure	1973	1974	1975	1976	1977	1978
Value added in the oil industry	17.9	44.6	34.5	36.6	38.5	35.3
Value added in the oil industry with 1972 terms of trade and output[a]	12.9	15.0	16.9	18.0	19.3	20.7
Extra value added	5.0	29.6	17.5	18.6	19.2	14.6
To Venezuelan agents[b]	1.9	25.7	20.0	18.6	19.2	14.6
Implicit transfers to domestic consumers of oil products	0.5	3.2	2.8	3.1	3.9	4.1
Total oil windfall	2.4	28.9	22.8	21.7	23.1	18.7
To government	1.9	25.7	20.0	15.2	15.8	11.4
To national oil companies	0	0	0	3.4	3.4	3.2
GDP without oil windfall	68.4	82.9	100.8	116.7	136.7	156.3
Oil windfall as a percentage of GDP excluding windfall	3.5	34.9	22.6	18.5	16.9	12.0

Note: The figures in the table probably underestimate the oil windfall immediately after the 1973 price increase and overestimate it for later years. But for the period as a whole the calculations should be approximately correct.
a. For details of the calculations, see Bourguignon (1985).
b. Sometimes larger than extra value added because of lags in payments made by the oil sector to the government.
Source: Bourguignon (1985).

oil *not* increased. This analysis uses a projection different from the one developed for comparative purposes in chapter 5 and more realistic for Venezuela. To make the projection, it is assumed that without the price rise both the volume of oil exports and their price relative to imports would have remained at their pre-1973 levels.[6] In table 15-1 computation of the windfall starts from the difference between the actual value added of the oil sector and its 1972 value added deflated by the import price index. This is then corrected for changes in the state's share of gross oil profits (the share was 100 percent after nationalization). Finally, account is taken of the fact that internal prices of oil products were only one-third of external prices after 1973; this substantial implicit transfer to domestic consumers is also considered part of the windfall. The resulting estimates of the windfall average 20 percent of GDP between 1974 and 1978, with a tendency to decline over time as export volume decreased and oil prices softened. Despite this, the windfall was still substantial in 1978.

Direct Uses of the Windfall

As table 15-1 shows, the government received the whole windfall until the nationalization of the oil companies, and most of it thereafter. The methodological problem in determining how the extra revenue was used is to infer what both the government and the oil companies would have spent had their oil receipts remained constant. For the government, a simple method would be to extrapolate the trends in real expenditures before 1973 and then to impute to the oil windfall the difference between actual expenditures and extrapolated figures. But such a solution would assume that the pre-1973 growth rate of government activity could have been sustained with no growth in oil receipts—not a tenable assumption. Although every set of assumptions has its drawbacks, this analysis is based on the following:

- The government's real investments and transfers would have remained constant (as they actually did between 1968 and 1972).
- The government's value added and intermediate consumption would have grown at a rate of 3 percent a year (about two-thirds of the average rate between 1968 and 1972, which was 4.4 percent). Three considerations enter into this assumption: (a) approximately 60 percent of the government's receipts would have been frozen in the absence of the oil windfall, whereas oil receipts had grown faster than the government's total income since 1968; (b) non-oil growth rates would have

been lower than their pre-1973 trend; and (c) current expenditures represented about two-thirds of total spending before 1973.

- Non-oil GDP could have grown at 5 percent a year in the absence of the windfall without producing larger current account deficits. Such an order of magnitude seems consistent with the 1958–72 experience.
- The huge financial investments of the national oil company after 1975 may be attributed to the windfall. In cases where the companies' share of the oil windfall proved larger than the actual net addition to their financial assets, the discrepancy has been imputed to their capital formation. This occurs only after 1978. Before then, net investments by national oil companies are rather low, which is consistent with the falling level of production. It is true, however, that under the assumption that oil output stayed at its 1972 level more investments would have been necessary. Thus these calculations probably slightly underestimate the share of the oil bonus made available by the oil companies to other domestic agents or to the rest of the world.

These assumptions, though arbitrary, lead to an approximately consistent set of estimates for the uses of the windfall. Fortunately, changes in actual public spending levels after 1973 are great enough for the results not to be too sensitive to the counterfactual projections.

The results of these calculations are clear. As recorded in table 15-2, the Venezuelan government used the windfall to raise wages, employment, and output in the public sector. Between 1973 and 1978 current expenditures increased by some 25 percent over their counterfactual levels. The annual growth in value added by the government rose from 4 percent in 1968–72 to 8.9 percent in 1973–78. The growth in gross direct investment by the government is even more dramatic: negligible before 1973, it reached more than 11 percent a year during the five years after the first oil price increase. In absolute terms, however, the impact on government investment was less than on current expenditures.

Transfers to households between 1974 and 1978 averaged roughly 7 percent of the government budget with the oil windfall excluded. These included transfers to public companies, most of which covered the deficit of the Marketing Board for Agricultural Products (about 1 percent of GDP). This deficit arose because in late 1974 the government, responding to rising inflation, implemented a broad policy of subsidies and of price controls that extended to nearly four-fifths of wage goods. In table 15-2 all transfers to households are imputed to the windfall. The same policy might have been implemented even in the absence of the extra oil revenue since it was one of President Pérez's 1973 campaign promises. But if so, the transfers would probably have been much smaller.

Spending lagged behind income. For the 1973–78 period the government used roughly 45 percent of its extra oil revenue, but up to 1975 it had used only 25 percent. Some of the windfall not used directly by the government, as well as some of that saved by the national oil companies, was converted to foreign assets; the rest was made available through financial channels to other Venezuelan economic agents. To separate these two uses of revenue, net loans to the rest of the world by the government and the nationalized oil companies are attributed to the oil windfall because the balance of capital exports and reserve accumulation became significant only from 1973 on.[7] The crucial distinctions between public and private and between net and gross flows are discussed below; here, only consolidated net capital flows are considered. These figures can therefore be misleading for two reasons: they refer to the Venezuelan economy as a whole, and they lump together net and gross flows. Strictly speaking, only positive changes in the net assets of the government (and of the oil companies after 1975) should be considered as investments made abroad out of the windfall, but heavy borrowing after 1976 may also be explained by the eagerness of international bankers to recycle petrodollars to oil exporters and importers alike.

In the first years after the oil price increase, almost all the oil windfall not used internally was saved abroad through the Venezuelan Investment Fund (FIV), which was created in 1974 to administer the public saving of oil revenue. After 1976, however, the Venezuelan public sector became a net borrower, even though the balance remained positive for the period as a whole (see table 15-2). Subtracting net loans from that part of the oil windfall not used directly yields the estimated amount of the windfall available to the rest of the economy. Among the secondary beneficiaries, one group is easy to identify—public non-oil companies, the rapid development of which must be attributed to the oil windfall.

As noted earlier, investments in such companies had increased substantially during the period of the fourth development plan (1970–74), which started shortly before the first oil price increase. They more than doubled under the fifth plan (1976–80), which was the first consistent program for using the oil windfall. The fifth plan, like the previous one, emphasized the construction of ambitious public steel and aluminum plants to promote nontraditional exports, to substitute imports of intermediate products, and to pro-

Table 15-2. Venezuela: Use of the Oil Windfall, 1973–78
(billions of bolivares)

Use of windfall	1973	1974	1975	1976	1977	1978
Imputed government expenditure						
Oil windfall received by the government	1.9	25.7	20.0	15.2	15.8	11.4
Additional current expenditures[a]	—	1.5	2.7	4.1	5.6	6.1
Percentage increase[a]		(12.4)	(19.4)	(27.3)	(33.0)	(32.0)
Compensation of employees[b]	—	1.2	2.2	3.4	4.6	4.9
Additional gross investment	—	—	3.2	1.8	2.4	3.9
Percentage increase[a]			(101.1)	(50.6)	(61.6)	(89.1)
Transfer to households, CMA, and other public companies[c]	—	1.8	2.1	1.9	2.3	1.9
Total imputed expenditures	—	3.3	8.0	7.8	10.3	11.9
Not imputed: net loans and capital transfers to public companies and the rest of the world	1.9	22.4	12.0	7.4	5.5	−0.5

Imputed windfall available to public non-oil companies, the private sector, and the rest of the world

Oil windfall not used by the government or national oil companies	1.9	22.4	12.0	10.8	8.9	2.7
Net change in foreign position of government and national oil companies	2.3	18.3	9.8	2.1	-2.3	-12.8
Oil windfall made available to public non-oil companies and private sector	-0.4	4.1	2.2	8.7	10.2	15.5
Imputed change in investments by public non-oil companies	—	—	—	5.6	9.3	10.3
Other	-0.4	4.1	2.2	3.1	0.9	5.2
Net change in foreign position of public non-oil companies and private sector	1.4	5.9	-0.7	-1.0	-11.3	-11.7
Imputed change in investment by private sector	—	-0.4	2.0	4.9	13.4	13.5
Imputed change in savings by non-oil sector[d]	1.8	1.4	-0.9	1.6	1.2	-3.4

— Not applicable.

Note: For details of the calculations, see Bourguignon (1985)

a. Figures in parentheses are estimated percentage increases over the hypothetical expenditures without the oil windfall.

b. Percentage increases are the same as for total current expenditures; see Bourguignon (1985).

c. The most important component is transfers to CMA, a public company in charge of the price controls and subsidy policy adopted for the agricultural sector in 1974. Households are the final beneficiaries of those transfers. Since most of the total transfers are imputed to the oil windfall, computing a rate of increase as in the previous lines would not make sense.

d. Computed as (net change in foreign position of public non-oil companies and private sector) + (change in investments by private sector) – (change in investments by private sector) – (other).

Source: Bourguignon (1985).

Table 15-3. Venezuela: Summary of the First Oil Windfall and Its Uses, 1973–78
(billions of bolivares)

Final beneficiary or main use	1973	1974	1975	1976	1977	1978	Total At 1973 prices^a	Percent
Total oil windfall	2.4	28.9	22.8	21.7	23.1	18.7	94.4	100.0
Net loans to the rest of the world[b]	3.7	24.2	9.1	1.1	−13.6	−24.5	7.0[g]	7.4
Domestic consumers of oil products	0.5	3.2	2.8	3.1	3.9	4.1	13.8	14.6
Government								
Current expenditures	—	1.5	2.7	4.1	5.6	6.1	15.0	15.9
Investment	—	—	3.2	1.8	2.4	3.9	8.4	8.9
Public companies (investment)[c]	—	—	—	6.0	9.3	10.3	18.3	19.4
Private sector								
Transfers from government to households	—	1.8	2.1	1.9	2.3	1.9	7.8	8.3
Other[d]	−1.8	−1.8	2.9	3.7	13.2	16.9	24.1	25.5
Investment[e]	—	−0.4	2.0	4.9	13.4	13.5	23.9	25.3
Total real expenditures imputed to the windfall[f]	—	2.9	10.0	18.7	33.0	35.7	73.5	77.9
Total investment imputed to the windfall	—	−0.4	5.2	12.7	25.1	27.7	50.7	53.7

— Not applicable.
a. Annual figures deflated by the consumer price index.
b. Aggregate net changes in the foreign position of public and private agents (see table 15-2).
c. Oil companies contributed only Bs0.4 billion in 1976.
d. Residual use of the oil windfall.
e. Private investment imputed to the oil windfall (see table 15-2).
f. Excludes transfers to domestic consumers of oil products.
g. Excludes interest revenues on loans.
Source: Bourguignon (1985).

vide the basis for a domestic capital goods industry; it also emphasized the lagging agricultural sector and basic infrastructure. If the difference between Venezuela's fourth and fifth development plans is imputed to the oil windfall, then the windfall resulted in more than $10 billion being invested in public companies in 1976–80—almost a trebling of nongovernment public investment and about a 30 percent rise in total investment.

The fifth plan also advocated increasing private investment by making more credit available through state-owned financial institutions. But table 15-2 shows that the amount of credit made available to the private sector was limited. Changes in expenditures by the private sector involve indirect (multiplier) as well as direct effects. Nevertheless, it is interesting to extend the imputing procedure used above to the private sector. The balance of the public use (including foreign savings) of the oil windfall—the line "other" in table 15-2—corresponds by definition to the excess of private investments and net loans to the rest of the world over private savings. The difference between actual investment and that corresponding to a growth trend of 5 percent is imputed to the windfall. Table 15-2 indicates how the dramatic increase in private investment after 1975 was financed—assuming, as before, that net capital flows from the rest of the world would have been negligible without the windfall. Foreign borrowing was the main component. Oil revenue made available by the government (which began to compensate for large flows of private savings abroad after 1978) played a secondary role.

Two points should be noted regarding the dramatic capital inflows from 1977 on. First, they include borrowing by public non-oil companies outside the official public budget. Venezuela's Public Credit Law of 1976 required that Congress approve all public sector borrowing, except for short-term working capital, which needed only the approval of the Ministry of Finance. After 1977 the administration, seeking to accelerate public programs, facilitated such borrowing. As a result, public companies and some decentralized government agencies contributed to a massive increase in short-term debt. In the heady boom years banks lent eagerly to Venezuela with little regard for the quality of investments financed by their loans.[8] Second, when net public and private capital flows are aggregated, they balance exactly over the 1973–78 period. *In aggregate terms, the entire oil windfall was fully used by the domestic economy.* The structure of the Venezuelan gross debt portfolio that resulted, however, would give rise to serious problems a few years later.

To provide a full picture of how the first oil windfall was used, table 15-3 regroups and aggregates the figures and uses the consumer price index as a deflator. About half the bonus net of transfers to consumers of domestic oil products was absorbed by the private sector and half by the public sector. As the last column indicates, more than half went to finance an unprecedented investment effort. Households also reaped benefits: additional public employment and direct or indirect transfers represent about 20 percent of the windfall. But this understates households' share for several reasons. First, they benefited from most of the subsidy on domestic consumption of oil derivatives. Second, they benefited from public services. Third, spending of the oil windfall had important multiplier effects for the private sector.

Indirect and Multiplier Effects

Several important measures adopted before 1974 or included in Pérez's campaign platform—and so initially independent of oil revenue—were bolstered by the unexpected prosperity. Employment and minimum wage laws passed before 1974 were reinforced, while price controls on consumer goods imposed when Pérez took office were maintained. It is difficult to assess the impact of these policies on the distribution of income and to guess what they would have achieved without the oil bonus. It is clear, however, that they contributed to the substantial increase in household real income between 1973 and 1978. The combined effect of controlling prices, providing subsidies, and allowing agricultural and manufactured imports to clear markets is indicated by the real effective exchange rate. This actually *depreciated* by 7 percent, relative to 1970–72, through the boom years of 1974–78 (see table 6-1).

With initial spare capacity in the non-oil economy, spending made possible by a windfall would be expected to have multiplier effects. But after some time, as the economy neared full capacity, wage and price inflation should have accelerated and non-oil GDP growth should have slowed down until new production capacity came on stream. Inflation should have affected nontraded goods the most, and the corresponding sectors should have attracted more investment than manufacturing or agriculture, which are caught between price controls and rising costs.

This is more or less what happened, as table 15-4 shows. Starting from just above 6 percent in 1972 and 1973, the growth rate of non-oil GDP accelerated to reach a record 11 percent in 1975, then decelerated sharply to 3.7 percent in 1978. Domestic inflation, as measured by the non-oil GDP deflator, rose faster than foreign inflation from 1976 on, and the share of imports in absorption began increasing dramatically. Nontraded sectors seem to have felt the pressure most; inflation in the manufacturing sector was notably lower than in the rest of the economy after 1975, largely because of the relaxation of import barriers. The year 1978 marked the point of full capacity; non-oil GDP growth slowed despite increasing demand. This interpretation is consistent with the high inflation differential with respect to import prices observed since 1977, with the decrease in the unemployment rate, and with continuing high levels of investment. The slower growth implies that the huge investments of the preceding years had not yet become operational. This is understandable for investments in infrastructure and public companies, which represented more than 60 percent of total investments between 1974 and 1977.[9] But it is more surprising for private investments and could indicate that they were adversely affected by bottlenecks in the whole production system.

Did the macroeconomic evolution of Venezuela modify the final distribution of the oil windfall? Although a full answer would require a complete model of the economy, some clues emerge from a few simple figures in table 15-4. The growth of private consumption was uniformly high from 1974 to 1978. One reason was price control, which kept increases in the consumer price index lower than those in the prices of non-oil domestic output. The consumer price index fell by 10 percent with respect to the non-oil GDP deflator between 1974 and 1978 (an effect that is also conspicuous in table 5-2). Other reasons were the government's *direct* transfer of oil proceeds and the wage and employment policy promoted even before the windfall.[10]

The same factors largely explain the rapid increase of the share of labor in non-oil GDP over 1973–78, which accentuates a secular trend in that direction. The labor share could rise despite a vigorous increase in investment because, with oil income and easy borrowing, there was no need for domestic non-oil savings to increase. Changes in the distribution of non-oil national income were therefore due to some exogenous policy measures and to the effects of the multiplier. Actually, this conclusion and those given earlier for private consumption seem valid until 1977; that is, while multiplier effects were dominant and capacity was not being fully used. But in 1978 excess demand may have produced some endogenous changes in the distribution of income, particularly in favor of wage earners, if the labor market proved an important bottleneck in the productive system.

An Assessment of the 1973–74 Oil Windfall

To appraise the economy of Venezuela on the eve of the second oil shock, table 15-5 compares economic aggregates and key stock variables for 1972 and 1978. Some important structural distortions per-

Table 15-4. Venezuela: Some Indicators of the Macroeconomic Consequences of the Windfalls, 1974–82
(percent)

Measure	1968–73 average	1974	1975	1976	1977	1978	1979	1980	1981	1982	1974–78 average	1979–82 average
Share of expenditures in non-oil GDP												
imputed to the oil windfall[a]	n.a.	4.2	11.9	19.2	28.1	26.3	14.7	6.6	11.2	7.9	17.9	10.1
Public expenditures[b]	n.a.	2.2	7.0	12.2	14.7	15.0	11.3	12.6	16.7	17.0	10.2	14.4
GDP rate of growth												
Non-oil GDP	5.4	9.7	11.0	9.2	8.0	3.7	0.1	−1.9	1.4	1.1	8.3	0.2
Manufacturing	6.6	9.2	12.0	11.8	3.8	5.6	4.4	1.7	−0.8	2.5	8.5	2.0
Agriculture	4.4	8.1	5.0	−2.4	7.3	6.8	4.2	−2.0	0.0	0.0	5.0	0.6
Construction	6.9	−3.3	19.4	18.9	25.0	10.9	−9.8	−16.4	−2.2	−4.5	14.2	−8.2
Government	n.a.	n.a.	n.a.	n.a.	n.a.	n.a.	4.2	3.0	3.9	3.8	8.9	3.7
Other sectors	n.a.	n.a.	n.a.	n.a.	n.a.	n.a.	−0.5	−2.6	2.1	0.8	7.8	−0.1
Ratio of imports to non-oil GDP	22.8	23.1	26.4	30.7	38.0	38.1	30.8	30.2	33.2	36.8	31.3	32.8
Private consumption rate of growth	5.9	17.7	13.6	9.6	11.8	10.2	4.7	2.3	1.0	2.7	12.6	2.7

Ratio of private consumption to non-oil GDP (current prices)	64.8	66.6	67.4	67.5	68.4	70.0	72.5	76.2	76.9	79.5	68.0	76.3
Investment rate of growth	8.6	-2.4	25.6	28.3	28.9	2.7	-17.3	-18.3	6.0	-1.3	16.6	-9.1
Private sector	7.8	2.1	9.7	27.9	33.3	-1.1	-16.6	-36.3	-15.6	-18.3	14.4	-21.7
Share of labor in non-oil GDP	49.3	51.5	52.0	52.9	52.6	53.9	51.9	55.3	54.6	52.4	52.6	53.6
Unemployment rate	n.a.	n.a.	7.2	6.0	4.8	4.7	5.4	6.0	6.2	7.0	5.7	6.2
Price inflation rate												
Non-oil GDP deflator	3.3	11.3	12.1	8.0	10.0	11.5	13.3	20.1	14.9	7.7	10.6	14.0
Manufacturing	2.8	16.1	10.3	6.2	5.6	10.2	11.6	16.0	11.6	7.5	9.7	11.7
Consumer price index	3.0	8.3	10.2	7.6	7.8	7.2	12.3	21.6	16.2	9.6	8.2	14.9
Import prices	8.6	16.7	12.8	6.0	7.3	7.1	15.4	15.6	11.9	7.3	11.1	12.6
Government wages	5.2	12.9	13.1	8.6	9.9	8.6	10.0	22.2	15.0	0.9	10.6	12.0

n.a. Not available.

a. Includes all imputed expenditures and transfers, with *negative* amounts for private investment after 1979.

b. Current expenditures and investments by the government and by all public companies.

Source: Bourguignon (1985)

Table 15-5. Venezuela: General Appraisal of the Oil Windfalls, 1972–82

Measure	Billions of bolivares				Growth rate (percent)					
					1972–78		1978–82		1972–82	
	1972	1978	1982	1982 modified	Total	Annual	Total	Annual	Total	Annual
GDP	53.4	77.2	77.1	n.a.	44.6	6.3	−0.1	−0.03	44.4	3.7
Non-oil GDP	43.4	70.4	70.9	n.a.	62.2	8.4	0.7	0.17	63.4	5.0
Agriculture	3.5	4.7	4.8	n.a.	32.1	4.8	2.1	0.5	37.1	3.2
Manufacturing	7.2	11.4	12.3	n.a.	58.7	8.0	7.9	1.9	70.8	5.5
Construction	2.8	6.1	4.3	n.a.	118.6	13.9	−29.5	−8.4	53.6	4.4
Government	6.0	9.5	11.0	n.a.	58.8	8.0	15.8	3.7	83.3	6.2
Other	23.9	38.7	38.5	n.a.	61.9	8.3	−0.5	−0.1	61.0	4.9
Private consumption	28.8	55.1	61.2	n.a.	91.3	11.4	11.1	2.7	112.5	7.8
Total capital stock	156	263	332	n.a.	68.6	9.0	26.2	6.0	112.8	7.8
Oil sector	24	27	39	n.a.	12.5	2.0	44.4	9.6	62.5	5.0
Nonoil sector	132	236	293	n.a	78.8	10.2	24.2	5.6	122.0	8.3
Private	x	x+56	x+81	n.a.	n.a.	n.a.	n.a.	n.a.	n.a.	n.a.
Public companies	x	x+29	x+53	n.a.	n.a.	n.a.	n.a.	n.a.	n.a.	n.a.
Government	x	x+18	x+27	n.a.	n.a.	n.a.	n.a.	n.a.	n.a.	n.a.

Total foreign assets	x	$x+68.0$	$x+129.0$	$x+117.0$	n.a.	n.a.	n.a.	n.a.	n.a.	n.a.	n.a.
Reserves in Central Bank and FIV[a]	1.7	25.9	49.7[b]	37.7	n.a.	n.a.	n.a.	n.a.	n.a.	n.a.	n.a.
Reserves in national oil companies	n.a.	21.0	10.9	10.9	n.a.	n.a.	n.a.	n.a.	n.a.	n.a.	n.a.
Other (private sector and non-oil public companies)	x	$x+22.8$	$x+70.1$[b]	$x+70.1$	n.a.	n.a.	n.a.	n.a.	n.a.	n.a.	n.a.
Total foreign liabilities	x	$x+68.0$	$x+105$	$x+105.0$	n.a.	n.a.	n.a.	n.a.	n.a.	n.a.	n.a.
Public debt	4.3	31.2	52.0[c]	85.0	n.a.	n.a.	n.a.	n.a.	n.a.	n.a.	n.a.
Direct	1.3	28.4	(30.3)[d]	n.a.	n.a.	n.a.	n.a.	n.a.	n.a.	n.a.	n.a.
Indirect	3.0	2.8	(10.6)[d]	n.a.	n.a.	n.a.	n.a.	n.a.	n.a.	n.a.	n.a.
Other	x	$x+41$	$x+57.2$[c]	24.2	n.a.	n.a.	n.a.	n.a.	n.a.	n.a.	n.a.

n.a. Not available.

x Signifies that there is no good estimate of the 1972 base value.

Note: Totals may not equal the sum of their parts because of rounding.

a. FIV is the Venezuelan Investment Fund.

b. Includes the revaluation of the stock of gold by approximately Bs12 billion in 1981, as well as the transfers to the Central Bank of savings abroad held by decentralized public agencies or non-oil public companies. Since the figure for the "other" agents is obtained as residual, it should correspond mostly to the private sector.

c. Does not include the short-run debt contracted in 1981 to cancel the outstanding debt of public companies and decentralized public agencies. At the end of 1982 it amounted to Bs33 billion, which should be added to the Bs52 billion in public debt and subtracted from the debt of "other" agents. The latter figure would thereby fall to Bs24.2 billion, corresponding to the liabilities of the private sector only.

d. 1981 figures.

Source: Bourguignon (1985).

sisted. Agriculture lagged behind the rest of the economy, while manufacturing grew at a rate slightly below that of non-oil GDP. These trends stand in sharp contrast to the pattern of development urged in Venezuela's fifth plan, which called for agriculture and manufacturing to be the fastest growing sectors. They also contrast with the "normal" pattern for countries at Venezuela's level of income per capita, which predicts an increase in the share of manufacturing in GDP (see table 6-3).

Although the accelerated growth of non-oil GDP coincided with a dramatic increase in investment, it was demand-led rather than supply-driven. As measured by capital stock estimates in table 15-5, capacity in the non-oil sector grew more than 10 percent a year between 1972 and 1978, exceeding output growth. Since most of the additional capital stock was installed only after 1975, the drop in productivity is not remarkable. But it seems to have been concentrated in the public sector. The consolidated accounts of nonfinancial public companies suggest an incremental capital-output ratio of approximately 5.6 between 1972 and 1978, a ratio that cannot be explained by technological considerations.[11] Between 1973 and 1978 the total gross investment of public manufacturing companies (the main ones being SIDOR for steel, VENALUM and ALCASA for aluminum, and PEQIVEN for chemical products) was about 10 billion bolivares (Bs) at 1968 prices, or one-third of total public investment outside the government and the oil sector. But value added by the public manufacturing sector in the same period increased at most by Bs0.3 billion (at 1976 prices). Such figures reflect poor management and marketing, plus substantial lags in maturation and overruns in construction time, as discussed below.

Although net foreign debt was about the same in 1978 as in 1972, gross assets and liabilities had dramatically increased (see table 15-5). Most of the assets were accumulated in the form of reserves held by the Central Bank, by the Venezuelan Investment Fund (FIV), and, after their nationalization, by the oil companies. Five years after the oil price increase, these entities had accumulated about $10 billion of foreign assets. An additional $5 billion had been invested abroad, partly by the private sector and partly by the public sector—but outside the Central Bank and the FIV. Available data suggest that the private sector dominated but do not reveal the composition of its portfolio.

With regard to liabilities, the extroverted nature of the Venezuelan capital market during the first boom is still more apparent. Venezuelan agents, as a whole, had no need to borrow abroad, but the government and public companies increased their debt by $6 billion between 1972 and 1978, and other agents borrowed some $10 bil-

lion. This situation reflected inefficiency in domestic financial intermediation, an openness to the North American capital market, and
inappropriate regulation, including the influence of the Public
Credit Law. It also reflected the exceptionally easy conditions
granted by international banks. The size of the gross capital flows
was fraught with potential danger. A drop in economic activity
could create serious problems in servicing short-term debt, while private assets held abroad could prove difficult to repatriate.

Several developments may have helped to reduce inequality in
the factoral distribution of income between 1972 and 1978: increases
in wages, a drop in unemployment, and price controls on wage
goods. Although adequate statistics on income distribution are not
available, there are some indications that these developments did
contribute to greater equality and less poverty among Venezuelan
households.[12] Bourguignon (1980a, b) arrived at that conclusion
using a macroeconomic framework in which only mean income differences between social groups and the demographic structure of
those groups were considered. Musgrove (1980) came to the same
conclusion using data from two consumer surveys in Caracas for
1970 and 1976. Both studies suggest that income inequality diminished marginally but that indexes remained rather high.

The differences between actual government expenditures on transfers and social uses and those projected by extrapolating the
pre-1973 trend are reported in table 15-6 for several sectors known
to have the greatest effect on redistribution. Except for transfers to
households through subsidies to agriculture, extra government
spending in these areas out of the oil windfall was quite limited—
despite the fact that all the social sectors listed in the table were recognized as priorities. In sum, although economic expansion along
with certain policy measures addressing wages, employment, and
prices contributed to some equalization of income distribution between 1973 and 1978, little was accomplished in crucial, long-
neglected social sectors. This issue was to be central in the presidential election of December 1978, as it had been in 1972.

The Second Oil Windfall, 1979–82

The two main political parties did not disagree on basic issues in
the 1978 campaign. Both advocated income redistribution. The
COPEI opposition, however, emphasized that little had actually been
done to improve social conditions. It argued, moreover, that too
many expensive projects had been launched at the same time and
in a disorganized manner—with the result that administrative inefficiency in the public sector had increased, corruption was on the

Table 15-6. Venezuela: Changes in Some Redistributive Expenditures by the Public Sector, 1974–78
(billions of bolivares)

Expenditure	1974	1975	1976	1977	1978
Education	0.2	0.5	0.4	0.7	0.4
Health	n.a.	0.3	0.5	0.9	0.6
Social assistance	n.a.	n.a.	0.3	0.2	0.6
Housing	0.7	−0.6	0.5	0.9	−0.7
Transfers to households[a]	1.8	2.1	1.9	2.3	1.9
Total	2.7	2.3	3.6	5.0	3.0
Total as a percentage of government windfall	10.5	11.5	23.7	31.6	25.3
Total as a percentage of actual government expenditures	15.3	9.6	15.7	17.3	9.4

n.a. Not available.

Note: The figures represent differences between actual figures and the pre-1973 extrapolated (real) trend. They include current as well as investment expenditures, but not implicit or explicit subsidies to households by public companies.

a. Essentially subsidies to the agricultural sector linked to the food price control policy.

Source: Bourguignon (1985).

rise, foreign borrowing had escaped public control, the economy was overheating, and a sharp acceleration in inflation threatened. It called, therefore, for a period of consolidation and of greater focus on urgent social needs. Partly because of the natural swing from the party in power, COPEI won the election and Luis Herrera Campins became president. However, the new president could not count on a firm majority in Congress, which was dominated by AD. The lack of unified political control led to conflicting policies, which in turn evoked distrust from the private sector and had a major— and unexpected—influence on the macroeconomic response to the second windfall.

Size and Uses of the Windfall

With 1972 again as the reference year, the extra revenue that accrued to Venezuela in 1979–82 and the main uses made of it are computed in table 15-7 as before. Including the implicit transfers to domestic consumers of oil products, the annual oil windfall averaged Bs56 billion between 1979 and 1982, corresponding to 27 percent of GDP excluding the windfall—slightly more than during the first boom.

The shares of the windfall going to domestic consumers of oil products and to national oil companies were substantially higher than in the earlier period. Domestic prices of oil products were held constant until 1981. The oil companies first began to reap some of the windfall in 1976. They invested progressively more for several reasons: investment had stagnated after nationalization in 1976; refining capacity had proved inadequate for some products; and the newly discovered reserves on the Orinoco fringe had to be evaluated. Still, the oil companies saved a substantial part of their share of the windfall abroad. Although their savings fell slightly in 1981 because of new investments, they rose by about Bs21.5 billion between 1979 and 1982.

As for government spending, additional current expenditures tended to stabilize at about Bs10 billion, but capital formation fell in 1979 and 1980 in line with the new administration's policy of restraint and did not recover to earlier levels until 1981. Additional transfers to households grew only moderately, with a smaller share channeled through food price subsidies. But other transfers that had been almost negligible during the first period became important. To estimate them, table 15-7 gives the net change in the foreign position of the government and the oil companies. As in the previous period, this net change was at first positive. But in 1982 almost Bs35 billion was obtained from the rest of the world by the government and the oil companies, so that the foreign balance for 1979–82 was more or less zero.

More of the total windfall was therefore made available to the rest of the economy in the second boom than in the first: 37 percent compared with 27 percent. Until 1981 investments in public non-oil companies absorbed most of this revenue. Until 1980 this was in accordance with the fifth plan. But despite the government's desire to moderate public spending—a desire reflected in the sixth plan, which otherwise echoed the previous one—investments in public non-oil companies continued to increase, amounting in 1981–82 to more than $6 billion. In addition, in 1981 and even more so in 1982, substantial amounts were transferred to public companies and the private sector, much of it to firms. Part went to public non-oil companies, enabling them to service and repay past debts— which they could not have done otherwise given their poor performance discussed below. Still more of the windfall was directed to public companies and the private sector through public financial intermediaries, assisted by the relaxation of domestic credit limits. These borrowings, defined as the residual of the identifiable uses of the oil bonus ("other" in table 15-7), were substantial in 1980 and reached the dramatic figure of Bs25 billion in 1982.

Table 15-7. Venezuela: The Second Oil Windfall and Its Uses
(billions of bolivares)

Windfall and uses	1979	1980	1981	1982	Total (1973 prices)	
					Bolivares	Percent
Total oil windfall	41.7	61.2	66.6	54.0	104.7	100.0
Implicit transfers to domestic consumers of oil products	7.5	13.8	15.9	17.0	24.7	23.6
Windfall received by oil companies	16.5	19.2	-1.1	8.8	22.3	21.3
Imputed investments by oil companies	1.9	3.8	7.5	10.2	10.2	9.7
Bonus received by government	17.7	28.2	51.8	28.9	57.8	55.2
Imputed additional current expenditures	7.2	8.9	10.9	10.6	17.5	16.7
Wages	6.0	7.4	9.0	8.7	14.5	13.8
Imputed additional investment	0.4	1.0	3.8	2.9	3.5	3.3
Imputed additional transfers to households	2.2	4.0	2.9	2.9	5.7	5.4
Net change in foreign position of government and oil companies	15.5	13.1	5.3	-34.9	4.5	4.3

Windfall made available to the rest of the economy	7.0	16.6	20.3	45.3	38.6	36.9
Imputed investments in public non-oil companies	8.0	9.1	12.5	14.8	20.4	19.5
Current transfers to public non-oil and private companies	0.7	0.9	4.9	5.8	5.2	5.0
Other	1.7	6.6	2.9	24.7	13.1	12.5
Net change in foreign position of private sector and public non-oil companies	−14.0	7.1	11.8	20.0	7.9	7.5
Imputed investments in the private sector	2.2	−15.8	−19.2	−29.4	−26.0	−24.8
Imputed change in savings by the private sector and public non-oil companies	−10.1	−15.3	−10.3	−34.1	−36.8	−35.1

Note: Reference year is 1972. For details of the calculations, see Bourguignon (1985).

Source: Bourguignon (1985).

The figures in the last three rows of table 15-7 are a sharp change from those of the earlier period and explain much of the crisis Venezuela later faced. In keeping with the convention of imputing to the oil shock the difference between actual private investment and a 5 percent real growth trend, private investment imputed to the windfall was negative after 1979. At the same time, a sudden reversal in capital movements occurred—for reasons to be discussed—with a vigorous and growing outflow of $9 billion over 1980–82. That the drop in investment was far larger than the outflow of capital points to a plunge in savings by both the private sector and non-oil public companies, a tendency already observed for 1978.

Given the assumptions, the loss in savings could have been as much as Bs10 billion in 1979 and 1981, Bs15 billion in 1980, and Bs34 billion in 1982. These figures may be overstated since one of the assumptions is a 5 percent annual growth rate for the whole non-oil sector in the absence of an oil boom. Of interest, however, is the discrepancy between changes in investment and changes in savings, and this figure is independent of the hypothetical value assigned to private investment without the oil windfall.

The steps are clear. First, the saving rate fell. Next, a strong capital outflow developed in the private sector. Then private firms and public non-oil companies borrowed from public financial entities to finance their investments or their current deficits. The public financial sector, in turn, drew down its reserves or borrowed abroad. In other words, *much of the second windfall was used to compensate for the drop in private and non-oil public savings and to permit massive capital exports by the private sector.*

In the aggregate, Venezuela actually saved abroad during the second windfall; net capital outflow was positive during 1979–82 (Bs12.4 billion at 1973 prices; see table 15-7). Yet, even more than in the first windfall, aggregating public and private net capital flows is misleading. In addition, as the notes to table 15-5 suggest, the official public reserve and debt figures are misleading for two reasons. First, reserves include the revaluation of the stock of gold possessed by the Central Bank by about Bs12 billion. This is unrelated to the use of oil revenue and should be subtracted, thereby reducing the value of foreign assets. Second, the public debt estimate for 1982 does not include borrowing by public companies and decentralized public agencies, which are included in the "other" entry. Their registered debt at the end of 1982 was Bs33 billion, which should be subtracted from the "other" entry and added to the public debt. The total liabilities of the public sector in the modified 1982 column in table 15-5 thus amounted to Bs85 billion ($20 billion) by December 1982. Its balance (after revaluation of gold reserves) was a deficit of about Bs35 billion ($8 billion). Imputing the remaining assets and liabilities to the private sector yields an estimated positive balance of Bs46 billion ($10 billion), with total liabilities of Bs24 billion ($5 billion).[13]

The Stagnation of the Economy after 1978

Four features capture the peculiarity of the 1979–82 period: the drop in savings already discussed, the sharp drop in private investment, the outflow of private capital, and the poor performance of non-oil public companies, which called forth current transfers. Each of these had a vital influence on the performance of Venezuela's non-oil economy, which grew at less than 0.2 percent in 1979–82.

What was the role of policy in shaping these features? In August 1979 the new government unveiled a program that consisted of five measures:

- Decontrol of prices on a wide range of consumer goods
- A sharp reduction in import duties, from up to 300 percent to a maximum of 100 percent
- Cuts in subsidies
- Sharp cuts in public spending by 10 percent in real terms in 1979
- Some increase in interest rates.

The government's objectives were to reduce overheating and regulation in the economy and to increase the degree of competition.

FALLING INVESTMENT LEVELS. The policy of moderating public investment and the drop in investment by public non-oil companies led in 1979 and 1980 to a decline in the share of the oil windfall going to direct public expenditures. Table 15-4 shows that, as a share of non-oil GDP, such expenditures fell from 15.0 percent in 1977–78 to 11.3 percent in 1979 and 12.6 percent in 1980. This may have caused a first negative shock, but the effect was greatly amplified by the abrupt drop in private investment (see table 15-7). This occurred for several reasons. First, private investment had reached an abnormal peak in 1976–77. Second, in December 1979 Congress passed a law calling for a 30 percent wage increase. It did so over the objections of the administration in response to union pressure, which was sparked by price increases following deregulation (the cost of living rose at an annual equivalent rate of 33.6 percent in the last trimester of 1979) and by the unexpected largesse of the second oil price increase. Profits were squeezed; as table 15-4 shows, the share of labor in non-oil GDP rose by 3.4 percentage points from 1979 to

1980, and private consumption as a share of non-oil GDP peaked in 1982. Receiving conflicting signals from the new government, and unaccustomed to foreign competition, private capital began to develop a wary attitude. The real effective exchange rate began to appreciate, rising by 8 percent in 1979–81 over the 1974–78 average. Third, the negative accelerator effect from a two-year stagnation of aggregate demand worsened the outlook for private investment, especially given the absence of non-oil exports. Non-oil GDP contracted in 1980. A further fall was avoided in 1981 and 1982 only because public expenditures and transfers out of the oil bonus increased.

CAPITAL FLIGHT. The poor outlook for private investment in turn encouraged the flight of private capital from Venezuela after 1978. Profits in the nontradable sectors dropped as demand slowed, while profits in manufacturing were squeezed by the wage push and real exchange rate appreciation. Between 1980 and 1982 domestic financial regulations provided additional incentives for private capital outflows. A usury law limiting the nominal interest rate to 12 percent caused the ratio between domestic and foreign rates to fall. In 1977 the ratio of the interest rate paid by mortgage companies in Venezuela to the rate on U.S. government bonds was 100; that ratio was 74.1 in 1980, 60 in 1981, and 80 in 1982. Real interest rates also fell short of those abroad after rates rose in the industrialized countries. The rise in administered nominal rates and the simultaneous drop in inflation in 1982 could close only part of this gap.

Private capital therefore flowed out—and did so with increasing speed when it become clear, in the aftermath of the Mexican debt crisis in July 1982, that the exchange rate was unsustainable because the public sector was unable to repay its large short-term debt. This had continued to mount despite the slowdown in public investment because the COPEI administration was reluctant to go to the AD-dominated Congress for approval of medium- and long-term borrowing by public entities and so continued to use the loophole in the Public Credit Law.

SUPPLY-SIDE FAILURE. Why did the output effects expected from the huge investments undertaken between 1975 and 1978 fail to materialize? One factor is that the stagnation of aggregate demand since 1979 prevented domestic firms in the nontraded sectors from using their recently installed capacity. Data on the sectoral breakdown of investments since 1973 are inadequate, but probably between 60 and 70 percent of the productive capacity installed between 1973 and 1978 was directly affected by the stagnation of domestic aggregate demand after 1979.[14]

A second factor is the poor performance of the public manufacturing companies. Manufacturing was the only sector (apart from government) exhibiting some growth after 1979. Yet at 1.9 percent its growth was low. This was due to a combination of inefficiency and a mismatch between investments and potential demand.

The cornerstone of the Venezuelan diversification strategy was an ambitious resource-based industrialization emphasizing steel and aluminum. With domestic markets insufficient to absorb output at full capacity, such plants were severely hit by the downturn in world markets in the 1980s. In addition, both the technologically ambitious nature of the plants and weaknesses in their management caused start-up and operating difficulties that adversely affected their competitiveness.

The national steel company, SIDOR, was responsible for much of public investment in manufacturing. The fifth plan called for expanding steel production from 1.2 to 4.8 million metric tons by 1984. Approximately two-thirds of public manufacturing investment between 1973 and 1981 was spent to meet that goal, but the average annual production in 1979–81 was only 1.4 million metric tons, less than 50 percent of the existing capacity, and output was even lower in 1982. The main problems were global overcapacity for steel production and strong international competition. After having reached a record figure of 0.5 million metric tons in 1979, Venezuelan steel exports fell continuously to 0.24 million metric tons in 1982. With its average cost of production high by international standards, SIDOR registered annual operating losses after 1978. Productivity improved somewhat in 1982, but the rate of return that could be expected in the following years remained extremely low.[15]

Much the same situation beset aluminum, the second largest public manufacturing sector. Its expansion, like that of the steel industry, was grounded on an anticipated comparative advantage over foreign competition. An investment of approximately Bs8 billion between 1974 and 1982 created an annual production capacity of more than 400,000 tons. But actual production between 1979 and 1982 was only 40 percent of capacity, partly because of technical problems with a new plant in 1981.

The huge excess capacity of these companies contributed to an abnormally low return on the investments in public manufacturing imputed to the oil windfall. At current prices, Bs30 billion was invested in the sector after 1973, half from the first windfall. Yet the gross value added by the public manufacturing sector averaged only Bs2.5 billion a year between 1980 and 1982. Such poor performance also explains the increasing direct and indirect transfers by the public financial sector to non-oil companies. Table 15-8 shows that

Table 15-8. Venezuela: Performance of Public Non-oil Companies, 1978–82
(billions of bolivares at current prices)

Measure	1978	1979	1980	1981	1982
Net value added[a]	4.8	4.9	5.3	6.8	10.3
Manufacturing	0.9	0.8	1.4	1.0	2.5
Wages paid	4.3	5.2	7.2	7.4	8.6
Manufacturing	1.1	1.4	2.1	2.2	2.7
Net interest payments	1.0	1.8	3.4	4.1	6.2
Manufacturing	0.4	1.1	1.9	1.9	1.3
Net savings	−0.5	2.1	−5.3	−4.7	−4.5
Manufacturing	−0.6	−1.7	−2.6	−3.1	−1.5

Note: Figures exclude financial intermediaries and commerce (essentially the CMA corporation responsible for food price controls and subsidies).

a. Excluding capital consumption.

Source: Bourguignon (1985).

from 1979 through 1982 the net value added by the public manufacturing sector never even covered wage payments. The same is true for the entire public non-oil sector, except for 1982. After interest payments, net savings were substantially negative. Much of the debt was short-term; the figures in table 15-8 thus underscore the acute need by public non-oil companies for substantial new lending throughout the 1979–82 period. (A law passed in 1982, however, transferred part of the debt of non-oil public companies to the government.) The poor results of these non-oil public companies also partly explain the overall drop in savings noted earlier.

A similar supply-side analysis is impossible for the private sector, but it is interesting to try to determine the scope for import substitution in manufacturing as a whole. Although the share of imports in demand for manufactured goods rose in 1974–78, the increase was less marked than expected, perhaps because of protection and previous spare capacity. Between 1973 and 1978, 60 percent of incremental demand was met by domestic producers, whose share of the market in 1973 was 72 percent. The relatively dynamic behavior of private manufacturing meant that little scope was left for import substitution even after 1978. Domestic manufacturers had lost no more than 10 percent of their market share. Thus with 1973 as the reference year, the potential growth of the domestic manufacturing sector after 1978, if total demand stagnated, was only 10 percent.

Another factor discouraging private manufacturing as well as private investment was the profit squeeze. As the real effective exchange rate appreciated, the share of imports submitted for licensing fell from 13 percent for 1972–74 to 5.5 percent for 1978–80 and to 1.8 percent in 1980.[16] Tariffs were reduced, the price of manufactured goods fell by about 14 percent with respect to the non-oil deflator from 1976 to 1982, and wages increased substantially in 1980. These conditions account for the sector's moderate performance since 1979, its inability to recover its pre-1973 market share, and the subsequent huge drop in investment.

An Assessment of Both Windfalls

Table 15-5 summarizes the performance of the Venezuelan economy in the decade since the first oil price increase in 1973. Between 1972 and 1982 GDP grew at a rate of 3.7 percent annually, about 1.5 percent below the average growth rate of the previous decade, when the Venezuelan terms of trade were at their lowest level since the war. The situation is no better when growth is evaluated in terms of non-oil GDP. But after 1973 consumption consistently grew faster than non-oil GDP, whereas before 1973 it had grown slower. Households therefore benefited to no small extent from the oil windfall, although this benefit has shown some signs of stagnation since 1981. Furthermore, the capital stock grew quickly, at an annual rate of almost 8 percent; this was mostly the result of huge investments in the oil sector and, after 1980, of ambitious public programs. The divergence between the growth rates of GDP and capital stock reflects the increase in excess capacity in public non-oil companies and in the (largely private) nonmanufacturing sectors.

The extra revenue generated by the second windfall was not entirely spent by 1982. Table 15-5 shows that the aggregate net accumulation of foreign assets exceeded liabilities by some Bs24 billion. This represented only 14 percent of the total windfall between 1979 and 1982, so that virtually all the oil windfall had been absorbed.[17] But this approximate balance masked strongly asymmetric behavior across various agents and a dangerous disequilibrium. Paradoxically, the public sector—the direct beneficiary of the oil bonus—ended up as a net debtor with respect to the rest of the world, whereas the private sector—which could borrow at home and abroad out of the oil revenue—ended up as a net creditor!

To assess the windfalls, two questions must first be answered. How valuable is the underutilized stock of domestic capital? And should the foreign assets of the private sector be considered as a positive entry? The answer to the first question depends on worldwide prospects for the steel and aluminum industries, which at present are not bright. As for the second question, from the perspective of the individual Venezuelans involved it makes sense to take into account foreign assets, but from a public and social point of view it is less justifiable to value them fully. This is especially true in light of the adverse effects of capital flight on domestic economic activity, which may be considered as a negative externality: "speculators" throw the burden of adjustment onto less mobile "workers," and the result is unemployed factors of production.

Finally, what was the effect of the windfalls on social services and income distribution? Notable achievements were made in the field of education. Illiteracy declined from about 20 percent of the total population at the start of the 1970s to 12 percent by 1981. Nevertheless, the illiteracy rate was three times as high in rural as in urban areas, and secondary school enrollment rates lagged behind those of poorer Latin American countries. Health care facilities and personnel increased markedly over the decade but were highly concentrated in major urban centers.

As for income distribution, the increase in household consumption as a share of non-oil GDP should correspond to some equalization of income distribution—a hypothesis consistent with the overall increase in the share of labor in non-oil GDP (see table 15-4). Indeed, a comparison of urban income distribution in 1970, 1979, and 1981 suggests a substantial decline in the Gini coefficient from 0.43 to 0.40 to 0.33. A similar decline is shown in the inequality of the distribution of household labor income between 1977 and 1981. By 1979 the inequality of the household income distribution was below that predicted from the Kuznets curve "norm."[18] But this favorable outcome could not be sustained without growth. In the early 1980s unemployment soared as the economy stagnated, and the share of labor in GDP began to decline. It also rested on continued absorption of labor by the public sector. Between 1977 and 1981 public sector employment grew at 4.2 percent, compared with 2.5 percent for the private sector.

Households did benefit greatly from the windfalls, even though in real terms potentially redistributive government expenditures stagnated after 1978. Because of price controls, because of the economic boom between 1974 and 1978, and to a lesser extent because of some moderate redistribution of income by the government, per capita consumption increased faster than ever before, rising by more than 50 percent between 1973 and 1982. But Venezuela has not succeeded in transforming the oil windfalls into a permanent acceleration of growth, so households have probably begun to lose what they had gained. This loss is likely to be greatest among those who are poorest and have fewest foreign assets. Unfortunately, the decade of windfall gains may not have brought about a permanent change for the better in the social conditions of the Venezuelan people.

The Exchange Crisis of 1983

With the weakening oil market in 1982 and large private capital outflows, the central government surplus of 2 percent of GDP in 1981 swung to a deficit of 2.6 percent in 1982. In November 1982 import restrictions were imposed, and the government moved to centralize control of foreign exchange reserves held by the state oil company. In February 1983 a multiple exchange rate system was instituted. The old rate, Bs4.3 per dollar, was retained for the petroleum and iron sectors, for debt service, and for "essential" imports. A rate of Bs6.0 per dollar was established for other export earnings that received subsidies and for approved "nonluxury" imports. Other transactions were to take place at a free rate, which stabilized at around Bs13 per dollar.

Although the balance of payments attained a slight surplus in 1983, Venezuela's adjustment has not been without cost. Unemployment reached 12 percent in 1983, and the non-oil economy contracted. By the end of that year it was one-third smaller than it would have been if expansion had continued in line with the pre-1973 trend.

Conclusion

What lessons can be drawn from the Venezuelan experience recounted here? Have the oil windfalls been a curse for Venezuela, to use the words of Pérez Alfonso, the Venezuelan founder of OPEC? Or have they been a blessing, with effects that have only temporarily vanished?

At the outset, the government intended to absorb its oil windfall very cautiously. It created the Venezuelan Investment Fund in 1974 to manage the large amount to be saved abroad. And indeed, not until 1976 did public investments accelerate sharply. By 1978 the government had still used only half of the first windfall *directly*. Perhaps it did not act cautiously enough, however, because it neglected the multiplier-accelerator process triggered by the initial increase in aggregate demand and funded by extraordinarily easy access to foreign loans. Thus the entire first windfall had been reintegrated into the domestic economy by the end of 1978. Venezuela's financial balance with the rest of the world was equilibrated, but its gross assets and liabilities had increased, and the latter had an unfavorable maturity structure.

The second windfall was handled very differently. In 1979 the government decided to put a brake on spending. This, and inconsistent policies, caused private investment to fall sharply to below its pre-1973 level. In fact, the reduction in public spending proved to be only moderate. Public projects failed to yield a normal rate of return and had to be subsidized. In addition, the government tried to compensate for the drop in the private saving rate and the surge in capital flight through further transfers. The flight of private capital was spurred in large part by policy-related factors: a ceiling on interest rates, an increasingly unsupportable exchange rate, and conflicting policies by the administration and Congress, which led to a profit squeeze. The result was the progressive shift of foreign assets from the public to the private sector.

The overall picture that emerges is one of a dramatic failure of economic policy under complex yet seemingly exceptionally favorable conditions. Nothing appears to have been gained from the windfalls in terms of non-oil GDP during 1973–82. Consumption has been the only winner, and even that gain is probably temporary.

Could this outcome have been avoided? The open and extroverted character of the Venezuelan capital market—combined with inappropriate policies for wages, interest rates, and exchange rates—had a significant negative effect on the evolution of the economy after 1973. Auty (1986a, b) concludes that the Venezuelan industrialization program was one of the most risky undertaken by an oil-exporting country—it was concentrated both in timing and in sectoral composition, there was little foreign participation, and the scale was far in excess of the domestic market. The emphasis on short-term financing only added to the risk. Finally, spending was much less cautious than intended because of social pressures on the government, the absence of control on borrowing abroad by public companies and the private sector, and the low return on public investment projects. In the second boom the contradiction in domestic policies led to a contraction in private investment, which in turn accelerated the government's use of the windfall in an attempt to prevent recession.

A more favorable outcome would therefore have required major changes in macroeconomic management, and possibly in political institutions. The results of the second boom can be considered as the outcome of a negative-sum game. Labor tried to appropriate the windfall at home. But capital took it abroad.

Notes

1. Almost all the statistical information used in this study is drawn from the statistical appendix of several issues of the *Informe Económico* published yearly by the Central Bank of Venezuela (BCV). Since 1981 that appendix has been published separately as the *Anuario de Series Estadísticas*. Data for years before 1968 are taken from *Treinta Anos de Historias Económicas* (Caracas: BCV, 1979). The brief survey of pre-1973 Venezuelan economic development also relies on Aranda (1977) and Salazar-Carrillo (1976).

2. For a survey of the historical development of the public sector and public companies in Venezuela, see Karl (1982, chap. 2). According to Karl, by 1970 there were more than 80 state enterprises in different areas of the economy and at least 146 mixed enterprises (that is, at least 25 percent state-owned). The development of the public sector is also documented by Bigler (1980).

3. The slight acceleration of inflation to almost 3 percent between 1969 and 1971 actually led Congress to oppose the 1972 fiscal budget as "inflationary."

4. In 1972 the Gini coefficient for incomes before transfers almost certainly exceeded 0.50, and little redistribution took place through transfers or public spending. For a survey of the statistical information available, see Bourguignon (1980a, b).

5. In an interesting confirmation of the importance of social issues in this election, AD attributed the defeat of COPEI to underestimating the "concern of the citizen with unemployment, the cost of living, and housing." A precise chronology of Venezuelan economic and political events is given in various articles in *Problèmes d'Amérique Latine* (La Documentation Française). The discussion here relies primarily on the following papers: P. Gilhodes, "Venezuela: trois ans de democratie chrétienne. Le gouvernement de M. Rafael Caldera" (vol. 25, pp. 5–44); F. Febrer, "La stratégie petrolière du Venezuela: des lois restrictives de 1970–1971 à la nationalisation" (vol. 37, pp. 7-53); F. Febrer, "Le quinquennal de Carlos Andrés Pérez au Venezuela (1974–1978)" (vol. 51, pp. 7–75).

6. In fact, the volume of Venezuela's oil production and exports fell substantially after 1974. The official explanation is that the gain in export revenue per barrel made conservation possible, but it is likely that oil production and exports would have fallen in any case because of the move toward nationalization and other factors. Still, it seems reasonable to assume that, over a longer period, Venezuela would have been able to maintain its export revenue.

7. Between 1968 and 1972 Venezuela's net loans to the rest of the world averaged less than $100 million a year; between 1973 and 1976 they skyrocketed to total $8 billion.

8. Asheshov (1980) captures the spirit of the boom years; loans were granted to Venezuelan public companies with almost no assurance of project completion and repayment. See also Karl (1982).

9. The structure of public investments (including public companies) during 1974–77 was: agriculture, 5 percent; petroleum and mines, 7 percent; manufacture, 22 percent; electricity, 20 percent; transport, 20 percent; and services, 26 percent.

10. Data on wages are scarce, but regular household surveys undertaken from 1975 on suggested a real annual growth rate of 10 percent in the average monthly earnings of those who worked.

11. The value added of non-oil public companies increased by approximately Bs5.5 billion in current prices between 1972 and 1978, for a total net investment roughly equal to Bs35 billion between 1972 and 1977. The ratio of 5.6 follows after conversion to constant 1968 prices. In comparison, the incremental capital-output ratio for the entire non-oil sector is only about 4.0.

12. After 1975 household surveys conducted twice a year yield some information on income distribution. But that information is not very reliable and is made available at too high a level of aggregation (seven broad monthly earnings brackets for the employed population). On the basis of simple linear extrapolations from the seven brackets, the Gini coefficient would have fallen from 0.33 in 1975 to 0.26 in 1978. Both figures are grossly underestimated, but the trend they indicate is less open to question.

13. The figures in the text follow from the aggregate accounts published in the *Informe Económico* by the Central Bank. More detailed information (CORDIPLAN 1983) suggests that the total liabilities of the consolidated public sector amounted to $27.5 billion. The estimate here, based on recorded annual variations of liabilities, yields an *increase* in the total liabilities of the economy of only $19 billion between 1972 and 1982. Because the unknown outstanding debt outside the public sector in 1972 cannot account for the difference between the two sources, there must be some inconsistency between the annual flow figures used and the revaluation of the stock in 1983. However, this does not invalidate the analysis of the oil windfall, which is based on the *net* movements of capital with respect to the rest of the world.

14. No sectoral breakdown of private investments is available since 1977; data for earlier years are incomplete, with "other activities" representing 60 percent of total investment. The weight of manufacturing in the private sector probably remained about the same as before 1973, since until 1978 the prices of manufactured goods changed little with respect to the prices of other goods and services. The share of manufacturing in total investments (excluding that by the government) was roughly 20 percent before 1973. For 1973–78, with the burgeoning of public manufacturing companies, that share may have been about 25 percent—or more, if only those investments imputed to the oil windfall are considered.

15. Information on the steel industry is taken from CORDIPLAN (1983) as well as various reports by the World Bank. According to the World Bank, the technical efficiency of the recent expansions of SIDOR was not in question. The problem lay rather in the low rate of utilization brought about by overestimating home and foreign markets.

16. More recent figures were not available at the time this study was completed.

17. The argument in the text ignores interest payments and receipts on foreign assets and liabilities related to the oil windfall. In aggregate terms and assuming identical rates on assets and liabilities, taking them into account would not change the assessment.

18. These observations are drawn from World Bank studies. Information on earnings provided by the biannual household surveys is of low quality and grossly underestimates income inequality. It may give some rough indication, however, of trends in the distribution of individual earnings:

	1975	1978	1979	1980	1981	1982
Gini coefficient	0.33	0.25	0.24	0.22	0.22	0.24

These figures refer to employed individuals; including the unemployed would make the rise in inequality more pronounced after 1980.

Bibliography

The word "processed" describes works that are reproduced from typescript by mimeograph, xerography, or similar means: such works may not be cataloged or commonly available through libraries, or may be subject to restricted circulation.

Aarrestad, Jostein. 1978. "Optimal Savings and Exhaustible Resource Extraction in an Open Economy." *Journal of Economic Theory* 19: 163–79.

Abey, A. Booth, and R. M. Sundrum. 1981. "Labour Absorption in Indonesian Agriculture." *Bulletin of Indonesian Economic Studies* (March): 36–64.

Acosta, Alberto. 1982. "Rasgos dominantes del Crecimento Ecuatoriano en las Ultimas Decadas." In Riffka (1982).

Adebayo, Robert Adeyinka. 1969. "The Truth about Tax Riots: Governor Adebayo Speaks." Ibadan: Government Printer.

Adelman, Irma, and C. T. Morris. 1973. *Economic Growth and Social Equity in Developing Countries*. Stanford, Calif.: Stanford University Press.

Adelman, M. A. 1986a. "The Competitive Floor to World Oil Prices." *The Energy Journal* 7: 9–35.

———. 1986b. "Oil-Producing Countries' Discount Rates."MIT Energy Laboratory Working Paper MIT-EL81-015WP. Cambridge, Mass., July.

———. 1983. "Oil-Exporting Developing Countries: Macroeconomic Policies and Adjustment Issues." Country Policy Department, World Bank. Processed.

Akinsanya, Adeoye A. 1981. "State Strategies Towards Nigerian and Foreign Business." Paper presented to the Conference on Nigeria, Johns Hopkins University, SAIS, Washington, D.C.

Alderman, Harold, and C. Peter Timmer. 1979. "Food Price Policy and Protein-Calorie Intake: Estimating Consumption Parameters for Indonesia." Harvard Institute for International Development, Cambridge, Mass., August. Processed.

Amemiya, Takeshi. 1974. "A Note on a Fair and Jaffee Model." *Econometrica* 42 (July): 759–62.

Amin, Samir. 1974. *Accumulation on a World Scale*. London: Monthly Review Press.

327

Amuzegar, Jahangir. 1982a. "Oil Wealth: A Very Mixed Blessing." *Foreign Affairs* 60: 814–34.

———. 1982b. *Oil Exporters' Economic Development in an Interdependent World.* IMF Occasional Paper 18. Washington, D.C.

———. 1983. "Managing Oil Wealth." *Finance & Development* 20 (3): 19–22.

Aranda, S. 1977. *La Economía Venezolana Siglo XXI.* Bogotá.

Arndt, H. W. 1977a. "Survey of Current Developments." *Bulletin of Indonesian Economic Studies* (July).

———. 1977b. "Indonesia: Survey of Recent Economic Developments." *Bulletin of Indonesian Economic Studies* (November): 1–33.

———. 1978. "Indonesia: Survey of Recent Developments." *Bulletin of Indonesian Economic Studies* (March): 1–29.

———. 1981. "Indonesia: Survey of Recent Developments." *Bulletin of Indonesian Economic Studies* (November): 1–24.

———. 1982. "Oil and the Indonesian Economy." Institute for Southeast Asian Studies, University of Singapore. Processed.

———. 1983. "Indonesia: Survey of Recent Developments." *Bulletin of Indonesian Economic Studies* (August): 1–26.

Arrow, K. J., and M. Kurtz. 1970. *Public Investment, the Rate of Return and Optimal Fiscal Policy.* Baltimore, Md.: Johns Hopkins University Press.

Asheshov, Nicholas. 1980. "Trying to Clean up the Venezuela Mess." *Institutional Investor* (April): 68–89.

Attiga, A. A. 1981a. "How Oil Revenues Can Destroy a Country." *Petroleum Intelligence Weekly*, Special Supplement, October 19.

———. 1981b. "Economic Development of Oil-Producing Countries." *OPEC Bulletin* (November).

Auty, Richard M. 1976. "Caribbean Sugar Factory Size and Survival." *Annals Association of American Geographers* 66: 76–88.

———. 1983. "Gas-Based Exports as an LDC Energy Strategy: Trinidad and Tobago." Unpublished working paper, Research Program in Development Studies, Woodrow Wilson School, Princeton University, February.

———. 1986a. "Entry Problems and Investment Returns in RBI: A Cross-Country Comparison." Report to Research Project 672–49. Development Research Department, World Bank. Processed.

———. 1986b. "Resource Based Industrialisation and Country Size: Venezuela and Trinidad and Tobago." *Geoforum* 17 (3): 325–38.

———. 1987. "Country Size and Efficiency Constraints on Resource Based Industrialization." Working Paper 50A. Harvard Institute for International Development, Harvard University, June.

———. Forthcoming. "External Causes of the Oil Exporters' Disappointing Diversification into Resource-Based Industry." *Energy Policy* 16.

Auty, Richard M., and Alan H. Gelb. 1986. "Oil Windfalls in a Small Parliamentary Democracy: Their Impact on Trinidad and Tobago." *World Development* 14 (9): 1161–75.

Baer, Werner. 1965. *Industrialization and Economic Development in Brazil*. Homewood, Ill.: Richard D. Irwin.

Balassa, Bela. 1964. "The Purchasing Power Parity Doctrine: A Reappraisal." *Journal of Political Economy* 72: 584–96.

Baldwin, R. E. 1966. *Economic Development and Export Growth: A Study of Northern Rhodesia, 1920–60*. Berkeley: University of California Press.

Balroya, E. A. 1979. "Oil Policies and Budgets in Venezuela." *Latin American Research Review* 9 (2): 28–72.

Banco Central. *See* Central Bank.

Banco de Desarrollo del Ecuador S.A. 1983. *Memoria*. Quito.

Barber, William J. 1961. *The Economy of British Central Africa: A Case Study of Development in a Dualistic Society*. Stanford, Calif.: Stanford University Press.

Barker, T. S. 1981. "De-Industrialisation, North Sea Oil and an Investment Strategy for the U.K." In Barker and Brailovsky (1981).

Barker, T. S., and V. Brailovksy, eds. 1981. *Oil or Industry? Energy, Industrialization and Economic Policy*. London: Academic Press.

Barnett, D. F., and Schorsch, L. 1983. *Steel: Upheaval in a Basic Industry*. Cambridge, Mass.: Ballinger.

Bates, Robert. 1981. *Markets and States in Tropical Africa*. Berkeley: University of California Press.

Baumgartner, Ulrich. 1980. "The Response of International Capital Markets to the 1973–74 Oil Price Increase." DM/80/48. Washington, D.C.: International Monetary Fund, July.

Beckford, G. L. 1972. *Persistent Poverty*. Oxford, Eng.: Oxford University Press.

Beer, Christopher. 1976. *The Politics of Peasant Groups in Western Nigeria*. Ibadan: University of Ibadan Press.

Beer, Christopher, and Gavin Williams. 1976. "The Politics of the Ibadan Peasantry." In Gavin Williams, ed., *Nigeria: Economy and Society*. London: Rex Collins.

Benassy, J. P. 1975. "Neo-Keynesian Disequilibrium Theory in a Monetary Economy." *Review of Economic Studies* 42 (October): 503–24.

Betancourt, Romulo. 1978. *Oil and Politics in Venezuela*. Boston: Houghton Mifflin.

Bienen, Henry. 1983. *Oil Revenues and Policy Choice in Nigeria*. World Bank Staff Working Paper 592. Washington, D.C., August.

———. 1985. "Politics and Agricultural Policy in Nigeria." Woodrow Wilson School, Princeton University. Processed.

Bienen, Henry, and V. P. Diejomaoh, eds. 1981. *The Political Economy of Income Distribution in Nigeria*. London and New York: Holmes and Meier.

Biersteker, Thomas B. 1978. *Distortion or Development: Contending Perspectives on the Multinational Corporation*. Cambridge, Mass.: MIT Press.

———. 1980. "Indigenization and the Nigerian Bourgeoisie: Dependent Development in an African Context." Unpublished paper, Yale University, November.

Bigler, G. E. H. 1980. "State Economic Control Versus Market Expansion: The Third Sector in Venezuelan Politics, 1928–78." Ph.D. diss., Johns Hopkins University.

Bird, Richard M. 1976., "Assessing Tax Performance in Developing Countries: A Critical Review of the Literature." *Finanzarchiv* 34 (2): 244–65.

Bitar, Sergio, and E. Troncoso. 1983. "Petróleo e Industrialización: La Experiencia Venezolana 1973–80." Wilson Center, Washington, D.C. Processed.

Black, J. K., H. I. Blutstein, K. T. Johnston, and D. S. McMorris. 1976. *Area Handbook for Trinidad and Tobago.* Washington, D.C.: American University.

Bobb, Euric. 1978. *Report of the Committee to Review Government Expenditure.* Port of Spain: Government Printer.

Bocco, Arnaldo. 1982. "Estado y Renta Petrolera en los Años Setenta." In Riffka (1982).

Boediono, 1980. "Indonesia: Survey of Recent Developments." *Bulletin of Indonesian Economic Studies* (July): 1–30.

Bond, M. E., and Adalbert Knobl. 1982. "Some Implications of North Sea Oil for the U. K. Economy." *International Monetary Fund Staff Papers* 29 (September): 363–97.

Booth, Anne, and Peter McCawley, eds. 1981. *The Indonesian Economy During the Suharto Era.* Kuala Lumpur: Oxford University Press.

Booth, Anne, and R. M. Sundrum. 1981. "Trends and Determinants of Income Distribution in Indonesia." In Ross Garnant and Peter McCawley, eds., *The Indonesian Connection.* Canberra: Australian National University.

Bordo, M. D. 1975. "John E. Cairnes on the Effects of the Australian Gold Discoveries 1851–73: An Early Application of the Methodology of Positive Economics." *History of Political Economy* 3: 337–59.

Bosson, Rex, and Bension Varon. 1977. *The Mining Industry and the Developing Countries.* New York: Oxford University Press.

Bourguignon, François, 1980a. "Oil and Income Distribution in Venezuela: 1968–76." In Jacques De Bandt and others, eds., *European Studies in Development.* London: Macmillan. 1980.

———. 1980b. "La Distribucción del Ingreso en Venezuela en el Periodo 1968–1976." *Revista de Hacienda* 77 (January).

———. 1981. "L'Utilisation du Surplus Petrolier au Venezuela: 1973–78." *Annales Economiques* 17: 145–68.

———. 1985. "Are Oil Windfalls a Curse or a Blessing? The Case of Oil in Venezuela." Report for RPO 672-49. Development Research Department, World Bank, January.

Bourguignon, François, Gilles Michel, and Didier Migueu. 1983. "Short-Run Distribution and Long-Run Adjustments in a Computable General Model of Income Distribution and Employment." *Journal of Development Economics* 13: 21–43.

Boutros-Ghali, Youssef. 1981. "The Single Export Dependent Economy Model." Ph.D. diss., Massachusetts Institute of Technology.

Brewster, Havelock. 1972. "The Growth of Employment under Export-Based Underdevelopment." *Social and Economic Studies* 21: 152–69.

Brittan, Samuel, and Barry Riley. 1978. "A People's Stake in North Sea Oil." *Lloyds Bank Review* 128 (April): 1–19.

Brown, Martin S., and others. 1983. *Worldwide Investment Analysis: The Case of Aluminum.* World Bank Staff Working Paper 603. Washington, D.C.

Bruno, Michael. 1976. "The Two-Sector Open Economy and the Real Exchange Rate." *American Economic Review* 66: 566–77.

Bruno, Michael, and Jeffrey Sachs. 1982. "Energy and Resource Allocation: A Dynamic Model of the Dutch Disease." *Review of Economic Studies* 49 (5): 845–59.

———. 1985. *Economics of Worldwide Stagflation.* Cambridge, Mass.: Harvard University Press.

Buiter, W. H., and Marcus Miller. 1981. "The Thatcher Experiment: What Went Wrong?" Paper prepared for the Brookings Panel on Economic Activity. Department of Economics, University of Bristol, September.

Buiter, W. H., and D. D. Purvis. 1983. "Oil, Disinflation and Export Competitiveness: A Model of the Dutch Disease." In Jagdeep S. Bhandari and others, eds., *Economic Interdependence and Flexible Exchange Rates.* Cambridge, Mass.: MIT Press.

Burns, Leland, and Leo Grebler. 1976. "Resource Allocation to Housing Investment: A Comparative Analysis." *Economic Development and Cultural Change* 25, no. 1 (October): 95–121.

Byatt, Ian, Nicholas Hartley, Rachel Lomax, Stephen Powell, and Peter Spenser. 1982. *North Sea Oil and Structural Adjustment.* Government Economic Services Working Paper 54/Treasury Working Paper 22. London: Her Majesty's Treasury.

Caroni Ltd. 1978. *Directors' Report and Accounts 1977.* Couva: Moonan Printers.

Central Bank of Ecuador. *Boletín Anuario,* various issues. Quito.

———. *Información Estadística, Boletín Quincenal,* various issues. Quito.

———. 1984. *Memoria del Gerente General.* Quito.

Central Bank of Trinidad and Tobago. 1981. *Annual Report.* Port of Spain. Processed.

———. 1982a. "Relationship between Inflation and Declining Productivity." Port of Spain. Processed.

———. 1982b. *Annual Report.* Port of Spain. Processed.

Central Bank of Venezuela (BCV). *Informe Económico,* various issues. Caracas.

———. *Anuario de Series Estadísticas,* various issues.

———. 1979. *Treinta Anos de Historias Económicas.* Caracas.

Chambers, George. 1982. Address to the 23rd Convention of the People's National Movement. Port of Spain, October 1. Processed.

———. 1984. Budget Speech. Port of Spain: Government Printer.

Chenery, Hollis B., and Michael Bruno. 1962. "Development Alternatives in an Open Economy: The Case of Israel." *Economic Journal* 72, no. 285 (March).

Chenery, Hollis B., and Arthur MacEwan. 1979. "Optimal Patterns of Growth and Aid: The Case of Pakistan." In Hollis B. Chenery, ed., *Structural Change and Development Policy*. New York: Oxford University Press.

Chenery, Hollis B., and A. M. Strout. 1966. "Foreign Assistance and Economic Development." *American Economic Review* 56, no. 4 (September).

Chenery, Hollis B., and Moises Syrquin. 1975. *Patterns of Development, 1950–1970*. Oxford, Eng.: Oxford University Press.

Chiriboga, Manuel. 1982. "La Pobreza Rural y la Producción Agropecuaria." In Riffka (1982).

Choksi, Armeane M. 1979. *State Intervention in Industrialization of Developing Countries: Selected Issues*. World Bank Staff Working Paper 341. Washington, D.C., July.

Citibank. 1979. *Trinidad and Tobago Investment Guide*. New York: Citibank.

Clark, C. 1972. "Calories and Proteins." *Bulletin of Indonesian Economic Studies*. July.

Coleman, James. 1964. *Nigeria: Background to Nationalism*. Berkeley: University of California Press.

Collier, Paul. 1985. "An Analysis of the Nigerian Labor Market." DRD Discussion Paper 155. Development Research Department, World Bank, February.

Collier, W. R., and others. 1982. "Acceleration of Rural Development in Java." *Bulletin of Indonesian Economic Studies* (November).

CONADE (Consejo Nacional de Desarrollo Económico). 1982. "Indicadores Socio-Económicos." Quito, May.

———. 1983. "Estadísticas Financieras del Sector Público Ecuatoriano, 1975–81." Quito. Processed.

Conway, Patrick. 1982. "Oil Rents and Development Strategy: A Case Study of Algeria." Report to RPO 672–49. Development Research Department, World Bank, July. Processed.

Conway, Patrick, and Alan H. Gelb. 1988. "Oil Windfalls in a Controlled Economy: A Fix-Price Equilibrium Analysis of Algeria." *Journal of Development Economics* 28: 63–81.

Corbo, Vittorio, Jaime de Melo, and James R. Tybout. 1984. "What Went Wrong with the Recent Reforms in the Southern Cone?" Development Research Department, World Bank. Paper presented at American Economic Association Meetings, December 26–28.

Corden, W. M. 1981a. "Exchange Rate Policy and the Resources Boom." Australian National University, March. Processed.

———. 1981b. "The Exchange Rate, Monetary Policy and North Sea Oil:

The Economic Theory of the Squeeze on Tradeables." *Oxford Economic Papers* 33 (July): 23–46.

———. 1982. "Exchange Rate Protection." In Kenen (1982).

———. 1984. "Booming Sector and Dutch Disease Economics: Survey and Consolidation." Oxford Economic Papers 36: 359–80.

Corden, W. M., and J. P. Neary. 1982. "Booming Sector and De-Industrialization in a Small Open Economy." *Economic Journal* 92 (December): 825–48.

CORDIPLAN (Oficina Central de Coordinación y Planificación de la Presidencia de la República). 1983. *Venezuela: Recent Economic Development and Medium-Term Prospects*. Caracas, March.

Cremer, Jacques, and Djaved Salehi-Isfahani. 1980. "Competitive Pricing in the World Oil Market: How Important Is OPEC? CARESS Working Paper 80-4. University of Pennsylvania. Processed.

Crockett, Andrew D., and Owen J. Evans. 1980. "Demand for Money in Middle Eastern Countries." *International Monetary Fund Staff Papers* (September): 543–77.

Cuddington, J. T. 1985. "Capital Flight: Issues, Estimates and Explanations." Development Research Department, World Bank, March. Processed.

Cuthbertson, A. B. 1982. "The Indonesian Export Certificate Scheme: Evaluation and Proposals." Report prepared for the Ministry of Trade and Cooperatives, Jakarta, July.

Dapice, David, and R. M. Sundrum. 1980. "Income Distribution 1970–77." *Bulletin of Indonesian Economic Studies* 1 (March): 86–91.

Dasgupta, Partha, Robert Eastwood, and Geoffrey M. Heal. 1978. "Resource Management in a Trading Economy." *Quarterly Journal of Economics* (May): 296–306.

Dasgupta, Partha, and Geoffrey M. Heal. 1980. *Economic Theory and Exhaustible Resources*. New York: Cambridge University Press.

Davis, J. M. 1983. "The Economic Effects of Windfall Gains in Export Earnings: 1975–78." *World Development* 11, no. 2 (February): 119-39.

Dean, Warren. 1966. "The Planter as Entrepreneur." *Hispanic American Historical Review* 46 (May).

Dervis, Kemal, Jaime de Melo, and Sherman Robinson. 1982. *General Equilibrium Models for Development Policy*. New York: Cambridge University Press.

Diejomaoh, V. P., and E. C. Anusionwu. 1981. "The Structure of Income Inequality in Nigeria: A Macro Analysis." In Bienen and Diejomaoh(1981).

Diewert, W. E. 1976. "Exact and Superlative Index Numbers." *Journal of Econometrics* 4 (May): 115–45.

Dornbusch, Rudiger. 1981. "Real Interest Rates, Home Goods and Optimal External Borrowing." Department of Economics, Massachusettes Institute of Technology, September. Processed.

Downey, Roger J., Steven Keuning, and others. 1983. "An Indonesian

SAM." Development Strategy Division Working Paper 83-5. Development Research Department, World Bank, June.

Drazen, Allan. 1980. "Recent Developments in Macroeconomic Disequilibrium Theory." *Econometrica* 48 (March): 283–306.

Drekonja, Gerhard, ed. 1978. *Ecuador Hoy* 21. Bogotá.

Dreze, Jacques. 1975. "Existence of an Exchange Equilibrium under Price Rigidities." *International Economic Review* 16 (June): 301–20.

Drud, Arne. 1983. "CONOPT: A GRC Code for Large Sparse Dynamic Nonlinear Optimisation." DRD Discussion Paper 59. Development Research Department, World Bank, August.

Dudley, B. J. 1973. *Instability and Political Order: Politics and Crises in Nigeria.* Ibadan: University of Ibadan Press.

Eastwood, R. K., and A. J. Venables. 1982. "The Macroeconomic Implications of a Resource Discovery in an Open Economy." *Economic Journal* 92 (June): 285–99.

El Serafy, Salah. 1981. "Absorptive Capacity, the Demand for Revenue and the Supply of Petroleum." *Journal of Energy and Development* 7, no.1 (Autumn): 73–88.

Emmerson, Donald K. 1978., "The Bureaucracy in Political Context: Weakness in Strength." In Jackson and Pye (1978).

Erb, G. F., and S. Schiavo-Campo. 1969. "Export Instability Level of Development and Economic Size of Less Developed Countries." *Bulletin of the Oxford Institute of Economics and Statistics* 31 (November): 363–83.

Fair, Ray C., and Dwight Jaffee. 1972. "Methods of Estimation for Markets in Disequilibrium. *Econometrica* 40: 497–514.

Fernandez, Ivan. 1982. "Estado y Clases Sociales en la Decada del Setenta." In Riffka (1982).

Financial Times (London). 1981. "Indonesia Survey." December 21.

Fineberg, R. A. 1982. "Chaos in the Capital: The Budget System in Crisis." Report by the Alaska Public Interest Group, Anchorage, Alaska.

Fischer, Stanley. 1980. "Seigniorage and the Case for a National Money." Department of Economics, Massachussetts Institute of Technology, September. Processed.

Fishlow, Albert. 1965. *American Railroads and the Transformation of the Ante-Bellum Economy.* Cambridge, Mass.: Harvard University Press.

Fitzgerald, E. V. U. 1980. "Capital Accumulation in Mexico." *Development and Change* 11, no. 3 (July).

Flemming, J. S. 1982. "U.K. Macro-Policy Response to Oil Price Shocks of 1974–75 and 1979–80." *European Economic Review* 18: 223–34.

Forsyth, P. J., and J. A. Kay. 1980. "The Economic Implications of North Sea Oil Revenues." *Fiscal Studies* 1 (3): 1–28.

———. 1981. "North Sea Oil and Manufacturing Output." *Fiscal Studies* 2 (2): 9–17.

Forsyth, P. J., and S. J. Nicholas. 1983. "The Decline of Spanish Industry and the Price Revolution: A Neoclassical Analysis." *Journal of European Economic History* 12 (Winter): 601–09.

Funkhouser, Richard, and P. W. MacAvoy. 1978. "A Sample of Observations on Comparative Prices in Public and Private Enterprises." *Journal of Public Economics* 11 (June).

Furtado, Celso. 1963. *The Economic Growth of Brazil: A Survey from Colonial to Modern Times.* Berkeley: University of California Press.

———. 1970. *Economic Development of Latin America.* London: Cambridge University Press.

Galbis, Vincente. 1979. "Money and Growth in Latin America." *Economic Development and Cultural Change* 27 (April): 423–43.

Garcia Araujo, M. 1982. "The Impact of Petrodollars on the Economy and the Public Sector of Venezuela." Paper delivered at the Tenth National Meeting of the Latin America Studies Association, Washington, D.C., March 4.

Gately, Dermot. 1984. "A Ten Year Perspective: OPEC and the World Oil Market." *Journal of Economic Literature* 22, no. 3 (September): 1100–14.

Geertz, Clifford. 1966. *Agricultural Involution: The Process of Ecological Change in Indonesia.* Berkeley: University of California Press.

Gelb, Alan H. 1979. "On the Definition and Measurement of Export Instability and the Cost of Buffering Export Fluctuations." *Review of Economic Studies* 46, no. 1 (January): 149–62.

———. 1981. *Capital-Importing Oil Exporters: Adjustment Issues and Policy Choices.* World Bank Staff Working Paper 475. Washington, D.C., August.

———. 1985a. "The Impact of Oil Windfalls: Comparative Statics with an Indonesia-Like Model." DRD Discussion Paper 133. Development Research Department, World Bank, October.

———. 1985b. "Are Oil Windfalls a Blessing or a Curse? Policy Exercise with an Indonesia-like Model." DRD Discussion Paper 135. Development Research Department, World Bank.

———. 1986a. "Adjustment to Windfall Gains: A Comparative Analysis of Oil-Exporting Countries." In Neary and van Wijnbergen (1986).

———. 1986b. "From Boom to Bust: Oil-Exporting Countries over the Cycle 1970–84." *IDS Bulletin* 17 (4): 22–29.

———. 1986c. "The Oil Syndrome: Adjustment to Windfall Gains in Oil-Exporting Countries." In Deepak Lal and Martin Wolf, eds., *Stagflation, Savings, and the State: Perspectives on the Global Economy.* New York: Oxford University Press.

Gillis, Malcolm. 1984. "Episodes in Indonesian Growth." In A. C. Harberger, ed., *World Economic Growth.* San Francisco, Calif.: Institute of Contemporary Studies.

Girvan, N. P. 1970. "Multinational Corporations and Dependent Underdevelopment in Mineral-Export Economies." *Social and Economic Studies* 19: 490–526.

Glassburner, Bruce. 1964. "High-Level Manpower for Economic Development: The Indonesian Experience." In Frederick H. Harbison and Charles A. Meyers, eds., *Education, Manpower, and Economic Growth: Strategies of Human Resource Development*. New York: McGraw-Hill, 1964.

————, ed. 1971. *The Economy of Indonesia*. Ithaca. N.Y.: Cornell University Press.

————. 1978a. "Indonesia's New Economic Policy and Its Socio-Political Implications." In Jackson and Pye (1978).

————. 1978b. "Political Economy and the Suharto Regime." *Bulletin of Indonesian Economic Studies* (November): 24–51.

————. 1984. "Oil, Public Policy and Economic Performance, Indonesia in the 1970's." Report for RPO 672-49. Development Research Department, World Bank, July.

Goffman, I. J., and D. J. Mahan. 1971. "The Growth of Public Expenditures in Selected Developing Nations: Six Caribbean Countries, 1940–65." *Public Finance* 26: 57–74.

Greenville, S. A. 1977. "Indonesia—Survey of Recent Developments." *Bulletin of Indonesian Economic Studies* (March): 1–31.

Gregory, R. G. 1976. "Some Implications of the Growth of the Mineral Sector." *Australian Journal of Agricultural Economics* 20, no. 2 (August): 71–93.

————. 1978. "Determinants of Relative Prices in the Manufacturing Sector of a Small Open Economy: The Australian Experience." In Wolfgang Kasper and Thomas G. Parry, eds., *Growth, Trade and Structural Change in an Open Australian Economy*. Kensington: Centre for Applied Economic Research, University of New South Wales.

Grenville, Stephen. 1981. "Monetary Policy and the Formal Financial Sector." In Booth and McCawley (1981).

Gupta, Syamaprasad. 1977. *A Model for Income Distribution, Employment, and Growth: A Case Study of Indonesia*. Baltimore, Md.: Johns Hopkins University Press.

Hablutzel, Rudolf. 1981a. *Development Prospects of Capital Surplus Oil-Exporting Countries*. World Bank Staff Working Paper 483. Washington, D.C.

————. 1981b. "Issues in Economic Development for the Oil-Rich Countries." *Finance & Development* 18, no. 2 (June): 10–13.

Hallwood, Paul, and Stuart Sinclair. 1981. *Oil, Debt and Development: OPEC in the Third World*. London: Allen and Unwin.

Handelman, Howard. 1980. "Ecuadorian Agrarian Reform: The Politics of Limited Change." American University Field Service Report 49. Hanover, N.H.: AUFS.

Handelman, Howard, and T. G. Sanders, eds. 1981. *Military Government and the Movement Towards Democracy in South America*. Bloomington: Indiana University Press.

Hanson, J. A. 1977. "Cycles, Growth, and Structural Change in Venezuela, 1950–74." In John D. Martz and David J. Meyers, eds., *Venezuela: The Democratic Experience*. New York: Praeger.

Harberger, A. C. 1983. "Dutch Disease—How Much Sickness, How Much Boon?" *Resources and Energy* 5: 1–20.

Hart, Gillian, and Daniel Sisler. 1978. "Aspects of Rural Labor Market Operations: A Javanese Case Study." *American Journal of Agricultural Economics* 65 (8).

Hausman, R., and C. Omiami. 1981. "The Realisation of the Venezuelan Oil Rent." Paper 8101. Paris: CEPREMAP, January.

Hayami, Yujiro, and Amwar Hafid. 1979. "Rice Harvesting and Welfare in Rural Java." *Bulletin of Indonesian Economic Studies* 2: 94–112.

Healy, B. T. 1981. "Indonesia: Survey of Recent Developments." *Bulletin of Indonesian Economic Studies* 1: 1–35.

Heckscher, E. F. 1963. *An Economic History of Sweden.* Cambridge, Mass.: Harvard University Press.

Helleiner, Gerald. 1966. *Peasant Agriculture, Government and Economic Growth in Nigeria.* Homewood, Ill.: Richard D. Irwin.

Heller, P. S. 1975. "A Model of Public Fiscal Behavior in Developing Countries: Aid, Investment and Taxation." *American Economic Review* 65 (June): 429–45.

Hicks, John. 1965. *Capital and Growth.* Oxford, Eng.: Oxford University Press.

Higgins, Benjamin. 1972. "Survey of Recent Developments." *Bulletin of Indonesian Economic Studies* (March).

Hill, Hal. 1980. "The Economies of Recent Changes in the Weaving Industry." *Bulletin of Indonesian Economic Studies* (July): 83–103.

Hirschman, Albert O. 1958. *The Strategy of Economic Development.* New Haven, Conn.: Yale University Press, 1958; New York: Norton, 1978.

———. 1981. *Essays in Trespassing: Economics to Politics and Beyond.* New York: Cambridge University Press.

———. 1984. "A Dissenter's Confession: 'The Strategy of Economic Development' Revisited." In Gerald M. Meier and Dudley Seers, eds., *Pioneers in Development.* New York, Oxford University Press.

Hodges, Donald C., and Ross Gandy. 1979. *Mexico 1910–1976: Reform or Revolution?* London: Zed Press.

Hoogvelt, Angie. 1979. "Indigenization and Foreign Capital: Industrialization in Nigeria." *Review of African Political Economy* 14.

Hotelling, Harold. 1931. "The Economics of Exhaustible Resources." *Journal of Political Economy* 2: 137–75.

Houghton, D. H. 1972. *The South African Economy.* Cape Town: Oxford University Press.

Hughes, Helen, and Shamsher Singh. 1978. "Economic Rent: Incidence in Selected Metals and Minerals." *Resources Policy* (June): 135–45.

Hunt, S. J. 1973. "Growth and Guano in Nineteenth Century Peru." Research Program on Economic Development, Discussion Paper 34, Princeton University, February.

Hunter, Alex. 1971. "The Indonesian Oil Industry." In Glassburner (1971).

Hurtado, Osvaldo. 1980. *Political Power in Ecuador*. Albuquerque: University of New Mexico Press.

ICF. 1982. *Alaska Natural Gas Develorment: An Economic Assessment of Marine System*. Washington, D.C.: ICF.

Idachaba, F. S. 1982. *The Political Economy of Nigeria's Green Revolution Program*. Ibadan: Food Policy Research Program, Department of Agricultural Economics, University of Ibadan.

Inter-American Development Bank. 1979. *Economic and Social Progress in Latin America*. Washington. D.C.

———. 1983. *Economic and Social Progress in Latin America*. Washington, D.C.

International Monetary Fund. *Annual Report*. Washington, D.C., various years.

Isard, Peter. 1977. "How Far Can We Push the 'Law of One Price'?" *American Economic Review* 67, no. 5 (December): 942–48.

Jackson, K. D., and L. W. Pye, eds. 1978. *Political Power and Communications in Indonesia*. Berkeley: University of California Press.

Jones, G. W. 1981. "Labor Force Developments since 1961." In Booth and McCawley (1981).

Joseph, Richard A. 1978. "Affluence and Under-development: The Nigerian Experience." *Journal of Modern African Studies* 16, no. 2 (June): 221–40.

Kahin, G. McT. 1952. *Nationalism and Revolution in Indonesia*. Ithaca, N.Y: Cornell University Press.

Kanbur, S. M. R. 1984. "How to Analyze Commodity Price Stabilisation? A Review Article." *Oxford Economic Papers* 36: 336–58.

Karl, T. L. 1982. "The Political Economy of Petrodollars: Oil and Democracy in Venezuela." Ph.D. diss., Stanford University.

Katouzian, M. A. 1978. "Oil versus Agriculture: A Case of Dual Depletion in Iran." *Journal of Peasant Studies* 5, no. 2 (April): 347–69.

Kendrick, David, and Lance Taylor. 1970. "Numerical Solution of Nonlinear Planning Models." *Econometrica* 38, no. 3 (May): 453–67.

Kenen, Peter, and others, eds. 1982. *The International Monetary System under Flexible Exchange Rates: Global, Regional, and National*. Cambridge, Mass.: Ballinger.

Keynes, J. M. [1930] 1950. *A Treatise on Money*. Vol. 2. London: Macmillan.

Khan, M. S. 1980. "Monetary Shocks and Dynamics of Inflation." *International Monetary Fund Staff Papers* 27, no. 2 (June): 250–84.

Kharas, Homi. 1984. "The Long-Run Creditworthiness of Developing Countries: Theory and Practice." *Quarterly Journal of Economics* (August).

Kornai, Janos. 1978. *The Economics of Shortage*. Amsterdam: North-Holland.

Kravis, Irving B., Alan Heston, and Robert Summers. 1978. *International Comparisons of Real Product and Purchasing Power*. Baltimore, Md.: Johns Hopkins University Press.

Kreinheder, Jack, and Leonard Steinberg. 1982. "State Budget Policy under Uncertain Revenue Forecasts: Options for Legislative Action." Alaska House Research Agency Report 82-B. Juneau.

Krueger, A. O. 1974. "The Political Economy of the Rent-Seeking Society." *American Economic Review* 64 (June): 291–303.

Leff, N. H. 1972. "Economic Development and Regional Inequality: Origins of the Brazilian Case." *Quarterly Journal of Economics* 86 (May): 243–62.

Levy, Walter J. 1978. "The Years That the Locust Hath Eaten: Oil Policy and OPEC Development Prospects." *Foreign Affairs* 57 (1–3): 287–305.

Lewis, W. A. 1950. "Industrial Development of the British West Indies." *Caribbean Economic Review* 2 (1): 1–61.

———. 1952. "Economic Development with Unlimited Supplies of Labor." *Manchester School of Economics and Social Studies* 20 (May): 139–91.

———. 1972. *Statement to the Second Annual Governor's Board Meeting, St. Lucia*. Barbados: Letterworth Press.

Liscom, W. L. 1982. *The Energy Decade*. Cambridge, Mass.: Ballinger.

Lotz, J. R., and E. R. Morss. 1977. "Measuring Tax Effort in Developing Countries." *International Monetary Fund Staff Papers* (November): 478–97.

Lowenthal, David. 1972. *West Indian Societies*. Oxford, Eng.: Oxford University Press.

Lim, David. 1980. "Income Distribution, Export Instability and Savings Behavior." *Economic Development and Cultural Change* 28 (2): 359–64.

MacBean, A. I. 1966. *Export Instability and Economic Development*. London: Allen and Unwin.

Macedo, J. Braga de. 1982. "Currency Diversification and Export Competitiveness: A Model of the Dutch Disease in Egypt." *Journal of Developing Economics* 11: 287–306.

Mackenzie, G. A. 1981. "The Role of Non-Oil Revenues in the Fiscal Policy of Oil-Exporting Countries." DM81/4. Washington, D.C.: International Monetary Fund, January.

Mackenzie, G. A., and S. M. Schadler. 1980. "Exchange Rate Policies and Diversification in Oil-Exporting Countries." DM80/33. Washington, D.C.: International Monetary Fund, May.

Mackintosh, John. 1966. *Nigerian Governmental Politics*. Evanston, Ill.: Northwestern University Press.

Malek, M. H. 1982. "OPEC Development Policies: Problems and Prospects." Paper presented to the Socialist Economist Conference, University of St. Andrews, September.

Malinvaud, Edmond. 1977. *The Theory of Unemployment Reconsidered*. Oxford. Eng.: Basil Blackwell.

340   Bibliography

Mallarde, E. 1975. *L'Algérie Depuis*. Paris: La Table Ronde.

Manning, Christopher, and Dipak Mazumdar. 1985. "Indonesian Labor Markets: An Overview." Development Research Department, World Bank, May.

Marshall-Silva, Jorge. 1984. "Ecuador: Quantification, Distribution and Effects of the Oil Bonus, 1973–82." Report for RPO 672-49. Development Research Department, World Bank, December.

Martin, Ricardo, and Sweder van Wijnbergen. 1986. "Shadow Prices and Intertemporal Aspects of Remittances and Oil Revenues in Egypt." In Neary and van Wijnbergen (1986).

Martinez, Luciano. 1983. "Capitalismo Agrario: Crisis e Impacto Social." In *Ecuador: Presente y Futuro*. 1983. Quito: Editorial el Conejo.

Mazri, Hamid. 1975. *Les Hydrocarbons dans l'Economie Algérienne*. Algiers: SNED.

Mazumdar, Dipak, and Sawit. 1986. "Trends in Rural Wages, West Java, 1977–83." *Bulletin of Indonesia Economic Studies* 22, no. 3 (December): 93–106.

McCawley, Peter. 1978. "Some Consequences of the Pertamina Crisis in Indonesia. *Journal of Southeast Asian Studies* (March).

McMillan, M. L., and K. H. Norrie. 1980. "Province-Building in a Rentier Society." *Canadian Public Policy* 6 (February): 213–20.

Mears, Leon A., and Sidik Moeljono. 1981. "Food Policy." In Booth and McCawley (1981).

Megatele, Abderrahmanne. 1980. *Investment Policies of National Oil Companies*. New York: Praeger.

Melo, Jaime de, and Kemal Dervis. 1977. "Modelling the Effects of Protection in a Dynamic Framework." *Journal of Development Economics* 4 (June): 149–72.

Mexico. Secretaría de Patrimonio y Fomento Industrial. 1980. *Programa de Energía: Metas a 1990 y Projeciones al Ano 2000*. Mexico City.

Meyer, Ronald K., and Scott R. Pearson. 1974. "Contribution of Petroleum to Nigerian Economic Development." In Scott R. Pearson and John Cownie, eds., *Commodity Exports and African Economic Development*. Lexington, Mass.: Lexington Books.

Michel, Gilles, and Didier Migueu. 1980. "Labor-Markets as Disequilibrium Factors in a Computable General Equilibrium Model Applied to Venezuela." Ecole Normale Supérieure, Laboratoire d'Economie Politique, Document 31. Paris: August.

Morgan, D. R. 1979a. "Fiscal Policies in Oil Exporting Countries." *International Monetary Fund Staff Papers* 26 (March): 55–86.

———. 1979b. "Fiscal Policy in Oil Exporting-Countries. 1972–78." *Finance & Development* (December): 14–17.

Morrison, Donald. 1981. "Inequalities of Social Rewards: Realities and Perceptions in Nigeria." In Bienen and Diejomaoh (1981).

Muellbauer, John, and Richard Portes. 1978. "Macroeconomic Models with Quantity Rationing." *Economic Journal* 88: 788–821.

Murphy, K. J. 1983. *Macroprojects in the Third World*. New York: Westwind Press.

Musgrove, Philip. 1980. "The Oil Price Increase and the Alleviation of Poverty: Income Distribution in Caracas, Venezuela, in 1966–1975." Washington, D.C.: Brookings Institution and ECIEL Program of Joint Studies of Latin American Integration, May. Processed.

Nankani, Gobindram T. 1979. *Development Problems of Mineral-Exporting Countries*. World Bank Staff Working Paper 354. Washington. D.C., August.

Neary, J. Peter, and D. D. Purvis. 1981. "Real Adjustment and Exchange Rate Dynamics." Paper presented to National Bureau of Economic Research Conference on Exchange Rates and International Macroeconomics, Cambridge, Mass., November 20–21.

Neary, J. Peter, and Sweder van Wijnbergen. 1984. "Can Higher Oil Revenue Lead to a Recession? A Comment on Eastwood and Venables." *Economic Journal* 94 (June): 390–95.

———, eds. 1986. *Natural Resources and the Macroeconomy*. Oxford, Eng.: Basil Blackwell.

Nelson, H. D., ed. 1979. *Algeria: A Country Study*. Washington, D.C.: American University.

Nestel, Barry. 1985. *Indonesia and the CGIAR Centers*. Consultative Group on International Agricultural Research Study Paper 10. Washington, D.C.: World Bank, November.

Newbery, David M. 1983. "Setting the Price of Oil in a Distorted Economy." Development Research Department, World Bank, September. Processed.

Newbery, David M., and Joseph E. Stiglitz. 1981. *The Theory of Commodity Price Stabilization: A Study on the Economics of Risk*. New York: Oxford University Press.

Nichols, D. A. 1970. "Land and Economic Growth." *American Economic Review* 60, no. 3 (June): 85–87.

Niehans, Jürg. 1981. "The Appreciation of Sterling: Causes, Effects, Policies." Volkswirtschaftliches Institut, Universität Bern, February. Processed.

Niering, F. S. 1982a. "Trinidad: Energy Policy in Transition." *Petroleum Economist* (September): 361–63.

———. 1982b. "Venezuela: Doubts over Long-Term Objectives." *Petroleum Economist* (March) 85–87.

Nigerian Economics Society. 1975. *Nigeria's Indigenization Policy*. Proceedings of the 1974 Symposium. Ibadan: Department of Economics, University of Ibadan.

Norton, Roger D. 1983. "Pricing Analyses for Nigerian Agriculture." Western Africa Regional Office, World Bank, September. Processed.

Olayide, S. O. 1980. "Agricultural Policy of the Military Era, 1966–1979." In Femi Kayode, ed., *The Nigerian Economy under the Military*. Proceedings of the 1980 Annual Conference of the Nigerian Economics Society. Zaria: Nigerian Economics Society.

Onage, Onatume F. 1975. "The Indigenization Decree and Economic Independence: Another Case of Bourgeois Utopianism." In Nigerian Economics Society (1975).

Onoh, J. K. 1983. *The Nigerian Oil Economy: From Prosperity to Glut*. London: Croom Helm; New York: St. Martin's Press.

Oyediran, Oyeleye. 1979. "Background to Military Rule." In Oyeleye Oyediran, ed., *Nigerian Government and Politics under Military Rule, 1966–79*. New York: St. Martin's Press.

Oyediran, Oyeleye. and W. A. Ajibola. 1975. "Nigerian Public Service in 1975." In Oyeleye Oyediran, ed., *Survey of Nigerian Affairs, 1975*. Ibadan: Oxford University Press.

Pachano, Abelardo. 1979. "Balance de la Situación Petrolera en el Ecuador." *Revista Cuestiones Económicas* (September/March).

Pakravan, Karim. 1981. "Government Intervention in the Industry of Iran, 1964–78." Hoover Institution, Stanford, California. Processed.

Palmer, Ingrid. 1978. *The Indonesian Economy since 1965: A Case Study of Political Earning*. London: Frank Case.

Panter-Brick, S. K., ed. 1970. *Nigerian Politics and Military Rule; Prelude to Civil War*. London: Athlone Press.

Pareja Diezcanseco, Alfredo. 1979. *Ecuador: La República de 1830 a Nuestras Días*. Quito: Editorial Universitaria.

Parsan, E. V. 1981. "An Evaluation of the Organisation and Development of the Fertilizer Industry in Trinidad and Tobago." M.Sc. thesis, University of the West Indies.

Pearson, Scott R. 1970. *Petroleum and the Nigerian Economy*. Palo Alto, Calif.: Stanford University Press.

Peil, Margaret. 1976. *The Nigerian Government: The People's View*. London: Cassell.

Pesaran, M. H. 1982a. "Macroeconomic Policy in an Oil-Exporting Economy." Trinity College, Cambridge University, May. Processed.

———. 1982b. "Dependent Capitalism in Pre- and Post-Revolutionary Iran." *International Journal of Middle East Studies* 14, no. 4 (November): 501–22.

Pesaran, M. H., and B. Pesaran. 1982. "Trends in Income Distribution in Urban Iran: 1959–78." Trinity College, Cambridge University, October. Processed.

Peterson, F. M., and A. L. Fisher. 1977. "The Exploitation of Extractive Resources: A Survey." *Economic Journal* 87 (December): 681–721.

Philip, George. 1980. "Oil and Politics in Ecuador: 1972–76." University of London Institute of Latin American Studies Working Papers 1.

Picard, Pierre. 1983. "Inflation and Growth in a Disequilibrium Macroeconomic Model." *Journal of Economic Theory* 30 (2): 266–95.

Pinto, Brian. 1987. "Nigeria during and after the Oil Boom: A Policy Comparison with Indonesia." *World Bank Economic Review* 1, no. 3 (May): 419–46.

Pitt, M. M., and L. F. Lee. 1981. "The Measurement and Sources of Technical Inefficiency in the Indonesian Weaving Industry." *Journal of Development Economics* 9 (1): 43–64.

Pollard, H. J. 1981a. "The Personal Factor in the Success of Agricultural Development Schemes." *Journal of Developing Areas* 15: 561–84.

———. 1981b. "Food Production and Trinidad's Home Market: An Unfulfilled Potential." *Journal of Tropical Geography* 51.

———. 1985. "The Erosion of Agriculture in an Oil Economy: The Case of Export Crop Production in Trinidad." *World Development* 13, no. 7 (July): 819–37.

Portes, Richard, and Sidney Winter. 1978. "The Demand for Money and Consumption Goods in Centrally Planned Economies." *Review of Economics and Statistics* 60 (February): 8–17.

———. 1980. "Disequilibrium Estimates for Consumption Goods in Centrally Planned Economies." *Review of Economic Studies* 47 (January): 137–57.

Pyatt, Graham, and others. 1972. "Comprehensive Employment Mission to Iran." Report for International Labour Organisation, World Employment Program, University of Warwick, February.

Quandt, Richard. 1976. "Testing Hypotheses in Disequilibrium Models." Princeton Econometric Research Program 197. Princeton University. Processed.

Quandt, William. 1971. *Revolution and Political Leadership: Algeria, 1954–1968*. Cambridge, Mass.: MIT Press.

Radetsky, Marian. 1985. *State Mineral Enterprises in Developing Countries: Their Impact on International Mineral Markets*. Baltimore, Md.: Johns Hopkins University Press.

Raffinot, Marc, and Pierre Jacquemot. 1977. *Le Capitalisme d'Etat Algérie*. Paris: Maspero.

Rampersad, Frank 1981a. "The Role of Agriculture in Trinidad's Oil-Producing Environment." In Jaycees, *Our Economy in Tomorrow's World*. Port of Spain: Jaycees, 1981.

———. 1981b. "On the Contribution of the Petroleum Industry to the Nation's Economy." Port of Spain, October. Processed.

Renaud, Bertrand. 1980. "Resource Allocation to Investment: Commitments and Results." *Economic Development and Cultural Change* 28 (2): 389–99.

Renwick, D. 1982. "A Future for the ONR." *Caribbean and West Indies Chronicle* (August): 12–29.

Report of the Commission of Inquiry into the Civil Disturbances Which

Occurred in Certain Parts of the Western State of Nigeria in the Month of December, 1968. 1968. Ibadan: Government Printer. (Known as the Ayoola Report.)

Resnick, S. A. 1970. "The Decline of Rural Industry under Export Expansion: A Comparison among Burma, Philippines, and Thailand, 1870–1938." *Journal of Economic History* 30 (March).

Reynolds, C. W. 1979. "Bankers as Revolutionaries in the Process of Development." In J. D. Aronson, ed., *Debt and the Less Developed Countries*. Boulder, Colo: Westview Press.

Richard, J. F. 1982. *Emerging Energy and Chemical Applications of Methanol: Opportunities for Developing Countries*. Washington, D.C.: World Bank.

Riffka, Sohel, coordinator. 1982. *Ecuador: El Mito de Desarrollo*. Quito: Editorial El Conejo.

Rimmer, Douglas. 1981. "Development in Nigeria: An Overview." In Bienen and Diejomaoh (1981).

Roemer, Michael. 1979. "Resource-Based Industrialization in the Developing Countries: A Survey." *Journal of Development Economics* 6, no. 2 (June).

————. 1983. "Dutch Disease in Developing Countries: Swallowing Bitter Medicine." Development Discussion Paper 156. Cambridge, Mass.: Harvard Institute of International Development, October.

Rosendale, Phyllis. 1980. "Indonesia: Survey of Recent Developments." *Bulletin of Indonesian Economic Studies* 1: 1–33.

Rupley, Lawrence A. 1981. "Revenue Sharing in the Nigerian Federation." *Journal of Modern African Studies* 19, no. 2 (June): 257–78.

Salazar-Carrillo, Jorge. 1976. *Oil in the Economic Development of Venezuela*. New York: Praeger.

Sandoval, J. M. 1983. "State Capitalism in a Petroleum-Based Economy: The Case of Trinidad and Tobago." In Fitzroy Ambursley and Robin Cohen, *Crisis in the Caribbean*. London: Heinemann.

Schatz, Sayre. 1981. "The Nigerian Petro-Political Fluctuation." Temple University, Philadelphia, Penn., unpublished.

Schatzl, L. H. 1969. *Petroleum in Nigeria*. Ibadan: Oxford University Press.

Scherr, S. J. 1984. "Agriculture and the Oil Syndrome The Role of Public Policy in Developing Petroleum Economies." Food Research Institute, Stanford University, Stanford, Calif. Processed.

Seers, Dudley. 1964. "The Mechanism of an Open Petroleum Economy." *Social and Economic Studies* 13 (2): 233–42.

Shann, E. W. 1981. "The Analysis of Mining Sector Growth." Paper presented to the Economic Society of Australia and New Zealand Tenth Conference, Australian National University, Canberra, August.

Shirley, Mary M. 1983. *Managing State-Owned Enterprises*. World Bank Staff Working Paper 577. Washington, D.C.

Sklar, Richard. 1966. *Nigerian Political Parties*. Princeton, N.J.: Princeton University Press.

Smith, Gordon W., and John T. Cuddington. eds. 1985. *International Debt and the Developing Countries*. Washington, D.C.: World Bank.

Smith, V. K. 1979. "Natural Resource Scarcity: A Strategic Analysis." *Review of Economics and Statistics* 61 (3): 423–26.

Southern, R. W. 1952. *The Makings of the Middle Ages*. London: Hutchinson.

Stauffer, T. R. 1975. *Energy-Intensive Industries in the Persian/Arabian Gulf: A New Ruhr without Water?* Cambridge, Mass.: Harvard Center for Middle Eastern Studies.

Sundararajan, Venkatramam, and Subhash Thakur. 1980. "Public Investment, Crowding Out and Growth: A Dynamic Model Applied to India and Korea." *International Monetary Fund Staff Papers* 27, no. 4 (December).

Tait, Alan, Wilfred Gratz, and Barry Eichengreen. 1979. "International Comparison of Taxation for Selected Developing Countries, 1972–76." *International Monetary Fund Staff Papers* 26 (March): 122–56.

Taylor, Lance. 1981. "Military Economics of the Third World." Paper prepared for the Independent Commission on Disarmament and Security Issues, Massachussettes Institute of Technology, October. Processed.

Timmer, C. Peter. 1975. "The Political Economy of Rice in Asia: Indonesia." *Food Research Institute Studies* 14 (3): 197–231.

———. 1985. "The Role of Price Policy in Rice Production in Indonesia: 1968–1982." Harvard Institute for International Development, Cambridge, Mass. Processed.

Tinker, Irene, and Millidge Walker. 1973. "Planning for Regional Development in Indonesia." *Asian Survey* 13, no. 12 (December): 1102–20.

Tobin, James. 1961. "Money, Capital and Other Stores of Value." *American Economic Review, Papers and Proceedings* 5, no. 1 (May): 36–37.

———. 1965. "Money and Economic Growth." *Econometrica* 33 (October): 671–84.

———. 1972. "Inflation and Unemployment." *American Economic Review* 62 (1): 1–18.

Trapido, P. J. 1982. "Agriculture in Venezuela: Trends in Production, Marketing and Trade in the 1970s." Washington, D.C.: U.S. Department of Agriculture. Processed.

Trinidad and Tobago. 1978. *White Paper on Agriculture*. Port of Spain: Government Printer.

———. 1981. *White Paper on Natural Gas*. Port of Spain, Government Printer.

———. 1982a. *Review of the Economy 1982*. Port of Spain: Government Printer.

———. 1982b. "Report of the Working Committee of the National Council on Productivity on Production Losses due to the Utilities and the Transport System and the Effect of Regulations and Procedures Which Impact on the Conduct of Business." April 30.

―――. 1983a. *Information Memorandum for the US$120 Million Loan*. Port of Spain: Government Printer.

―――. 1983b. *Review of the Economy 1983*. Port of Spain: Government Printer.

―――. 1984. *National Transportation Policy Study*. Port of Spain: Government Printer.

―――. Agricultural Statistics Section. 1983. "Statistical Review 1983." Port of Spain. Processed.

―――. Minister of State Enterprises. 1982. "Address to the National Petroleum Manufacturing Company." Port of Spain, September 10. Processed.

―――. Ministry of Agriculture. 1978. "White Paper on Agriculture." Port of Spain, December.

―――. Ministry of Agriculture. 1983. "Food and Agricultural Policy." Port of Spain: Government Printer. Processed.

―――. Ministry of Energy and Mineral Resources. 1982. "The Trinidad and Tobago Petroleum Industry: Mid-Year Review 1982." Port of Spain: Government Printer. Processed.

―――. Ministry of Finance. 1980. *Accounting for the Petrodollar*. Port of Spain: Government Printer.

―――. Ministry of Petroleum. 1971. "A Study of a Trinidad LNG Plant." Port of Spain. Processed.

―――. NEC (National Energy Corporation). 1979. *Annual Report of the National Energy Corporation*. Port of Spain. Processed.

―――. NEC. 1981. "Gas-Based Industry." Press release. Port of Spain, July 8.

"Trinidad's Oil Problems." *Caribbean Contact* 10, no. 6 (October 1982).

Tugwell, Franklin. 1975. *The Politics of Oil in Venezuela*. Stanford, Calif.: Stanford University Press.

Turner, L., and J. M. Bedare. 1979. *Middle Eastern Industrialisation*. London: Saxon House.

Tussing, A. R. 1982. "Alaska's Oil-Based Economy in National and International Perspective." University of Alaska, September. Processed.

U.S. Department of Energy. 1981. *Energy Industry Abroad*. Washington, D.C.: September.

―――. Office of International Affairs. 1977. *The Role of Foreign Governments in the Energy Industry*. Washington. D.C.: October.

U.S. Department of State. 1981. *Indonesia in the 1980s: Proceedings of a Conference, May 4*. Washington, D.C. Processed.

U.S. Embassy, Jakarta. 1982. "Indonesia's Petroleum Sector." Jakarta, June. Processed.

U.S. Energy Information Administration. 1983. *The Petroleum Resources of Venezuela and Trinidad and Tobago*. Washington, D.C.: EIA.

Vais, J. A. 1982. Primary Aluminum Demand and Supply in the 1980s." Paper presented to the Second Aluminum Congress, Monte Carlo, September.

van Ginneken, W. 1980. *Socio-Economic Groups and Income Distribution in Mexico*. London: Croom Helm.

van Wijnbergen, Sweder. 1982. "A Note on Infinite Horizon and Equivalent Finite Horizon Optimal Control Programs." Development Research Department, World Bank, January. Processed.

————. 1984a. "The 'Dutch Disease': A Disease After All?" *Economic Journal* 94 (March): 41–55.

————. 1984b. "Inflation, Employment and the Dutch Disease in Oil Exporting Countries: A Short-Run Disequilibrium Analysis." *Quarterly Journal of Economics* 99: 233–50.

————. 1984c. "The Optimal Investment and Current Account Response to Oil Price Shocks under Putty-Clay Technology." *Journal of International Economics* 17 (August): 139–47.

————. 1985a. "Optimal Capital Accumulation and Investment Allocation over Traded and Nontraded Sectors in Oil-Exporting Countries." *The Scandinavian Journal of Economics* 87: 89–101.

————. 1985b. "Optimal Taxation of Imported Energy under Price Uncertainty." *Oxford Economic Papers* 37 (March): 83–92.

Varas, Augusto, and Fernando Bustamante. 1978. *Fuerzas Armadas y Politica en Ecuador*. Quito: Ediciones Latinoamerica.

Verba, Sidney, Norman H. Nie, and Jae-On Kim. 1978. *Participation and Political Equality: A Seven Nation Comparison*. New York: Cambridge University Press.

Verleger, P. K. 1982. "The Determinants of Official OPEC Crude Prices." *Review of Economics and Statistics* 2 (May): 177–83.

von Lazar, Arpad, and Althea Duerstein. 1976. "Energy Policy and Patterns of National Development and Social Change: Lessons from Venezuela, Nigeria and Trinidad-Tobago." Paper for International Political Science Association Congress, Edinburgh, August 16–21.

Vos, Rob. 1981. "Ecuador: External Dependence and Capital Accumulation." ISS–PREALC Research Paper 1. Quito: Institute of Social Studies–PREALC. December.

————. 1982. "Access to Basic Services and Public Expenditure Incidence, Ecuador, 1970–80." Quito, October. Processed.

Vos, Rob, Arjen Vos, and Sietse van de Werff. 1982. "Rural Development Supply and Access to Basic Public Services, Province of Bolivar." Quito, May. Processed.

Vreeland, Nena, and others. 1975. *Area Handbook for Indonesia*. Washington, D.C.: American University.

Watkins, M. H. 1963. "A Staple Theory of Economic Growth." *Canadian Journal of Economics and Political Science* 29 (May).

Warr, Peter G. 1986. "Indonesia's Other Dutch Disease: Economic Effects of the Petroleum Boom." In Neary and van Wijnbergen (1986).

Watts, Michael. 1983. *Silent Violence: Food, Famine, and Peasantry in Northern Nigeria*. Berkeley: University of California Press.

Wells, Jerome G. 1974. *Agricultural Policy and Economic Growth in Nigeria, 1961–1968*. Ibadan: Oxford University Press.

Wheeler, David. 1980. *Human Resource Development and Economic Growth in Developing Countries: A Simultaneous Model*. World Bank Staff Working Paper 407. Washington, D.C., July.

Williams, E. N. 1970. *The Ancien Regime in Europe*. New York: Penguin.

Williams, Eric. 1981. *Budget Speech*. Port of Spain: Government Printer.

World Bank. 1979. *World Development Report 1979*. New York: Oxford University Press.

———. 1980a. *World Development Report 1980*. New York: Oxford University Press.

———. 1980b. *Indonesia: Employment and Income Distribution in Indonesia*. Country Study. Washington, D.C., July.

———. 1984. *Indonesia: Wages and Employment*. Country Study. Washington, D.C.

———. 1985. *Ecuador: An Agenda for Recovery and Sustained Growth*. Country Study. Washington, D.C.

Worswick, G. D. N. 1980. "North Sea Oil and the Decline of Manufacturing." *National Institute Economic Review* 94: 22–27.

Wright, B. 1982. "A Microstudy of Caricom Production and Export Incentives." New Haven, Conn.: Yale University Economic Growth Center. Processed.

Yotopoulos, P. M., and J. B. Nugent. 1976. *Economics of Development: Empirical Investigations*. New York: Harper and Row.

Zartman, I. W. 1975. "The Elites of the Maghreb: A Review Article." *International Journal of Middle East Studies* 6, no. 4 (December).

Zavallos Vicente, J. 1981. *El Estado Ecuatoriano y las Transnacionales Petroleras*. Quito: Ediciones Universidad Católica.

Index

Absorption of windfall, 32–45, 70–71; in Algeria, 59–60, 74; allocation of funds for, 56–77; country differences for 74; in Ecuador, 59–60, 170–96; effect of political structure on, 138–39; influence of special interests on, 204; in Mexico, 74; nationalization and, 135–36; public policy choices for, 37–45; in Trinidad and Tobago, 268–71, 274–77

Absorption structure, for countries studied, 59–60, 74

Adebayo, Robert A., 257

Adelman, Irma, 36

Adelman, Morris A., 13 n3, 21, 35

Agriculture: in Algeria, 90, 95, 159; in countries studied, 89–93; in Ecuador, 89, 91, 93, 192–95; farmer revolt in Nigeria and, 257; in Indonesia, 89, 90–92, 215–20; in Nigeria, 90–92, 103–04, 228, 229–32, 245–47, 251–53; in Trinidad and Tobago, 90, 266, 279–80; in Venezuela, 90–91, 93, 308

Ajibola, W. A., 241

Akinsanya, Adeoye A., 260 n7

Algeria: absorption structure in, 59–60, 74; agriculture in, 90, 95, 159; benefits from windfalls in, 166–68; consumption in, 148, 149–50, 151, 166; credit to public enterprise in, 154–55; currency policy in, 160–62; deficit in, 75; Dutch disease index in, 162; economic structure in, 150–52; exchange rates in, 82–83, 160, 162; exports from, 152, 158; fiscal policy in, 61–75; fix-price model of economy in, 151, 163–66, 167; foreign borrowing in, 147, 148, 166; gas and LNG industry in, 102, 115, 155, 158; government stability in, 150; growth in, 162–63, 167; hydrocarbon industry in, 94, 155; imports of, 159–60; nationalization in, 150–52, 155, 163, 167–68; nonmining sector in, 162; non-oil traded sector in, 90, 152, 159–63; political structure in, 148–50; public investment in, 95, 102, 154–62; rationing in, 167; response to first price shock in, 147; role of SONATRACH in, 155, 158; seigniorage in, 82–83, 161, 169 n11; state control in, 163, 167; traded sector in, 169 n13; wages in, 83; use of windfalls in, 152–54

Aluminum industry: in Trinidad and Tobago, 270, 281, 283; in Venezuela, 105

Amuzegar, Jahangir, 8

Anusionwu, E. C., 255

Aranda, S., 323 n1

Arndt, H. W., 217, 225 n14

Asheshov, Nicholas, 323 n8